CW01081956

The Illustrated History of

LMS

STANDARD
COACHING STOCK

III: Non-Corridor, Special Purpose and Self-Propelled Vehicles

David Jenkinson and Bob Essery

OPC

Oxford Publishing Co

With the introduction of the new Mersey-Wirral stock in 1938 (see Chapter 8), the LMS took a great step forward in electric multiple-unit (EMU) design as far as our main line railways were concerned. London Transport excepted, these were the first British sliding-door electrics to go into service, but their large picture windows and excellent seating provision made them superior in amenity to most LT stock. Apart from some similar LMS types on the Southport route a few years later and some excellent LNER designs for the Shenfield route, nothing remotely similar was to appear on the main British railway network until over a generation later.

Note on Picture Credits
All uncredited photographs and carriage diagrams used in this book are from official sources made freely available to the authors via British Railways London Midland Region in the late 1960s. Such pictures as have survived (probably the majority) have now been transferred to the National Railway Museum (NRM) to which all enquiries should be made regarding the possibility of obtaining copies. All other pictures are credited where known and apologies offered in advance for any mistakes, notification of which should be addressed to the publishers. Copies of the LMS carriage diagram book are held at the NRM and the Public Record Office at Kew but it is regretted that neither authors nor publisher are able to supply copies of any of the images used in this book.

First published 2000

ISBN 0 86093 452 7

Published by Oxford Publishing Company

an imprint of Ian Allan Publishing Ltd, Terminal House, Shepperton, Surrey TW17 8AS.
Printed by Ian Allan Printing Ltd, Riverdene Business Park, Hersham, Surrey KT12 4RG.

Code: 0007/A2

Contents

List of Figure Drawings

List of Summary Tables

Authors' Introduction to Volume III

It is now some six years since the second volume of our revised third edition of this survey was published, during which time the cumulative effects of the early 1990s trade recession and the changing nature of the specialised book trade itself have more than once caused us to wonder whether it would ever appear at all . . . We were therefore delighted when the new owners of OPC asked us, late in 1998, whether we were still interested in completing our half-finished work. 'Does a duck swim?' seemed the most appropriate response and it is with some pleasure, not to say keeping faith with those loyal readers who have bombarded us with enquiries about when the final volume would appear, that we offer this completion of the story.

The book itself follows the structural parameters established with the first two revised volumes in 1991 and 1994 — ie all available carriage diagrams are now included (a few are missing), together with full pre-1933 renumbering data where applicable, and pictures of as many carriage varieties as we have been able to find. At the same time, it is probably worth repeating, not least for the avoidance of misunderstanding, that the 'draughtsmanship quality' of the London, Midland & Scottish Railway (LMS) diagram drawings deteriorated rapidly in the early 1930s for reasons given in the Introduction to Volume II — made even more cruelly obvious by the 4mm=1ft scale in which all were offered in that volume. Things were no different as far as the diagrams for this volume were concerned — in some cases even worse(!) — so we have, therefore, exercised what we like to think is a bit more aesthetic judgement on this occasion by confining 4mm scale images to those diagrams whose quality of line justifies such treatment. The sub-standard diagrams have been reproduced to smaller scales and we hope this compromise proves satisfactory.

As for the rest, those readers who have the original single-volume OPC edition of 1977 (reprinted 1984) will clearly recognise quite a lot of the material within this book, but as with both the previous volumes in this expanded version, we have considerably expanded the detail coverage (probably by more than 50%) even if the introductory narratives remain largely the same. In the latter context, not much more of general substance remains to be said; but as we stated in our Introduction to Volume I, it hardly seemed possible in the context of the 1960s, when we first started out on this road, that one day we would be able to offer what amounted to a fully illustrated diagram book of every carriage type which the LMS ever built. That we have finally been able to do so (in spite of many vicissitudes on the way) says much for the sort of information which modern-day railway enthusiasts tend to expect — not to say the ever-increasing willingness of publishers to offer such data in spite of all the problems. For our part, we are simply pleased to be able to offer some part of this story.

Finally, given that the delay in appearance of this volume causes it to come out in what is mathematically the last year of the 20th century, it is highly tempting to try to appraise the story of LMS carriages in the context of that century. On the whole, we are inclined to think that this great company, drawing mainly (but not exclusively) upon its inheritance from those two pre-1923 English giants, the London & North Western (LNWR) and Midland Railways (MR), probably took railway carriage development further forward than any other single 'operator' (however defined) during the 20th century, when viewed as a totality. Its carriages were not always better than the others, nor did it have a monopoly of good ideas, but when one looks at the current nature of the modern British express train in particular, it is hard to see it as being *conceptually* any better than that which the LMS was offering over 60 years earlier, even though it may now go a bit faster — and on that we rest our case . . .

DJ, RJE
Easingwold/Rolleston-on-Dove, 2000

The ill-fated 1939 'Coronation Scot' train (see Chapter 4) never ran in revenue service as such and this official view is one of very few known pictures of the carriages actually running in Britain at all. It shows the complete American tour train undergoing final track tests in 1939 prior to its shipment to the USA. Three only of the five planned articulated 'twins' were sent to America and these lead the formation, followed by the staff sleeping car and the club brake. The locomotive is No 6229 *Duchess of Hamilton*, masquerading as No 6220 *Coronation* and already fitted with the headlamp and bell which were a legal requirement for running over North American lines.

Explanation of Terms

DIAGRAMS AND LOTS

LMS coaches were built to various *diagrams*. Basically the diagram was a drawing which defined the precise type of coach which was to be built although not, in itself, a working drawing. The various diagrams have identifying numbers, not necessarily in consecutive sequence through the years, and in this book will be referred to throughout as Dxxxx. Several diagrams were current for a number of years and each separate batch of coaches built to a particular diagram was given an identifying *lot number*. In general, lot numbers, while not always consecutively numbered on a particular diagram, were in ascending order as the years went by. Thus Lot 954 of D1915 would represent later coaches than Lot 843 of the same diagram.

Whenever a design was changed — even to a minor extent — a fresh diagram was almost always issued. As far as can be ascertained there were very few exceptions to this policy and these have been noted. Diagrams have been used extensively as illustrative material in this book.

PLATING

This term will be used to refer to the LMS practice of putting works plates on the coach. These were carried on the solebar and on the coach end. The solebar plate generally gave details of the works where built and the date of building, including lot numbers from 1934/5, while the plate on the coach end was a dimension plate giving length, width and tare weight, to the nearest ton. Sometimes the plates were slightly at variance with the official diagram version. The policy in this book will be to give the diagram version, drawing attention where necessary to any discrepancies in the coach plating details as observed in traffic.

DIMENSIONS

Unless otherwise stated, basic coach dimensions will be given as follows:

Height: Rail level to top of roof, not counting roof ventilators.

Length: Over headstocks — with LMS coaches, which almost always had flat ends, this dimension was some 1in to 1½ in less than the body length of the coach.

Width: Over projections — ie a coach with a 9ft 0in wide body but with projecting handles would be quoted as 9ft 3in if this dimension was the width over the handles.

STRUCTURAL TERMS

The following definitions have been adopted as a standard for this work.

Beading: Raised wooden strips covering the panel joints on wood-panelled stock.

Cantrail: The point at which the coach side meets the roof.

Cornice: The moulding, often of slightly ornamental nature, which was frequently found along the line of the cantrail.

Chassis: The complete underframe together with bogies, buffing, draw gear, etc.

Gutter: The rainwater channel along the top of the cornice.

Headstock: The end section of the underframe which carried the buffing and draw gear.

Light: A generic term for a carriage window, sub-classified as follows:

      Droplight: An opening window which moves in the vertical plane — usually wood framed but there were aluminium frame and frameless variants.

      Fixed Light: A window which will not open.

      Quarterlight: The small fixed light flanking the doors of all compartments which had outside doors.

      Toplight: A small window situated between the cantrail and the top of the main carriage window.

Panelling: A generic term relating to the method of covering the exterior of the coach — eg wooden panelling, steel panelling, flush panelling, etc. The following principal sub-classifications should be noted:

      Eaves Panel: The section of the body panelling located between the window top and the cantrail.

      Flush Panelling: Used to refer to any coach which did not have any form of raised body projections in the form of wooden beading.

      Matchboarding: The name used in reference to the type of coach and panelling which consisted of a series of tongue-and-groove boarding running vertically from roof level to headstocks. This was a technique generally confined to coaches with an 'all wood' exterior finish.

      Tumblehome: The incurving portion of the bodyside panelling as it approaches the solebar.

      Waist Panel: The portion of the body panelling situated immediately below the windows and on LMS coaches, having a depth of some 8in. Waist panelling was generally confined to high-waisted fully beaded coaches of wood-panelled style.

Roof Types: The LMS, for the most part, adopted two types of roof as follows:

      Rainstrip roof: This was of wood and canvas construction with a continuous rainstrip from end to end and on each side of the roof.

      Ribbed roof: This was the Stanier-pattern metal-clad roof with a series of strengthening ribs from one side of the coach to the other, rainstrips, if present at all, being generally confined to the section of the roof directly above the doors. Some coaches had flush welded roof panels without external transverse ribs.

Semi-elliptical: This is a term used to refer to the roof profile above the cantrail when in the form of a semi-ellipse.

Solebar:	The heavy section forming the main side members of the coach underframe. On LMS-design coaches this was a steel channel section, generally with the channel facing outwards.
Truss-rods:	The angle section fixed underneath the underframe between the bogies, giving additional strength to the underframe itself and acting as a support for some ancillary fittings.
Underfame:	The supporting frame of the coach on which the body was mounted, but not counting the bogies, buffers, ancillary fittings, etc.
Ventilators:	The following principal sub-classifications should be noted:

	Door ventilators:	These were the ventilators situated on outside doors above the droplight, either hooded or louvred.
	Hooded ventilators:	External ventilators (generally on doors or above windows) which were covered by a plain metal 'hood'.
	Louvre ventilators:	External ventilators (usually mounted over door drop-lights) which consisted outwardly of a series of horizontal wooden louvres, usually three.
	Shell and Torpedo ventilators:	The two types of roof ventilator generally used by the LMS. Torpedo ventilators were of several styles and the differences are best appreciated by comparing pictures of the various types.
	Sliding ventilators:	The type of ventilator used in the upper part of the big side windows of Stanier-pattern gangwayed coaches.
	Stones ventilators:	These were ventilators generally placed above the main windows of coaches in the eaves panel. They had swivelling glass vanes (six or nine elements) which could be adjusted by the passenger to 'face' or 'trail' the airstream past the coach.
	Dewel ventilators:	Similar to Stones ventilators but even shorter (five moving vanes).

TYPES OF COACH

The following definitions will be adopted throughout:

Corridor coach:	A coach with a side corridor for all or part of its length and with gangway connections to adjacent vehicles.
Dining car:	A vestibule coach containing a kitchen as well as passenger seating accommodation.
Vestibule coach:	An open coach with gangway connections to adjacent vehicles. Note that a vestibule coach used exclusively for dining purposes but *not* having a kitchen was referred to as a 'vestibule dining coach' and was *not* called a dining car.
Non-corridor coach:	Any coach without gangway connections.
Lavatory coach:	A non-gangwayed coach with toilets serving individual compartments either directly or from a short side corridor.

The nomenclature of other types of coaches is self explanatory.

COACH CODING

Where it seems appropriate, the standard British Railways coach codes have been adopted for ease of reference. These are, in fact, based on the old London & North Eastern Railway (LNER) system but the familiarity of present-day usage will, it is felt, make them easier to understand for most readers than the official LMS codes. Full details are given on page 10, together with the old LMS code letters.

COACH NUMBERING

Until 1932, new standard LMS coaches were numbered somewhat haphazardly in the gaps available between the various batches of Pre-Grouping coaches which themselves, apart from the ex-MR vehicles, had been numbered in blocks in 1923. The ex-MR coaches retained their Pre-Grouping numbers except for the Midland & Glasgow & South Western Railways (M&GSWR) and Midland & North British Railways (M&NBR) Joint Stock vehicles which were given vacant numbers in the ex-MR allocation, generally at the end of this series.

From 1933, the whole coaching stock (pre-Grouping and standard) was renumbered systematically by generic vehicle types and these 1933 numbers are the ones which are used throughout this book. Details of the renumbering principles are given on pages 10 and 11. At Nationalisation, LMS coaches generally retained their numbers and newly built coaches to LMS/LMR (London Midland Region) diagrams were given numbers in the appropriate LMS series. From 1948 until 1951, the LMS number was prefixed by a letter 'M' to denote the company/region of origin of the design. At about the time of the introduction of BR standard coaching stock, the prefix/suffix system was introduced. The prefix letter now denoted the region of allocation; the suffix letter was introduced as the identification of the vehicle's origin. Thus, for example, LMS coach No 1234 would first have become M1234 in 1948 and then, if allocated to, say, Scotland, would have finally become Sc1234M. For the sake of consistency, it will be the policy of this book to omit the prefix/suffix letters in all references to LMS/LMR coaches — even those which entered service carrying such letters.

Basic Dimensions and Assumptions

In the chapters following this, the various generic types of coach built by the LMS are described and listed. Because of the high degree of standardisation of LMS coaches it is possible to take as read many basic features of the design and thus confine the description of the types and the tabulated data to those aspects peculiar to the coaches under discussion. It is hoped that this will simplify the understanding of the subject.

DIMENSIONS

The following basic table of dimensions can be taken as standard for all coaches of the lengths specified:

Length over headstocks	69ft	68ft	65ft	62ft	60ft	58ft	57ft	54ft	51ft	50ft
Bogie type	6wh	6wh	4wh	4wh	4wh	4wh	4wh	4wh	4wh	4wh
Bogie wheelbase	12ft 6in	12ft 6in	9ft 0in	9ft 0in	9ft 0in	9ft 0in	9ft 0in	9ft 0in	9ft 0in	9ft 0in
Bogie centres	46ft 0in	45ft 0in	48ft 0in	45ft 6in	43ft 6in	41ft 6in	40ft 6in	37ft 6in	34ft 6in	33ft 6in
Buffer type oval (O) or round (R)	O	O	O	O	R	R	R	R	R	R

Because of this standardised pattern, the only dimensions quoted in the summary tables will be length over headstocks, width over projections and height from rails to rooftop.

Typical window and panel dimensions of all three periods of design are given in Volume I, page 6, viz: Period I: 1923-30; Period II: 1930-1932/3; Period III: 1933 onwards.

ASSUMPTIONS

Unless stated otherwise, it may safely be assumed that the following styling and other features were common to all LMS coaches to be described:

Period I coaches:	Body:	High-waisted, wood-panelled, fully beaded sides and matchboard ends.
	Roof:	Wood construction with canvas covering and carrying an-end-to-end longitudinal rainstrip at each side.
	Roof vents:	Torpedo pattern.
	Door vents: locks/handles, etc.	Three-element louvre type; but hooded metal on coaches built with MR
	Corridor connections:	British standard (scissor type).
	Livery when new: red coach ends.	Fully lined out, original insignia styles and placings, grey and black roof,

Period II coaches:	Body:	a. Gangway stock: Low-waisted 'square windowed', wood- or steel-panelled. The type of panelling and presence or absence of beading will be specified in the narrative.
		b. Non-corridor: High-waisted, steel-panelled, 'square windows'.
	Roof:	Wood/Canvas/Rainstrip.
	Roof vents:	Torpedo pattern.
	Door vents:	Hooded metal (steel panelling), louvre type (wood panelling).
	Corridor connections:	British standard (scissor type).
	Livery when new:	Fully lined out but without waist panel, stretched scroll figures and later insignia placing, grey and black roof, red coach ends.

Period III coaches:	Body:	Totally flush clad without raised window mouldings, rounded window corners, steel panelled.
	Roof:	Metal clad 'ribbed' pattern.
	Roof vents:	Shell pattern.
	Door vents:	Hooded metal.
	Window vents:	Sliding type with *o* moving elements.
	Corridor connections:	British standard (suspended gangway type).
	Livery:	Simplified lining, shaded block-style figures and later insignia placing, metallic roof finish (prewar), grey roof finish (postwar), black ends from late 1936, 'straw' lining from 1946.

The principal exceptions to the above summary were the early Stanier coaches. Some of these came out in full livery and some had the earlier sliding ventilator with one moving element. A few had torpedo ventilators and there were other slight points of difference. All these aspects are covered in the summary tables. Stanier coaches in full livery generally carried unshaded block-style figures.

In all subsequent chapters, the various coaches are listed in the form of standardised summary tables at the end of the narrative. These give details supplementary to those which may be deduced from the above list of assumptions.

In most summary tables, the first and last withdrawal dates for each coach 'lot' are given. The dates are London Midland Region four-week periods and relate to the normal planned coach withdrawals. They do not generally take account of premature withdrawals due to accident or wartime enemy action.

Standard Codes for Coaching Stock

The BR system of coding coach types is based on the old LNER system and the following parts of it are relevant to LMS standard coaches discussed in this book, the LMS codes being given for comparison:

Dining and Kitchen Vehicles	BR Code	LMS Code
First Class Kitchen Dining car	RF	First RKC
Composite " "	RC	Compo RKC
Third Class " "	RT	Third RKC
Unclassified " "	RU	Common RKC
Kitchen Buffet car	RB or RKB	BRC
Kitchen only car	RK	KC
First Class vestibule dining coach	RFO	QL (Dining)
Composite " " "	RCO	VC (Dining)
Third Class " " "	RTO	QF (Dining)
Unclassified " " "	RUO	–

Sleeping Cars		
First Class	SLF	SC
Composite	SLC	CSC
Third Class	SLT	SCT
" " (twin berth)	SLT (T)	–

Vestibule Stock		
Vestibule First Class	FO	QL
" Composite	CO	VC
" Third Class	TO	QF
" Third Class Brake	BTO	VH
Semi-open First Class (Corridor Vestibule)	Semi-FO or Semi-RFO	CQL
Semi-open Third Class (Corridor Vestibule)	Semi-TO or Semi-RTO	–

Corridor Stock	BR Code	LMS Code
First Class	FK	CL
" " Brake	BFK	E
Composite	CK	CBC
" Brake	BCK	CBB
Third Class	TK	CF
" " Brake	BTK	CH

Non-corridor Stock		
First Class	F	L
" " (with lavatory)	FL	LM
Composite	C	BC
" (with lavatory)	CL	L&C
Third Class	T	F
" " Brake	BT	H
" " " (with lavatory)	BTL	LH

Other Coaching Stock		
Passenger full brake with gangway	BG	CBR
Six-wheel passenger full brake with gangway	BGZ	CR " "
" " " without gangway	BZ	R
Post Office Sorting Van	POS	POR
Post Office Tender (Stowage Van)	POT	PPR

Notes:
1. Articulated stock is prefaced by the word 'Twin' or 'Triple' in the BR system.
2. Codes exist for multiple-unit stock but have not been employed in this book.

A Note on the 1923 LMS Coaching Stock Numbers

When the LMS was formed in 1923, the ex-Midland carriages mostly kept their old numbers and the former M&GSWR/M&NBR Joint stock was eventually assimilated into this series in 1923 and 1928 respectively. The other pre-Grouping companies were then allocated blocks of new numbers following on in sequence, each company being kept together before going on to another company. Thus, for example, the LNWR/WCJS (West Coast Joint Stock) carriages were allocated the 4301-10700 block, followed by the LYR (Lancashire & Yorkshire Railway), etc. Non-passenger coaching stock was numbered in a separate series with the ex-MR vehicles again at the head of the list (retaining their numbers) followed by the other pre-Grouping fleets.

For the most part, new LMS carriage numbers for pre-Grouping carriages were allocated in ascending diagram page order and the coaches on any particular diagram were usually numbered in pre-Grouping number order. Although this system was not particularly refined it did, in most cases, collect all coaches of any particular type and diagram into one consecutive number series — often for the first time, given the somewhat random numbering principles followed by most LMS constituents. The basic fault was that inadequate provision was made for the numbering of newly built LMS standard coaches.

The general principle was to use appropriate gaps in the pre-Grouping lists but this was not wholly successful. Where a complete series of old pre-Grouping carriages had been scrapped, this would normally, of course, vacate a fully consecutive LMS number series (given the 1923 renumbering principles) but even when this was added to the existing gaps in the sequence, the blocks of numbers selected in 1923 were frequently too small to absorb the sheer numbers of new carriages. In consequence, the pre-1933 numbers of new coaches could either be found in short consecutive batches (existing gaps or replacing withdrawn pre-Grouping stock) or randomly scattered anywhere in the whole LMS series where any gap (even one only) was to be found. Even this did not suffice and the LMS itself eventually had to resort to an old LNWR principle of 'cyphering' the running numbers of still existing pre-Grouping carriages. This was done by adding a 'O' prefix to many 1923 LMS numbers, thus freeing the originals for reuse.

By 1932/3, the situation had become so confusing that the LMS felt obliged to introduce a completely new and systematic numbering scheme whose principles are outlined below. It is felt that this may have been the main reason for introducing sans serif carriage number insignia — mainly to allow easy differentiation of new from old numbers during the changeover.

The 1932/3 LMS Coach Renumbering Scheme

The 1932/3 renumbering scheme grouped all coaching stock (pre- and post-Grouping) into systematic number blocks according to coach type. Within the pre-Grouping allocations, the numbering order was generally as follows: LNWR (which carried the lowest numbers); MR; LYR; FR (Furness Railway); CR (Caledonian Railway): GSWR; and HR (Highland Railway) (which carried the highest numbers). Generally speaking, the LMS standard coaches were numbered consecutively upwards from the start of the block and the pre-Grouping coaches were numbered backwards from the end of the block. The pre-Grouping numbers were allocated in such a way that the complete pre-Grouping block of coaches generally occupied the last and highest numbers in any series. This usually left a gap between the end of the LMS standard block and the start of the pre-Grouping block which was available for new construction. In some cases the 1932 planners underestimated the size of the number blocks they would need and certain coaches overflowed into the other blocks — these are annotated below:

1-99	**First Class Kitchen/Dining Cars**	
	1-44	LMS Standard types
	45-58	Vacant
	59-99	Pre-Grouping types
100-199	**Third Class Kitchen/Dining Cars and Buffet Cars**	
	100-148	LMS Standard types
	147-199	Pre-Grouping types (including first 147/8)
200-299	**Composite Kitchen/Dining Cars**	
	200-221	Ex-Pullman cars (mostly Scottish)
	222-252	LMS Standard types
	253-270	Sundry post-1947 cafeteria conversions of LMS coaches
	241-299	Original Pre-Grouping allocation

300-499	**First Class Sleeping Cars**	
	300-402	LMS Standard types
	403-437	Vacant
	438-496	LNWR (with a few gaps)
	497-499	Vacant
500-699	**Third Class Sleeping Cars**	
	500-599	LMS Standard SLT
	600-624	LMS types SLT(T)
	625-699	Vacant
700-799	**Composite Sleeping Cars**	
	700-724	LMS Standard types
	725-789	Vacant
	790-799	LNWR — NB: second 798/9 later given to HM The King's and HM The Queen's Saloons.

800-999	**Special Saloons — mainly Pre-Grouping varieties**	

1000-1199   **Corridor Firsts and Semi-open Firsts**
1000-1128   LMS Standard types
1128-1199   Pre-Grouping types (including first 1128)

1200-3399   **Corridor Thirds**
1200-2516   LMS diagrams
2235-3399   Pre-Grouping types (including first 2235-2516)

3400-3499   **Push-Pull conversions of older gangwayed stock — both pre-Grouping and LMS Standard types** (some of the pre-Grouping examples were built as push-pull vehicles)

3500-4999   **Corridor Composites**
3500-4514   LMS Standard types
4357-4999   Pre-Grouping types (including first 4357-4514)
second 4800-4899   LMS Standard types

5000-5199   **Corridor First Brakes and Open First Brakes**
5000-5004   LMS Standard Lounge (open) brakes
5005-5077   LMS Standard BFKs
5078-5144   Vacant
5145-5199   Pre-Grouping types

5200-6599   **Corridor Third Brakes**
5200-6038   LMS diagrams
5990-6599   Pre-Grouping types (including first 5990-6038)

6600-7399   **Corridor Composite Brakes**
6600-6876   LMS Standard types
6877-6956   Vacant
6957-7399   Pre-Grouping types

7400-7599   **Vestibule Firsts (both FO and RFO)**
7400-7575   LMS Standard types (Note: first 7465-89 were later downgraded and the numbers in part used again for later standard coaches)
7556-7599   Pre-Grouping types (including first 7556-7575)

7600-9699   **Vestibule Thirds (both TO and RTO)**
7600-9518   LMS Standard types
9519-9561   Vacant
9562-9699   Pre-Grouping types

9700-9799   **Vestibule Composites (both CO and RCO)**
9700-9758   LMS Standard types
9759-9791   Vacant
9792-9799   Ex-LYR

9800-9999   **Vestibule Brake Thirds**
9800-9999   LMS Standard types
9971-9999   Pre-Grouping types — first coaches with these numbers

Note: This concluded the initial allocation of numbers for passenger-carrying non-articulated gangwayed stock. Extra batches built after the number series filled up were as follows:

Corridor Thirds: 12750-13184
Corridor Composites: 24500-24739
Corridor Brake Thirds: 26100-27095*
Vestibule Thirds: 27100-27449*
Vestibule Third Brakes: 27900-27956*

* These were also originally used to renumber pre-Grouping gangwayed stock to clear the original series for standard construction.

10000-10699   **Non-corridor Firsts**
10000-10131   LMS Standard types
10132-10308   Vacant
10309-10699   Pre-Grouping types

10700-15799   **Non-corridor Thirds**
10700-12267   LMS Standard types
12268-12277   Downgraded composites from 160xx series
12278-12283   Ex-MSJA trailers (converted 1954)
12284-13610   Vacant (12750-13184 used for overflow numbering of TKs and 13610 downwards used for various downgraded vehicles)
13611-15799   Pre-Grouping types

15800-15999   **Non-corridor Thirds — Motor Fitted**
15800-15857   Pre-Grouping types
15858-15906   LMS Standard types
15907-15996   Vacant
15997-15999   LMS Standard types (converted)

16000-17899   **Non-corridor Composites**
16000-16325   LMS Standard types (16000-16006 originally compo. seconds)
16326-16330   Vacant — allocated initially to 17900-4 (Push-Pull version)
16331-16796   LMS Standard types
16797-16876   GWR designs built post-1947 and given LMS series numbers

16000-17899   **Non-corridor Composites** (*cont.*)
16850-16937   Originally part of the vacant series but later used in part (post-1947) for ex-CLC stock and marked down Pre-Grouping firsts
16938-17899   Pre-Grouping types

17900-17999   **Non-corridor Composites — Motor Fitted**
17900-17942   LMS Standard types
17943-17957   Vacant but some later used for conversions
17958-17999   Pre-Grouping types

18000-18199   **Non-corridor Lavatory Firsts**
18000-18029   LMS Standard types
18030-18161   Vacant
18162-18199   Pre-Grouping types

18200-18999   **Non-corridor Lavatory Thirds**
No LMS Standard designs built but 18614-18999 were Pre-Grouping coaches

19000-19999   **Non-corridor Lavatory Composites**
19000-19199   LMS Standard types
19200-19386   Originally vacant but 19377-86 were given to non-lavatory Cs to Lot 1450 (Motor-fitted coaches — D1921A)
19387-19999   Pre-Grouping types, also first 19385/6

20000-24399   **Non-corridor Third Brakes**
20000-21251   LMS Standard types
21252-22214   Vacant (22196-202 later used for ex-North London area LMS Standard brake seconds and 22203-14 for other downgraded coaches)
22215-24399   Pre-Grouping types (24317-31 later used again for Push-Pull driving trailers — 1950)

24400-24499   **Non-corridor Driving Trailer Thirds**
24400-24459   LMS Standard types
24460-24499   Pre-Grouping types and LMS standard conversions

24500-24799   **Non-corridor Composite Brakes**
24500-24717   Vacant (no LMS designs) but later used for overflow numbering of Period III CKs 24500-24739
24718-24799   Pre-Grouping types (including first 24718-24739)

24800-24899   **Non-corridor Driving Trailer Composites**
24800-24895   Vacant (no LMS Standard types)
24896-24899   Ex-MR and Ex-LYR

24900-24999   **Non-corridor Second Brakes**
24900-24906   LMS Standard designs for North London sets — later downgraded and renumbered 22196-202
24907-24999   Vacant but 24989-99 later used for marked up BTs (Pre-Grouping) which were later marked down again

25000-25699   **Non-corridor Lavatory Third Brakes**
25000-25272   LMS Standard types
25273-25507   Vacant
25508-25699   Pre-Grouping types

25700-25999   **Non-corridor Lavatory Composite Brakes**
25700-25777   Vacant (no LMS Standard design)
25778-25999   Pre-Grouping types

26000-27999   **Pre-Grouping four/six-wheel passenger-carrying coaches — all types**
Note: Survivors of this block again renumbered 26000-99 when the 'overflow' numbering began.

28000-29899   **Electric Multiple-Unit Stock**
The number allocation in these blocks was a little complex and is best appreciated by studying Chapter 8.

29900-29999   **Miscellaneous Railcars, etc.**

30000-30199   **Kitchen Cars**
30000-30106   LMS Standard types
30107-30196   Vacant
30197-30199   Ex-LNWR

30200-30399   **Post Office Vehicles**
The numbering in this group was completely haphazard — see Chapter 6

30400-32899   **Bogie Corridor Full Brakes**
30400-32019   LMS Standard types and LMS-built conversions from other coaches. There were vacant numbers
32020-32899   Pre-Grouping types built as full brakes

32900-33499   **Six-Wheel Corridor Full Brakes**
32900-33019   LMS Standard types
33020-33441   Vacant
33442-33499   Pre-Grouping types

33500-44999   **Non-passenger-carrying coaching stock**

45xxx numbers   **Chairman's and Engineer's Saloons**

50000 Upwards   **Articulated coaches**

These two views typify almost the opposite ends of the operating spectrum as far as LMS non-corridor stock was concerned. The earlier view (above), taken at the Yorkshire end of Standedge Tunnel in 1936, shows 'Horwich Mogul' No 2862 in charge of an unidentified stopping passenger train headed in the direction of Huddersfield and Leeds on the old LNWR main line from Manchester. The carriages which can be seen (there may well have been others in the tunnel) form a typical three-coach Period I Inter-District lavatory set and this fact alone hints that the service concerned was of sufficiently reasonable distance to justify the use of these, by LMS standards, somewhat uncommon vehicles.

By contrast, the second view taken just after Nationalisation offers a view of that wonderful Aladdin's cave of sidings (flanked by Platforms 7 and 8) which used to lurk, often unnoticed by most travellers, between the main arrival and departure sides of 'old' Euston in the years before its major rebuilding in 1962-3. On the left is a typically endless string of non-corridor, non-lavatory Period III types, probably bound 'all stations' for Bletchley in due course, while to the right can be seen some of the many vacuum-fitted vans which were used for the considerable amount of 'non-passenger coaching stock' traffic which Euston handled at that time.

Chapter 1 - 57ft Non-corridor Stock

57ft Lavatory Stock; 57ft Non-lavatory Stock, North London Sets; Push-Pull Stock

With but a few exceptions (see Chapter 2), all general service non-corridor coaches built by the LMS were mounted on 57ft chassis. Apart from external style changes which followed the usual LMS sequence, the layout of non-corridor stock hardly varied at all from the early Period I standard coaches to the end of the Stanier phase. Since there was so little change, the best way to appreciate what actually did take place is to consider coaches by their generic types rather than by design periods. The bulk of 57ft stock does not seem to have been designed to run in sets and was generally supplied against a divisional requirement for 'x' seats. It is therefore not readily possible to do more than describe the types built. However, there were a few small batches of 57ft coaches built for the North London services which were supplied in set formations. As these coaches also differed slightly in layout from the standard general service coaches, they have been considered and tabulated separately.

57FT LAVATORY STOCK

The LMS was not a great builder of non-corridor lavatory stock and produced only three basic 57ft designs. No 57ft lavatory stock was built after 1930; moreover, only 50 coaches were built after the close of Period I. It seems from a study of the coach construction minutes that by 1930 it was becoming LMS policy to use older corridor stock for its intermediate cross-country services. These would give rather better accommodation than non-corridor coaches, especially in relation to toilet facilities, and the company presumably felt that this aspect of the situation was more important than the newness of any non-corridor coaches.

First class lavatory coaches were built only during Period I and totalled 30 vehicles to D1761. Built in 1927, they were seven-compartment coaches with two separated lavatories to which four compartments could gain access. These compartments had only seven seats and a short corridor connecting two compartments was located alongside each lavatory.

Composite coaches were eight-compartment vehicles built to one basic design although they appeared with both Period I and Period II styling (D1686/D1736). They again had two lavatories, this time placed side by side to which access was gained from two first class and two third class compartments by intermediate short corridors.

The remaining 57ft lavatory designs were third brakes with one lavatory accessible from two of the five compartments. They were again built with both Period I and Period II styling to D1685 and D1737. Another detail difference was the offset toilet window in the Period I type but centred in the Period II version.

The lavatory full firsts were used for general service and mixed somewhat indiscriminately amongst older vehicles. However, the composites and brake thirds were, in theory, designed as two, three or four-coach Inter-District lavatory sets formed CL + BTL; BTL + CL + BTL or BTL + CL + CL + BTL respectively.

From contemporary observers' reports, it would seem that this tidy pattern was rarely witnessed and many of the LMS lavatory coaches were simply used as replacements for older stock. For example, local sets might be composed of an ex-LNWR BTL plus an LMS standard CL or perhaps two LMS standard BTLs flanking a Midland CL. According to one extremely reliable source, the formations were too untidy to suggest any deliberate attempt to deliver them as sets but they may have been made into sets as required. They were also mixed with non-lavatory stock.

A few more non-corridor lavatory composite coaches were built on 54ft chassis but these were all for the Tilbury section and are considered in the next chapter.

NOTE: In order to simplify the presentation of this chapter, it seems slightly more logical to complete the survey of lavatory stock prior to moving on to the more complex non-lavatory 57ft carriages. Accordingly, the next few pages will be devoted to the completion of this story by way of tabulations of types (including the 1933 renumbering) and the type-by-type survey.

TABLE 1a: SUMMARY TABLE OF LMS STANDARD 57FT NON-CORRIDOR LAVATORY STOCK
Note: This table should be read in conjunction with the list of standard dimensions and details on page 8.

Type	*Diag*	*Lot*	*Qty*	*Date*	*Built*	*Dimensions* (L x W x H)	*Weight*	*Period*	*Running Numbers*	*Withdrawals First*	*Withdrawals Last*	*Remarks*
FL	1761	249	30	1927	Wolverton	57ft x 9ft 3in x 12ft 4¾in	28T	I	18000-18029	4/57	2/64	The only LMS design of FL.
CL	1686	126	20	1926/7	Derby	57ft x 9ft 3in x 12ft 4¾in	26T	I	19026-19045*	5/59	2/64	The so-called 'Inter-District' composites.
		389	50	1929	Wolverton		28T		19046-19095	5/59	13/64	It is doubtful if many were formed up with
		446	75	1929	Wolverton		28T		19096-19170	5/59	9/64	the BTLs into strict sets.
CL	1736	529	25	1930	Wolverton	57ft x 9ft 2¼in x 12ft 4¼in	30T	II	19171-19195	5/59	7/64	The Period II version of D1686.
BTL	1685	127	50	1926/7	Derby	57ft x 9ft 3in x 12ft 4¾in	26T	I	25000-25049	5/59	8/67†	Again 'Inter-District' coaches. Lot 127
		290	50	1927	Ntn Hth		26T		25050-25099	5/59	1/65	was plated 27T.
		398	73	1928/9	Ntn Hth		26T		25100-25172	3/58	8/64	
		448	75	1928/9	Ntn Hth		26T		25173-25247	5/59	4/65	
BTL	1737	530	25	1930	Ntn Hth	57ft x 9ft 3¼in x 12ft 4¾in	27T	II	25248-25272	5/59	8/64	The coaches were plated 9ft 3in although the diagram shows 9ft 3³⁄₁₆in for some reason. The Period II version of D1685. Plated 28T.

* The numbering of the composites started at 19026. The numbers between 19000 and 19025 were occupied by 54ft composites built for the LT&S sets and listed in Table 2a.

† One survivor only to this date (25048). Remainder scrapped before 1965.

TABLE 1b: THE 1933 RENUMBERING OF LMS 57FT LAVATORY STOCK

All the LMS 57ft lavatory stock was built prior to the 1933 renumbering, the full lists being given below in the same carriage order as Table 1a.

Column 1

New Number	Old Number
Lavatory First Class	
D1761	
18000	15424
18001	15459
18002	15466
18003	15517
18004	15520
18005	15536
18006	15701
18007	15910
18008	15917
18009	15926
18010	15927
18011	15937
18012	15944
18013	15945
18014	15975
18015	15999
18016	16109
18017	16124
18018	16195
18019	16233
18020	16246
18021	16355
18022	16384
18023	16401
18024	16430
18025	16476
18026	16536
18027	16543
18028	16871
18029	16881
Lavatory Composite	
D1686	
19026	15402
19027	15469
19028	15478
19029	15660
19030	15775
19031	15838
19032	15871
19033	15886
19034	16279
19035	16280
19036	16303
19037	16325
19038	16392
19039	16403
19040	16494
19041	16603
19042	16745
19043	16775
19044	16957
19045	17156
19046	2830
19047	2846
19048	2988
19049	2991
19050	3346
19051	3365
19052	3514
19053	3577
19054	3578
19055	3582
19056	3586
19057	3614
19058	3701
19059	9290
19060	9340
19061	9351
19062	9381
19063	9392
19064	9394
19065	9398
19066	9415
19067	11031
19068	11586
19069	11587
19070	11594
19071	11597

Column 2

New Number	Old Number
19072	11601
19073	11606
19074	11607
19075	11608
19076	11609
19077	11610
19078	11611
19079	11612
19080	11613
19081	11614
19082	11615
19083	11616
19084	11617
19085	11618
19086	11622
19087	11642
19088	11695
19089	15603
19090	15766
19091	15802
19092	15855
19093	15916
19094	15986
19095	15993
19096	62
19097	340
19098	452
19099	546
19100	925
19101	983
19102	1124
19103	1382
19104	1387
19105	1628
19106	1639
19107	1660
19108	1662
19109	1677
19110	1777
19111	1787
19112	3472
19113	3551
19114	3593
19115	3704
19116	3705
19117	6225
19118	6226
19119	6227
19120	8796
19121	9489
19122	9492
19123	9494
19124	15606
19125	15632
19126	15681
19127	15697
19128	15808
19129	15919
19130	15936
19131	16181
19132	4162
19133	4163
19134	4164
19135	4165
19136	4166
19137	4167
19138	4168
19139	4169
19140	4170
19141	4171
19142	4172
19143	4173
19144	4174
19145	4175
19146	4176
19147	4177
19148	4178
19149	4179
19150	4180
19151	4181
19152	4182

Column 3

Number New	Number Old
19153	4183
19154	4184
19155	4185
19156	4186
19157	4187
19158	4188
19159	4189
19160	4190
19161	4191
19162	4192
19163	4193
19164	4194
19165	4195
19166	4196
19167	4197
19168	4198
19169	4199
19170	4200
D1736	
19171	11053
19172	11054
19173	11055
19174	11057
19175	11058
19176	11060
19177	11061
19178	11063
19179	11064
19180	11065
19181	11066
19182	11067
19183	11068
19184	11073
19185	11074
19186	11076
19187	11077
19188	11079
19189	11080
19190	11082
19191	11083
19192	11085
19193	11144
19194	11145
19195	11146
Lavatory Brake Third	
D1685	
25000	15076
25001	15077
25002	15078
25003	18921
25004	18925
25005	18926
25006	18927
25007	18930
25008	18931
25009	18932
25010	18933
25011	18934
25012	18935
25013	18936
25014	18937
25015	18938
25016	18940
25017	18941
25018	18943
25019	18944
25020	18947
25021	18949
25022	18950
20523	18952
25024	18953
25025	18954
25026	18955
25027	18956
25028	18958
25029	18959
25030	18960
25031	18961
25032	18962

Column 4

Number New	Number Old
25033	18963
25034	18964
25035	18965
25036	18966
25037	18973
25038	18974
25039	18976
25040	18981
25041	18982
25042	18983
25043	18985
25044	18986
25045	18987
25046	18988
25047	18989
25048	19010
25049	19013
25050	1683
25051	2734
25052	3581
25053	5311
25054	5312
25055	6247
25056	7621
25057	7623
25058	7624
25059	7626
25060	7659
25061	7669
25062	7681
25063	7718
25064	7728
25065	8790
25066	9498
25067	9499
25068	9500
25069	9896
25070	15390
25071	15414
25072	15607
25073	15620
25074	15624
25075	15636
25076	15644
25077	15985
25078	15987
25079	16139
25080	16149
25081	16206
25082	16230
25083	16239
25084	16273
25085	16274
25086	16285
25087	16396
25088	16425
25089	16433
25090	16437
25091	16447
25092	16452
25093	16457
25094	16625
25095	16703
25096	16877
25097	16915
25098	16940
25099	16943
25100	14071
25101	14072
25102	14074
25103	14075
25104	14078
25105	14080
25106	14081
25107	14083
25108	14084
25109	14085
25110	14087
25111	14093
25112	14094
25113	14095

Column 5

Number New	Number Old
25114	14097
25115	14100
25116	14102
25117	14105
25118	14106
25119	14109
25120	14111
25121	14116
25122	14121
25123	14123
25124	14127
25125	14128
25126	14129
25127	14130
25128	14131
25129	14135
25130	14136
25131	14137
25132	14140
25133	14142
25134	14143
25135	14145
25136	14147
25137	14149
25138	14150
25139	14151
25140	14153
25141	14154
25142	14155
25143	14157
25144	14158
25145	14159
25146	14160
25147	14161
25148	14162
25149	14163
25150	14164
25151	14165
25152	14166
25153	14167
25154	14168
25155	14169
25156	14170
25157	14171
25158	14173
25159	14174
25160	14177
25161	14180
25162	14181
25163	14182
25164	14196
25165	14199
25166	14201
25167	14202
25168	14203
25169	14205
25170	14207
25171	14208
25172	14209
25173	73
25174	125
25175	184
25176	196
25177	254
25178	292
25179	687
25180	707
25181	723
25182	836
25183	840
25184	868
25185	899
25186	964
25187	978
25188	1003
25189	1044
25190	1058
25191	1061
25192	1228
25193	1239
25194	1344

Column 6

Number New	Number Old
25195	1347
25196	1404
25197	1438
25198	1666
25199	1688
25200	1713
25201	1741
25202	1744
25203	1759
25204	1771
25205	1772
25206	1779
25207	1786
25208	1820
25209	5834
25210	6175
25211	15633
25212	16090
25213	16111
25214	16174
25215	16252
25216	16265
25217	16338
25218	16407
25219	16409
25220	16440
25221	16442
25222	16445
25223	16518
25224	16557
25225	16605
25226	16623
25227	16652
25228	16907
25229	16929
25230	16949
25231	16960
25232	16966
25233	16968
25234	16971
25235	16974
25236	16975
25237	16985
25238	16987
25239	17007
25240	17094
25241	17163
25242	17172
25243	17212
25244	17236
25245	17274
25246	17283
25247	17284
D1737	
25248	864
25249	885
25250	7902
25251	7904
25252	7905
25253	7907
25254	7908
25255	7909
25256	7925
25257	7929
25258	7930
25259	7931
25260	7938
25261	7940
25262	15462
25263	15524
25264	15525
25265	15532
25266	15647
25267	16402
25268	16405
25269	16422
25270	16455
25271	16459
25272	16463

NB. The type-by-type survey of 57ft lavatory stock follows on the next five pages

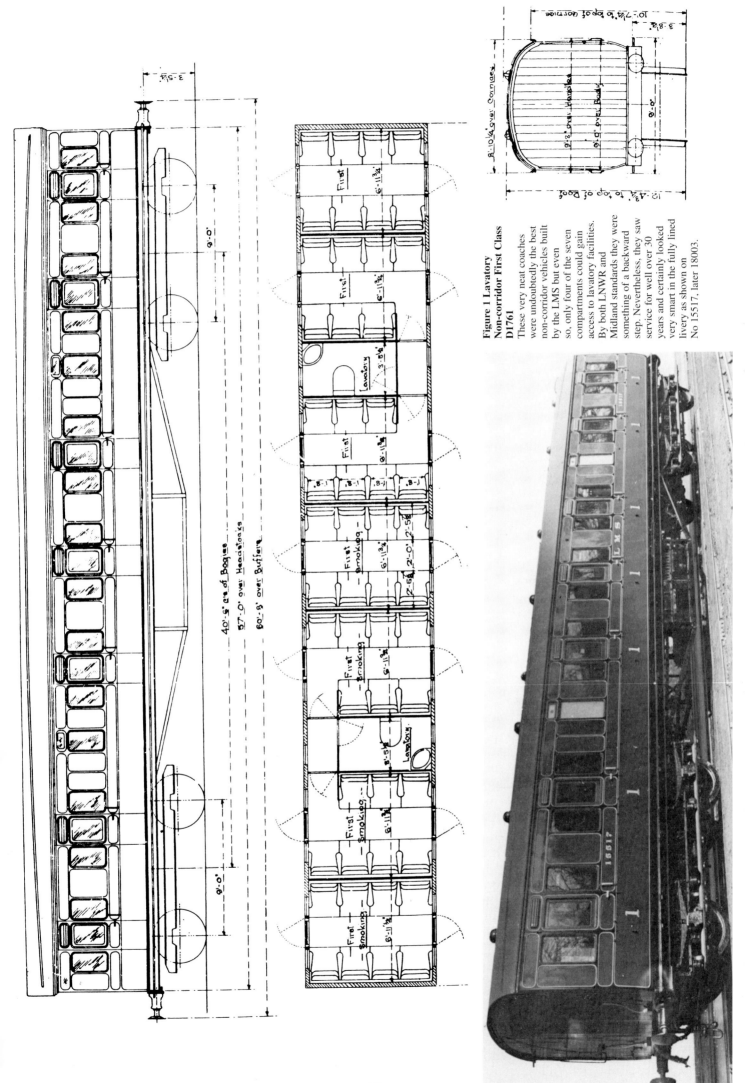

Figure 1 Lavatory Non-corridor First Class D1761

These very neat coaches were undoubtedly the best non-corridor vehicles built by the LMS but even so, only four of the seven compartments could gain access to lavatory facilities. By both LNWR and Midland standards they were something of a backward step. Nevertheless, they saw service for well over 30 years and certainly looked very smart in the fully lined livery as shown on No 15517, later 18003.

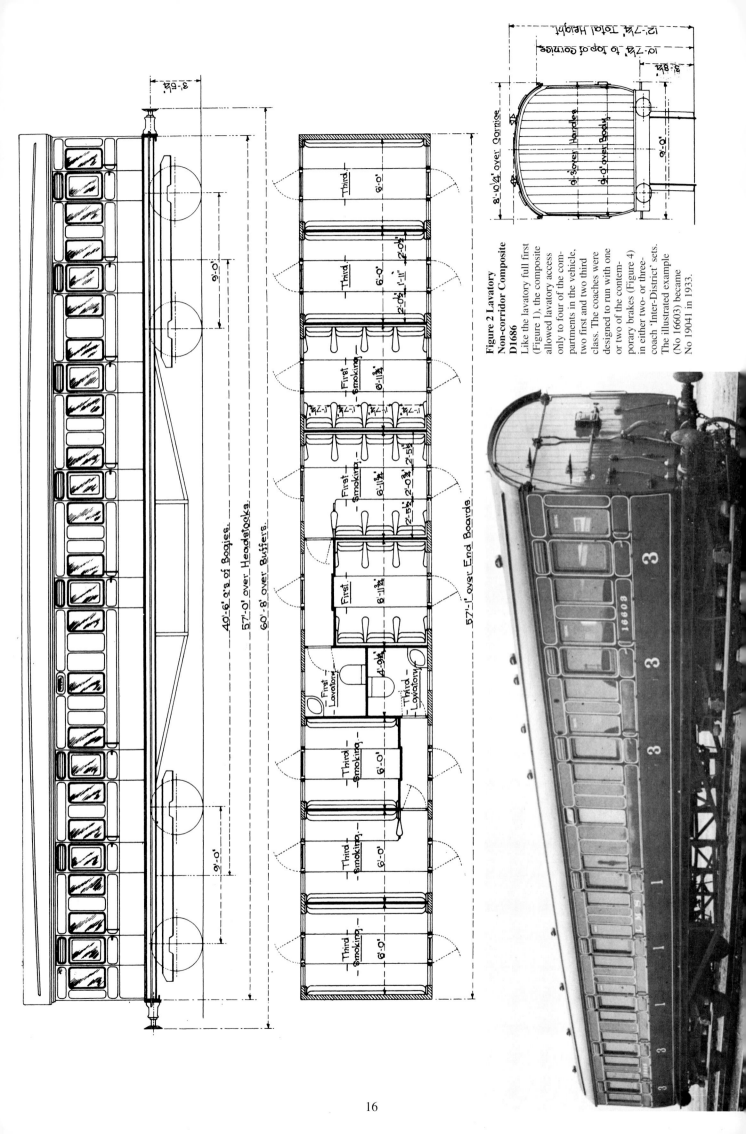

Figure 2 Lavatory Non-corridor Composite D1686

Like the lavatory full first (Figure 1), the composite allowed lavatory access only to four of the compartments in the vehicle, two first and two third class. The coaches were designed to run with one or two of the contemporary brakes (Figure 4) in either two- or three-coach 'Inter-District' sets. The illustrated example (No 16603) became (No 19041 in 1933.

3'-5½"

9'-0"

9'-0"

40'-6" c's of Bogies.

57'-0" over Headstocks.

60'-8" over Buffers.

9'-0"

9'-0"

Third. 6'-0"

Third. 6'-0" 1'-11"

2'-0½" 2'-0"

First smoking. 6'-11¾"

1'-7½" 1'-7½" 1'-7½" 1'-7¾"

First Smoking. 6'-11¾"

2'-5½" 2'-0¾" 2'-5½"

First. 6'-11¾"

First Lavatory.

Third Lavatory.

4'-9¾"

Third Smoking. 6'-0"

Third Smoking. 6'-0"

Third Smoking. 6'-0"

57'-1" over End Boards.

12'-7¾" Total Height.

10'-7½" to top of cornice.

3'-8½"

8'-10¼" over Cornice.

9'-3" over Handles.

9'-0" over Body.

9'-0"

16

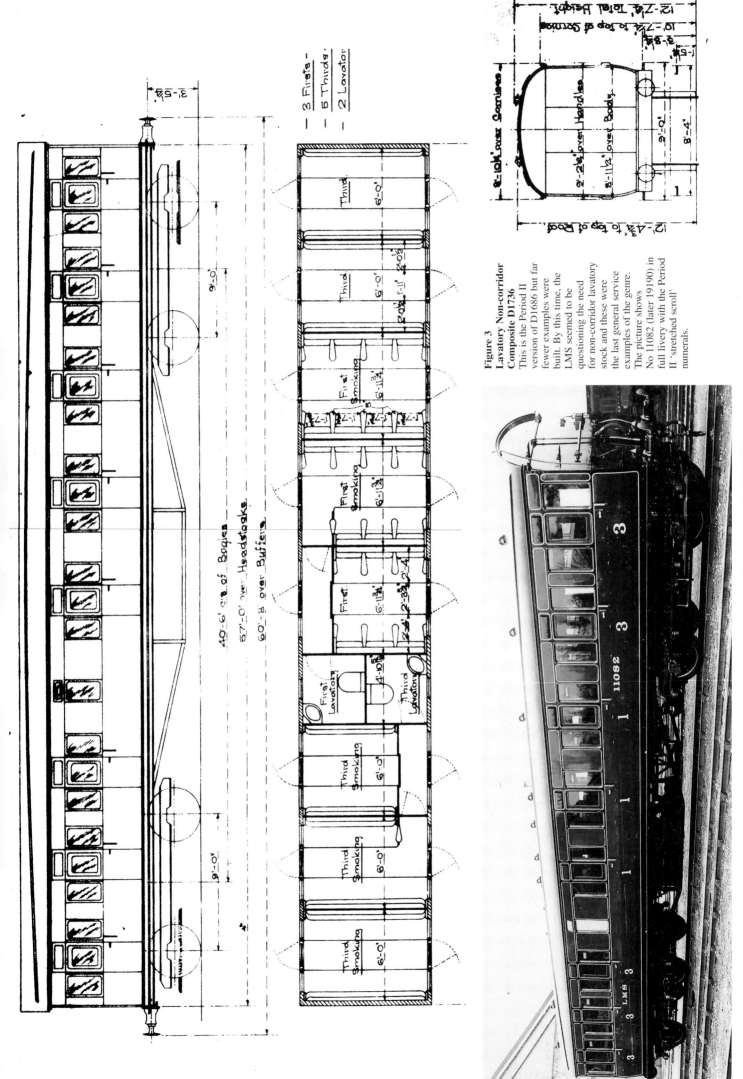

Figure 3
Lavatory Non-corridor Composite D1736
This is the Period II version of D1686 but far fewer examples were built. By this time, the LMS seemed to be questioning the need for non-corridor lavatory stock and these were the last general service examples of the genre. The picture shows No 11082 (later 19190) in full livery with the Period II 'stretched scroll' numerals.

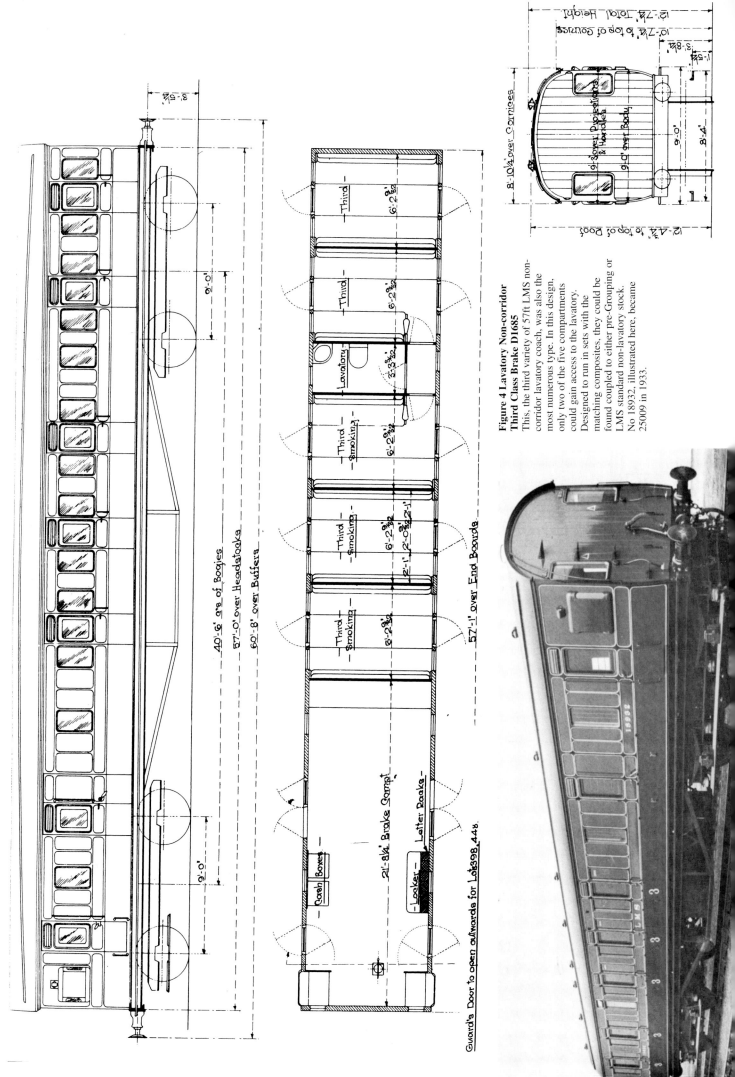

3'-0⅜"

9'-0"

9'-0"

40'-6" c's of Bogies

57'-0" over Headstocks

60'-8" over Buffers

Third — 6'-2³⁄₃₂"

Third — 6'-2³⁄₃₂"

Lavatory — 3'-3³⁄₃₂"

Third Smoking — 6'-2³⁄₃₂"

Third Smoking — 6'-2³⁄₃₂"

Third Smoking — 6'-2³⁄₃₂" — 2'-1" — 2'-0"₂'-1"

Coach Boxes

21'-8¼" Brake Compt

Looker — Letter Boxes

57'-1" over End Boards

Guard's Door to open outwards for Lot 398, 448.

8'-10½" over Cornices

9'-3" over Projections & Handles

9'-0" over Body

9'-0"

8'-4"

3'-8¼"

1'-5¾"

10'-7¼" to top of cornice

12'-7¾" Total Height

12'-4¾" to top of Roof

Figure 4 Lavatory Non-corridor Third Class Brake D1685

This, the third variety of 57ft LMS non-corridor lavatory coach, was also the most numerous type. In this design, only two of the five compartments could gain access to the lavatory. Designed to run in sets with the matching composites, they could be found coupled to either pre-Grouping or LMS standard non-lavatory stock. No 18932, illustrated here, became 25009 in 1933.

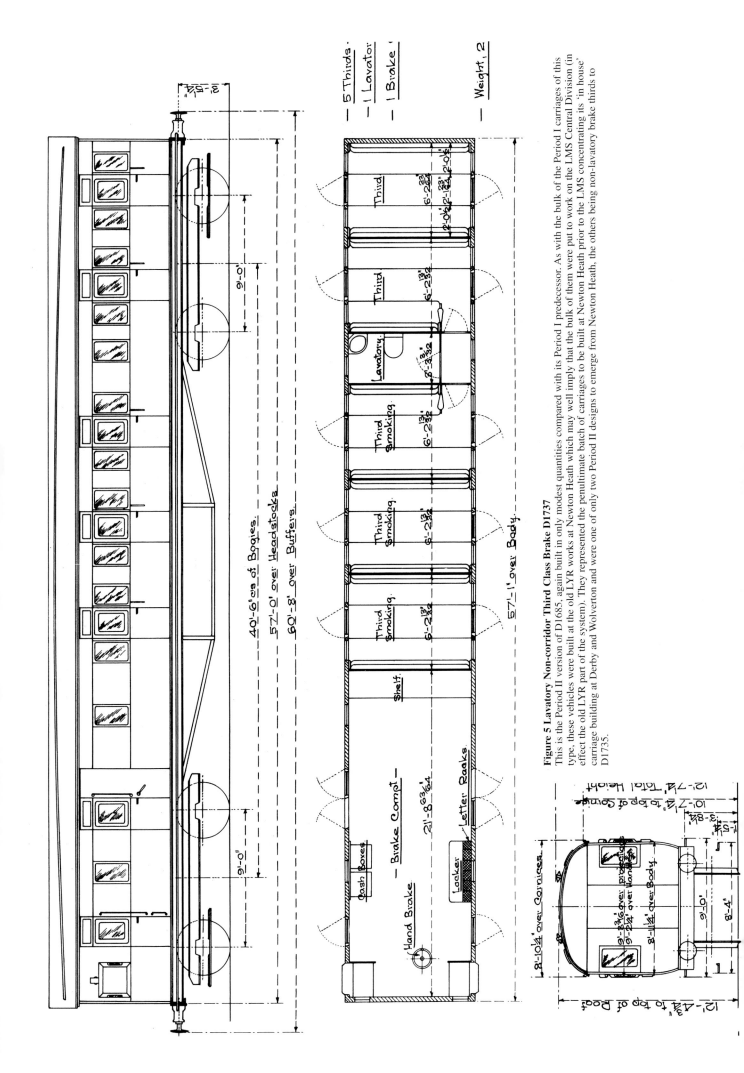

Figure 5 Lavatory Non-corridor Third Class Brake D1737

This is the Period II version of D1685, again built in only modest quantities compared with its Period I predecessor. As with the bulk of the Period I carriages of this type, these vehicles were built at the old LYR works at Newton Heath which may well imply that the bulk of them were put to work on the LMS Central Division (in effect the old LYR part of the system). They represented the penultimate batch of carriages to be built at Newton Heath prior to the LMS concentrating its 'in house' carriage building at Derby and Wolverton and were one of only two Period II designs to emerge from Newton Heath, the others being non-lavatory brake thirds to D1735.

19

57FT NON-LAVATORY STOCK

First Class

All LMS non-corridor firsts were eight-compartment coaches, mostly built during Period I (D1702). None was built during Period II but a handful of Period III versions were built in the 1930s. These were, technically, the last of the LMS non-corridor firsts, but, somewhat surprisingly, a further group of 15 were built after Nationalisation in 1951. These seem to have been used in Scotland on the downgrading of the five-a-side Cathcart Circle first class coaches (see Chapter 2) and may have been a contributory factor to the non-appearance of a BR standard non-corridor full first.

Third Class

Non-corridor thirds were built in great quantity in all three design periods and continued to be built until 1951. All were nine-compartment 108-seat vehicles and the only real change, apart from the exteriors, was the occasional reshuffling of the non-smoking compartments. Some of the coaches, especially the later ones, were either fitted for or converted to push-pull working.

Third brakes were almost equally consistent, being six-compartment coaches seating 72 passengers. They were again built in quantity during all three periods and continued in production until 1951/2. Many were fitted for push-pull use.

There were two principal exceptions to the normal LMS standard non-corridor brake third. One was a six-compartment brake *second* for the North London sets (D1723/D1797) while the North London brake third was a *seven*-compartment vehicle (D1733/D1783). These coaches are considered in more detail below.

Composite

Once again, the standard layout never varied from Grouping until 1950. LMS-design non-corridor composites for general service were nine-compartment coaches arranged, like their LNWR ancestors, with three first class compartments in the centre. Again they were built in all three periods and contained their quota of push-pull vehicles. Because of the first class compartments, the third class compartments in the composites were shorter between partitions than they were in the full thirds and brake thirds.

The only LMS-designed variation was an eight-compartment coach containing six first class compartments of somewhat larger dimensions between partitions. The other two compartments were either second class (D1731/D1786) or third class (D1732/D1785). They were again designed for use on the North London section and are considered below.

The final composites to be given LMS series numbers were to D2189. These were built at Swindon to GWR design after Nationalisation. Apparently, Derby and Wolverton were fully occupied with work and the coaches were urgently needed. They had four first class compartments with five-a-side seating and were 59ft 2in over frames. Included in this survey merely for the sake of completeness, they were built to GWR Diagram E156 (GW lots 1749/1772).

Period II BT No 16630, later 20526 (D1735). This coach was one of the last Period II vehicles to be built (1932) and the slightly simplified form of the fully lined livery between the windows probably anticipated the early Stanier style.

Period III non-corridor first No 10124 built in 1951 to a 1938 diagram (D1997). Note the unlined BR red livery and BR-type torpedo ventilators.

Period III non-corridor composite to D1921A, No 16751 built in 1949. This coach, apart from the lack of company initials, was outshopped in final LMS livery, and did not carry the figure '3' on any compartment doors. Slightly shorter third class compartments were provided in the composite coaches than in the full thirds.

TABLE 1c: SUMMARY TABLE OF LMS STANDARD 57ft NON-CORRIDOR (NON-LAVATORY) STOCK FOR GENERAL SERVICE

Note: This table should be read in conjunction with the list of standard dimensions and details on page 8.

Type	Diag	Lot	Qty	Date	Built	Dimensions (L x W x H)	Weight	Period	Running Numbers	Withdrawals First	Last	Remarks
F	1702	32	4	1924	Wolverton	57ft x 9ft 3in x 12ft 4¾in	28T	I	10027-10030	5/58	1/60	The most common non-corridor first class coach to LMS design.
		121	25	1926	Wolverton		27T		10031-10055	7/58	9/64	Lot 32 had MR fittings and was 9ft 1½in wide. No 9ft 1½in issued.
		248	20	1927	Wolverton		28T		10056-10075	8/58	13/62	Lots 248/321 plated 27T. 10000-26 were 54ft coaches — see Table
		321	30	1928	Wolverton		28T		10076-10105	10/58	13/62	2a.
F	1858	693	4	1933	Derby	57ft x 9ft 3in x 12ft 4¾in	30T	III	10106-10109	12/61	4/66	Period III version of D1702. Lot 693 had full livery when new.
		778	1	1934	Derby		30T		10110	-	10/64	10111-2 were 54ft coaches — see Table 2a.
F	1997	1048	4	1938	Wolverton	57ft x 9ft 3in x 12ft 4¾in	30T	III	10113-10116	2/62	4/65	Identical to D1858 except for the disposition of non-smokers and
		1632	15	1951	Wolverton		30T		10117-10131	3/64	4/66	the slightly increased height over ventilators. Lot 1048 plated 1937. Lot 1632 had postwar-type torpedo vents and was outshopped in BR crimson livery.
C	1701	33	49	1925	Wolverton	57ft x 9ft 3in x 12ft 4¾in	28T	I	16028-16076	5/59	1/64	The standard Period I composite, matching D1702/D1703. Lot 81
		81	8	1927	Derby		26T		16077-16084	5/59	3/65	seems to have been ordered for eight three-car sets with Lot 82 (BT
		122	80	1926	Wolverton		27T		16085-16164	10/57	7/64	— D1703) and was built with short buffers. They were not
		247	51	1926/7	Wolverton		27T		16165-16215	5/59	12/63	marshalled with Lot 82! 16000-6 were NL stock (see Table 1d) and
		322	80	1927	Wolverton		27T		16216-16295	2/58	11/65	16007-27 were 51ft and 54ft stock (Table 2a).
C	1767	229	30	1926/7	Ntn Hth	57ft x 9ft 3in x 12ft 4¾ in	26T	I	16296-16325	5/59	6/65	An odd batch with slightly different compartment dimen-sions from the otherwise identical D1701. The firsts were a little larger and the thirds a little smaller. They were built without dynamos to run with BTs 20206-20235 (D1703) and the arrangement of non-smoking compartments differed from D1701.
C	1734	526	43	1930/1	W'ton	57ft x 9ft 2¼ in x 12ft 4¾ in	27T	II	16331-16368	5/59	7/64	The Period II version of D1702. Some at least of Lot 526 were
									17900-17904*	3/61	9/64	plated 29T.
		581	100	1931/2	W'ton		29T		16369-16468	8/58	10/65	*Motor-fitted coaches, originally allocated 16326-30.
C	1849	650	20	1932	Wolverton	57ft x 9ft 3in x 12ft 4¾ in	30T	II	16469-16488	6/59	1/65	This was an interesting diagram. It was a Period II diagram but
		684	55	1933	Derby		30T	III	16496-16535	2/62	1/66	Lots 684/704 were actually Period III coaches. All carried full
									17905-17919*	4/62	12/65	livery and Lots 684/704 were some of the few Stanier coaches to
		704	34	1933	Derby		30T	III	16536-16569	4/63	12/65	be given torpedo ventilators before the adoption of the shell type. Coach layout identical to D1734 but with slightly modified compartment dimensions. 16489-95 were NL stock (see Table 1d). *Motor-fitted coaches.
C	1921	741	25	1933/4	Derby	57ft x 9ft 3in x 12ft 4¾ in	30T	III	16570-16594	9/62	7/64	The genuine Period III diagram but otherwise no difference from
		742	20	1934	Derby		30T		16595-16614	9/62	1/66	the Period I and II predecessors. All are believed to have had simple
		849	32	1935	Derby		30T		16615-16644	9/62	12/65	livery but Lot 741 is not confirmed.
									17920-17921*	3/64	13/64	*Motor-fitted coaches.
C	1921A	901	27	1936	Derby	57ft x 9ft 3in x 12ft 4¾ in	30T	III	16645-16671	4/63	6/66	3in less over stepboards and 3⁄16in higher over roof vents than
		1047	36	1938	Wolverton		30T		16672-16706	4/63	2/66	D1921. Lot 1449 had simple LMS livery but no LMS markings.
									17922*			Lot 1450 was probably similar. Lot 1576 believed to have had BR
		1102	40	1939	Wolverton		30T		16707-16746	7/63	9/66	livery from new. Lots 1450/1576 seem to have had postwar
		1449	50	1949	Derby		28T		16747-16796	2/64	12/66	torpedo-type ventilators. Lot 1102 plated 1938; Lot 1576 plated
		1450	20	1949	Derby		28T		17923-17942*	1/64	7/66	29T.
		1576	10	1950	Wolverton		28T		19377-19386‡	2/64	11/66	*Motor-fitted coaches. ‡Motor-fitted coaches given vacant overflow numbers in the lavatory composite series.
C	2189	1648	45	1952/3	Swindon	59ft 2in x 9ft 3in x 12ft 3¼in	29T	see	16797-16841	6/64	6/66	GWR-style coaches built after Nationalisation to a resuscitated
							29T	notes				prewar design. Their numbers had an M prefix and W suffix with BR
		1661	35	1953	Swindon		29T		16842-16816	1/64	11/67	livery from new. GWR Diagram E156 — Lots 1749/1772.
T	1700	102	38	1925	Wolverton	57ft x 9ft 3in x 12ft 4¾ in	27T	I	10850-10887	5/59	12/63	The standard Period I full third. Lot 510 was for the North London
		103	20	1925	Ntn Hth		28T		10888-10907	2/60	12/63	sets — see Table 1d.
		124	42	1925	Ntn Hth		28T		10908-10949	8/58	5/63	*Conversions to motor-fitted stock:*
		231	50	1926	Ntn Hth		27T		10950-10999	2/58	13/64	11170 to 15998 c1935
		305	50	1927/8	Ntn Hth		26T		11000-11049	7/58	13/63	11284 to 15999 c1935
		361	100	1928	Wolverton		27T		11050-11149	11/58	11/64	
		390	50	1928	Wolverton		27T		11150-11199	9/58	12/63	*Plating discrepancies:*
		410	68	1928/30	Derby		26T		11200-11267	11/58	4/65	Lot 231 plated 28T; Lot 305 plated 27T and all plated 1927.
		447	50	1929	Wolverton		28T		11268-11317	5/59	9/64	
		492	50	1930	Ntn Hth		28T		11318-11367	5/59	11/64	
		510	6	1930	Derby		27T		11368-11373	2/62	7/64	
T	1784	523	50	1930/1	Derby	57ft x 9ft 2¼ in x 12ft 4¾ in	28T	II	11374-11423	5/59	9/64	The Period II version of D1700. Lots 544/642 were for the North
		528	78	1930	Wolverton		28T		11424-11501	2/59	11/64	London sets — see Table 1d. Lot 554 had bodies built at Newton
		554	4	1931	see notes		29T		11502-11505	3/61	3/64	Heath on Derby-built chassis. 11606-23 were 54ft coaches (Table
		580	100	1932	Derby		28T		11506-11605	6/59	12/65	2a).
		642	4	1932	Derby		28T		11624-11627	10/60	1/64	*Conversions to motor-fitted stock:* 11403 to 15997 c1935

Type	*Diag*	*Lot*	*Qty*	*Date*	*Built*	*Dimensions* (L x W x H)	*Weight*	*Period*	*Running Numbers*	*Withdrawals First*	*Withdrawals Last*	*Remarks*
T	1906	682	50	1933	Derby	57ft x 9ft 3in x 12ft 4⅝ in	30T	III	15858-15859*	11/62	2/64	Period III version of D1700. Note the reversion to this diagram in 1939 after a number of coaches had been built to D1906A. *Motor-fitted; Lot 683 may also have been originally intended as a motor-fitted batch. 11705-16 were 54ft coaches (Table 2a).
									11628-11675	4/62	6/66	
		683	4	1933	Derby		30T		11676-11679	4/62	11/63	
		743	25	1934	Derby		30T		11680-11704	7/63	3/66	
		847	25	1935	Derby		29T		11717-11741	4/63	2/67	
		1194	40	1939	Wolverton		30T		12158-12197	12/63	12/66	
		1195	30	1939/40	Wolverton		30T		12198-12227	7/60	8/66	
T	1906A	906	55	1936	Wolverton	57ft x 9ft 3in x 12ft 4⅝ in	30T	III	11742-11796	4/62	12/66	Identical to D1906 except for rearranged smoking/non-smoking and very minor dimension differences. The frame of one of Lot 1094 was used for one vehicle of the BR XP64 demonstration train! *Motor-fitted
		907	55	1936	Wolverton		30T		11797-11851	11/61	9/67	
		1036	60	1937	Derby		29T		11852-11911	10/63	9/67	
		1043	55	1937	Wolverton		30T		11912-11966	3/62	8/67	
		1044	55	1937	Wolverton		30T		11967-12021	12/61	9/67	
		1094	67	1938	Wolverton		30T		12022-12087	12/63	9/67	
									15860*	-	7/64	
		1095	70	1938	Wolverton		30T		12088-12157	12/61	13/66	
T	2124	1451	30	1949	Derby	57ft x 9ft 3in x 12ft 4⅝ in	28T	III	15862-15891	13/63	Not known	Generally as per D1906A but with roof vents closer together. No apparently good reason for the change in diagram but as the first two lots were built motor-fitted, the diagram change may have been for this reason. Lot 1633 was plated 1950. All are thought to have had postwar torpedo ventilators and the following ex-works livery: Lot 1451 — LMS simple livery, no LMS markings. Lot 1578 — BR lined out crimson. Lot 1633 — BR unlined crimson.
		1578	15	1950	Wolverton		28T		15892-15906	12/63	9/66	
		1633	40	1951	Wolverton		28T		12228-12267	1/64	11/66	
BT	1703	82	16	1927	Derby	57ft x 9ft 3in x 12ft 4¾ in	26T	I	20140-20155	5/59	7/64	The standard Period I coach. Lot 82 emerged very late for such a low lot number and Lot 141 was also a late arrival. Lot 82 may have been ordered with Lot 81 (C-D1701) for a particular need for three-coach sets which failed to materialise and was thus held back until needed for general service. They were general service coaches when they did enter service. 20299 was later used as a Morecambe-Heysham driving trailer (1950). 20000-139 were 54ft coaches (Table 2a).
		141	50	1927	Derby		27T		20156-20205	5/59	2/63	
		230	30	1926/7	Ntn Hth		27T		20206-20235	5/59	1/65	
		289	51	1927	Ntn Hth		27T		20236-20286	11/58	1/64	
		335	50	1928	Ntn Hth		27T		20287-20336	7/58	11/64	
		356	50	1928	Ntn Hth		27T		20337-20386	8/58	4/66	
BT	1735	part 527	33	1930	Derby	57ft x 9ft 3 1/16 in x 12ft 4¾ in	27T	II	20540-20572	5/59	8/65	The Period II version of D1703 but again with a change to Period III styling at Lot 681 without a change of diagram. Lots 681/687 had full livery and torpedo ventilators. *Motor-fitted conversions:* 20553-24472; 20554-24467; 20557-24468; 20564-24462; 20565-24460; 20597-24470; 20602-24471; 20461-24473; 20469-24464; 20470-24465; 20471-24466.
		562	40	1930/1	Ntn Hth		27T		20387-20426	3/60	10/65	
		621	45	1931/2	Derby		28T	-	20427-20471	5/60	5/65	
		647	15	1932	Derby		28T		20472-20486	11/59	13/64	
		649	50	1932	Derby		28T		20487-20536	3/60	4/65	
		681	20	1933	Wolverton		29T	III	20700-20719	6/61	4/66	
		687	122	1933	Wolverton		29T		20577-20699	12/59	1/67	
		1147	1	1938	Wolverton		29T		20584	-	13/63	Lot 1147 was a one-for-one replacement of an accident victim destroyed in 1937 at Birmingham. *Plating discrepancies:* Lot 562 plated 28T.
BT (Driving)	1790	part 527	7	1930	Derby	57ft x 9ft 3in x 12ft 4¾ in	27T	II	24403-24409	7/59	1/64	The driving trailer version of D1735. The post-1932 conversions to driving trailers of D1735 closely resembled D1790 except that they had flush glazing on the control end windows rather than the Period II windows of D1790. The D1790 coaches were built as normal BTs on D1735 and altered to motor-fitted in 1930-2. It is not clear if many saw service as normal BTs between these dates (probably only 24403/4).
BT (Driving)	1856	688	17	1933	Wolverton	57ft x 9ft 3in x 12ft 4⅝ in	30T	III	24410-24426	5/63	12/65	The Period III driving trailer although the Diagram is Period II. Lot 688 had full livery with torpedo ventilators. The length was quoted as 57ft 1in on the works plate — technically correct but it was more common to quote 57ft only, omitting the odd inch.
		part 850	2	1935	Derby		29T		24427-24428	1/64	4/66	
		part 1037	1	1937	Derby		29T		24429	-	2/64	
BT	1907	744	30	1934	Wolverton	57ft x 9ft 3in x 12ft 4⅝ in	29T	III	20720-20749	12/61	7/65	The Period III version of D1703. 20781-4 were 54ft coaches (Table 2a).
		745	31	1934	Wolverton		29T		20750-20780	6/61	6/66	
		part 850	30	1935	Derby		29T		20785-20814	1/62	9/65	
BT	1964	900	64	1936	Derby	57ft x 9ft 3 3/16 in x 12ft 4⅝ in	28T	III	20815-20878	Not known	2/67	As for D1907 but the guard's van end was altered to have two pairs of double doors. Plated 30T.
BT	1964A	part 1037	49	1937/8	Derby	57ft x 9ft 3 3/16 in x 12ft 4⅝ in	28T	III	20879-20927	12/61	1/67	Identical to D1964 but with roof vents closer together. The official reason for the change in diagram was the alteration in position of the non-smoking areas. This may have been the reason for D1921/D1921A and D1906/D1906A (above) but has not been confirmed. Lot 1441 — simple LMS livery but no LMS marks. Lots 1485/1634 — postwar torpedo vents and BR livery. 20966 was used as a Morecambe-Heysham trailer in 1950.
		1086	44	1938	Derby		28T		20928-20971	11/63	2/66	
		1087	50	1938	Derby		28T		20972-21021	4/61	1/67	
		1441	60	1949	Wolverton		28T		21022-21081	12/63	8/67	
		1485	50	1951	Glos C&W		28T		21082-21131	13/63	6/67	
		1634	120	1951	Wolverton		28T		21132-21251	12/63	9/67	
BT (Driving)	2122	1442	30	1949	Wolverton}	57ft x 9ft 3in x 12ft 4⅝ in	29T	III	24430-24459	1/64	7/66	As for D1856 but van doors slightly altered in position. Postwar torpedo ventilators. Lot 1442 — LMS livery but no LMS marks; Lot 1577 — BR livery.
		1577	15	1950	Wolverton}		29T		24317-24331	3/64	13/66	

NORTH LONDON SETS

As already stated, the vast majority of 57ft stock built by the LMS was for general service and not formed into strict sets of coaches. However, the North London passenger stock inherited at the Grouping was a pretty gruesome collection of semi-museum pieces and it was not too long before the LMS put into service some new sets of standard 57ft coaches for the Broad Street-Alexandra Park services. Externally they matched the general service stock of the day but because of the different nature of the services, they were formed into sets. Five types of coaches were provided of which the full thirds were to standard LMS diagrams although built as separate North London lots. The other four types differed slightly as outlined above and thus necessitated new diagrams. The provision of second class accommodation was unique on the LMS except for the NCC, but the coaches themselves seem to have been little different from their third class contemporaries. Three classes survived on these and the related LNER suburban services until 1938. There is evidence that the seating might have been a little softer than in the thirds but the seating capacity was the same and the amount of knee room was also identical to that in the thirds.

Sufficient coaches were provided to make up seven six-coach sets. Three sets were Period I in styling and delivered in 1930 while there were four Period II sets delivered, two each in 1931 and 1932. The coaches were formed up as follows: BT/T/T/C(third-first)/C(first-second)/BS. Of the seven sets, the coaches delivered to Lots 55x in 1931 have been confirmed in this formation and, from this, the likely composition of the remainder has been deduced (Table 1d). At a later date, the second class branding was abolished (c1938) and the brake seconds were renumbered in the brake third series. The first/second composites were downgraded but retained their numbers as no separate series had been allocated to them.

TABLE 1d: SUMMARY TABLE OF SEPARATE DIAGRAMS RAISED FOR NORTH LONDON 57ft STOCK TOGETHER WITH TRAIN SET FORMATIONS

Note: This table should be read in conjunction with the list of standard dimensions and details on page 8

Type	*Diag*	*Lot*	*Qty*	*Date*	*Built*	*Dimensions* (L x W x H)	*Weight*	*Period*	*Running Numbers*	*Withdrawals First*	*Withdrawals Last*	*Remarks*
C(1/2)	1731	512	3	1930	Derby	57ft x 9ft 3in x 12ft 4¾in	27T	I	16000-16002	8/60	6/63	The eight-compartment composite with six first- and two second- class compartments.
C(1/2)	1786	556	2	1931	see notes		28T	II	16003-16004	11/62	2/64	Lot 556 had bodies built at Newton Heath with bogies/underframe built at Derby. The Period II version of D1731.
		644	2	1932	Derby	57ft x 9ft 2¼in x 12ft 4¾in	28T		16005-16006	12/62	5/63	
C(1/3)	1732	511	3	1930	Derby	57ft x 9ft 3in x 12ft 4¾in	27T	I	16489-16491	5/59	10/62	The first/third version of D1731.
C(1/3)	1785	555	2	1931	see notes	57ft x 9ft 2¼in x 12ft 4¾in	29T	II	16492-16493	7/61	6/64	The Period II version of D1732. Lot 555 built as for Lot 556 — see above.
		643	2	1932	Derby		28T		16494-16495	10/41	1/62	
BS	1723	513	3	1930	Derby	57ft x 9ft 3in x 12ft 4¾in	27T	I	24900-24902	13/62	4/64	Six-compartment brake seconds but otherwise identical to the general service D1703 brake third. Downgraded to BT and renumbered 22196-8 c1938.
BS	1797	557	2	1931	see notes	57ft x 9ft 3 3/16in x 12ft 4¾in	28T	II	24903-24904	3/63	8/63	The Period II version of D1723. Lot 557 plated 27T and built as for Lot 556 — see above. Downgraded to BT and renumbered 22199-202 c1938.
		645	2	1932	Derby		28T		24905-24906	9/61	2/64	
BT	1733	509	3	1930	Derby	57ft x 9ft 3in x 12ft 4¾in	27T	I	20537-20539	7/63	10/63	The seven-compartment brake third — otherwise identically styled to the general service D1703.
BT	1783	553	2	1931	see notes	57ft x 9ft 3 3/16in x 12ft 4¾in	27T	II	20573-20574	7/59	6/61	The Period II version of D1733. Lot 553 built as for Lot 556 — see above.
		641	2	1932	Derby		27T		20575-20576	12/62	7/64	

Note: Fourteen all thirds were built for these services but these coaches were identical to the general service all thirds and are listed under these diagrams in Table 1c. Their running numbers were as follows:
Period I coaches (Lot 510): 11368-11373 (D1700)
Period II coaches (Lot 554): 11502-11505 (D1784)
Period II coaches (Lot 642): 11624-11627 (D1784)
Lot 554 was built as for Lot 556 — see note to D1785 (above).

North London six-coach sets (confirmed individual coaches shown in italic numerals)

Set Number	*Brake*	*Third*	*Third*	*Compo*	*Compo*	*Brake*	*Remarks*
	Third			*(1/3)*	*(1/2)*	*Second*	
	20537	11368	11369	16490	16000	24900 (later 22196)	The three Period I sets of coaches
	20538	11372	11371	16491	16002	24902 (later 22198)	
N.18	*20539*	*11373*	*11370*	*16489*	*16001*	*24901 (later 22197)*	
N.16	*20573*	*11502*	*11503*	*16492*	*16003*	*24903 (later 22199)*	The four Period II sets of coaches
N.17	*20574*	11504	11505	*16493*	*16004*	*24904 (later 22200)*	
	20575	11624	11625	16494	16005	24905 (later 22201)	
	20576	11626	11627	16495	16006	24906 (later 22202)	

PUSH-PULL STOCK

As explained in Volume 1, the LMS never designed any separate motor-fitted vehicles and all the LMS standard push-pull stock was identical in styling to the contemporary non-corridor stock. Push-pull vehicles were usually listed on the same diagrams as the normal coaches while in many cases, normal non-corridor LMS coaches were later converted to motor-fitted style with little if any changes in appearance except for the windows in the driving end. Although these conversions, etc are listed in the summary tables, it has been thought desirable to give a separate list of all motor-fitted coaches either built or rebuilt to LMS standard designs and this information is appended below.

There were also push-pull conversions of LMS-design gangway stock but these were relatively few in number and no diagrams have been located for them. The conversions took place in the 1950s and involved coaches from the following diagrams:

BTK D1851 (originally built 1932)   TO D1692 (originally built 1929)   TO D1807 (originally built 1932)

Such details as are known are given in the 'Remarks' columns of Tables 3a and 4a of Volume 2.

TABLE 1e: SUMMARY OF LMS STANDARD MOTOR-FITTED STOCK

Note: This table only includes details of motor-fitted stock which was of standard LMS-pattern non-corridor design. It does, however, include all vehicles which were converted to motor-fitted form although built as standard non-corridor coaches. Undated conversions are all believed to have been c1934.

Driving Trailers

Running Numbers	Date built/ converted	Lot	Type/Remarks
24400-24402	1927	part 79	54ft Period I coaches converted 1927 — the only 54ft LMS Standard motor-fitted vehicles
24403-24409	1930-2	part 527	57ft Period II coaches converted 1930-2 but 24405-9 probably entered service motor-fitted
24410-24429	1932-8	688, 750 1087	Period III coaches built as driving trailers to D1856
24430-24459	1949	1442	57ft postwar Period III driving trailers to D2122
24317-24331	1950	1577	57ft as per 24430-24459
24460		527	57ft Period II coach converted from 20565
24462		527	57ft Period II coach converted from 20564
24464	c1934	621	57ft Period II coach converted from 20469
24665	c1934	621	57ft Period II coach converted from 20470
24466	c1934	621	57ft Period II coach converted from 20471
24467		527	57ft Period II coach converted from 20554
24468		527	57ft Period II coach converted from 20557
24470	c1935	687	57ft Period III coach converted from 20597
24471	c1935	687	57ft Period III coach converted from 20602
24472	c1935	527	57ft Period II coach converted from 20553
24473	1934	621	57ft Period II coach converted from 20461

Note: The missing 244xx series numbers were carried by pre-Grouping vehicles

All Thirds

Running Numbers	Date built/ converted	Lot	Type/Remarks
15858-15859	1933	682	57ft Period III built new
15860	1938	1094	57ft Period III built new
15861	c1938	1044	57ft Period III ex-12010
15862-15891	1949	1451	57ft Period III built new
15892-15906	1950	1578	57ft Period III built new
15997	c1935	523	57ft Period II ex-11403
15998		390	57ft Period I ex-11162
15999		447	57ft Period I ex-11284

Composites

Running Numbers	Date built/ converted	Lot	Type/Remarks
17900-17904	1931	526	Originally allocated 16326-30 in compo list but converted to push-pull before getting these numbers 57ft Period II coaches
17905-17919	1933	684	57ft Period III coaches built new. Full livery and torpedo ventilators
17920-17921	1935	849	57ft Period III coaches built new
17922	1938	1047	57ft Period III coach built new
17923-17942	1949	1450	57ft Period III coaches built new
17944		650	57ft Period II coach ex-16478
17946		33	57ft Period I coach ex-16066
17947		526	57ft Period II coach ex-16343
17948		581	57ft Period II coach ex-16432
17949		581	57ft Period II coach ex-16434
17950		581	57ft Period II coach ex-16435
17951		526	57ft Period II coach ex-16356
17952		122	57ft Period I coach ex-16101
17954	c1935	684	57ft Period III coach ex-16523
17955	c1935	684	57ft Period III coach ex-16522
17956	c1935	684	57ft Period III coach ex-16521
17597	1934	526	57ft Period II coach ex-16347
19377-19386	1950	1576	57ft Period III coaches built new

Note: Except for 17943, which was never used, the missing 179xx numbers were carried by pre-Grouping vehicles.

TABLE 1f: THE 1933 RENUMBERING OF LMS 57ft NON-LAVATORY STOCK

The following list is given in the same carriage diagram order as Tables 1c and 1d. It is, of course, applicable only to Period I and Period II designs, the North London stock — Table 1d — being listed separately from the general batches and suffixed (NL).

New Number	Old	New Number	Old	New Number	Old	New Number	Old	New Number	Old	New Number	Old	New Number	Old
First Class		10087	18233	16052	3473	16115	9249	16178	15893	16241	17725	16301	18596
D1702		10088	18234	16053	3476	16116	9256	16179	15895	16242	17726	16302	18598
		10089	18235	16054	3480	16117	9257	16180	15930	16243	17727	16303	18600
10027	16691	10090	18236	16055	3503	16118	9258	16181	16084	16244	17729	16304	18601
10028	16783	10091	18237	16056	3510	16119	9261	16182	16188	16245	17730	16305	18602
10029	16785	10092	18238	16057	3512	16120	9267	16183	16189	16246	17732	16306	18603
10030	16790	10093	18239	16058	3513	16121	9268	16184	16200	16247	17733	16307	18604
10031	9344	10094	18241	16059	3518	16122	9272	16185	16245	16248	17734	16308	18605
10032	10093	10095	18242	16060	3520	16123	9273	16186	16328	16249	17735	16309	18606
10033	10094	10096	18243	16061	3526	16124	9276	16187	16360	16250	17736	16310	18607
10034	10095	10097	18244	16062	3533	16125	9277	16188	16366	16251	17738	16311	18609
10035	10096	10098	18245	16063	3535	16126	9279	16189	16373	16252	17739	16312	18610
10036	10097	10099	18246	16064	3547	16127	9281	16190	16393	16253	17740	16313	18611
10037	10098	10100	18247	16065	3548	16128	9283	16191	16412	16254	17742	16314	18612
10038	10099	10101	18248	16066	3553	16129	9360	16192	16497	16255	17744	16315	18613
10039	10100	10102	18249	16067	3556	16130	9897	16193	16576	16256	17745	16316	18637
10040	10101	10103	18250	16068	3568	16131	9898	16194	16587	16257	17746	16317	18638
10041	10102	10104	18251	16069	3570	16132	9899	16195	16599	16258	17747	16318	18639
10042	10103	10105	18254	16070	3576	16133	9900	16196	16645	16259	17748	16319	18642
10043	10245			16071	3601	16134	9901	16197	16653	16260	17749	16320	18643
10044	10246	**First/Second**		16072	3714	16135	9902	16198	16656	16261	17750	16321	18645
10045	10260	**Composite**		16073	8717	16136	9903	16199	16714	16262	17751	16322	18646
10046	10261	D1731 (NL)		16074	8718	16137	9904	16200	16753	16263	17752	16323	18647
10047	10262			16075	9259	16138	9905	16201	16767	16264	17753	16324	18648
10048	10263	16000	1426	16076	9263	16139	9906	16202	16792	16265	17754	16325	18650
10049	10264	16001	1429	16077	2881	16140	9907	16203	16803	16266	17755		
10050	10265	16002	7857	16078	3397	16141	9908	16204	16809	16267	17756	D1734	
10051	10266			16079	3519	16142	9909	16205	16839	16268	17757		
10052	10267	D1786 (NL)		16080	3573	16143	9910	16206	16885	16269	17758	16331	3012
10053	10268			16081	3695	16144	9911	16207	16891	16270	17759	16332	3014
10054	10269	16003	11149	16082	3697	16145	9912	16208	16914	16271	17760	16333	3015
10055	10270	16004	11152	16083	3708	16146	9913	16209	16994	16272	17780	16334	3016
10056	18694	16005	3162	16084	3710	16147	9914	16210	17013	16273	17781	16335	3017
10057	18697	16006	3252	16085	8720	16148	9915	16211	17042	16274	17803	16336	3018
10058	18698			16086	8721	16149	9916	16212	17125	16275	17806	16337	3019
10059	18699	**First/Third**		16087	8724	16150	9922	16213	17341	16276	17808	16338	3020
10060	18702	**Composite**		16088	8725	16151	9923	16214	17342	16277	17814	16339	3021
10061	18710	D1701		16089	8726	16152	9924	16215	17432	16278	17820	16340	3041
10062	18711			16090	8727	16153	9925	16216	17579	16279	17822	16341	3042
10063	18712	16028	2809	16091	8728	16154	9926	16217	17580	16280	17824	16342	3043
10064	18713	16029	2942	16092	8729	16155	9927	16218	17581	16281	17920	16343	3044
10065	18723	16030	2950	16093	8730	16156	9928	16219	17643	16282	17954	16344	3045
10066	18725	16031	2951	16094	8731	16157	9929	16220	17650	16283	17955	16345	3046
10067	18727	16032	2953	16095	8732	16158	9930	16221	17659	16284	17956	16346	3047
10068	18729	16033	2955	16096	8733	16159	9931	16222	17705	16285	17957	16347	3048
10069	18730	16034	2956	16097	8734	16160	9932	16223	17706	16286	17958	16348	3049
10070	18733	16035	2957	16098	8735	16161	9933	16224	17707	16287	17959	16349	3050
10071	18734	16036	2958	16099	8736	16162	9934	16225	17708	16288	17960	16350	3051
10072	18735	16037	2960	16100	8737	16163	9935	16226	17709	16289	17961	16351	3052
10073	18739	16038	2968	16101	8738	16164	9936	16227	17710	16290	17962	16352	3053
10074	18740	16039	2969	16102	8739	16165	1641	16228	17711	16291	17963	16353	3054
10075	18741	16040	2973	16103	8740	16166	2996	16229	17712	16292	17964	16354	3055
10076	18213	16041	2976	16104	8741	16167	3678	16230	17713	16293	17965	16355	3087
10077	18217	16042	2985	16105	8742	16168	3688	16231	17714	16294	17966	16356	3088
10078	18218	16043	3309	16106	8743	16169	15465	16232	17715	16295	17967	16357	3089
10079	18219	16044	3310	16107	8744	16170	15601	16233	17717			16358	3090
10080	18220	16045	3301	16108	8745	16171	15622	16234	17718	D1767		16359	3092
10081	18221	16046	3409	16109	8791	16172	15733	16235	17719			16360	3093
10082	18222	16047	3433	16110	9231	16173	15735	16236	17720	16296	18591	16361	3094
10083	18225	16048	3442	16111	9243	16174	15795	16237	17721	16297	18592	16362	3095
10084	18226	16049	3454	16112	9244	16175	15823	16238	17722	16298	18593	16363	3096
10085	18228	16050	3466	16113	9245	16176	15840	16239	17723	16299	18594	16364	3097
10086	18229	16051	3471	16114	9247	16177	15884	16240	17724	16300	18595	16365	3143

New Number	Old Number
16366	3595
16367	3596
16368	3647
16369	84
16370	1795
16371	2443
16372	3003
16373	3060
16374	3061
16375	3062
16376	3076
16377	3079
16378	3102
16379	3120
16380	3122
16381	3131
16382	3137
16383	3138
16384	3141
16385	3142
16386	3145
16387	3147
16388	3150
16389	3151
16390	3152
16391	3157
16392	3159
16393	3161
16394	3164
16395	3166
16396	3167
16397	3174
16398	3178
16399	3181
16400	3186
16401	3187
16402	3190
16403	3191
16404	3193
16405	3200
16406	3204
16407	3211
16408	3212
16409	3224
16410	3269
16411	3270
16412	3271
16413	3275
16414	3277
16415	3287
16416	3561
16417	3589
16418	3592
16419	3615
16420	3720
16421	3723
16422	3731
16423	3844
16424	3852
16425	3853
16426	5691
16427	7732
16428	8599
16429	8635
16430	9438
16431	9742
16432	10703

New Number	Old Number
16433	10728
16434	11292
16435	11792
16436	11818
16437	12056
16438	12063
16439	12086
16440	12203
16441	12293
16442	12374
16443	12576
16444	12643
16445	12650
16446	12724
16447	12964
16448	13138
16449	13161
16450	13188
16451	13302
16452	13925
16453	13926
16454	14755
16455	14781
16456	14813
16457	14816
16458	14818
16459	14829
16460	14831
16461	14952
16462	15694
16463	15854
16464	16115
16465	16369
16466	16874
16467	17107
16468	17811

D1849

New Number	Old Number
16469	70
16470	1413
16471	1414
16472	1794
16473	3170
16474	3176
16475	3179
16476	3182
16477	3189
16478	3192
16479	3194
16480	7662
16481	7671
16482	7692
16483	7763
16484	7834
16485	7953
16486	9442
16487	9448
16488	11165

D1732 (NL)

New Number	Old Number
16489	1147
16490	1162
16491	1211

D1785 (NL)

New Number	Old Number
16492	8630
16493	8631
16494	2778
16495	2900

Third Class
D1700

New Number	Old Number
10850	5814
10851	5832
10852	5836
10853	5837
10854	5838
10855	5840
10856	5847
10857	5862
10858	5877
10859	5878
10860	5879
10861	5880
10862	5883
10863	5887
10864	5888
10865	5890
10866	5894
10867	5895
10868	5898
10869	5924
10870	5936
10871	5951
10872	5952
10873	5953
10874	5954
10875	5956
10876	5957
10877	5961
10878	5962
10879	5963
10880	5964
10881	5966
10882	5968
10883	5969
10884	5970
10885	5972
10886	5974
10887	5975
10888	13914
10889	13924
10890	13933
10891	13941
10892	13963
10893	13974
10894	13997
10895	14039
10896	14069
10897	14077
10898	14101
10899	14103
10900	14114
10901	14117
10902	14119
10903	14125
10904	14152
10905	14176
10906	14184
10907	14224
10908	13915

New Number	Old Number
10909	13920
10910	13942
10911	13945
10912	13948
10913	13958
10914	13964
10915	13979
10916	13987
10917	13995
10918	14010
10919	14018
10920	14019
10921	14021
10922	14024
10923	14062
10924	14064
10925	14065
10926	14066
10927	14073
10928	14076
10929	14090
10930	14099
10931	14104
10932	14107
10933	14108
10934	14112
10935	14115
10936	14118
10937	14122
10938	14126
10939	14139
10940	14141
10941	14146
10942	14148
10943	14156
10944	14172
10945	14179
10946	14197
10947	14206
10948	14210
10949	14214
10950	10717
10951	12922
10952	12974
10953	13840
10954	14175
10955	15376
10956	15378
10957	15391
10958	15474
10959	15486
10960	15674
10961	15695
10962	15756
10963	15792
10964	15877
10965	15880
10966	16097
10967	16344
10968	16410
10969	16426
10970	16556
10971	16593
10972	16650
10973	16662
10974	16692
10975	16697

New Number	Old Number
10976	16727
10977	16773
10978	16779
10979	16789
10980	16817
10981	16818
10982	16995
10983	17187
10984	17232
10985	18922
10986	18923
10987	18924
10988	18928
10989	18942
10990	18945
10991	18946
10992	18948
10993	18951
10994	18957
10995	18970
10996	18979
10997	18980
10998	18984
10999	18990
11000	18256
11001	18257
11002	18258
11003	18259
11004	18260
11005	18265
11006	18266
11007	18269
11008	18276
11009	18278
11010	18279
11011	18280
11012	18281
11013	18327
11014	18330
11015	18342
11016	18355
11017	18356
11018	18359
11019	18360
11020	18361
11021	18362
11022	18363
11023	18364
11024	18366
11025	18367
11026	18371
11027	18372
11028	18414
11029	18415
11030	18416
11031	18417
11032	18418
11033	18464
11034	18465
11035	18558
11036	18579
11037	18580
11038	18583
11039	19007
11040	19008
11041	19011
11042	19012

New Number	Old Number
11043	19014
11044	19015
11045	19016
11046	19018
11047	19019
11048	19020
11049	19021
11050	35
11051	252
11052	278
11053	373
11054	431
11055	443
11056	446
11057	602
11058	721
11059	993
11060	1035
11061	1090
11062	1097
11063	1208
11064	1306
11065	1310
11066	1350
11067	1397
11068	1634
11069	1636
11070	1638
11071	1644
11072	1646
11073	1649
11074	1653
11075	1654
11076	1657
11077	1663
11078	1673
11079	1674
11080	1678
11081	1682
11082	1689
11083	1690
11084	1717
11085	1774
11086	1778
11087	1780
11088	1791
11089	1797
11090	1802
11091	1806
11092	1807
11093	1824
11094	3896
11095	6092
11096	6381
11097	7657
11098	16098
11099	16110
11100	16119
11101	16127
11102	16129
11103	16132
11104	16143
11105	16160
11106	16166
11107	16168
11108	16172
11109	16175

New Number	Old Number
11110	16176
11111	16179
11112	16182
11113	16192
11114	16193
11115	16194
11116	16204
11117	16205
11118	16208
11119	16214
11120	16217
11121	16219
11122	16223
11123	16226
11124	16234
11125	16240
11126	16241
11127	16259
11128	16266
11129	16272
11130	16277
11131	16286
11132	16287
11133	16288
11134	16293
11135	16295
11136	16315
11137	16378
11138	16381
11139	16388
11140	16399
11141	16419
11142	16469
11143	16528
11144	16545
11145	16552
11146	16573
11147	16637
11148	16671
11149	16765
11150	19
11151	256
11152	262
11153	394
11154	467
11155	478
11156	545
11157	599
11158	621
11159	624
11160	625
11161	973
11162	1082
11163	1084
11164	1197
11165	1204
11166	1630
11167	1635
11168	1686
11169	1692
11170	1698
11171	1715
11172	1742
11173	1773
11174	1825
11175	1855
11176	6026

New Number	Old	New Number	Old	New Number	Old	New Number	Old	New Number	Old	New Number	Old	New Number	Old
11177	6087	11244	14376	11311	6203	11375	2366	11442	1127	11509	96	11576	1227
11178	7827	11245	14377	11312	6210	11376	2367	11443	1137	11510	100	11577	1233
11179	14004	11246	14378	11313	6211	11377	2368	11444	1345	11511	109	11578	1236
11180	14009	11247	14380	11314	6212	11378	2369	11445	1401	11512	111	11579	1237
11181	14011	11248	14381	11315	6215	11379	2370	11446	1403	11513	121	11580	1248
11182	14015	11249	14382	11316	6116	11380	2371	11447	1442	11514	182	11581	1258
11183	14032	11250	14383	11317	6217	11381	2372	11448	1809	11515	192	11582	1261
11184	14204	11251	14384	11318	251	11382	2373	11449	1813	11516	257	11583	1273
11185	14211	11252	14385	11319	314	11383	2374	11450	1818	11517	258	11584	1284
11186	14272	11253	14386	11320	381	11384	2375	11451	1819	11518	556	11585	1285
11187	14290	11254	14387	11321	713	11385	2376	11452	1823	11519	668	11586	1290
11188	14315	11255	14388	11322	726	11386	2377	11453	1835	11520	674	11587	1311
11189	14393	11256	14389	11323	734	11387	2378	11454	1839	11521	678	11588	1326
11190	14397	11257	14390	11324	736	11388	2379	11455	1840	11522	686	11589	1328
11191	14417	11258	14391	11325	942	11389	2380	11456	1842	11523	704	11590	1332
11192	15968	11259	14392	11326	1231	11390	2381	11457	1844	11524	705	11591	1333
11193	16085	11260	14394	11327	1351	11391	2382	11458	1845	11525	717	11592	1335
11194	16257	11261	14395	11328	1377	11392	2383	11459	1846	11526	743	11593	1337
11195	16444	11262	14396	11329	1378	11393	2384	11460	2422	11527	787	11594	1339
11196	16454	11263	14398	11330	1388	11394	2385	11461	2423	11528	812	11595	1340
11197	16506	11264	14399	11331	1814	11395	2386	11462	3554	11529	832	11596	1343
11198	16884	11265	14400	11332	1822	11396	2387	11463	4282	11530	835	11597	1362
11199	16948	11266	14401	11333	1828	11397	2388	11464	4283	11531	841	11598	1373
11200	14332	11267	14402	11334	1829	11398	2389	11465	4284	11532	854	11599	1415
11201	14333	11268	241	11335	1843	11399	2390	11466	4285	11533	882	11600	1416
11202	14334	11269	318	11336	1849	11400	2391	11467	10648	11534	913	11601	1621
11203	14335	11270	377	11337	1945	11401	2392	11468	10649	11535	967	11602	1624
11204	14336	11271	388	11338	6178	11402	2393	11469	10650	11536	974	11603	1625
11205	14337	11272	480	11339	6184	11403	6276	11470	10652	11537	982	11604	1626
11206	14338	11273	498	11340	6185	11404	6292	11471	10653	11538	994	11605	1627
11207	14339	11274	514	11341	6186	11405	12054	11472	10656	11539	998	11606	1847
11208	14340	11275	541	11342	6188	11406	12059	11473	10658	11540	1001	11607	9425
11209	14341	11276	618	11343	6190	11407	12085	11474	10659	11541	1005	11608	14042
11210	14342	11277	777	11344	6193	11408	12122	11475	10661	11542	1006	11609	14043
11211	14343	11278	874	11345	6194	11409	12131	11476	10662	11543	1007	11610	14046
11212	14344	11279	929	11346	6195	11410	12134	11477	10664	11544	1010	11611	14047
11213	14345	11280	943	11347	6269	11411	12150	11478	10665	11545	1012	11612	14740
11214	14346	11281	956	11348	7656	11412	12153	11479	10667	11546	1015	11613	14741
11215	14347	11282	970	11349	7773	11413	12195	11480	10669	11547	1021	11614	14743
11216	14348	11283	1027	11350	7817	11414	12205	11481	10670	11548	1022	11615	15237
11217	14349	11284	1039	11351	11718	11415	12214	11482	10671	11549	1025	11616	17623
11218	14350	11285	1245	11352	12607	11416	12216	11483	10672	11550	1032	11617	17625
11219	14351	11286	1247	11353	13758	11417	12217	11484	10673	11551	1040	11618	17627
11220	14352	11287	1629	11354	15250	11418	12219	11485	10675	11552	1043	11619	17641
11221	14353	11288	1633	11355	15689	11419	12221	11486	10676	11553	1047	11620	17884
11222	14354	11289	1637	11356	16385	11420	12230	11487	10677	11554	1051	11621	17888
11223	14355	11290	1640	11357	16563	11421	12235	11488	10678	11555	1075	11622	17889
11224	14356	11291	1642	11358	16591	11422	12281	11489	11787	11556	1103	11623	17939
11225	14357	11292	1645	11359	16617	11423	12270	11490	12206	11557	1104	11624	60
11226	14358	11293	1650	11360	16660	11424	69	11491	12653	11558	1108	11625	207
11227	14359	11294	1651	11361	16988	11425	107	11492	13063	11559	1114	11626	1859
11228	14360	11295	1658	11362	17093	11426	147	11493	15271	11560	1117	11627	3106
11229	14361	11296	1661	11363	17124	11427	214	11494	15316	11561	1121		
11230	14362	11297	1667	11364	17154	11428	220	11495	16389	11562	1125		
11231	14363	11298	1668	11365	17188	11429	249	11496	16441	11563	1129		
11232	14364	11299	1679	11366	17196	11430	265	11497	16981	11564	1130		
11233	14365	11300	1684	11367	17208	11431	300	11498	17147	11565	1144		
11234	14366	11301	1687	11368	789	11432	731	11499	17158	11566	1170		
11235	14367	11302	1694	11369	797	11433	818	11500	18582	11567	1187		
11236	14368	11303	1695	11370	800	11434	829	11501	18716	11568	1188		
11237	14369	11304	1696	11371	1138	11435	838	11502	17940	11569	1192		
11238	14370	11305	1751	11372	6182	11436	852	11503	17941	11570	1216		
11239	14371	11306	1792	11373	7686	11437	867	11504	17943	11571	1218		
11240	14372	11307	1832			11438	880	11505	17944	11572	1219		
11241	14373	11308	6199	D1784		11439	890	11506	27	11573	1220		
11242	14374	11309	6201			11440	891	11507	86	11574	1225		
11243	14375	11310	6202	11374	2365	11441	960	11508	95	11575	1226		

Third Class Brake

D1703

New Number	Old
20140	2854
20141	3474
20142	3489
20143	3515
20144	3534
20145	3545
20146	3558
20147	3563
20148	3585
20149	3677

New Number	Old Number
20150	3683
20151	3687
20152	3694
20153	3696
20154	3709
20155	3711
20156	16075
20157	16101
20158	16131
20159	16156
20160	16187
20161	16196
20162	16210
20163	16215
20164	16225
20165	16232
20166	16238
20167	16258
20168	16301
20169	16302
20170	16317
20171	16340
20172	16346
20173	16423
20174	16428
20175	16458
20176	16465
20177	16474
20178	16481
20179	16514
20180	16537
20181	16550
20182	16564
20183	16592
20184	16597
20185	16654
20186	16664
20187	16673
20188	16700
20189	16711
20190	16747
20191	16756
20192	16764
20193	16770
20194	16777
20195	16786
20196	16853
20197	16855
20198	16865
20199	16873
20200	16982
20201	16986
20202	16993
20203	17180
20204	17215
20205	17334
20206	18621
20207	18641
20208	18644
20209	18649
20210	18651
20211	18652
20212	18653
20213	18695
20214	18696
20215	18700
20216	18701
20217	18703
20218	18705
20219	18706
20220	18707
20221	18708
20222	18709
20223	18714
20224	18715
20225	18717
20226	18718
20227	18719
20228	18720
20229	18721
20230	18722
20231	18724
20232	18726
20233	18736
20234	18737
20235	18802
20236	46
20237	159
20238	385
20239	468
20240	903
20241	958
20242	965
20243	985
20244	1252
20245	6066
20246	6742
20247	7632
20248	7651
20249	7658
20250	7739
20251	7740
20252	8566
20253	9359
20254	9386
20255	14728
20256	7701
20257	9388
20258	9430
20259	9439
20260	15361
20261	15380
20262	15382
20263	15404
20264	15408
20265	15410
20266	15416
20267	15476
20268	15477
20269	15625
20270	15627
20271	16117
20272	16154
20273	16169
20274	16212
20275	16231
20276	16249
20277	16276
20278	16305
20279	16310
20280	16375
20281	16394
20282	16496
20283	16569
20284	16629
20285	16867
20286	16917
20287	2553
20288	2568
20289	11604
20290	11605
20291	13155
20292	13156
20293	14190
20294	14192
20295	14193
20296	14194
20297	15605
20298	15978
20299	15979
20300	16216
20301	16218
20302	16227
20303	16251
20304	16255
20305	16256
20306	16261
20307	16562
20308	16913
20309	16932
20310	16939
20311	18357
20312	19022
20313	19023
20314	19024
20315	19025
20316	19026
20317	19027
20318	19029
20319	19030
20320	19031
20321	19032
20322	19033
20323	19034
20324	19036
20325	19037
20326	19038
20327	19039
20328	19040
20329	19041
20330	19042
20331	19048
20332	19050
20333	19051
20334	19052
20335	19053
20336	19054
20337	13946
20338	13947
20339	13949
20340	13950
20341	13951
20342	13952
20343	13953
20344	13954
20345	13955
20346	13956
20347	13957
20348	13959
20349	13960
20350	13961
20351	13962
20352	13965
20353	13966
20354	13967
20355	13968
20356	13969
20357	13970
20358	13971
20359	13972
20360	13973
20361	13975
20362	13976
20363	13977
20364	13978
20365	13980
20366	13981
20367	13982
20368	13983
20369	13984
20370	13985
20371	13986
20372	13989
20373	13990
20374	13991
20375	13992
20376	13993
20377	13994
20378	13996
20379	13998
20380	13999
20381	14000
20382	14001
20383	14002
20384	14003
20385	14113
20386	14200

D1735

New Number	Old Number
20387	802
20388	949
20389	1143
20390	1148
20391	1161
20392	1163
20393	1166
20394	1854
20395	1868
20396	1869
20397	1870
20398	1871
20399	1872
20400	1873
20401	1874
20402	1875
20403	1876
20404	1877
20405	1878
20406	1879
20407	1880
20408	1881
20409	1882
20410	1883
20411	2235
20412	2256
20413	7429
20414	7625
20415	7757
20416	7777
20417	11819
20418	11898
20419	11946
20420	12211
20421	12359
20422	12611
20423	12976
20424	13507
20425	15238
20426	17942
20427	226
20428	493
20429	608
20430	711
20431	1118
20432	1444
20433	1862
20434	1885
20435	1887
20436	1888
20437	1893
20438	1908
20439	1918
20440	1920
20441	1928
20442	1936
20443	1943
20444	1960
20445	1961
20446	1966
20447	1978
20448	1982
20449	2119
20450	2166
20451	5690
20452	6253
20453	6254
20454	6256
20455	6287
20456	6306
20457	6308
20458	6371
20459	6372
20460	6373
20461	6374
20462	7684
20463	7688
20464	11905
20465	12075
20466	13154
20467	14810
20468	16079
20469	16323
20470	16705
20471	16720
20472	754
20473	1991
20474	3743
20475	3745
20476	3843
20477	4054
20478	5310
20479	5655
20480	6324
20481	6326
20482	6342
20483	6356
20484	7724
20485	8447
20486	9841
20487	15668
20488	15684
20489	15692
20490	15698
20491	15729
20492	15732
20493	15743
20494	15760
20495	15809
20496	15816
20497	15827
20498	15831
20499	15843
20500	15852
20501	15860
20502	15869
20503	15907
20504	15909
20505	15911
20506	15920
20507	15929
20508	15931
20509	15939
20510	15941
20511	15969
20512	15970
20513	15973
20514	15981
20515	16153
20516	16253
20517	16387
20518	16448
20519	16451
20520	16453
20521	16462
20522	16521
20523	16529
20524	16533
20525	16628
20526	16630
20527	16646
20528	16802
20529	16812
20530	16911
20531	16930
20532	16936
20533	16937
20534	16958
20535	16959
20536	16962
20540	17120
20541	17121
20542	17123
20543	17126
20544	17127
20545	17136
20546	17137
20547	17138
20548	17141
20549	17142
20550	17144
20551	17145
20552	17146
20553	17149
20554	17151
20555	17152
20556	17153
20557	17155
20558	17157
20559	17159
20560	17161
20561	17165
20562	17168
20563	17182
20564	17183
20565	17184
20566	17186
20567	17190
20568	17191
20569	17192
20570	17193
20571	17194
20572	17197

D1790 (motor driving)

New Number	Old Number
24403	17148
24404	17195
24405	17114
24406	17115
24407	17117
24408	17118
24409	17119

Second Class Brake
D1723 (NL)

New Number	Old Number
24900	6200
24901	6213
24902	7891

D1797 (NL)

New Number	Old Number
24903	733
24904	1400
24905	3280
24906	3739

Third Class Brake
D1733 (NL)

New Number	Old Number
20537	6180
20538	6181
20539	7806

D1783 (NL)

New Number	Old Number
20573	7749
20574	7750
20575	7
20576	17

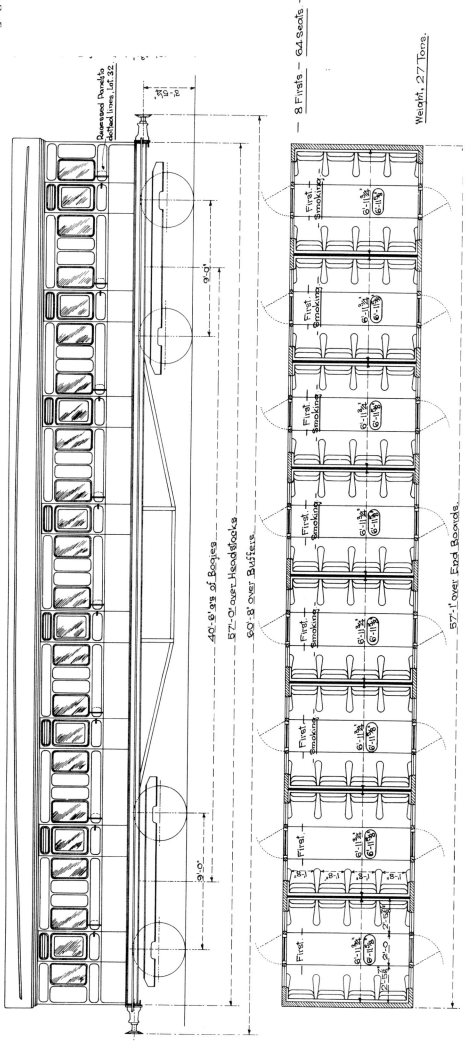

8 Firsts — 64 Seats

Weight, 27 Tons.

Recessed Panels to dotted lines, Lot 32.

40'-6" c'rs of Bogies
57'-0" over Headstocks
60'-8" over Buffers
57'-1" over End Boards

First. Smoking

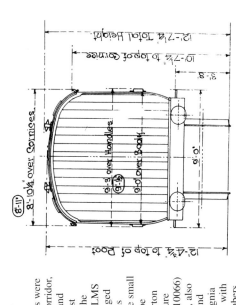

12'-7¾" Total Height
10'-7¼" to top of Cornice
8'-11" over Cornices
8'-10¾" over Body
9'-3" over Handles
9'-0" over Body
9'-0"
12'-4¾" to Top of Roof

Figure 6 Non-corridor
First Class D1702

These attractive vehicles were the only Period I non-corridor, non-lavatory full firsts and also represented the most numerous examples of the genre during the whole LMS period. Note that the ringed compartment dimensions apply to Lot 32 only, the small batch built with MR-type fittings, albeit at Wolverton (see Table 1c). The picture shows No 18725 (later 10066) of Lot 248 in full livery, also showing the first style and disposition of LMS insignia — ie LMS in the centre with two sets of running numbers per side.

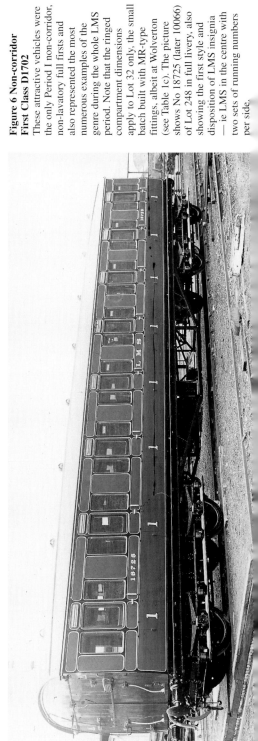

30

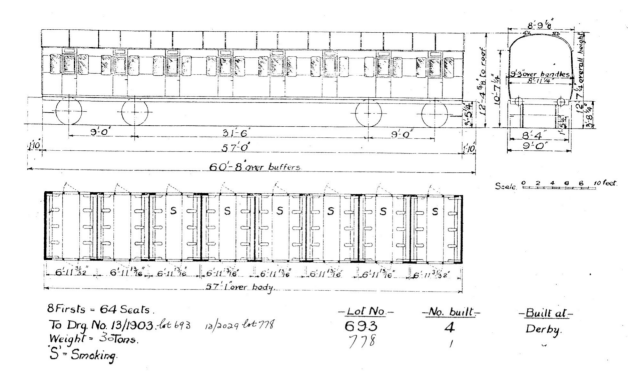

8 Firsts = 64 Seats.
To Drg. No. 13/1903. *lot 693*   13/2029 *lot 778*
Weight = 30 Tons.
'S' = Smoking.

— Lot No. —	— No. built —	— Built at —
693	4	Derby.
778	1	

Figures 7/8 Non-corridor First Class D1858/1997

These two diagrams, differing only in the disposition of smoking compartments and a slightly higher dimension over roof ventilators in the later D1997 version, were the only LMS non-corridor full firsts built after Period I and it is hard to see the justification for two separate diagrams. Numbering but 24 examples between both of them, of which no fewer than 15 were built by BR — for some strange reason as late as 1951 (picture, page 21) — they reflect the diminishing role of the non-corridor first class in LMS thinking down the years as the company made increasing use of 'cascaded' corridor types for its intermediate services. They are also the first two examples in this book of what became a somewhat 'basic' style of diagram presentation compared with earlier days and for this reason are reproduced at a smaller scale — for views see overleaf.

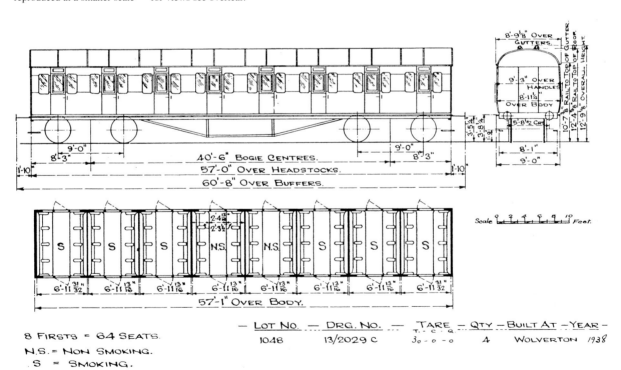

8 FIRSTS = 64 SEATS.
N.S. = NON SMOKING.
S = SMOKING.

— LOT NO. —	— DRG. NO. —	— TARE —			— QTY —	— BUILT AT —	— YEAR —
		T.	C.	Q.			
1048	13/2029 C	30	0	0	4	WOLVERTON	1938

The upper photograph on this page shows the exterior of one of the handful of Period III non-corridor firsts built by the LMS itself — No 10113, the first example of D1997 in 1938 and, no doubt, the reason why it was photographed. It is typical of the bland and unenterprising non-corridor carriages which the LMS continued to build until the very end, albeit that compartment dimensions were not ungenerous for a non-corridor type compared with other companies. It is painted in the simplified post-1933 livery with black ends.

The second view shows the interior of the 1951 BR continuation via No 10124 of Lot 1632 — see also the exterior view, page 21. The interior gives little evidence that it was of LMS design and the upholstery itself is rendered in a sort of blue/grey moquette which was soon to become familiar in the BR standard Mk I stock later that year.

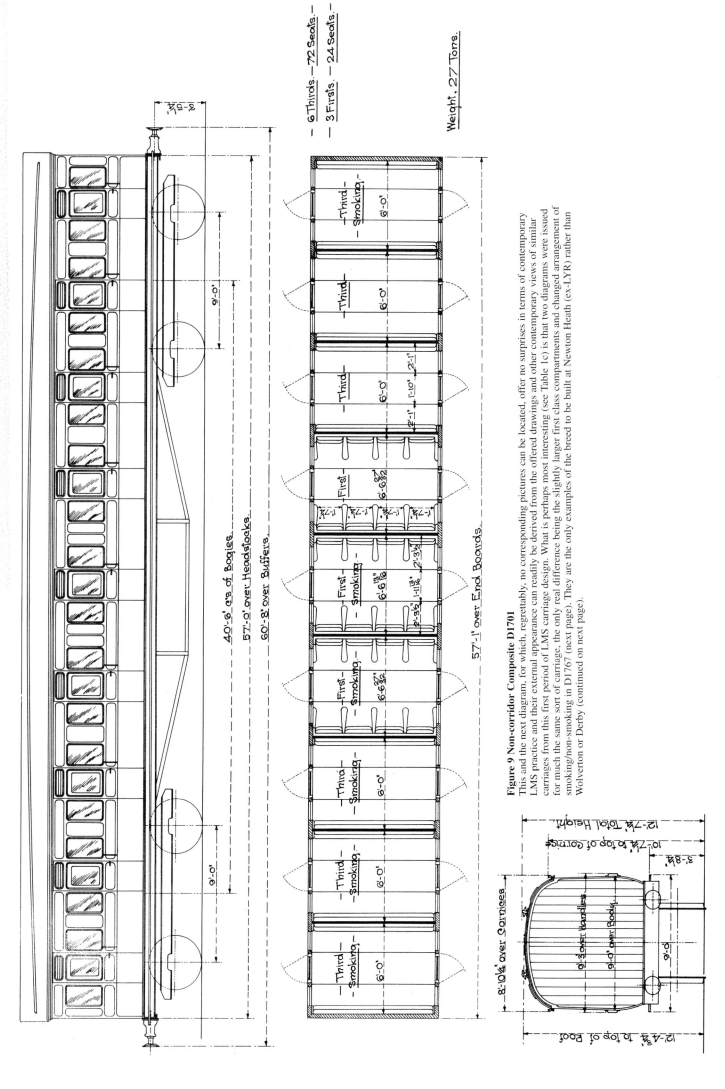

- 6 Thirds. – 72 Seats. –
- 3 Firsts. – 24 Seats. –

Weight, 27 Tons.

Figure 9 Non-corridor Composite D1701

This and the next diagram, for which, regrettably, no corresponding pictures can be located, offer no surprises in terms of contemporary LMS practice and their external appearance can readily be derived from the offered drawings and other contemporary views of similar carriages from this first period of LMS carriage design. What is perhaps most interesting (see Table 1c) is that two diagrams were issued for much the same sort of carriage, the only real difference being the slightly larger first class compartments and changed arrangement of smoking/non-smoking in D1767 (next page). They are the only examples of the breed to be built at Newton Heath (ex-LYR) rather than Wolverton or Derby (continued on next page).

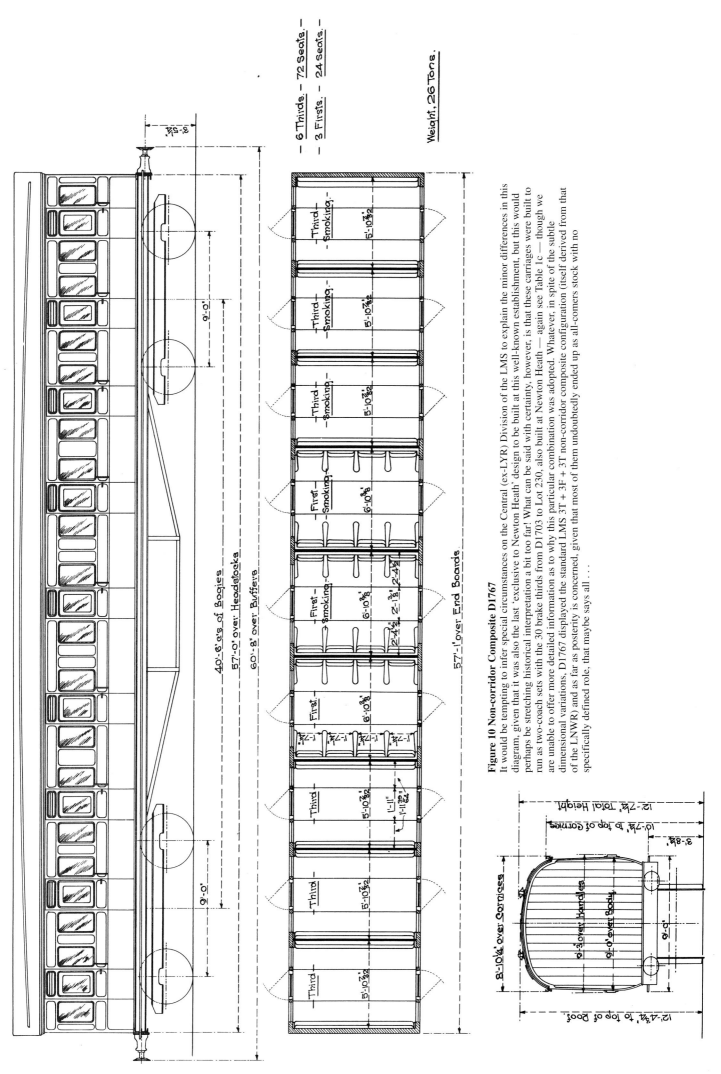

Figure 10 Non-corridor Composite D1767

It would be tempting to infer special circumstances on the Central (ex-LYR) Division of the LMS to explain the minor differences in this diagram, given that it was also the last 'exclusive to Newton Heath' design to be built at this well-known establishment, but this would perhaps be stretching historical interpretation a bit too far! What can be said with certainty, however, is that these carriages were built to run as two-coach sets with the 30 brake thirds from D1703 to Lot 230, also built at Newton Heath — again see Table 1c — though we are unable to offer more detailed information as to why this particular combination was adopted. Whatever, in spite of the subtle dimensional variations, D1767 displayed the standard LMS 3T + 3F + 3T non-corridor composite configuration (itself derived from that of the LNWR) and as far as posterity is concerned, given that most of them undoubtedly ended up as all-comers stock with no specifically defined role, that maybe says all . . . .

34

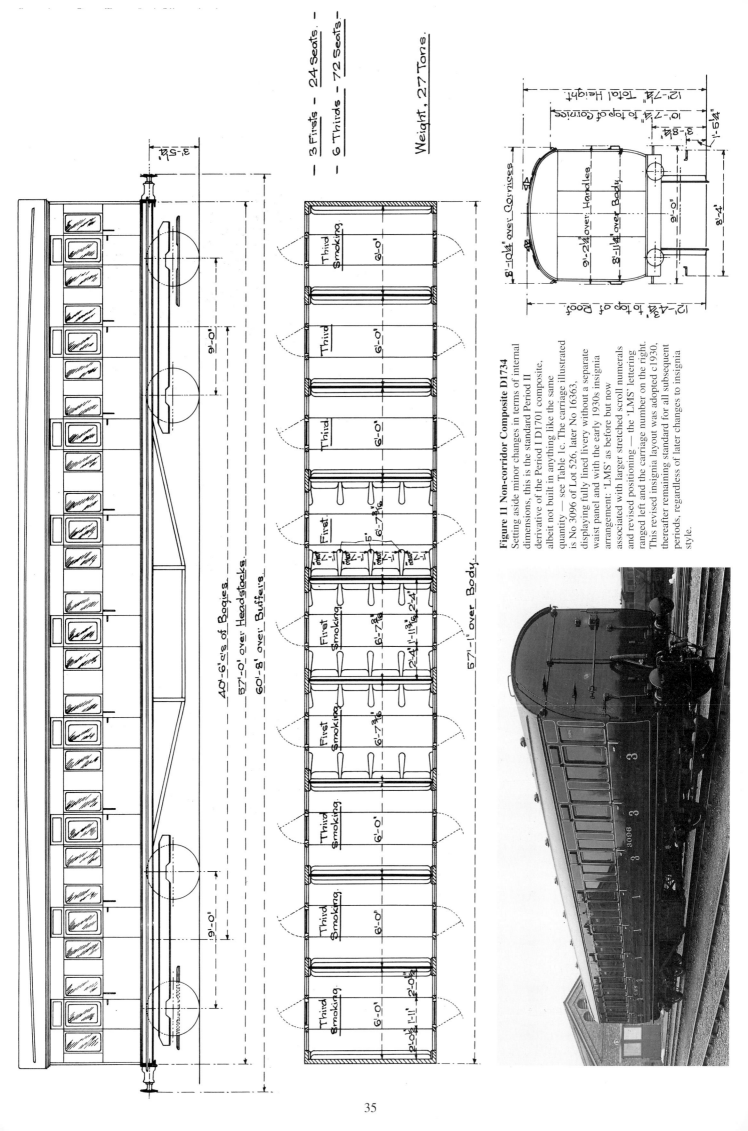

3 Firsts — 24 Seats
6 Thirds — 72 Seats

Weight, 27 Tons.

3'-5½"

40'-6' c's of Bogies.

57'-0' over Headstocks.

60'-8' over Buffers.

9'-0'

9'-0'

2'-0½" 1'-11" 2'-0½"

Third Smoking. 6'-0'

Third Smoking. 6'-0'

Third Smoking. 6'-0'

First Smoking. 6'-7³⁄₁₆'

First Smoking. 6'-7³⁄₁₆'

First. 6'-7³⁄₁₆'

Third. 6'-0'

Third. 6'-0'

Third Smoking. 6'-0'

2'-4" 1'-11³⁄₁₆' 2'-4"

5"

1'-7' 1'-7' 1'-7' 1'-7'

57'-1' over Body.

12'-7¾' Total Height.

10'-7½" to top of Cornice.

3'-8½"

1'-5¾"

8'-10¼" over Cornices

9'-2¼" over Handles

8'-11¼" over Body

9'-0"

8'-4"

12'-2¾' to top of Roof.

Figure 11 Non-corridor Composite D1734
Setting aside minor changes in terms of internal dimensions, this is the standard Period II derivative of the Period I D1701 composite, albeit not built in anything like the same quantity — see Table 1c. The carriage illustrated is No 3096 of Lot 526, later No 16363, displaying fully lined livery without a separate waist panel and with the early 1930s insignia arrangement: 'LMS' as before but now associated with larger stretched scroll numerals and revised positioning — the 'LMS' lettering ranged left and the carriage number on the right. This revised insignia layout was adopted c1930, thereafter remaining standard for all subsequent periods, regardless of later changes to insignia style.

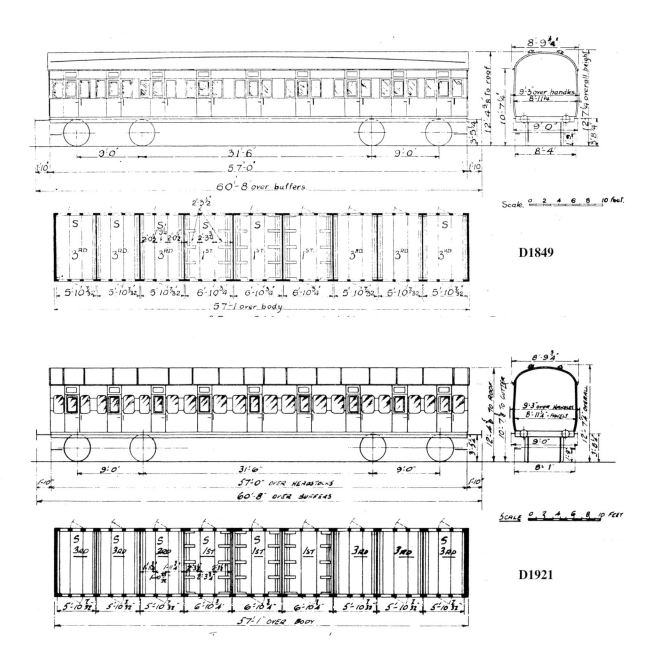

D1849

D1921

Figures 12-14 Non-corridor Composite D1849/1921/1921A
These three typically basic diagrams, all reproduced at c2mm=1ft scale, represent the final LMS-design non-corridor composites — more details on the next two pages.

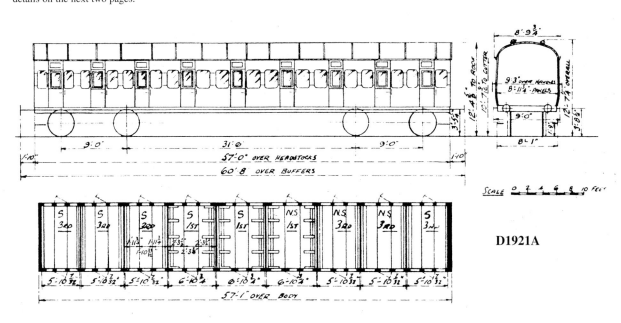

D1921A

Period III Non-corridor Composites

The opposite page gives the essential diagram details of the final orthodox 57ft LMS-design non-corridor composites, none differing in any significant dimensional respects from their predecessors, or from each other for that matter, thus making it hard to understand why three different diagrams were offered. The first of them (D1849), in spite of the new style 'economic' draughtsmanship, does imply Period II features and the first 20 carriages to this diagram were indeed to Period II style (Lot 650, Table 1c). But the later batches of D1849 were wholly Period III in exterior styling which makes it all the more surprising that D1921 and D1921A were issued later to cover far less significant external changes in style than those which took place without change of diagram in the early 1930s — all very curious and we are unable to offer a sensible explanation. The pictures on this spread represent the first and last diagrams of this type.

The initial pair of views show the first and third class interiors of the first Period III batch built to D1849 — carriage No 16502 of Lot 684. The round-cornered windows are clear to see but the use of dark wood finishes and traditional upholstery patterns is more characteristic of Period II. The next view shows the third class interior of No 16717 to Lot 1102 of D1921A, built in 1939, a typical Period III design of the immediate prewar era. Note the lighter woodwork and more modern upholstery in what was an otherwise unchanged compartment arrangement.

Period III Non-corridor Composites (cont)

This exterior view of composite No 16717 to D1921A shows the orthodox Period III arrangement of simplified livery and post-1934 insignia. Note too the use of welded bogies — increasingly common but never 100% exclusive in later LMS days.

Figure 15 Non-corridor Composite D2189

For the sake of completion we offer this final 'GWR'-style diagram (scale 2mm=1ft) built to LMS order after Nationalisation and included in the LMS/LMR diagram book. We are unable to offer a picture, nor any further details other than those already given on page 20 and in Table 1c.

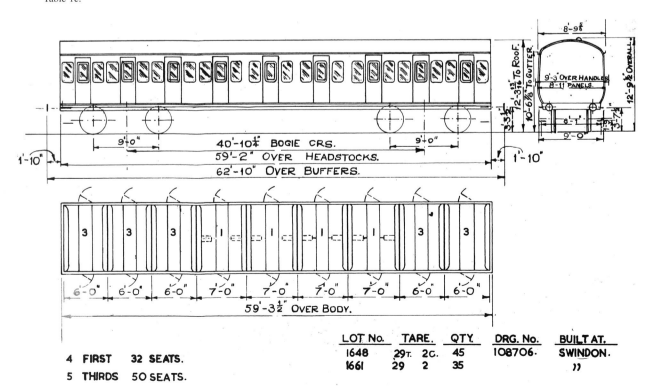

4 FIRST 32 SEATS.
5 THIRDS 50 SEATS.

LOT No.	TARE.		QTY.	DRG. No.	BUILT AT.
1648	29 T.	2 C.	45	108706.	SWINDON.
1661	29	2	35		,,

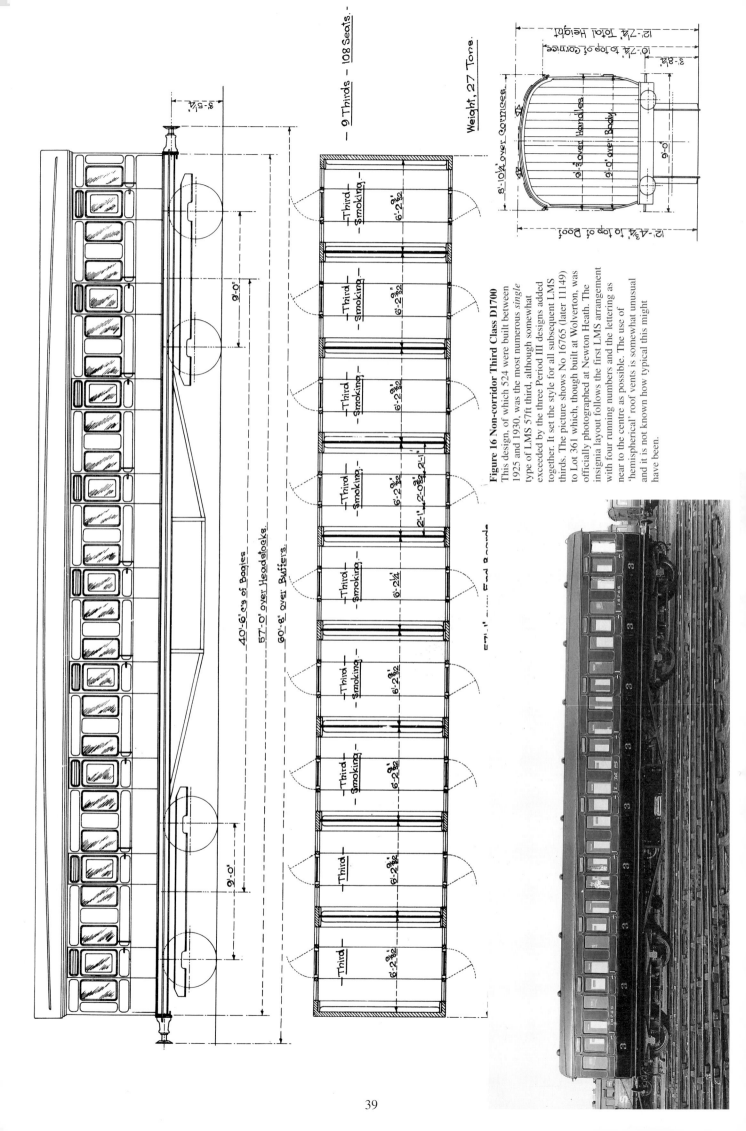

Figure 16 Non-corridor Third Class D1700

This design, of which 524 were built between 1925 and 1930, was the most numerous *single* type of LMS 57ft third, although somewhat exceeded by the three Period III designs added together. It set the style for all subsequent LMS thirds. The picture shows No 16765 (later 11149) to Lot 361 which, though built at Wolverton, was officially photographed at Newton Heath. The insignia layout follows the first LMS arrangement with four running numbers and the lettering as near to the centre as possible. The use of 'hemispherical' roof vents is somewhat unusual and it is not known how typical this might have been.

9 Thirds – 108 Seats.

Weight, 27 Tons.

8'-5¼"

9'-0"

40'-6" c's of Bogies.

57'-0" over Headstocks.

60'-8" over Buffers.

57'11" over End Boards.

Third Smoking 6'-2³²/₃₂"

Third 6'-2³²/₃₂"

8'-10¼" over Cornices.

9'-3" over Handles

9'-0" over Body

9'-0"

10'-7¼" to top of Cornice.

12'-7¼" Total Height

3'-8¼"

12'-4³/₄" to top of Roof.

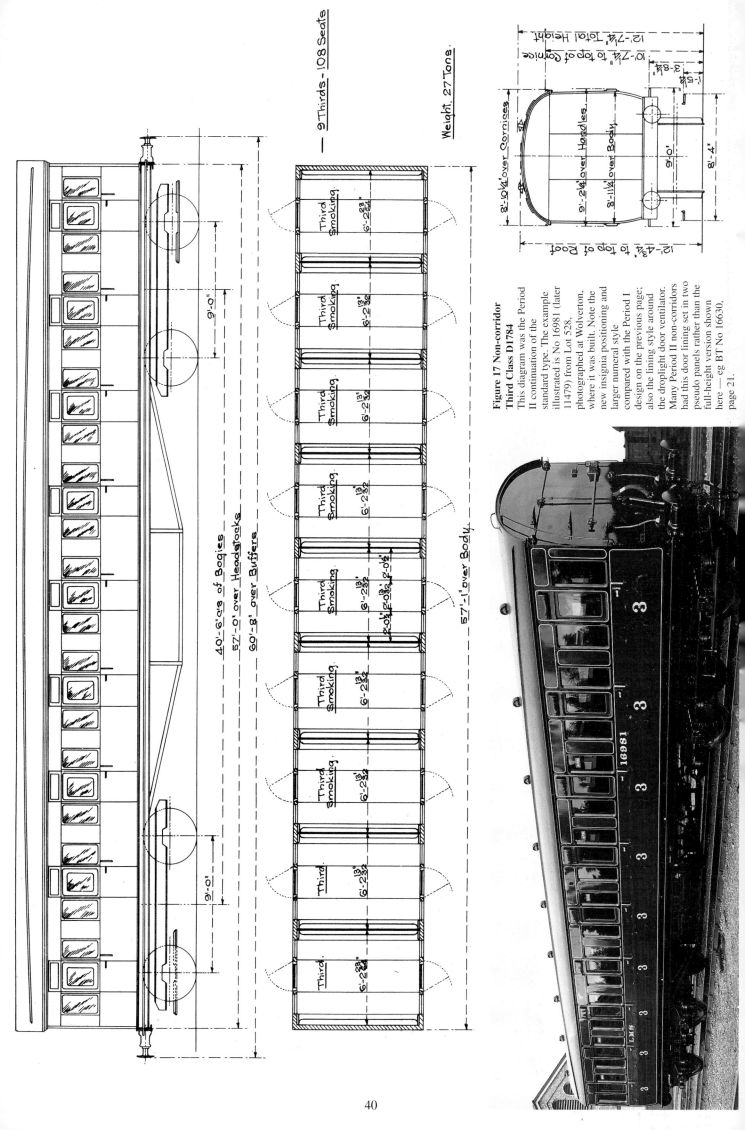

9 Thirds - 108 Seats

Weight, 27 Tons.

9'-0"

40'-6" c'rs of Bogies
57'-0" over Headstocks
60'-8" over Buffers
57'-1" over Body

Third Smoking 6'-2¹³⁄₃₂"
Third Smoking 6'-2¹³⁄₃₂"
Third Smoking 6'-2¹³⁄₃₂"
Third Smoking 6'-2¹³⁄₃₂"
Third Smoking 6'-2¹³⁄₃₂"
Third Smoking 6'-2¹³⁄₃₂" 2'-0½" 2'-0½"
Third Smoking 6'-2¹³⁄₃₂"
Third Smoking 6'-2¹³⁄₃₂"
Third 6'-2¹³⁄₃₂"
Third 6'-2²³⁄₆₄"

8'-10¼" over Cornices
9'-2¼" over Handles
8'-11¼" over Body
9'-0"
12'-7¼" Total Height
10'-7¼" to top of Cornice
3'-8¾"
1'-5¼"
8'-4"
12'-4¾" to top of Roof

Figure 17 Non-corridor Third Class D1784

This diagram was the Period II continuation of the standard type. The example illustrated is No 16981 (later 11479) from Lot 528, photographed at Wolverton, where it was built. Note the new insignia positioning and larger numeral style compared with the Period I design on the previous page; also the lining style around the droplight door ventilator. Many Period II non-corridors had this door lining set in two pseudo panels rather than the full-height version shown here — eg BT No 16630, page 21.

40

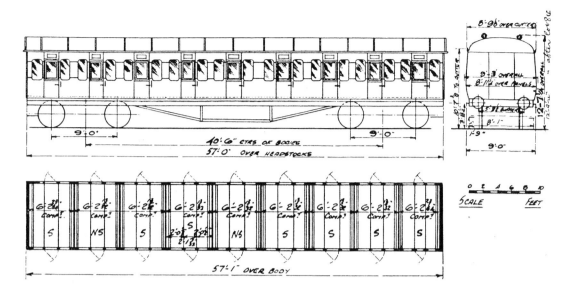

Figure 18 Non-corridor Third Class D1906/1906A

These two diagrams were near-identical (see Table 1c) and since the only version of D1906A available to the authors is so bad as to be incapable of reproduction at any scale(!), the D1906 version given above at c2mm=1ft scale must serve for both. The D1906A version had both non-smoking compartments in the centre (third and fourth from the left as shown in this plan) and this is the only variation we can find — but this is not much help when one looks at the pictures overleaf!

The views below show, on the left, the interior of No 12049, built in 1938 to D1906A, while on the right is No 12194 to D1906, after reversion to this type (whatever the difference) in 1939. Yet more upholstery patterns are revealed but as with all LMS types in this and previous volumes, we have been unable to find any official records of their colour schemes. Note the ARP notice, the instruction of which preceded the fitting of blackout shields. Exterior views are overleaf.

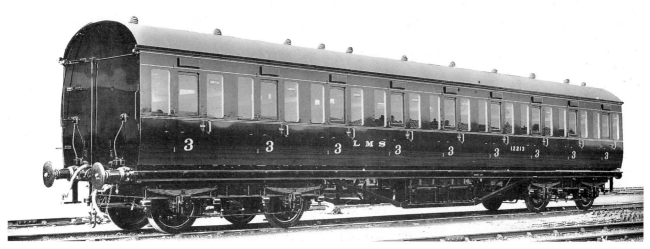

These four views show, top to bottom, Nos 12194 and 12213 from D1906 (both from the post-D1906A build in 1939/40), followed by Nos 11916 and 12049 from D1906A, itself from 1937/8. We are unable to see any significant differences. All four have welded bogies (not unexpected at the time) while the reversion to D1906 was accompanied by a change to all-welded underframe on the examples shown; but if that was the difference, the diagram does not say so. The non-smokers are in the same position in both types (so much for the diagram difference) while what seem to be apparent slight differences in roof ventilator positions do not seem to be consistent between any of them . . .

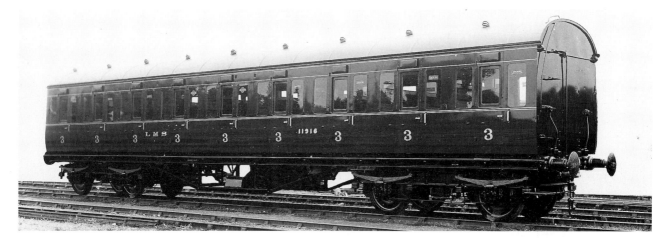

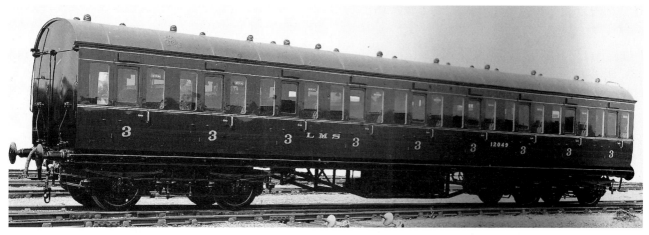

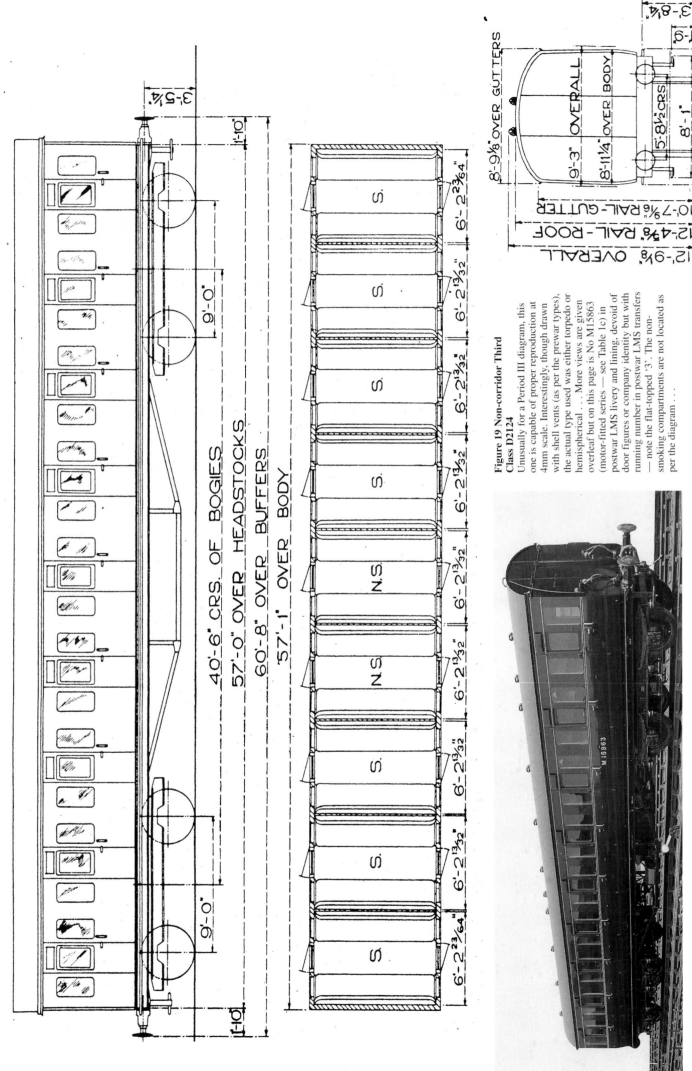

**Figure 19 Non-corridor Third
Class D2124**

Unusually for a Period III diagram, this one is capable of proper reproduction at 4mm scale. Interestingly, though drawn with shell vents (as per the prewar types), the actual type used was either torpedo or hemispherical . . . More views are given overleaf but on this page is No M15863 (motor-fitted series — see Table 1c) in postwar LMS livery and lining, devoid of door figures or company identity but with running number in postwar LMS transfers — note the flat-topped '3'. The non-smoking compartments are not located as per the diagram . . .

9'-3⅛" OVER GUTTERS

9'-3" OVERALL

8'-11¼" OVER BODY

3'-8¼"

1'-9"

5'-8½" CRS

8'-1"

9'-0"

12'-4⅜" RAIL-ROOF

10'-7⁹⁄₁₆" RAIL-GUTTER

12'-9⅝" OVERALL

3'-5¼"

1'-10"

9'-0"

40'-6" CRS. OF BOGIES

57'-0" OVER HEADSTOCKS

60'-8" OVER BUFFERS

57'-1" OVER BODY

S.

S.

S.

S.

N.S.

N.S.

S.

S.

S.

6'-2²³⁄₆₄"   6'-2¹³⁄₃₂"   6'-2¹³⁄₃₂"   6'-2¹³⁄₃₂"   6'-2¹³⁄₃₂"   6'-2¹³⁄₃₂"   6'-2¹³⁄₃₂"   6'-2¹³⁄₃₂"   6'-2²³⁄₆₄"

M 15863

43

These views show the two later lots of D2124. The two detailed pictures show the Lot 1578 version with lined BR livery, the end view showing No M15893 (motor-fitted series), the close-up door detail being from an unidentified example from the same lot. Both are entirely characteristic of Period III non-corridors. Albeit official, the lined-out non-corridor stock BR livery was by no means universal as the final view of the general service example No M12235 to Lot 1633 clearly shows. It displays BR hemispherical vents, as did some (all?) of Lot 1578, compared with the LMS-type torpedo vents on Lot 1451 (page 43). All three lots had fully welded underframes and bogies.

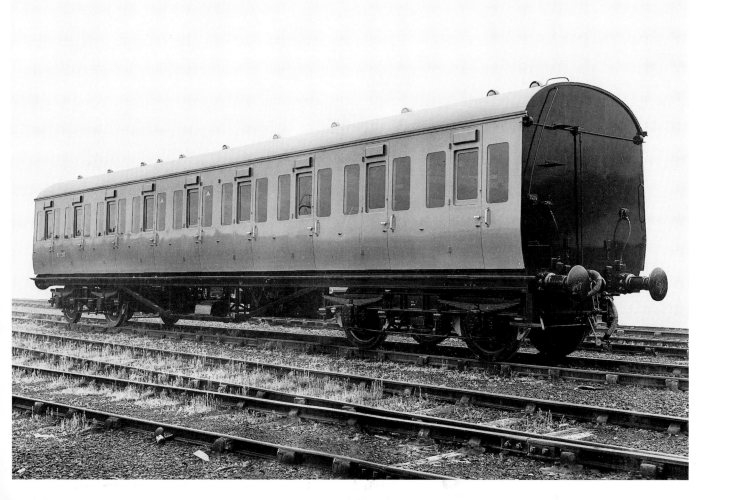

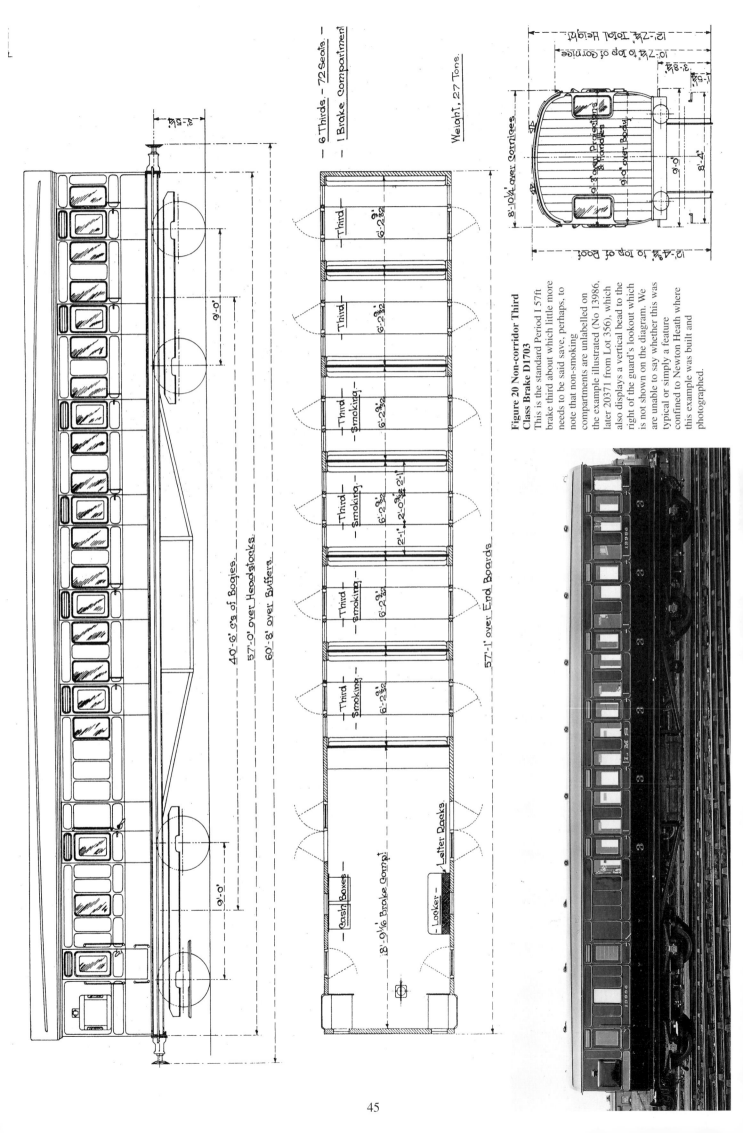

12'-2¾' Total Height

10'-7¾' to top of Cornice

3'-8¾'

1'-5¾'

8'-10¼' over Cornices

9'-3' over Projections & Handles

9'-0' over Body

9'-0'

8'-4'

12'-4¾' to top of Roof

6 Thirds - 72 Seats

1 Brake Compartment

Weight, 27 Tons.

Third 6'-2 3/32"

Third 6'-2 3/32"

Third Smoking 6'-2 3/32"

Third Smoking 6'-2 3/32"

Third Smoking 6'-2 3/32"

Third Smoking 6'-2 3/32"

2'-1' 2'-0¾' 2'-1'

57'-1' over End Boards

Cash Boxes

18'-0 11/16' Brake Comp't

Locker

Letter Racks

3'-6½'

9'-0'

40'-6' c's of Bogies.

57'-0' over Headstocks.

60'-8' over Buffers.

9'-0'

Figure 20 Non-corridor Third Class Brake D1703

This is the standard Period I 57ft brake third about which little more needs to be said save, perhaps, to note that non-smoking compartments are unlabelled on the example illustrated (No 13986, later 20371 from Lot 356), which also displays a vertical bead to the right of the guard's lookout which is not shown on the diagram. We are unable to say whether this was typical or simply a feature confined to Newton Heath where this example was built and photographed.

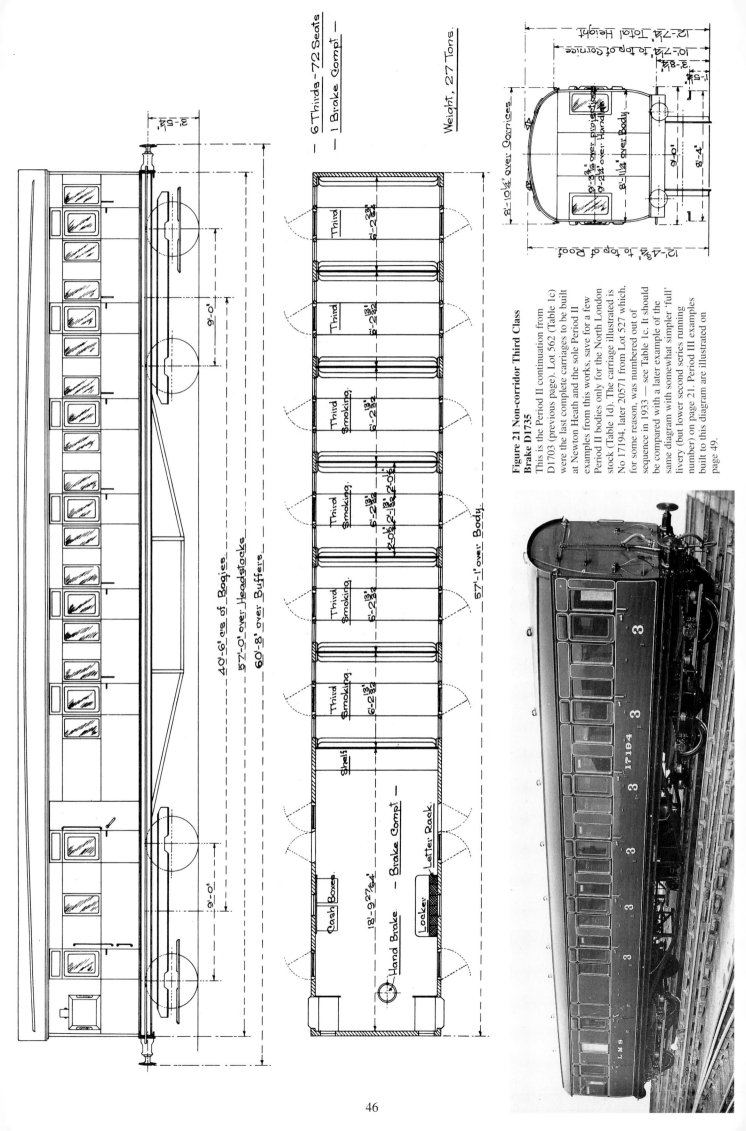

6 Thirds – 72 Seats

1 Brake Compt

Weight, 27 Tons.

3'-5½"

9'-0"

40'-6" c'rs of Bogies

57'-0" over Headstocks

60'-8" over Buffers

57'-1" over Body

9'-0"

Third 6'-2 13/64"

Third 6'-2 13/64"

Third Smoking 6'-2 13/64"

Third Smoking 6'-2 13/64"

2'-0½"-13-2'-0½"

Third Smoking 6'-2 13/64"

Third Smoking 6'-2 13/64"

Shelf

Cash Boxes

Brake Compt 18'-9 27/64"

Hand Brake

Locker

Letter Rack

8'-10¾" over Cornices

12'-7¾" Total Height

10'-7¾" to top of Cornice

3'-8¾"

9'-3⅝ over Engine

9'-2¼ over Hand

8'-11¼ over Body

9'-0"

8'-4"

12'-4¾" to top of Roof

Figure 21 Non-corridor Third Class Brake D1735

This is the Period II continuation from D1703 (previous page). Lot 562 (Table 1c) were the last complete carriages to be built at Newton Heath and the sole Period II examples from this works, save for a few Period II bodies only for the North London stock (Table 1d). The carriage illustrated is No 17194, later 20571 from Lot 527 which, for some reason, was numbered out of sequence in 1933 — see Table 1c. It should be compared with a later example of the same diagram with somewhat simpler 'full' livery (but lower second series running number) on page 21. Period III examples built to this diagram are illustrated on page 49.

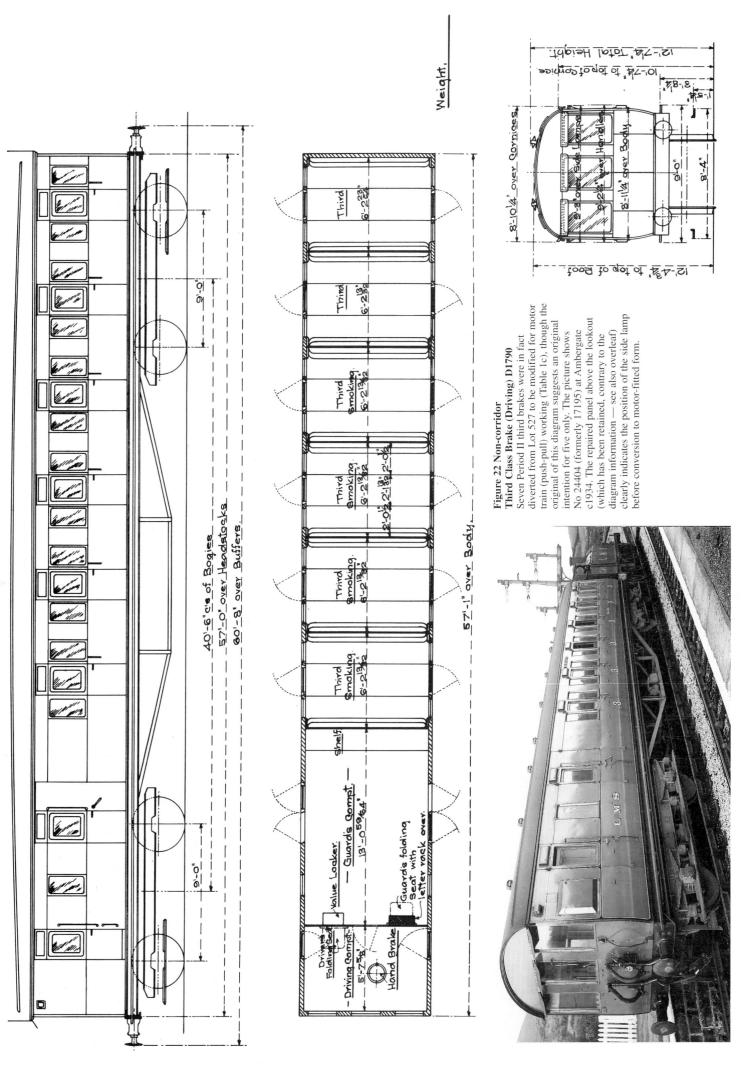

Weight.

40'-6" c's of Bogies
57'-0" over Headstocks
60'-8" over Buffers.

9'-0"

9'-0"

Third
6'-2⅔"

Third
6'-2³⁄₃₂"

Third
Smoking
6'-2³⁄₃₂"

Third
Smoking
6'-2³⁄₃₂"

2'-0½" 2'-1⅛" 2'-0½"

Third
Smoking
6'-2³⁄₃₂"

Third
Smoking
6'-2³⁄₃₂"

Third
Smoking
6'-2³⁄₃₂"

Shelf

Value Locker

Guards Compt.
13'-0⁵⁹⁄₆₄'

Driving Compt.
5'-7⁵⁄₈'

Driving
Folding Seat

Guard's folding
seat with
letter rack over.

Hand Brake

57'-1" over Body.

12'-7¾". Total Height.

10'-7¾" to top of cornice

3'-8¾"

1'-2"

9'-0"

8'-4"

8'-10¼" over Cornices

2'-3" over Side Lamps

9'-2¼" over Handrails

8'-11¼" over Body

12'-4⅜" to top of Roof

Figure 22 Non-corridor
Third Class Brake (Driving) D1790
Seven Period II third brakes were in fact diverted from Lot 527 to be modified for motor train (push-pull) working (Table 1c), though the original of this diagram suggests an original intention for five only. The picture shows No 24404 (formerly 17195) at Ambergate c1934. The repaired panel above the lookout (which has been retained, contrary to the diagram information — see also overleaf) clearly indicates the position of the side lamp before conversion to motor-fitted form.

47

Non-corridor Third Class Brake (Driving) D1790 (cont)

The somewhat sub-standard exterior view below of No 17115 (later 24406), also taken at Ambergate but this time in 1932, shows a D1790 driving trailer in a simpler and more low-waisted form of full livery and without lookouts. It is believed that five D1790 carriages were built to this form from new (probably those which became No 24405-9 after 1933), the two extras (see page 47) being converted from erstwhile orthodox brakes very soon afterwards. The interior view shows the driving compartment of No 24404 (page 47), one of these two conversions. *Authors' Collection*

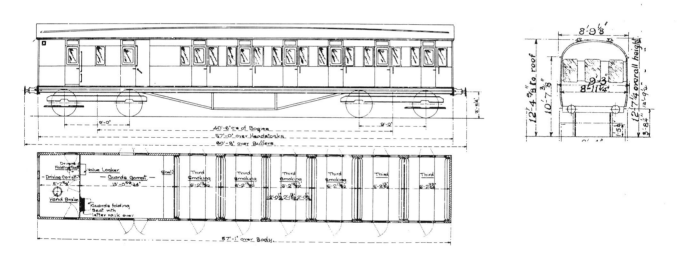

Figure 23 Non-corridor Third Class Brake (Driving) D1856

In spite of appearances, this was in fact a Period III diagram (issued at the start of the 'economy' period in the drawing office) and eventually included 20 examples, most of which emerged at the very start of Period III in full livery with torpedo ventilators, the example illustrated, No 24413, being one such. Note that, like the 'genuine' Period II version (above), there is no guard's lookout.

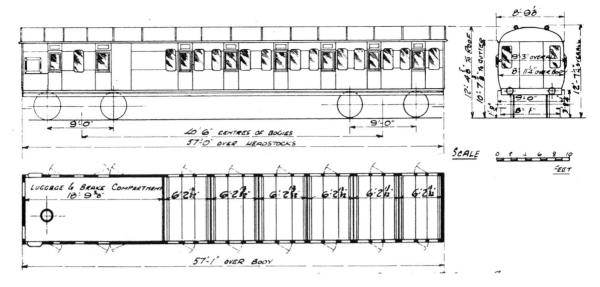

Figure 24 Non-corridor Third Class Brake D1907

As recorded, the first Period III third brakes were actually inserted on to D1735, but the genuine D1907 continuation was dimensionally identical and differed significantly only by way of having shell ventilators and simple livery. We have been unable to obtain pictures of the D1907 version, so instead we offer two views of the Period III brakes which appeared on D1735, Nos 20609 and 20704, both in full livery with torpedo ventilators. No 20609 (Lot 687) has a side lamp above the lookout which is not present on No 20704. D1907 was similar to No 20704, this being the time that the LMS began to remove the side lamps from brake-ended passenger carriages.

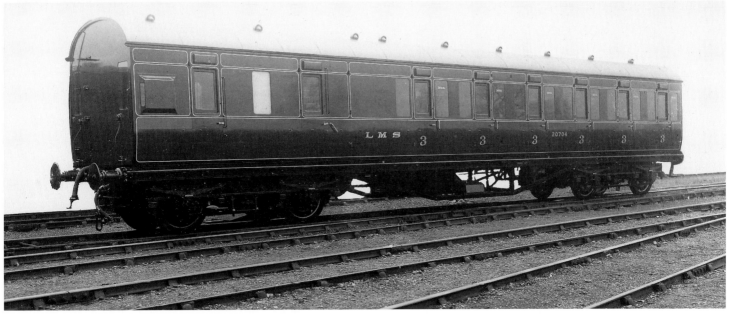

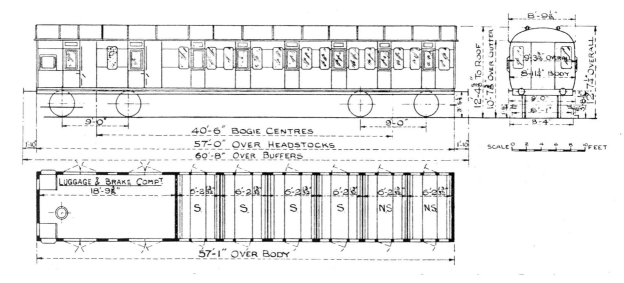

Figures 25/26 Non-corridor Third Class Brake D1964/1964A

These two diagrams were identical save for the repositioning of the non-smoking compartments which is given as the official reason for D1964A — not dissimilar, in fact, to the contemporary full thirds to D1906/1906A (page 41). This time, however, there was a structural change from the earlier Period III type in the form of two pairs of double doors at the van end which thereafter remained standard for Period III non-corridor general service third class brakes.

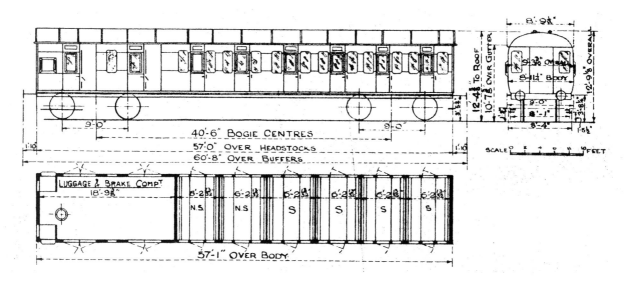

These two pictures (below and opposite) show the exterior of No 20958 and the van interior of No 21034, both to D1964A — again note the use of welded underframe and bogie, by now becoming normal LMS custom.

50

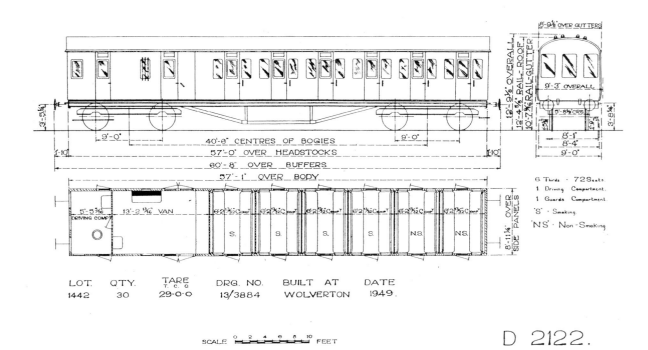

LOT.   QTY.   TARE   DRG. NO.   BUILT AT   DATE
1442   30   29·0·0   13/3884   WOLVERTON   1949.

SCALE |0 2 4 6 8 10| FEET

D 2122.

Figure 27 Non-corridor Third Class Brake (Driving) D2122
The survey of general service 57ft stock is concluded with this BR-built push-pull type for which, unfortunately, no picture has been located. In general it followed the layout of D1856 (page 48) but with the double van doors moved slightly towards the compartments. The design also had a side window in the driver's compartment and no raised lookout. Note too that although the general service brake thirds had by now received two pairs of double doors at the van end, the push-pull version retained the older single pair of double doors.

(end of general service 57ft stock, North London sets follow)

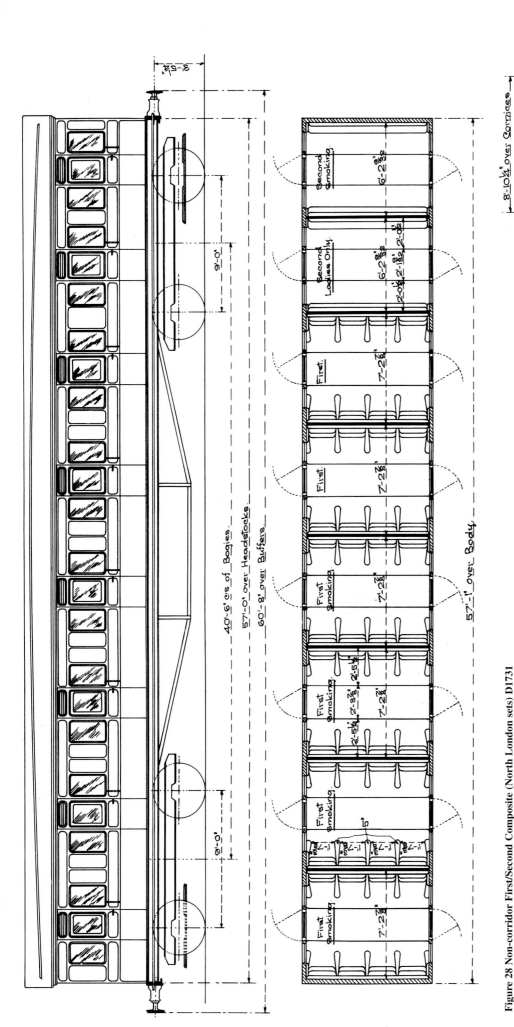

Figure 28 Non-corridor First/Second Class Composite (North London sets) D1731

These vehicles were amongst the relatively few LMS standard types to offer second class accommodation, three-class travel being retained, for historic reasons, on the former North London Railway (NLR) suburban services until well into the 1930s. As far as can be determined, the second class compartments showed no significant differences from the contemporary thirds and were left unchanged after the eventual downgrading to all third in the late 1930s. No pictures have been located of the Period I types but their detail was in every way identical to other contemporary Period I non-corridors.

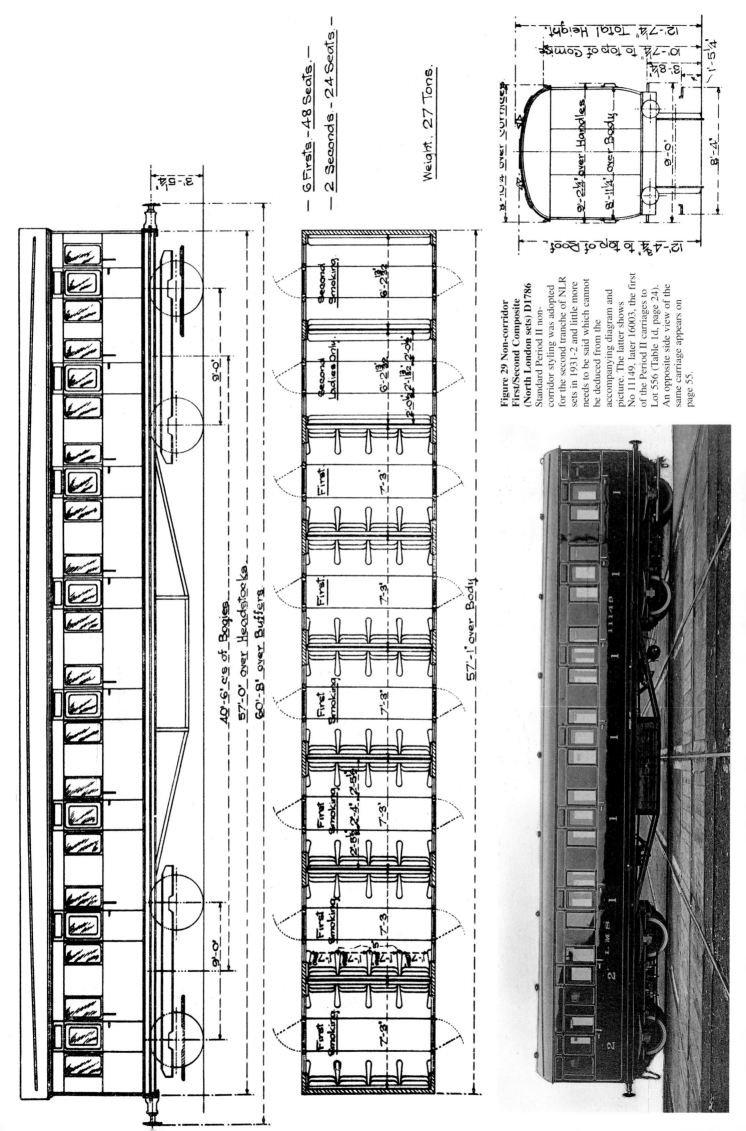

3'-5¼"

9'-0"

40'-6' c's of Bogies

57'-0' over Headstocks

60'-8' over Buffers

9'-0"

6 Firsts - 48 Seats
2 Seconds - 24 Seats

Weight. 27 Tons.

First Smoking — 7'-3'
First Smoking — 7'-3'
First Smoking — 7'-3'
First — 7'-3'
First — 7'-3'
Second Ladies Only — 6'-2½'
Second Smoking — 6'-2½'

2'-5½' 2'-4' 2'-5½'
2'-0½' 2'-1½' 2'-0½'

57'-1' over Body

8'-10¼" over carriage

9'-2¼" over Handles
8'-11¼" over Body

9'-0"

8'-4'

1'-5¼"

3'-8¼"

10'-7¾" to top of Cornice
12'-7⅜" Total Height.

12'-4⅜" to top of Roof.

Figure 29 Non-corridor First/Second Composite (North London sets) D1786
Standard Period II non-corridor styling was adopted for the second tranche of NLR sets in 1931-2 and little more needs to be said which cannot be deduced from the accompanying diagram and picture. The latter shows No 11149, later 16003, the first of the Period II carriages to Lot 556 (Table 1d, page 24). An opposite side view of the same carriage appears on page 55.

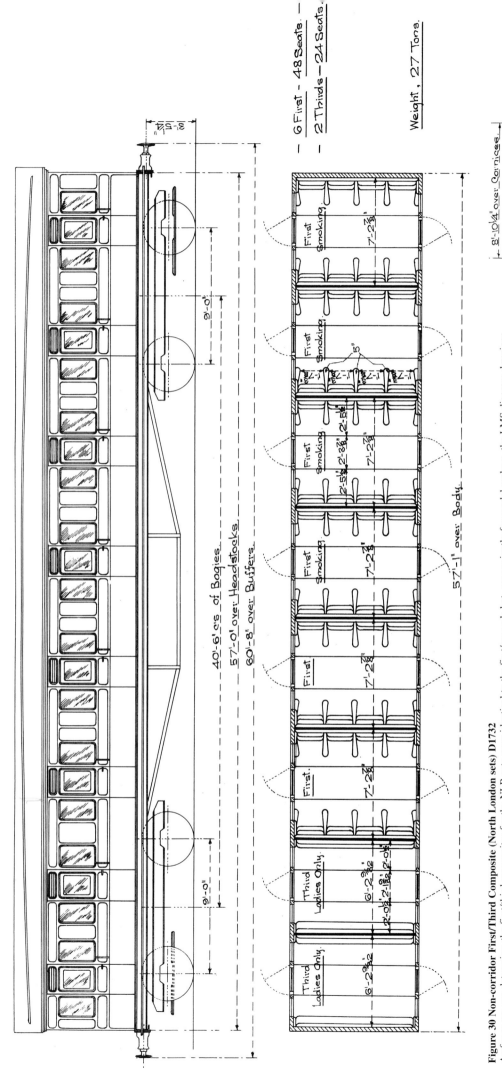

Figure 30 Non-corridor First/Third Composite (North London sets) D1732

As far as we can determine, the first/third composites for the NLR sets were identical to the first/seconds but, conveniently for model makers, the LMS diagram drawings show them from the opposite side, probably because they were marshalled into sets with the first class sections of each type together — see footnote to Table 1d. The two third class compartments in this and the next design were for ladies only — believed to be the only carriages thus marked as far as LMS standard types were concerned.

54

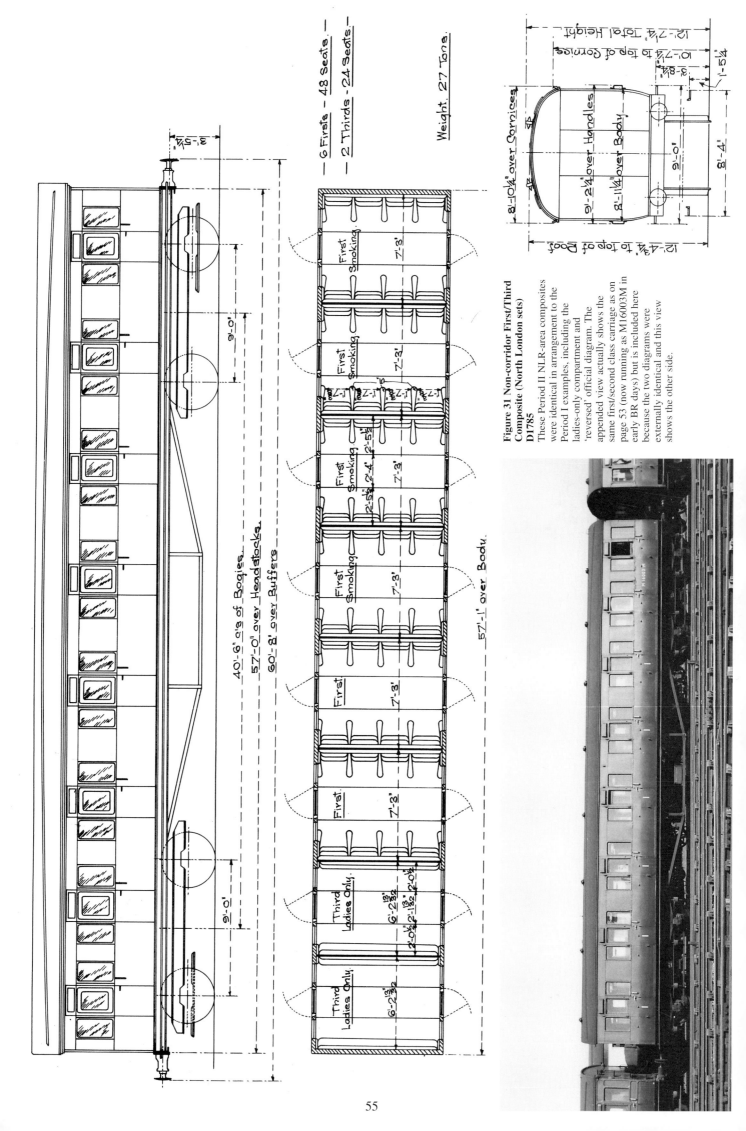

Figure 31 Non-corridor First/Third Composite (North London sets) D1785

These Period II NLR-area composites were identical in arrangement to the Period I examples, including the ladies-only compartment and 'reversed' official diagram. The appended view actually shows the same first/second class carriage as on page 53 (now running as M16003M in early BR days) but is included here because the two diagrams were externally identical and this view shows the other side.

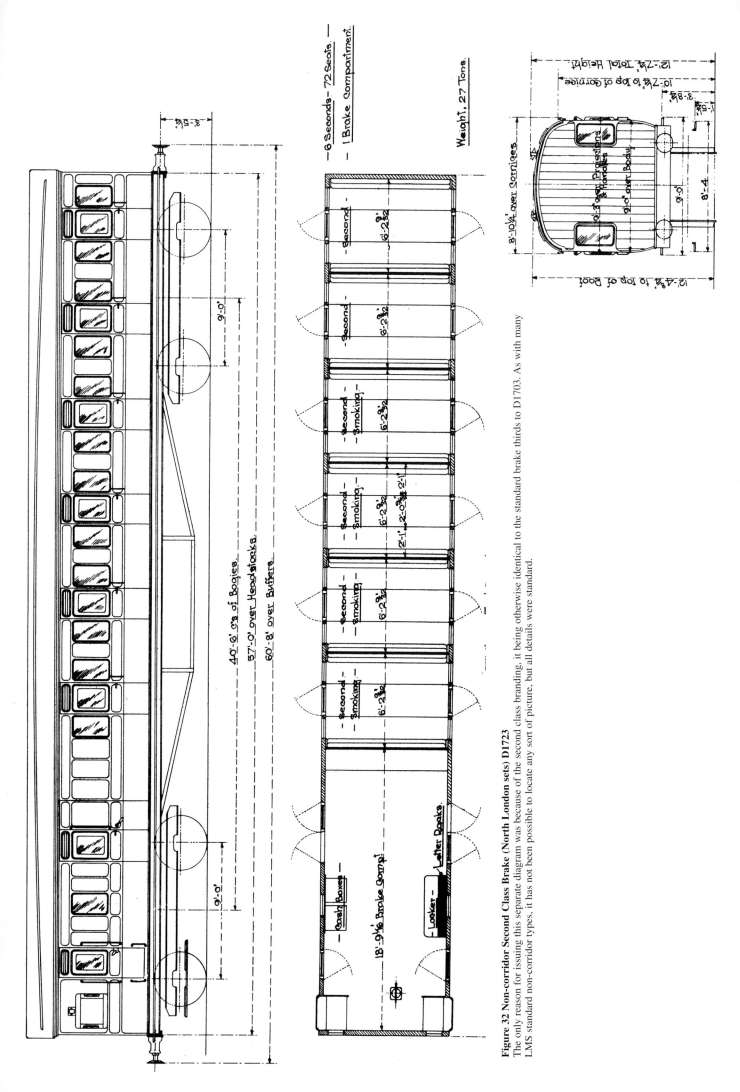

Figure 32 Non-corridor Second Class Brake (North London sets) D1723
The only reason for issuing this separate diagram was because of the second class branding, it being otherwise identical to the standard brake thirds to D1703. As with many LMS standard non-corridor types, it has not been possible to locate any sort of picture, but all details were standard.

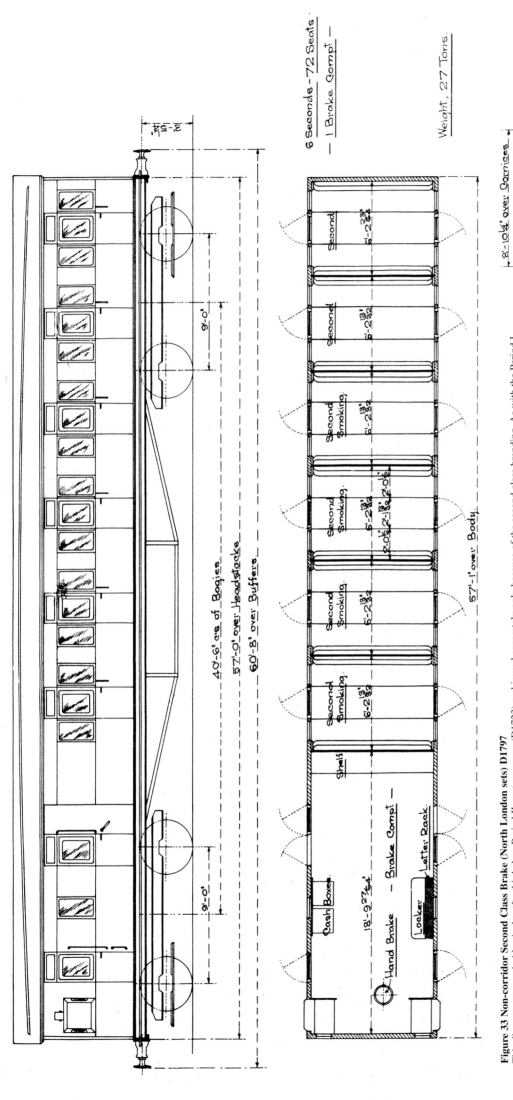

Figure 33 Non-corridor Second Class Brake (North London sets) D1797
This diagram was again identical to the third class Period II contemporary (D1723) and issued separately only because of the second class branding. As with the Period I equivalents, these brakes were renumbered on downgrading to third class (see Table 1d) whereas the first/second composites (pages 52-3) retained their 1933 numbers.

57

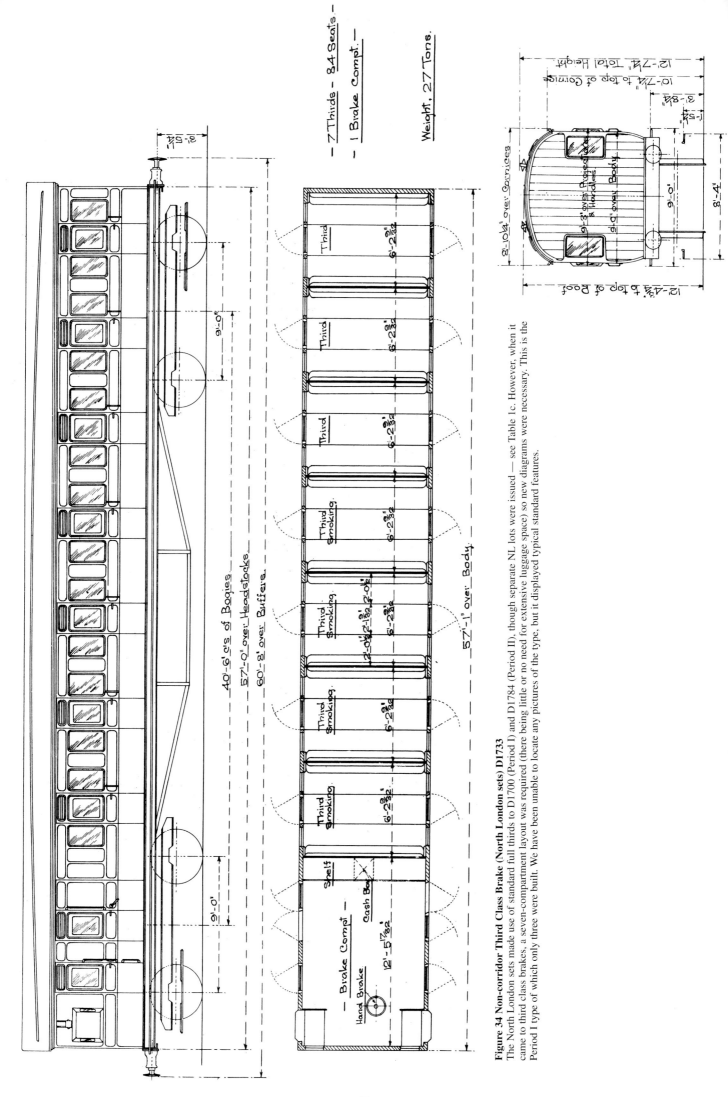

Figure 34 Non-corridor Third Class Brake (North London sets) D1733

The North London sets made use of standard full thirds to D1700 (Period I) and D1784 (Period II), though separate NL lots were issued — see Table 1c. However, when it came to third class brakes, a seven-compartment layout was required (there being little or no need for extensive luggage space) so new diagrams were necessary. This is the Period I type of which only three were built. We have been unable to locate any pictures of the type, but it displayed typical standard features.

- 7 Thirds - 84 Seats -
- 1 Brake Compt. -

Weight, 27 Tons.

58

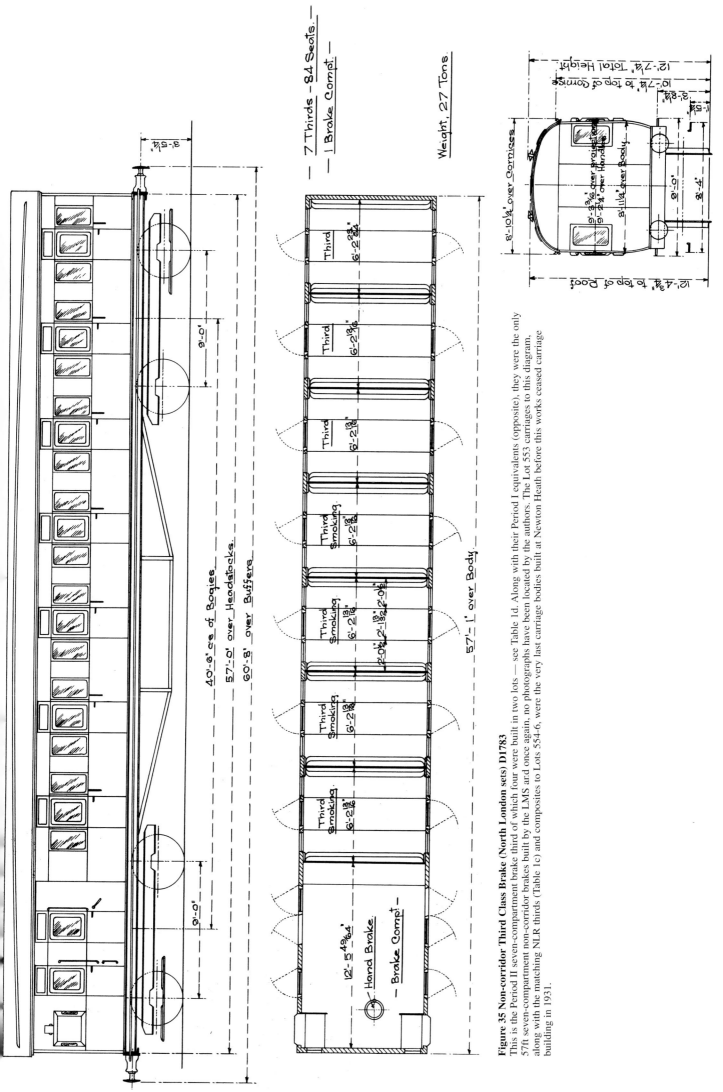

7 Thirds – 84 Seats.
1 Brake Compt.

Weight, 27 Tons.

Figure 35 Non-corridor Third Class Brake (North London sets) D1783
This is the Period II seven-compartment brake third of which four were built in two lots — see Table 1d. Along with their Period I equivalents (opposite), they were the only 57ft seven-compartment non-corridor brakes built by the LMS and once again, no photographs have been located by the authors. The Lot 553 carriages to this diagram, along with the matching NLR thirds (Table 1c) and composites to Lots 554-6, were the very last carriage bodies built at Newton Heath before this works ceased carriage building in 1931.

59

Chapter 2 - 51ft and 54ft Non-corridor Stock

Introduction; Period I designs; Period II and III designs; The London, Tilbury & Southend Sets;
Cathcart Circle Stock; General Service Stock.

It is often assumed that the LMS built two lengths of non-corridor stock (57ft and 54ft) more or less indiscriminately but this is not quite true. The general policy was to build only 57ft coaches and with but a few exceptions, shorter stock was built only for specific services in specific areas. Thus, the analysis of the shorter stock is closely linked to the services for which they were designed. Therefore, in addition to describing the vehicles, this chapter will also concern itself with the services for which they were built.

Virtually all the short non-corridor coaches were on a 54ft underframe, this length being traceable back to the Midland Railway. The only exception to this length was a batch of 51ft composite coaches built for the Cathcart Circle suburban services in Glasgow during 1926. These were the only 51ft passenger-carrying vehicles ever built by the LMS. Although most of the short stock was built for these services in Glasgow or for the Tilbury section, there was, in addition, a small number of general service 54ft coaches but these represent an insignificant total when compared with the 57ft general service non-corridor stock. They may, however, have been built to satisfy a preference in parts of the system for a 54ft as opposed to a 57ft length. Three of these 54ft coaches were used for motor train working.

Like their 57ft contemporaries, the shorter coaches were built only to four basic types: firsts, composites, thirds and brake thirds. The LMS never designed a standard non-corridor brake first or brake composite.

PERIOD I DESIGNS

By far the largest number of short coaches were built during Period I and they included the only general service representatives of the length.

Full firsts were eight-compartment coaches, most for the London, Tilbury & Southend Railway (LT&S) services and the wood-panelled coaches were built to two diagrams (D1759/D1762). The earlier diagram had the MR 9ft 1½in width while D1762 was the 9ft 3in LMS version. Two more identical coaches to D1759 were also built with some of the compartment walls thickened to provide a composite version. This was to D1764 and the reasons for this rather odd and quite unique conversion are explained later, when the formation of the LT&S sets is discussed.

There was, of course, an orthodox Period I wood-panelled 54ft composite and these coaches were also confined to the Tilbury section. They contained lavatories and there were two diagrams. D1763 was a seven-compartment coach and had the MR-style fittings with the two lavatories separated, one towards each end of the vehicle. The later version to D1765 with the LMS 9ft 3in width and eight compartments had both lavatories placed side by side in the centre of the coach and this layout of lavatory composite remained standard on the LT&S lines until the end of the LMS responsibility for providing coaches.

The thirds and brake thirds were, like the firsts, 54ft coaches, the main difference being the reduced compartment size necessitated by the 54ft underframe. The full thirds still retained nine compartments while the brake ends had either six or seven compartments. The six-compartment version was for general service while the wood-panelled seven-compartment design was for use on the LT&S section. There were again diagrams covering both 9ft 1½in widths in both thirds and brake thirds (thirds — D1768/D1769; brake thirds — D1770/D1771/D1772).

It was during Period I that the Cathcart Circle stock was introduced. This differed from the normal Period I short stock in having steel panelling. Thus, the coaches were exactly similar in appearance to the orthodox Period II coaches and may, perhaps, be regarded as the prototype Period II non-corridor vehicles. However, the Cathcart Circle coaches were given full Period I livery with painted waist panel and this, initially, distinguished them from the true Period II coaches.

The Cathcart Circle stock was provided in three types (first, brake third and composite), all built by outside manufacturers. The full firsts to D1760 were identical to the fully beaded D1762 (above), but had five-a-side seating and no armrests. The brake thirds were built to the same seven-compartment diagram as the LT&S stock (D1772) but did not, of course, have the raised beading and wood panelling of the Tilbury coaches.

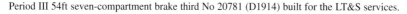

Period III 54ft seven-compartment brake third No 20781 (D1914) built for the LT&S services.

The composites were the only 51ft coaches built to an LMS diagram (D1766). They were eight-compartment vehicles identical in layout to the second design of LT&S centre lavatory composite (D1765) except for the omission of the lavatories which was the reason for the reduced length. The first class compartments were again devoid of armrests and seated five-a-side. Like their matching five-a-side full firsts, the coaches were later written down to third class and renumbered. They were the shortest LMS standard locomotive-hauled single-unit passenger-carrying coaches.

PERIOD II AND III DESIGNS

All Period II and III designs for short non-corridor coaches were 54ft vehicles and all were for the LT&S services. The only really curious feature about them was the fact that the Period III coaches were actually built to Period II diagrams with the exception of the brake thirds. Why this was so is not known but it may be compared with the 57ft stock where in some cases there was a change from Period II to Period III on the same diagram — see Table 1c, pages 22-3. By 1930, the make-up of the LT&S sets had been standardised and the 54ft coaches of Periods II and III were built only to four specific types: full first, full third, lavatory composite and seven-compartment brake third. In terms of compartment layout they were identical to the final Period I designs.

THE LONDON, TILBURY & SOUTHEND SETS

The 54ft vehicles, for this section of the LMS, were built to form 17 semi-close coupled sets of 11 coaches. The sets were generally branded 'F&S 2xx' (the F&S standing for Fenchurch Street and Southend) and the make-up for one set was generally as follows: BT/T/T/T/CL/F/CL/T/T/T/BT. The 54ft length was probably adopted because of platform or loop lengths on the Tilbury line.

The first two sets (F&S 241/2) were not quite of this standard layout as they each contained two full firsts and only one composite, the latter being of the 'separated' lavatory type. It seems that the Operating Department must have felt that this formation gave too much first class space and requested a reduction in future sets. However, the next two sets (F&S 243/4) were already building at the time and the only way to reduce the first class space would be to turn one of the firsts into a composite. This seems the most likely explanation for the curious conversion of only two coaches to D1764 mentioned above. If the coaches had not been built, there would have been no good reason why two more of the lavatory composites could not have been substituted for the two unwanted firsts. Moreover, if the conversion of the two firsts to composite took place *after* the coaches entered service one would have logically expected two coaches from sets F&S 241/2 to be likewise altered and this was never done.

By the time subsequent sets were in production, the new centre lavatory composite had been designed and two of these replaced one of the firsts and the older staggered lavatory composite. It seemed hardly worth while having lavatories at all, for only two compartments — one first and one third — were served, a total of four out of the entire set.

The diagrams show that some of the 54ft LT&S coaches were built with four short buffers and some with short buffers at one end and long buffers at the other. In general, the short-buffered ends were semi-permanently coupled together while the long buffers were provided where the sets were divided into shorter units at off-peak hours. Although in later years the splitting of sets and the reversal of sections caused the pattern to be somewhat confused (too much so to analyse here), the general principles seem to be as outlined below.

The basic 11-coach set was divided as follows: BT+T/T+T+CL+F/CL+T/T+T+BT, the long buffers being at the outer ends of these sections. The most general off-peak reduction was to remove the three-coach CL+T+T portion, leaving an eight-coach unit. Frequently, the detached three-coach sections would be coupled in pairs with two loose brakes to form further sets. One can only presume that this splitting was to reduce the average daily mileage of any specific vehicle of these intensively used coaches so as to lengthen the period between overhauls. Table 2a lists the LT&S sets as they were when originally built as running until at least 1939. After the war, they became a little split up but sufficient coaches have been verified in the original sets by eye witnesses to establish that the overall pattern hardly changed at all.

CATHCART CIRCLE STOCK

The Cathcart Circle coaches were built to form eight five-coach sets with spare vehicles. The formation of a set was as follows: BT/C/F/C/BT with a total of 160 first class seats and 264 thirds. Unfortunately, it has not been possible to confirm the running numbers of the coaches in each individual set but published information at the time shows that seven sets came from Hurst Nelson and one set and eight spare coaches from Pickering & Co. There could have been a further set made from the spares but whether this was done is not known. Table 2a includes an attempt to reconstruct the probable formation of the Cathcart Circle sets but has not been confirmed. In about 1938, nine composites were marked down to thirds and renumbered, followed in about 1941 by the 10 firsts and in 1953 by the remaining composites. Details are given with Table 2a.

GENERAL SERVICE STOCK

The 54ft coaches not accounted for by the LT&S/Cathcart Circle sets were 78 thirds to D1768 and 94 brake thirds to D1770/D1771. These seemed to be fairly widespread in use and, no doubt, were more acceptable than the 57ft coaches in many parts of the Midland Division because of their 54ft length. Nevertheless, they seem to have been indiscriminately mixed with 57ft stock when in service and some fairly typical observed formations on the Midland Division using the 54ft coaches would include 54ft BT/57ft CL/57ft BT or 54ft BT/57ft CL/57ft BTL as local sets and 54ft BT/54ft T/54ft T/57ft T/54ft BT as an excursion set.

There were a few motor-fitted 54ft coaches and these are covered on page 25 although details are also included in the summary table to this chapter.

Period III 54ft lavatory composite No 19196 (D1788) built for the LT&S services. These coaches, of which only four were built, were the only Period III non-corridor lavatory vehicles.

TABLE 2a: SUMMARY TABLE OF LMS STANDARD 51ft AND 54ft NON-CORRIDOR STOCK

Type	Diag	Lot	Qty	Date	Built	Dimensions (L x W x H)	Weight	Period	Running Numbers	Withdrawals First	Withdrawals Last	Remarks
F	1759	12	4	1924	Derby }	54ft x 9ft 1½in x 12ft 5½in	26T	I	10000-10003	6/61	12/63	LT&S stock with MR fittings and with alternate long/short buffers. Lot 12 for sets F&S 241/2; Lot 96 for F&S 243/4.
		part 96	2	1924	Derby }		26T	I	10004-10005	11/60	13/62	
F	1760	212	7	1926	Hurst Nelson }	54ft x 9ft 3in x 12ft 4¾in	27T	I (steel panelled)	10017-10023	7/59	6/61	The Cathcart Circle coaches with five-a-side seating. Downgraded to third class (c1941).
		213	3	1926	Pickering }		27T		10024-10026	11/60	2/62	
F	1762	129	2	1926	Derby }	54ft x 9ft 3in x 12ft 4¾in	26T	I	10006-10007	1/45	2/62	LT&S stock with LMS standard fittings. Otherwise identical to D1759 and fitted with alternative long/short buffers. One each in sets F&S 245-252.
		331	2	1927	Derby		26T		10008-10009	5/61	3/62	
		394	2	1928	Derby		26T		10010-10011	-	2/62	
		432	2	1929	Derby }		26T		10012-10013	2/62	3/62	
F	1787	558	3	1931	see notes }	54ft x 9ft 2¼in x 12ft 4¾in	28T	II	10014-10016	2/62	5/62	LT&S stock with alternate long/short buffers. Lot 558 was built at Newton Heath on Derby chassis. Note change to Period III on same diagram. Lot 558 was for sets F&S 253-5; Lot 819 for F&S 264/5.
		819	2	1934	Derby }		29T	III	10111-10112	9/61	3/62	
CL	1763	13	2	1924	Derby }	54ft x 9ft 1½in x 12ft 5½in	25T	I	19022-19023	9/61	12/61	The first LT&S-style CL with separated lavatories. All with short buffers and one each in sets F&S 241-4. Diagram shows 9ft 1½in width but some coaches may not have had MR-pattern locks/handles. No reason can be given why they were numbered after D1765/D1788.
		97	2	1924	Derby }		25T		19024-19025	11/61	12/61	
C	1764	part 96	2	1924	Derby	54ft x 9ft 1½in x 12ft 5½in	26T	I	16026-16027	-	2/62	These were the coaches modified from D1759 to have thicker compartment walls and hence smaller third class compartments. Although built to 9ft 1½in diagram, they did not have MR-pattern handles, etc. One each in sets F&S 243-4.
C	1766	216	14	1926	Hurst Nelson }	51ft x 9ft 3in x 12ft 4¾in	27T	I (steel panelled)	16007-16020	2/60	13/61	Cathcart Circle coaches with five-a-side firsts. Downgraded to third class (c1938/1953).
		217	5	1926	Pickering }		27T		16021-16025	6/60	6/64	
CL	1765	130	4	1926	Derby }	54ft x 9ft 3in x 12ft 4¾in	26T	I	19000-19003	6/61	3/62	LT&S stock with the centre lavatory and LMS fittings. Replaced D1763 and had one more first class compartment. Two from each lot had long/short buffers, two all short. Two coaches per set in F&S 245-252.
		332	4	1927	Derby		26T		19004-19007	5/59	4/62	
		395	4	1928	Derby		26T		19008-19011	6/61	12/61	
		433	4	1929	Derby }		26T		19012-19015	3/62	6/62	
CL	1788	559	6	1930	see notes }	54ft x 9ft 2¼in x 12ft 4¾in	28T	II	19016-19021	6/61	6/62	The Period II and III versions of D1765. Lot 559 built as for Lot 558 (above). Buffers as per D1765. Lot 559 was for sets F&S 253-5; Lot 820 for F&S 264/5.
		820	4	1935	Derby }		29T	III	19196-19199	7/61	4/62	
T	1768	14	12	1924	Derby }	54ft x 9ft 1½in x 12ft 5½in	26T	I	10700-10711	5/61	6/62	The official 9ft 1½in version but Lot 78 did not have MR handles and was 9ft 3in wide. Lots 14/98 may have been similar and were the LT&S coaches. These had four of each lot with long/short buffers and eight with all short buffers. Six coaches into each of sets F&S 241-244. Lots 60/78 were the general service lots and Lot 60 was 9ft 1½in.
		98	12	1924	Derby		26T		10712-10723	8/60	4/62	
		60	40	1924/5	Ntn Hth		27T		10772-10811	5/59	1/64	
		78	38	1924	Derby }		26T		10812-10849	5/59	13/62	
T	1769	131	12	1926	Derby }	54ft x 9ft 3in x 12ft 4¾in	26T	I	10724-10735	5/58	4/62	These were the official 9ft 3in coaches and all for LT&S sets (six each to F&S 245-252). Eight of each lot had long/short buffers and four all short — a reversal of D1768.
		333	12	1927	Derby		26T		10736-10747	9/59	4/62	
		396	12	1928	Derby		26T		10748-10759	6/61	4/62	
		434	12	1929	Derby }		26T		10760-10771	6/61	4/62	
T	1789	560	18	1931/2	see notes }	54ft x 9ft 2¼in x 12ft 4¾in	29T	II	11606-11623	7/60	4/62	The Period II/III LT&S coaches. Buffers as per D1769. Lot 560 plated 27T and built as for Lots 558/559 (above). F&S sets 253-5/264/5.
		821	12	1935	Derby }		29T	III	11705-11716	4/61	2/62	
BT	1770	15	4	1924	Derby }	54ft x 9ft 1½in x 12ft 5½in	26T	I	20091-20094	7/61	12/61	The 9ft1½in diagram but Lot 61 (at least) plated 9ft 3in and the others may have been similar. Lots 15/99 were LT&S (F&S sets 241-4) with alternate long/short buffers & 7 comps. Lot 61 had six compartments and was probably plated 27T.
		61	20	1925	Ntn Hth }		24T		20000-20019	7/58	7/62	
		99	4	1924	Derby }		26T		20095-20098	4/61	2/62	
BT	1771	79	24	1925	Derby }	54ft x 9ft 3in x 12ft 4¾in	26T	I	20020-20040	5/59	1/64	The official 9ft 3in six-compartment general service coaches, plated 1924. *Driving Trailers, converted 1927.
									24400-24402*	9/60	1/64	
		128	50	1925	Derby }		26T		20041-20090	10/58	3/64	
BT	1772	132	4	1926	Derby	54ft x 9ft 3in x 12ft 4¾in	26T	I	20099-20102	2/62	2/62	The 9ft 3in seven-compartment coaches for LT&S and Cathcart Circle sets. Note that in this case a separate diagram was raised for the seven-compartment version. Lots 214/5 were Cathcart Circle, remainder LT&S. LT&S coaches had long buffers at brake end, short at opposite end and were for sets F&S 245-252.
		214	14	1926	Hurst Nelson		26T	I (flush)	20103-20116	6/59	13/62	
		215	5	1926	Pickering		26T	I (flush)	20117-20121	1/60	6/60	
		334	4	1927	Derby		26T	I	20122-20125	3/60	4/62	
		397	4	1928	Derby		26T		20126-20129	6/61	4/62	
		435	4	1929	Derby		26T		20130-20133	11/61	3/62	
BT	1841	561	6	1932	see notes }	54ft x 9ft 2¼in x 12ft 4¾in	27T	II	20134-20139	4/61	6/62	This time, two diagrams were raised for the Period II/III stock, the van of D1914 being slightly shorter. Lot 561 was built as for Lots 558-560 (above). Coaches for F&S sets 253/5; 264/5.
BT	1914	822	4	1934	Derby }	54ft x 9ft 3in x 12ft 4⅝in	29T	III	20781-20784	7/60	2/62	

London, Tilbury & Southend set formations

Date in service	Set No	Third Brake	Third	Third	Third	Lavatory	First Compo	Lavatory Compo	Third	Third	Third	Third Brake	Remarks
1924	F&S 241	20091	10700	10701	10702	19022*	10000	10001†	10703	10704	10705	20092	These were the non-standard Period I sets.
1924	F&S 242	20093	10706	10707	10708	19023*	10002	10003†	10709	10710	10711	20094	* 'separated' Cls.
1924	F&S 243	20095	10712	10713	10714	19024*	10004	16026+	10715	10716	10717	20096	† full firsts, no lavatories.
1924	F&S 244	20097	10718	10719	10720	19025*	10005	16027+	10721	10722	10723	20098	+ converted composites, no lavatories.
1926	F&S 245	20101	10730	10731	10732	19002	10007	19003	10733	10734	10735	20102	The standard Period I sets. Set 246
1926	F&S 246	20099	10724	10725	10726	19000	10006	19001	10727	10728	10729	20100	emerged before set 245 and had the lower-
1927	F&S 247	20122	10736	10737	10738	19004	10008	19005	10739	10740	10741	20123	numbered coaches.
1927	F&S 248	20124	10742	10743	10744	19006	10009	19007	10745	10746	10747	20125	
1928	F&S 249	20126	10748	10749	10750	19008	10010	19009	10751	10752	10753	20127	
1928	F&S 250	20128	10754	10755	10756	19010	10011	19011	10757	10758	10759	20129	
1929	F&S 251	20130	10760	10761	10762	19012	10012	19013	10763	10764	10765	20131	
1929	F&S 252	20132	10766	10767	10768	19014	10013	19015	10769	10770	10771	20133	
1931	F&S 253	20134	11606	11607	16908	19016	10014	19017	11609	11610	11611	20135	The Period II sets.
1931	F&S 254	20136	11612	11613	11614	19018	10015	19019	11615	11616	11619	20137	
1931	F&S 255	20138	11618	11617	11620	19020	10016	19021	11621	11622	11623	20139	
1934	F&S 264	20781	11705	11706	11707	19196	10111	19197	11708	11709	11710	20782	The Period III sets.
1934	F&S 265	20783	11711	11712	11713	19198	10112	19199	11714	11715	11716	20784	

Note: For some reason, coaches 11617/9 were placed in the wrong sets and appeared to stay there.

Cathcart Circle sets

The following table gives the probable composition of the sets as first built.

Third Brake	Compo	First	Compo Brake	Third	Remarks	Spare Coaches and Renumbering
20103	16007	10017	16008	20104	The Hurst Nelson sets	1. The following Pickering coaches were probably the initial spare vehicles:
20105	16009	10018	16010	20106		
20107	16011	10019	16012	20108		First: 10025/6
20109	16013	10020	16014	20110		Compos: 16023-5
20111	16015	10021	16016	20112		*Brakes: 20119-21*
20113	16017	10022	16018	20114		
20115	16019	10023	16020	20116		
20117	16021	10024	10022	20118	The Pickering set	2. On downgrading, the firsts and composites received the following numbers:

16007-25 became 13468-70; 12268-70; 13471-3; 12271-2; 13474-5; 12273; 13476; 12274-7 in the same order. The 134xx series was the 1938 batch and the 122xx series the 1953 batch.

10017-26 became 13426-35 in the same order. The downgrading took place c1941 but some of the renumbering was as late as 1950.

Table 2b: 1933 RENUMBERING OF LMS 51ft/54ft NON-CORRIDOR STOCK

The following list is given in the same carriage diagram order as Table 2a and is, of course, applicable only to Period I and Period II designs.

New Number	Old Number	New Number	Old Number	New Number	Old Number	New Number	Old Number
First Class		D1787		16019	15883	19020	15545
D1759				16020	15892	19021	15547
		10014	9836	16021	15896		
10000	2620	10015	9838	16022	15918	**Third Class**	
10001	2621	10016	15740	16023	15982	D1768	
10002	2622			16024	15990		
10003	2630	**Composite**		16025	16001	10700	4225
10004	2639	D1763 (lavatory)				10701	4226
10005	2641			D1765 (lavatory)		10702	4227
		19022	2631			10703	4228
D1760		19023	2632	19000	2651	10704	4229
		19024	2633	19001	2653	10705	4230
10017	15368	19025	2634	19002	2654	10706	4231
10018	15393			19003	2795	10707	4232
10019	15403	D1764		19004	2495	10708	4233
10020	15425			19005	2496	10709	4234
10021	15426	16026	2640	19006	2497	10710	4235
10022	15428	16027	2642	19007	2498	10711	4236
10023	15430			19008	4156	10712	4237
10024	15456	D1766		19009	4157	10713	4238
10025	15487			19010	4158	10714	4239
10026	15490	16007	15597	19011	4159	10715	4240
		16008	15619	19012	2342	10716	4241
D1762		16009	15702	19013	2418	10717	4242
		16010	15768	19014	2421	10718	4243
10006	2649	16011	15774	19015	2434	10719	4244
10007	2650	16012	15790			10720	4245
10008	2796	16013	15794	D1788 (lavatory)		10721	4246
10009	2797	16014	15799			10722	4247
10010	2798	16015	15818	19016	15535	10723	4248
10011	4155	16016	15867	19017	15537	10772	14461
10012	2499	16017	15872	19018	15538	10773	14462
10013	2500	16018	15875	19019	15543	10774	14463

New Number	Old Number	New Number	Old Number	New Number	Old Number	New Number	Old Number
10775	14464	**D1769**		20001	13944	20066	16768
10776	14465			20002	14005	20067	16769
10777	14466	10724	4249	20003	14017	20068	16778
10778	14467	10725	4250	20004	14079	20069	16780
10779	14468	10726	4251	20005	14082	20070	16781
10780	14469	10727	4252	20006	14086	20071	16791
10781	14470	10728	4253	20007	14088	20072	16814
10782	14471	10729	4254	20008	14089	20073	16824
10783	14472	10730	4255	20009	14091	20074	16828
10784	14473	10731	4256	20010	14092	20075	16830
10785	14474	10732	4257	20011	14096	20076	16831
10786	14475	10733	4258	20012	14098	20077	16832
10787	14476	10734	4259	20013	14110	20078	16833
10788	14477	10735	4260	20014	14120	20079	16838
10789	14478	10736	4266	20015	14124	20080	16841
10790	14479	10737	4267	20016	14132	20081	16848
10791	14480	10738	4268	20017	14133	20082	16849
10792	14481	10739	4269	20018	14134	20083	16857
10793	14482	10740	4270	20019	14144	20084	16858
10794	14483	10741	4271	20091	3873	20085	16860
10795	14484	10742	4272	20092	3882	20086	16861
10796	14485	10743	4273	20093	3883	20087	17100
10797	14486	10744	4274	20094	3884	20088	17134
10798	14487	10745	4275	20095	3885	20089	19124
10799	14488	10746	4276	20096	3886	20090	19129
10800	14489	10747	4277	20097	3887	24400	7702
10801	14490	10748	2419	20098	3888	24401	7730
10802	14491	10749	2424			24402	7837
10803	14492	10750	2425	**D1771**			
10804	14493	10751	2426			**D1772**	
10805	14494	10752	2427	20020	6954		
10806	14495	10753	2428	20021	7111	20099	3889
10807	14496	10754	4278	20022	7606	20100	3890
10808	14497	10755	4279	20023	7607	20101	3891
10809	14498	10756	4286	20024	7608	20102	3892
10810	14499	10757	4287	20025	7612	20103	16236
10811	14500	10758	4288	20026	7667	20104	16362
10812	950	10759	4289	20027	7677	20105	16729
10813	1206	10760	2347	20028	7687	20106	16757
10814	2688	10761	2348	20029	7699	20107	16774
10815	2691	10762	2349	20030	7703	20108	16787
10816	2695	10763	2350	20031	7716	20109	16788
10817	2697	10764	2351	20032	7719	20110	16815
10818	2702	10765	2352	20033	7813	20111	16835
10819	2705	10766	2353	20034	8739	20112	16836
10820	2709	10767	2354	20035	16068	20113	16866
10821	2732	10768	2355	20036	16069	20114	16870
10822	2733	10769	2356	20037	16555	20115	16878
10823	2735	10770	2357	20038	16638	20116	16882
10824	2736	10771	2358	20039	16647	20117	16893
10825	2737			20040	17408	20118	16904
10826	2738	**D1789**		20041	15630	20119	16920
10827	2852			20042	16088	20120	17018
10828	3435	11606	1847	20043	16152	20121	17135
10829	3457	11607	9425	20044	16185	20122	3874
10830	3477	11608	14042	20045	16316	20123	3875
10831	3506	11609	14043	20046	16351	20124	3876
10832	3509	11610	14046	20047	16353	20125	3877
10833	3525	11611	14047	20048	16357	20126	4160
10834	3527	11612	14740	20049	16361	20127	4161
10835	3569	11613	14741	20050	16363	20128	4280
10836	3679	11614	14743	20051	16427	20129	4281
10837	3681	11615	15237	20052	16477	20130	2721
10838	3689	11616	17623	20053	16489	20131	2722
10839	3691	11617	17625	20054	16490	20132	2723
10840	3692	11618	17627	20055	16495	20133	2724
10841	3700	11619	17641	20056	16505		
10842	16064	11620	17884	20057	16604	**D1841**	
10843	16065	11621	17888	20058	16631		
10844	16066	11622	17889	20059	16632	20134	2400
10845	16067	11623	17939	20060	16643	20135	2401
10846	16202			20061	16648	20136	2402
10847	16784	**Third Class Brake**		20062	16655	20137	2403
10848	16793	**D1770**		20063	16698	20138	2404
10849	16895			20064	16741	20139	2405
		20000	13938	20065	16746		

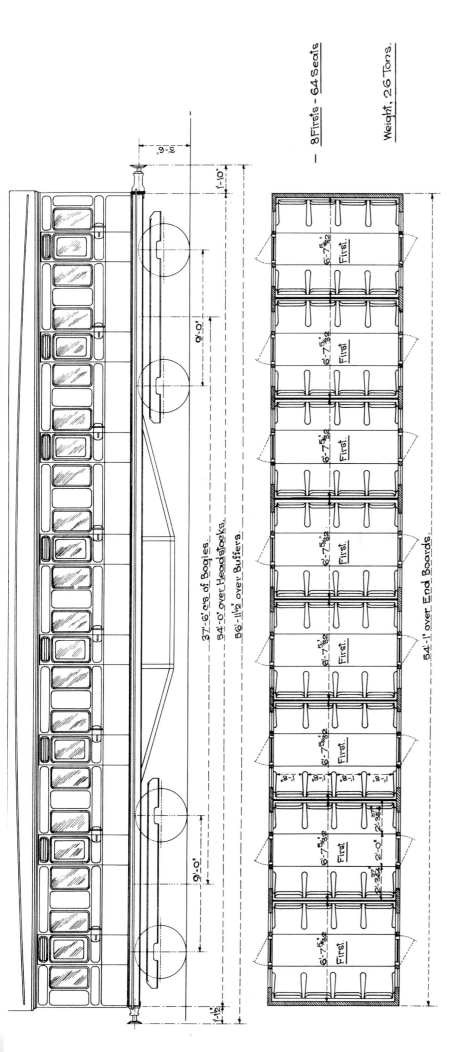

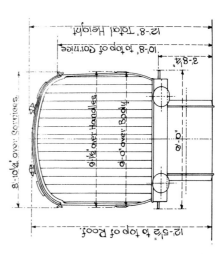

8Firsts — 64 Seats

Weight, 26 Tons.

Figure 36 Non-corridor First Class D1759

This diagram was issued for the first few LT&S sets of 1924 — see Table 2a — and was distinguished from the later Period I examples by its Midland-pattern recessed door handles which reduced its overall width. Note too the alternate long and short buffers. Two more otherwise identical carriages were put into service as composites — see Figure 41, page 70.

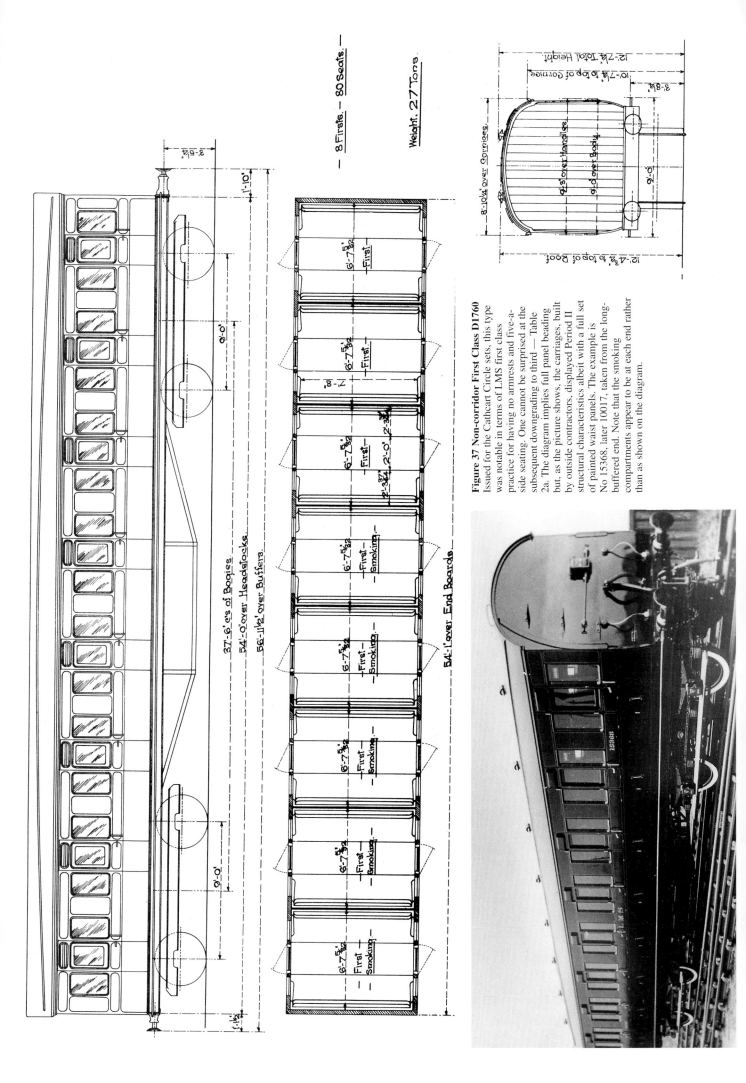

— 8 Firsts. — 80 Seats. —

Weight. 27 Tons

3'-6¼"

1'-10"

9'-0"

37'-6' c's of Bogies.

54'-0" over Headstocks.

56'-11½' over Buffers.

6'-7⁵/₃₂"
First

6'-7⁵/₃₂"
First

2'-0"

6'-7⁵/₃₂"
First

2'-3¾". 2'-0'. 2'-3¾".

6'-7⁵/₃₂"
First
Smoking

6'-7⁵/₃₂"
First
Smoking

6'-7⁵/₃₂"
First
Smoking

6'-7⁵/₃₂"
First
Smoking

6'-7⁵/₃₂"
First
Smoking

54'-' over End Boards.

9'-0"

8'-10¼" over Cornices.

9'-3" over Handles.

9'-0" over Body.

9'-0"

3'-8¾"

10'-7¾' to top of Cornices.

12'-7¾' Total Height.

12'-4¾' to top of Roof.

Figure 37 Non-corridor First Class D1760
Issued for the Cathcart Circle sets, this type was notable in terms of LMS first class practice for having no armrests and five-a-side seating. One cannot be surprised at the subsequent downgrading to third — Table 2a. The diagram implies full panel beading but, as the picture shows, the carriages, built by outside contractors, displayed Period II structural characteristics albeit with a full set of painted waist panels. The example is No 15368, later 10017, taken from the long-buffered end. Note that the smoking compartments appear to be at each end rather than as shown on the diagram.

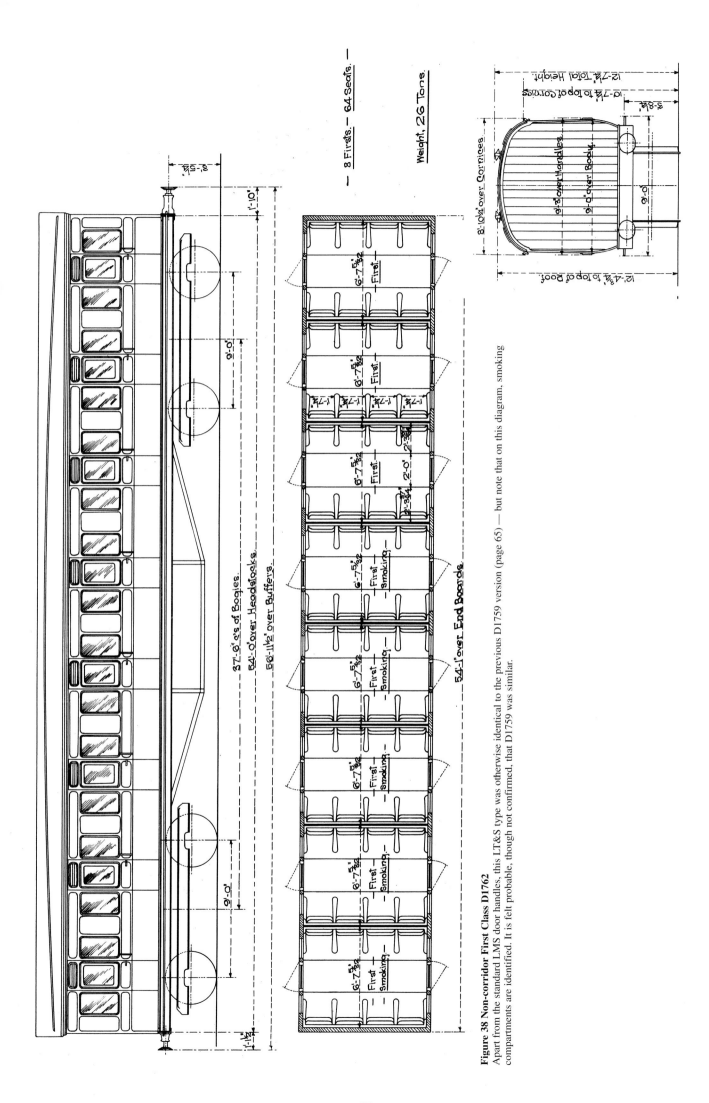

Figure 38 Non-corridor First Class D1762

Apart from the standard LMS door handles, this LT&S type was otherwise identical to the previous D1759 version (page 65) — but note that on this diagram, smoking compartments are identified. It is felt probable, though not confirmed, that D1759 was similar.

— 8 Firsts. — 64 Seats. —

Weight, 26 Tons.

67

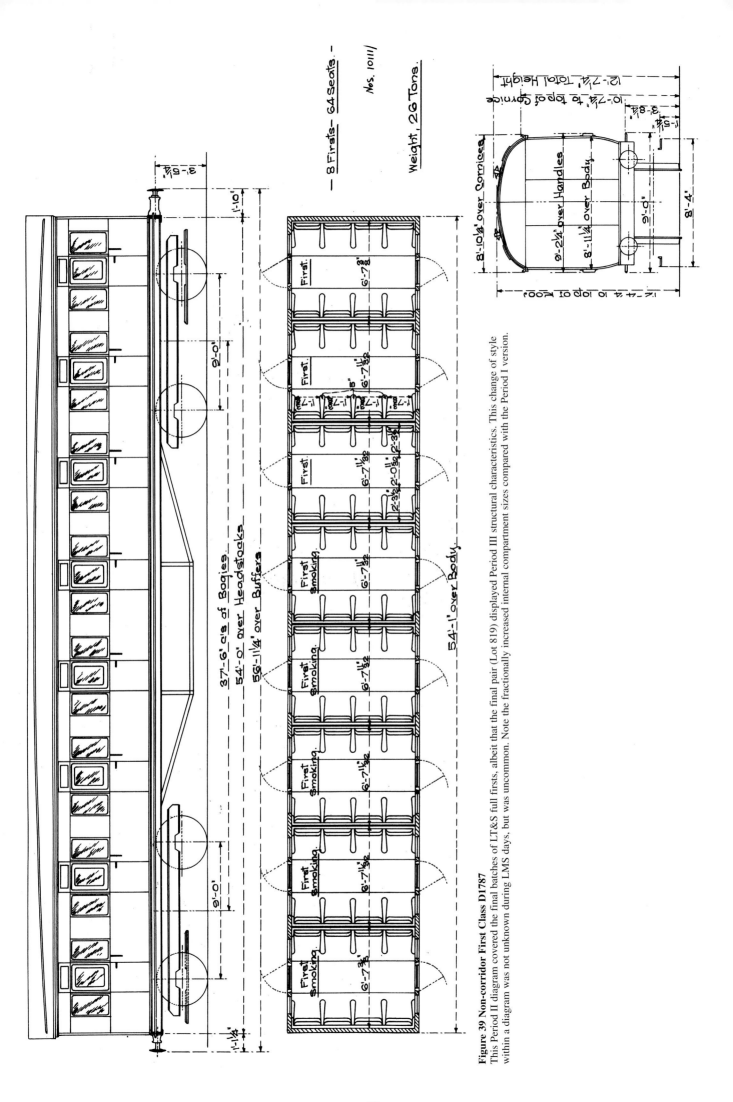

Figure 39 Non-corridor First Class D1787

This Period II diagram covered the final batches of LT&S full firsts, albeit that the final pair (Lot 819) displayed Period III structural characteristics. This change of style within a diagram was not unknown during LMS days, but was uncommon. Note the fractionally increased internal compartment sizes compared with the Period I version.

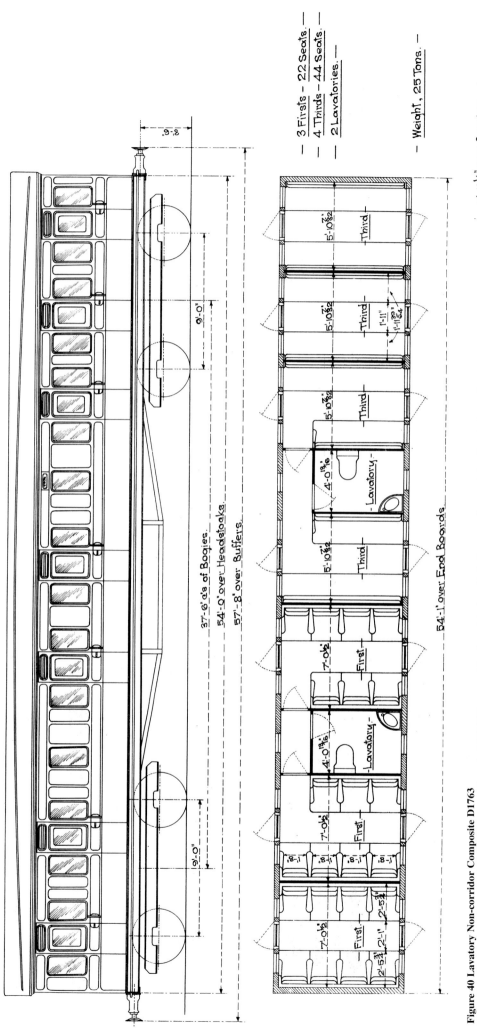

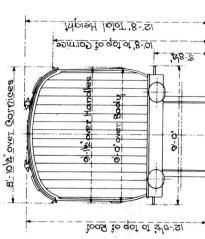

— 3 Firsts – 22 Seats.
— 4 Thirds – 44 Seats.
— 2 Lavatories.

— Weight, 25 Tons.

Figure 40 Lavatory Non-corridor Composite D1763

These four attractive carriages for the LT&S sets were the only LMS 54ft types with what might be called adequate toilet provision, but the internal arrangement was not repeated in later sets. Although shown with long buffers they are all believed to have had the short variety. There is some evidence — see 'Remarks' column in Table 2a — that the second batch may have had conventional LMS-pattern door handles. Smoking compartments are not identified but are likely to have been present.

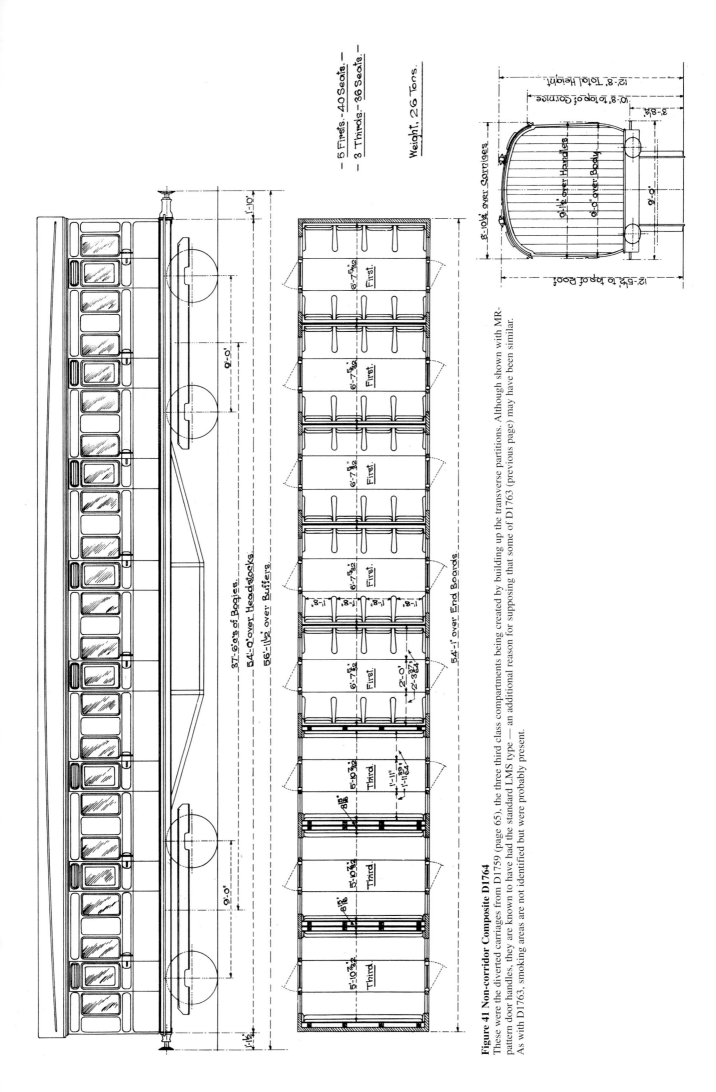

Figure 41 Non-corridor Composite D1764

These were the diverted carriages from D1759 (page 65), the three third class compartments being created by building up the transverse partitions. Although shown with MR-pattern door handles, they are known to have had the standard LMS type — an additional reason for supposing that some of D1763 (previous page) may have been similar. As with D1763, smoking areas are not identified but were probably present.

5 Firsts. - 40 Seats.
3 Thirds. - 36 Seats.

Weight, 26 Tons.

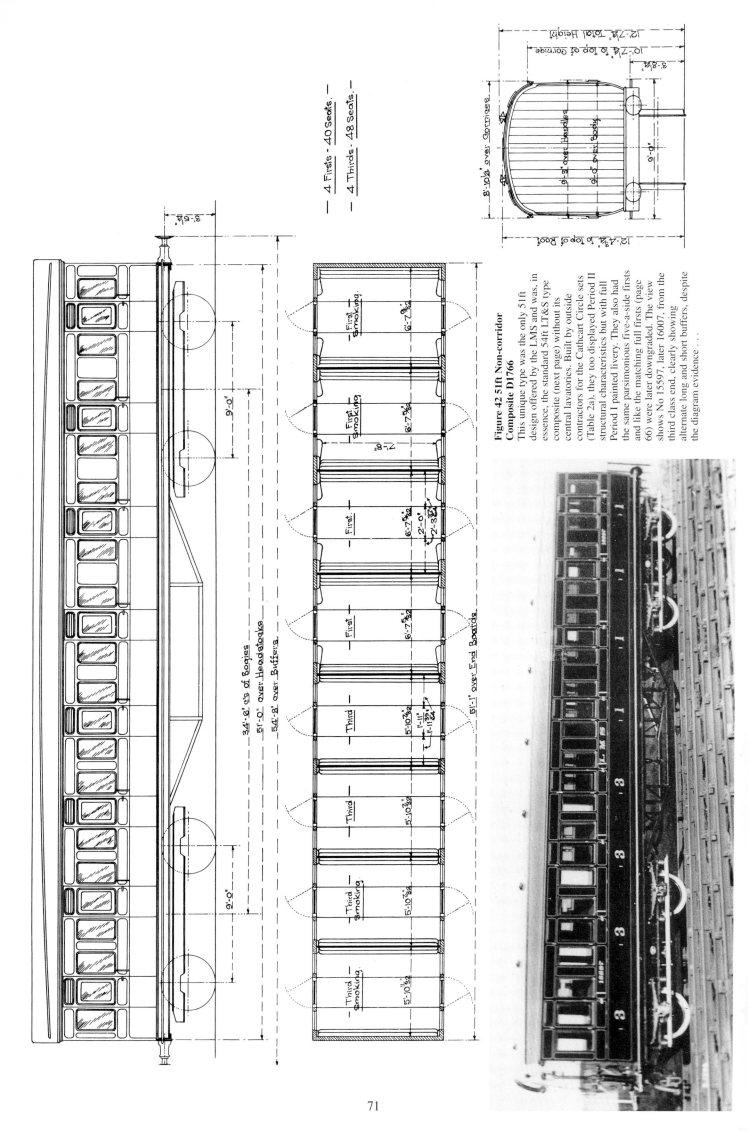

4 Firsts - 40 Seats.
4 Thirds - 48 Seats.

8'-5½"
9'-0"
9'-0"
34'-6" c's of Bogies
51'-0" over Headstocks
54'-8" over Buffers.

12'-7¾" Total Height
10'-7¼" to top of cornice
8'-8½"
9'-3" over Cornices
9'-0" over Body
9'-0" over Handles
8'-10½" over Cornices
9'-0"
12'-4¾" to top of Roof.

First Smoking. 6'-7⁷₃₂
First Smoking. 6'-7⁷₃₂
8'-2"
First. 6'-7⁵₃₂
First. 6'-7⁵₃₂
2'-0"
2'-3³₃₂
Third 5'-10⁷₃₂
Third 5'-10⁷₃₂
1'-11"
1'-39"
1'-11²⁴
Third Smoking. 5'-10⁷₃₂
Third Smoking. 5'-10½"
51'-1" over End Boards.

Figure 42 51ft Non-corridor Composite D1766

This unique type was the only 51ft design offered by the LMS and was, in essence, the standard 54ft LT&S type composite (next page) without its central lavatories. Built by outside contractors for the Cathcart Circle sets (Table 2a), they too displayed Period II structural characteristics but with full Period I painted livery. They also had the same parsimonious five-a-side firsts and like the matching full firsts (page 66) were later downgraded. The view shows No 15597, later 16007, from the third class end, clearly showing alternate long and short buffers, despite the diagram evidence . . . .

71

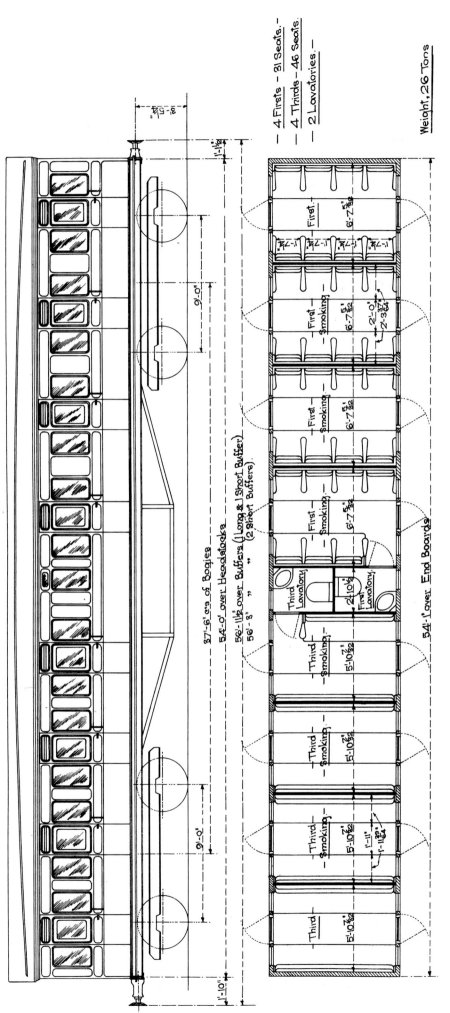

4 Firsts – 31 Seats.
4 Thirds – 46 Seats.
2 Lavatories.

Weight, 26 Tons.

Figure 43 Lavatory Non-corridor Composite D1765
This was the standard Period I LT&S lavatory composite, which set the layout for both the Period II and Period III versions. The reduction of lavatories compared with D1763 (page 69) allowed the provision of an extra first class compartment, which may have been important in context — see also the main narrative regarding the slight variations within the LT&S sets and 'Remarks' column of Table 2a concerning the buffer variations within this type.

72

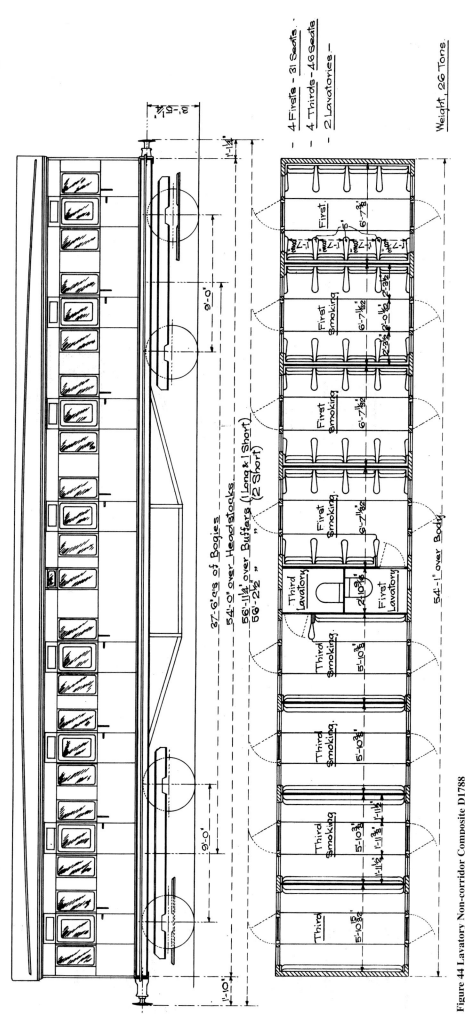

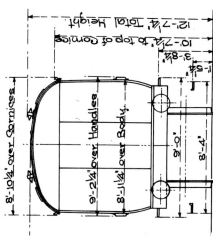

Figure 44 Lavatory Non-corridor Composite D1788

This Period II design for the LT&S also covered the small number of Period III examples of the type, the first of which is illustrated on page 62. One can only suppose (as with D1767, page 68) that the relatively small number of Period III examples, plus the fact that Period III 54ft carriages were built only for the LT&S sets and were identically dimensioned to their predecessors (save for the brake thirds — page 80), made a new diagram redundant.

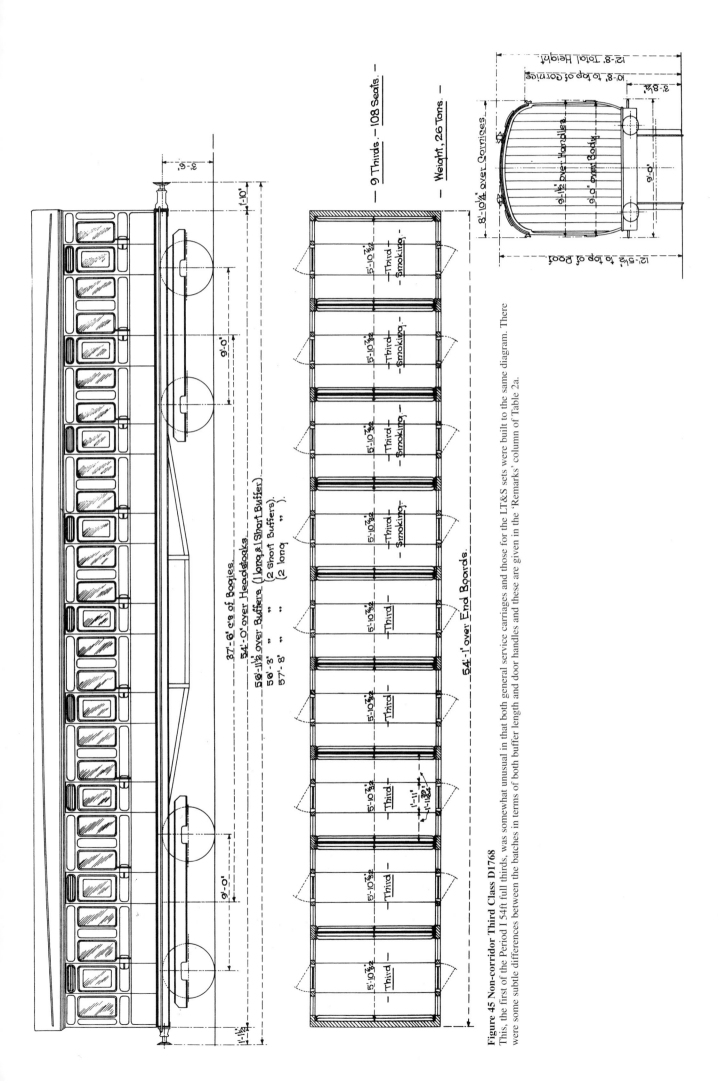

Figure 45 Non-corridor Third Class D1768

This, the first of the Period I 54ft full thirds, was somewhat unusual in that both general service carriages and those for the LT&S sets were built to the same diagram. There were some subtle differences between the batches in terms of both buffer length and door handles and these are given in the 'Remarks' column of Table 2a.

74

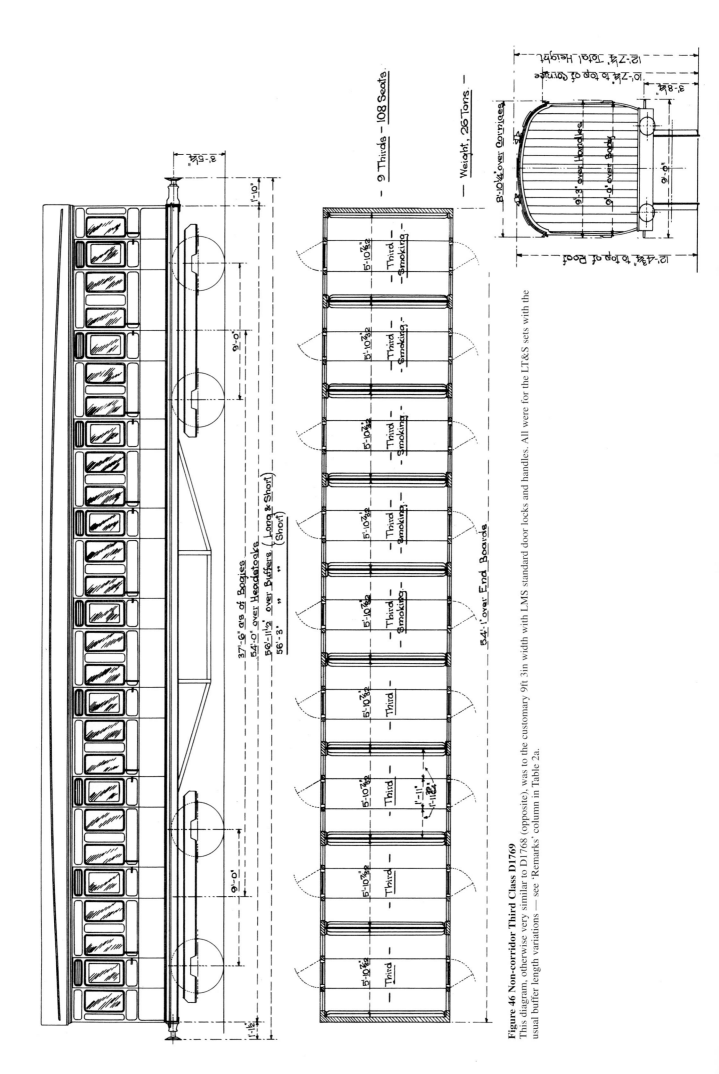

Figure 46 Non-corridor Third Class D1769

This diagram, otherwise very similar to D1768 (opposite), was to the customary 9ft 3in width with LMS standard door locks and handles. All were for the LT&S sets with the usual buffer length variations — see 'Remarks' column in Table 2a.

75

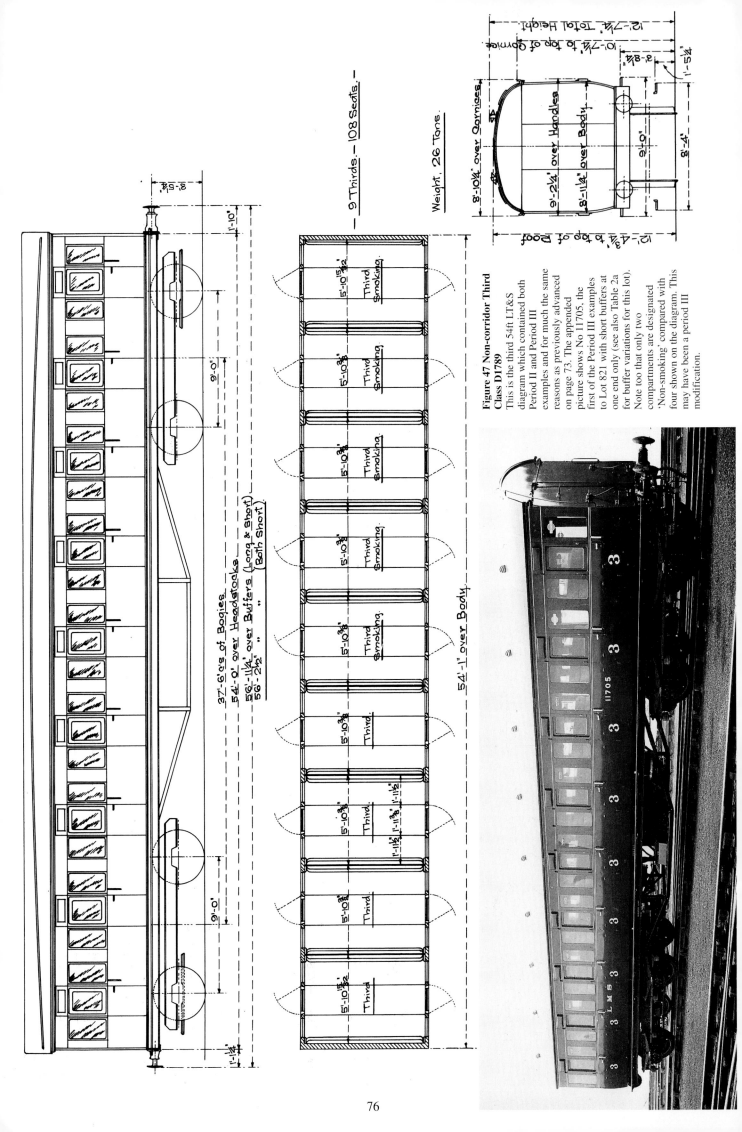

Figure 47 Non-corridor Third Class D1789

This is the third 54ft LT&S diagram which contained both Period II and Period III examples and for much the same reasons as previously advanced on page 73. The appended picture shows No 11705, the first of the Period III examples to Lot 821 with short buffers at one end only (see also Table 2a for buffer variations for this lot). Note too that only two compartments are designated 'Non-smoking' compared with four shown on the diagram. This may have been a period III modification.

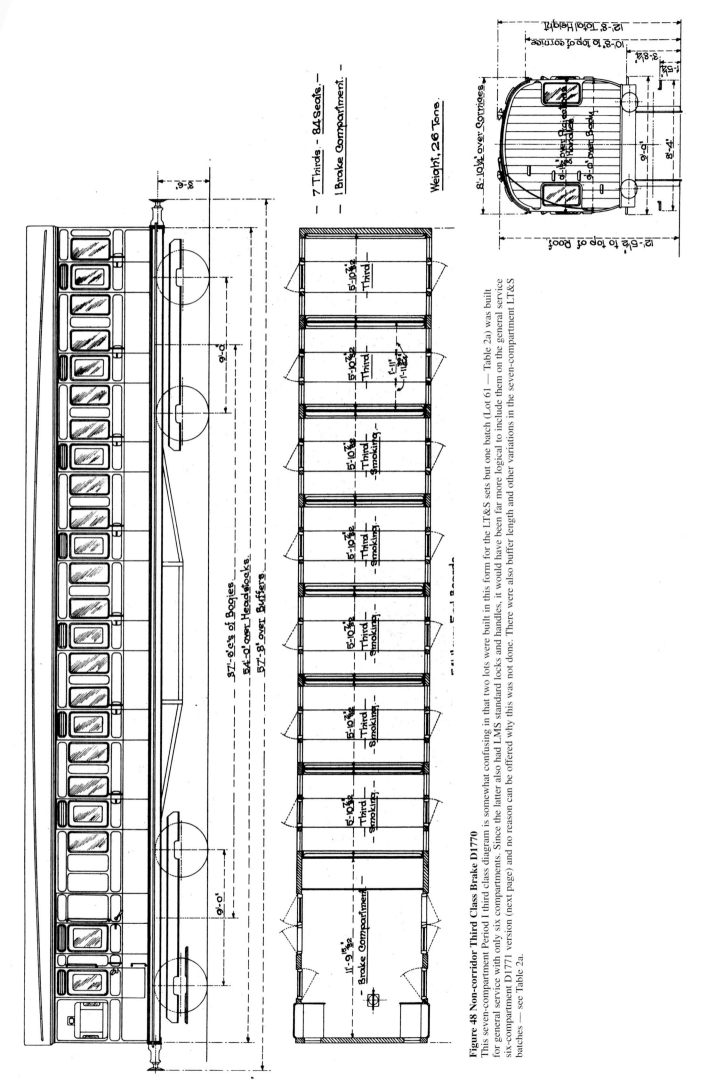

Figure 48 Non-corridor Third Class Brake D1770

This seven-compartment Period I third class diagram is somewhat confusing in that two lots were built in this form for the LT&S sets but one batch (Lot 61 — Table 2a) was built for general service with only six compartments. Since the latter also had LMS standard locks and handles, it would have been far more logical to include them on the general service six-compartment D1771 version (next page) and no reason can be offered why this was not done. There were also buffer length and other variations in the seven-compartment LT&S batches — see Table 2a.

77

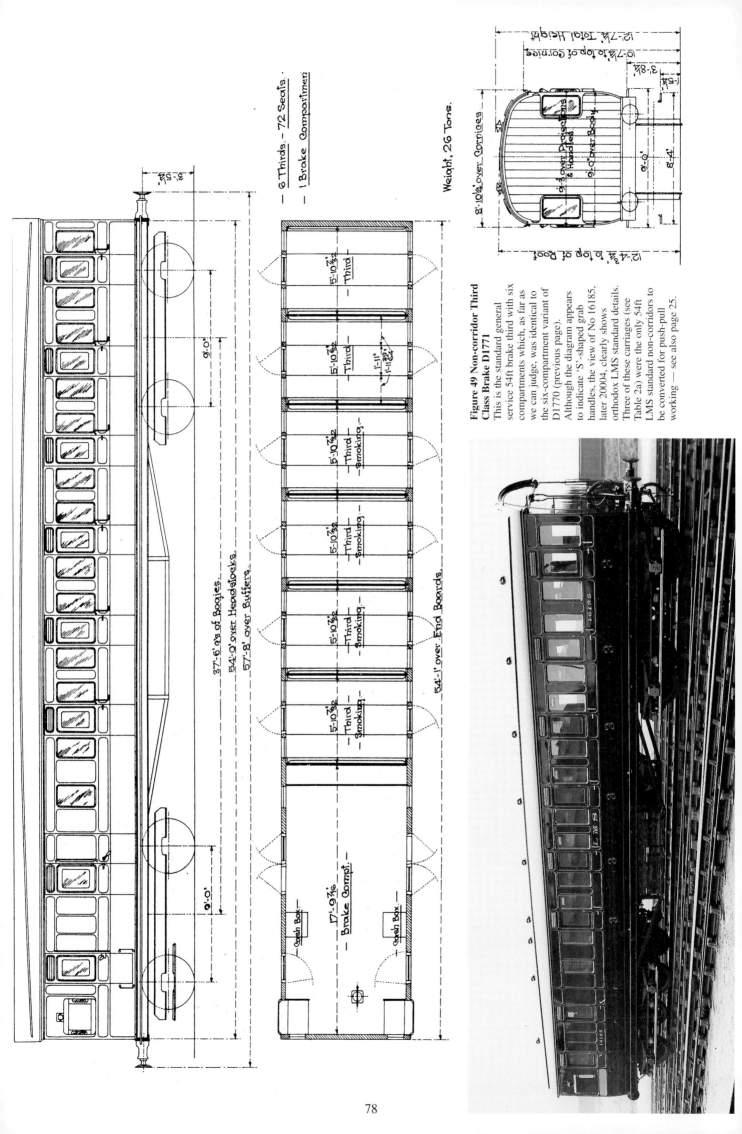

6 Thirds - 72 Seats.
1 Brake Compartment

Weight, 26 Tons.

3'-0½'

9'-0"

37'-6' C's of Bogies.
54'-0' over Headstocks.
57'-8' over Buffers.

9'-0"

5'-10¾₂' Third

5'-10¾₂' Third

5'-10¾₂' Third Smoking

5'-10¾₂' Third Smoking

5'-10¾₂' Third Smoking

5'-10¾₂' Third Smoking

1'-11" 23"
1'-11" 24"

17'-9⅞₆' Brake Compt.

Sash Box.
Sash Box.

54'-1' over End Boards.

12'-7¾' Total Height.
10'-7¾' to top of cornice.
3'-8¼'
6½'
9'-3' over Projections & Handrail
9'-0' over Body
9'-0'
8'-4'
8'-10¼' over Cornices
12'-4¾' to top of Roof.

Figure 49 Non-corridor Third Class Brake D1771
This is the standard general service 54ft brake third with six compartments which, as far as we can judge, was identical to the six-compartment variant of D1770 (previous page). Although the diagram appears to indicate 'S'-shaped grab handles, the view of No 16185, later 20004, clearly shows orthodox LMS standard details. Three of these carriages (see Table 2a) were the only 54ft LMS standard non-corridors to be converted for push-pull working — see also page 25.

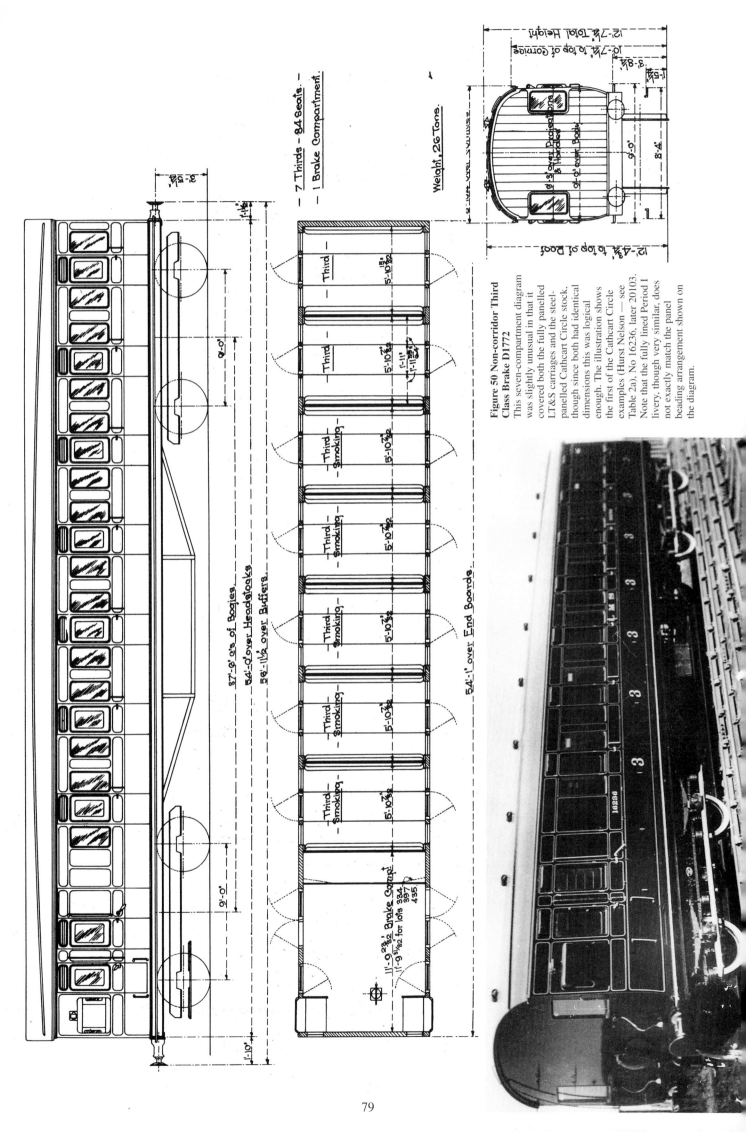

Figure 50 Non-corridor Third Class Brake D1772
This seven-compartment diagram was slightly unusual in that it covered both the fully panelled LT&S carriages and the steel-panelled Cathcart Circle stock, though since both had identical dimensions this was logical enough. The illustration shows the first of the Cathcart Circle examples (Hurst Nelson — see Table 2a), No 16236, later 20103. Note that the fully lined Period I livery, though very similar, does not exactly match the panel beading arrangement shown on the diagram.

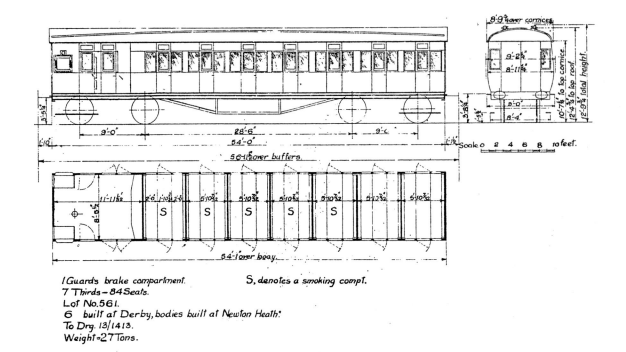

I Guard's brake compartment.
7 Thirds – 84 Seats.
Lot No.561.
6 built at Derby, bodies built at Newton Heath.
To Drg. 13/1413.
Weight=27 Tons.

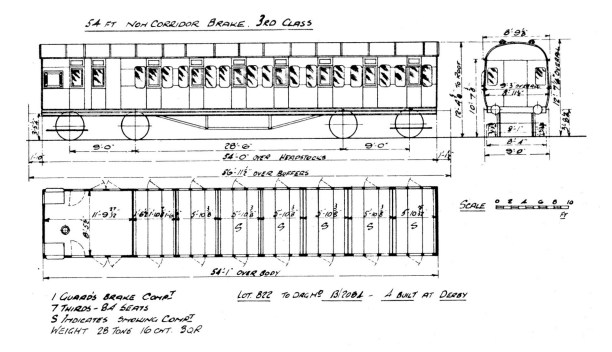

54 FT NON CORRIDOR BRAKE. 3RD CLASS

I GUARD'S BRAKE COMP.
7 THIRDS – 84 SEATS
S INDICATES SMOKING COMP.
WEIGHT 28 TONS 16 CWT. 3QR

LOT. 822 TO DRGN. 13/2081 – 4 BUILT AT DERBY

Figures 51/52 Non-corridor Third Class Brake D1841/1914
These sub-standard diagrams date from the early 1930s — see Table 2a — and show the final LT&S seven-compartment brakes. As far as can be judged, compared with the contemporary firsts, composites and thirds (see earlier pages) the only reason for issuing a separate Period III diagram (D1914) on this occasion (illustrated on page 60) was to cover the slight reduction in van length and other minor dimensional variations.

Chapter 3 - Articulated General Service Stock

Introduction; Historical Background; The Inter-District Sets; The 10-coach Vestibule Sets;
Conclusions; Summary of Coaches Built.

Unlike the LNER where articulation of passenger stock was commonplace, the LMS did not make great use of the articulated principle. However, this was not for want of trying and the vehicles of the type which were built during 1937 shed interesting light on to the operating and other problems which faced the LMS during the mid-1930s. Thanks to the existence of much contemporary correspondence which has been made available to the authors, a good deal of the background to the LMS articulated stock is known and can be recorded.

LMS articulated coaches fell into two categories: the general service coaches of 1937 and the special vehicles built for the second 'Coronation Scot' train of 1939/40. The story of this latter train is sufficiently complex to merit special treatment so this chapter merely concerns itself with the general service articulated stock.

HISTORICAL BACKGROUND

The first relevant references to articulation come in correspondence between various departments in 1935. On 9 April of that year a letter was sent from the commercial side to Stanier, relevant extracts from which are quoted:

'It appears . . . that if we are to advance in effecting material economies in coal consumption with our passenger trains . . . and keep the size of locomotives within reasonable limits . . . it is necessary that serious consideration should be given to reducing the weight per seat of our vehicles. I know that you have given considerable thought to this question and . . . that it has been under the consideration of the research department for some time. It is a matter of complex nature because it is essential that the amenities and comfort to the travelling public should not be reduced.

'I detail below the weight, seating and weight per seat of the vestibule, corridor and non-corridor stock it is proposed to build in 1936 . . .

Type	Weight	No of	Weight per seat		
	Tons	seats	T	Cwt	Qrs
Vestibules					
First	30	42		14	1
Third	31	60		10	1
Corridor					
First	30	33		18	1
Composite	33	42		15	3
Third	31	42		14	3
Non-Corridor					
Composite	27	96		5	3
Third	27	108		5	0

'The fact that a corridor third vehicle weighs 14cwt 3qrs per seat is . . . a very serious matter, and I may say that in a conversation the Vice-President had with me the other day he mentioned a figure of 5cwts per seat as being the ideal to be aimed at.

'So far as the 1936 building programme is concerned . . . there is insufficient time to make any radical change in the design . . . and I shall feel much obliged if you will kindly see what steps can be taken in the 1937 Carriage Building Programme on the lines set out in this letter. . .'

This enquiry partially coincided with Stanier's own views and, in fact, he had already asked Vice-President Sir Harold Hartley the previous week for permission to conduct experiments in articulation using pre-Grouping stock:

'The question of providing articulated train sets has arisen from time to time, and the more recently in connection with vestibule excursion sets and sleeping cars, and in order that some experience may be obtained with this type of stock it is recommended that a three-coach set be prepared for experimental purposes by converting three existing vehicles, and providing the same with two articulated bogies and two heavy bogies for the leading and trailing ends.'

This letter was forwarded to the commercial department and the two separated lines of thought were fused in a letter to Vice-President E. J. H. Lemon which, *inter alia*, contained the following paragraph:

'Articulation may be the means of reducing the weight per seat and on this account I think it would probably be sound to carry out the experiment suggested by Mr Stanier to Sir Harold Hartley in his letter of April second.'

The upshot of all this was that the experimental work was given the go-ahead by Sir Harold Hartley while Vice-President Lemon expressed his own views to the commercial side as follows:

'I am obliged to you for your letter of the 9th and note your views regarding the articulation of sleeping cars and excursion sets. I do not think we need trouble too much regarding the former, as in view of the number of sleeping cars compared with our total carriage stock the benefits from articulation would not be material.

'As regards the excursion sets, I can see the difficulty which would arise from a loading and unloading point of view*. I think, however, a more profitable line of attack would be our three-coach sets and combinations of such for suburban and local train working. We have a considerable number of three-coach sets and articulation might mean a reduction of 10 tons per set, which is appreciable.'

*The original design scheme for the vestibule 10-coach set was for 'loose' brake ends and twin open third articulated pairs. The latter would have but one centre door on each side compared with two per side on the standard stock. This was thought to be a disadvantage on a frequently stopping excursion-type train.

The experimental three-coach set involved using normal pre-Grouping stock and in view of the trial nature of the project, the design showed only a 1-ton saving over the separated vehicles and not the envisaged 10-ton saving. This caused a little heart-searching until Stanier pointed out that the experiment was to try out the articulation principle and that new vehicles of the type would show the desired savings in coach weight. The approval for the conversion was given on 23 May 1935, and, on the same day, diagrams were also requested of the CME for the following production types of articulated stock:

a. Inter-District three-coach set comprising

	Seating		
	First	Third	
Non-corridor Third Brake		72	(6 compartments)
Non-corridor Composite	24	72	(3+6 compartments)
Non-corridor Third Brake		72	(6 compartments)
Total	24	216	

b. 10-coach articulated vestibule train made up as follows:

Vestibule Third Brake ⎫
Vestibule Third ⎬ three-coach set, articulated
Vestibule Third ⎭
Vestibule Third ⎫ two-coach set, articulated
Vestibule Third ⎭
Vestibule Third ⎫ two-coach set, articulated
Vestibule Third ⎭
Vestibule Third ⎫
Vestibule Third ⎬ three-coach set, articulated
Vestibule Third Brake ⎭

Meanwhile, the experimental set chosen for conversion was the MR four-coach St Pancras and Bedford set No 37, built in 1910. The new articulated bogies were provided on three coaches while the fourth vehicle was unaltered. The set went into Derby Works in June 1935 and the formation was thus:

Brake Third	No 23198 ⎫
Third	No 14234 ⎬ articulated
First	No 10529 ⎭
Brake Third	No 23217 left unaltered

There was some delay in providing the diagrams for the new sets and in November 1935 a reminder was sent by the commercial staff to the CME who replied that 'we are not now working on the lines of the memorandum of the meeting held on 23 May'. Diagrams were submitted by Stanier but he pointed out that precise weights could not be determined until the 'proposed experimental vestibule coach has been designed and built'.

It would appear that the commercial side was not aware of the proposal to build an experimental coach and it went to some pains to inform the CME that too much delay was undesirable:

'It is very desirable that the question of building 10-coach articulated vestibule trains should be sufficiently advanced to enable a definite conclusion to be arrived at when consideration is given to the 1937 Carriage Renewal Programme early next year.'

Stanier was, however, in a position to reassure the commercial department that the design work would be finished in time. The experimental 'one-off' vestibule coach cannot be traced in the diagram book, but there was an experimental corridor brake third built to D1971 (Coach No 5844) which employed the centrally trussed frame used on the articulated stock and tared some 3-4 tons less than a conventional coach. Although not in service until December 1937, this may have been the vehicle referred to in the correspondence since it carried a lower lot number than the articulated stock.

The centrally trussed experimental brake third to D1971, No 5844, which was almost certainly the experimental vehicle built to evaluate the underframe for the articulated stock.

Non-corridor articulated triple BT+C+BT Nos 60003/4/5 (D1995). Note the conventional trussing of these coaches compared with the vestibule stock and also the oval buffers.

There were certain minor aspects of the layout of the proposed three-coach unit for Inter-District services which were not liked by HQ at first. These were mainly in the nature of compartment sizes and whether or not to have identically sized brake compartments at each end. However, it is clear that by the end of 1935, the decision had been made to build articulated stock during 1937 and the proposed layouts were therefore submitted to the Operating Divisions for their comments on the proposed layout of the sets and their general suitability. The 10-coach excursion set diagrams were sent in December 1935 and the three-coach Inter-District set were submitted to the Divisions in January 1936. From this point it is simpler to consider the two designs separately.

THE INTER-DISTRICT SETS

The original proposal for the divisions to scrutinise was not quite the same as the original study requested on 23 May 1935. The final proposal was for a reduction of the composite from nine to eight compartments thus enabling the commercial department's wish for larger third class compartments to be provided in the composite coach. Thus the envisaged three-coach unit was to be in the form BT+C+BT seating 72 thirds, 24 firsts plus 60 thirds, and 72 thirds respectively. There was an alternative suggestion for a version with five thirds in one brake end and seven thirds at the opposite end. The replies from the Divisional Managers were somewhat revealing and the relevant extracts are worth quoting:

Midland Division	'As you know, most of the local services of this Division are scheduled to consist of two-coach sets, supplemented by extras where required. The occupation of coaches has been analysed, and it is found that the introduction of the proposed three-coach unit would definitely involve more coaches . . . I suggest that for this Division a suitable two-coach unit could be provided, ie composite seating 24 first, 60 thirds and a third brake seating 72 thirds and giving a brake compartment 16ft 9in long.'
Western Division	'So far as the Western Division is concerned I consider that a three-car Inter-District articulated set is what is required and not a two-car set, which I understand is suggested would be the right formation for the Midland Division.'
Central Division	'I cannot recommend the building of any three-coach articulated sets for use on this Division for the reason that none of the three-coach sets which are in general traffic on the Division remain at that formation but are made up to as many as nine or ten vehicles during some part of their workings.

'I should, however, be prepared to accept 15 four-coach articulated sets for use on the Manchester and Oldham Branch, these sets could be formed as follows:

Third Brake ⎫
Third   ⎬ To seat 24 firsts and 312 third class passengers
Composite ⎪
Third Brake ⎭

. . . two-coach units of the type suggested by the Midland Division would offer too much first class accommodation for general use on this Division.'

Northern Division	'It is suggested that the brake compartment at each end be reduced in size sufficient to admit an additional third class compartment in each coach and that the centre coach instead of having three first and five third class compartments should have four firsts and four third class compartments.

The effect of these proposals would increase the seating capacity of the train to 32 first class and 216 third class seats, and there would be ample brake van accommodation for luggage, etc.'

In the event, the design was still further modified and was built with only seven compartments in the centre coach (4F+3T), although the Scottish suggestion of seven compartments in the brake ends was adopted. As far as is known, the coaches were mostly employed in Scotland. Photographs show some sets in use on Euston-Northampton services, although these workings are not thought to have lasted long. More information would be welcomed by the authors on workings by the three-coach non-corridor articulated sets.

The wide measure of divisional disagreement, and in some cases, scarcely veiled antipathy towards these articulated sets must almost certainly have been a major factor behind the building of only one batch to D1995, details of which are appended at the end of the chapter.

Articulated twin TO+CO Nos 55000/12 (D1967) as built. Note the somewhat deeper than usual eaves panel for a Period III design.

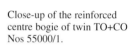

Close-up of the reinforced centre bogie of twin TO+CO Nos 55000/1.

A constructional view of the centrally trussed underframe of one of the vestibule sets, viewed from the articulated end.

THE 10-COACH VESTIBULE SETS

The original proposal submitted for divisional comment envisaged an all-third train formed BTO+TO+TO/ /TO+TO/ /TO+TO/ /TO+TO+BTO. All would be 57ft coaches except for the centre vehicles of the triplets which were designed as 48ft 3in sections. The lengths were determined partially by the length of point locking bars (45ft) which affected the bogie centre dimensions and secondly by the overhang which might cause running restrictions. In general they were designed to run on lines cleared for the 60ft stock. Unlike the case of the non-corridor sets, the comments from the Divisions were more in unison:

Midland Division	The Midland Division stated that the train was too big. The division in the proposed trains for including kitchen cars was regarded as 'useless from a Dining Car Department point of view, as they will not serve meals more than two vehicles away from the Kitchen'. The Division also felt that there should be first class accommodation and that each coach should have a sliding door to enable separate parties of up to about 30 to be accommodated in one vehicle. Finally, the Midland Division felt that the proposed lavatories at one end only of the vehicle were not suitable where two parties were accommodated in the same vehicle.
Western Division	This division also recommended eight-car trains with an extra composite or first class coach to provide first class seating. It was also felt that the lavatories should be rearranged.
Central Division	The Central Division did not feel that the train was the wrong length but like the Midland and Western Divisions recommended repositioned lavatories and suggested 18 first class seats in one of the 10 coaches. Like the Midland Division, the absence of internal partitions was not favoured.
Northern Division	'So far as the Northern Division is concerned, I think the unit will be suitable and if one train is included in the building programme for Scotland it will be kept continuously employed, at any rate during the summer months'. The Division felt that it would be unnecessary to provide first class seating in the train.

As a result of these suggestions, the proposed scheme was altered to a 10-coach configuration of articulated pairs to the following scheme: BTO+TO/ /TO+TO/ /TO+CO/ /TO+TO/ /TO+BTO. The dropping of the short centre vehicle of the triplet scheme enabled all coaches to be the same 54ft length (actually 54ft 3in) and thus enabled the design staff to incorporate the suggested modifications to toilet layout. Interior partitions and first class seating were also provided and in this form the coaches were built to D1965/D1966/D1967. Bogie centres were 46ft 6¾ in.

This might have been the end of the matter but in March 1937 a fresh list of running restrictions was stipulated over and above those applicable to the 60ft stock, which restrictions had hitherto been the only ones envisaged. This caused mild panic at Euston House when Stanier informed the commercial staff of the Chief Engineer's decision. The comments from the Commercial Manager were curt and to the point:

'. . . I would point out, however, that the restrictions at and near Preston and at Blackpool and Morecambe will practically mean that the sets, although built for the heavy excursion traffic at those points, will not be capable of running thereto, and the restriction at Chester will also considerably hamper us in the manipulation of the heavy excursion traffic at the peak periods.

'The list of restrictions generally is a formidable one for vehicles engaged in excursion traffic and is one which we certainly did not anticipate when the diagrams were signed . . .

'I shall be glad if you will kindly again approach the Engineer and see whether . . . it is possible to give us more latitude in the working of the sets.'

This plea seems to have had some effect and the Chief Engineer relented a little although not at Chester. He did, however, point out that the tendency to enlarge coaching stock and thus diminish clearances did make more urgent the necessity for improving the matter of clearances on the line as a whole.

When the Divisions were finally advised of the restrictions, some amusing side effects followed. At Shilton, between Nuneaton and Rugby, it was stated that the signalman would not be aware which trains were conveying the new stock and it was therefore suggested that the articulated coaches be totally banned from the Rugby-Nuneaton line. This was not thought desirable and the upshot was that a decrepit and unused milk loading stage at Shilton, which was the feature fouling the loading gauge of the articulated sets, was removed. This enabled other restrictions on out-of-gauge loads on the up slow line between Nuneaton No 1 and Rugby No 7 boxes to be removed as well.

The restrictions on working into Blackpool and Morecambe were waived because the vehicles were fitted with windows of a type which 'prevented the passenger from putting his head through' and as the stations were termini, the speed of the coaches would be slow.

The Chester restriction was more serious and the Western Division Superintendent of Operations commented:

'So far as the restriction on the new articulated sets is concerned, I am afraid this will entirely preclude the use of these sets in working to or from North Wales, the Wirral or Birkenhead. Although there are two other up roads and down roads, and an up and down platform line over which such trains could be worked, it would be exceedingly difficult to identify the trains which were conveying these articulated sets in order to ensure that they were run through Chester station over one of the other roads and not over the restricted roads.

'You will appreciate the restricted roads are the two roads through the "yard" over which we normally work a large number of excursion trains on which the articulated stock would be expected to run.'

As if to pile Ossa upon Pelion, the other three companies also put forward a fearsome list of restrictions for the LMS articulated sets. The LNER excluded them from all its lines in Scotland, England north of Northallerton, large parts of the West Riding and many areas of East Anglia. The Southern would not have them at all (!) and many GWR branches were excluded. Not surprisingly, the original batches were not repeated and all the 11 sets were allocated to the Central Division, virtually confined to LMS lines.

CONCLUSIONS

The LMS articulated experiment cannot really be considered a success. It was not that the coaches were no good in themselves but the widely differing requirements of the Divisions, coupled with the widespread running restrictions — which applied equally to both vestibule and non-corridor sets although probably affecting the vestibule sets more often — militated against the general service aspect of their design. They were lighter than comparable general service vehicles and gave identical standards of accommodation but the LMS in general never really took to them.

Nevertheless, the special circumstances of the 'Coronation Scot' train caused the LMS to look again at articulation as a means to save weight, this time on high-speed services over its principal main line. These 1939/40 trains had as complex a history as their general service precursors and are considered in the next chapter.

Plans were in hand for the construction of further general service articulated stock from 1940 onwards which, presumably, would have been based on the constructional principles of the 'Coronation Scot' sets. These were to have included three, four, five and six-car sets of non-corridor type made up from twin and triplet units. These plans were shelved because of the war and were never revived afterwards.

TABLE 3: SUMMARY OF ARTICULATED GENERAL SERVICE COACHES BUILT DURING 1937

Note: All coaches were built at Derby, all were Period III style with simple livery.

Type	*Diag*	*Lot*	*No of Sets*	*Wt*	*Dimensions* (L x W x H)	*Running Numbers*	*Withdrawals First*	*Last*	*Remarks*
Triple BT+C+BT	1995	1038	11	76T	162ft 4½in x 9ft 3in x 12ft 4⅝ in	60000-60032	5/63	10/64	The non-corridor sets. The brake ends were 56ft 4¼ in long and the centre vehicle was 47ft 6in long. The numbers of the individual coaches ran consecutively in threes thus 60000+60001+60002 and the composites always had the middle number of the three. Bogie centres were 48ft 7½ in, underframes were conventionally trussed.
Twin BTO+TO	1965	1000	22	49T	109ft 7½in x 9ft 3in x 12ft 2 9/16 in	52500-52543	1/64	4/65	Both elements were 54ft 3in long and the even numbers of each pair were the open third end, odd numbers the brake end.
Twin TO+TO	1966	1001	22	49T	109ft 7½in x 9ft 3in x 12ft 2 9/16 in	50000-50043	11/63	2/65	Only one end had a non-smoking compartment and this was the even numbered end of the pair.
Twin TO+CO	1967	1002	11	49T	109ft 7½in x 9ft 3in x 12ft 2 9/16 in	55000-55021	11/63	3/65	The first class section had two and one seating and there was, initially, no non-smoking area in the set. The even numbers of the pairs were the third class ends. The third class saloon next to the first class section had one seat less adjacent to the partition because of the offset gangway to the first class area.

Footnotes:

1. Initially, the vestibule sets were formed into 11 ten-coach excursion sets classified as Central Division Extra Trains and branded on the ends 'CEN DIV ET'. They were numbered 250-60 but only set 256 has been confirmed in full formation. Some were incorrectly plated.
2. There were no real innovations in the coaches themselves except for the centrally trussed underframes of the vestibule sets which effected a slight reduction in height. Bodies and interiors of both varieties of coach were conventionally arranged and the first class bays in the vestibule sets differed from the thirds solely in having two and one seating. Leg room and bay length were identical to the thirds.

Following on the next two pages are drawings of the LMS articulated stock. In the case of the non-corridor sets, this is in the form of the usual diagram, but we have been unable to locate copies of the official diagrams for the vestibule sets in any form which will allow satisfactory reproduction. We are therefore including a dimensioned line drawing of these types prepared by one of the authors which, although it has been reproduced elsewhere, does at least allow the essential details to be offered. The caption detail for this drawing (Figure 54 — which fills page 88) is given opposite with that for Figure 53. Additionally, the view appended below will give some idea of the very different nature of the underframes of the articulated vestibule stock.

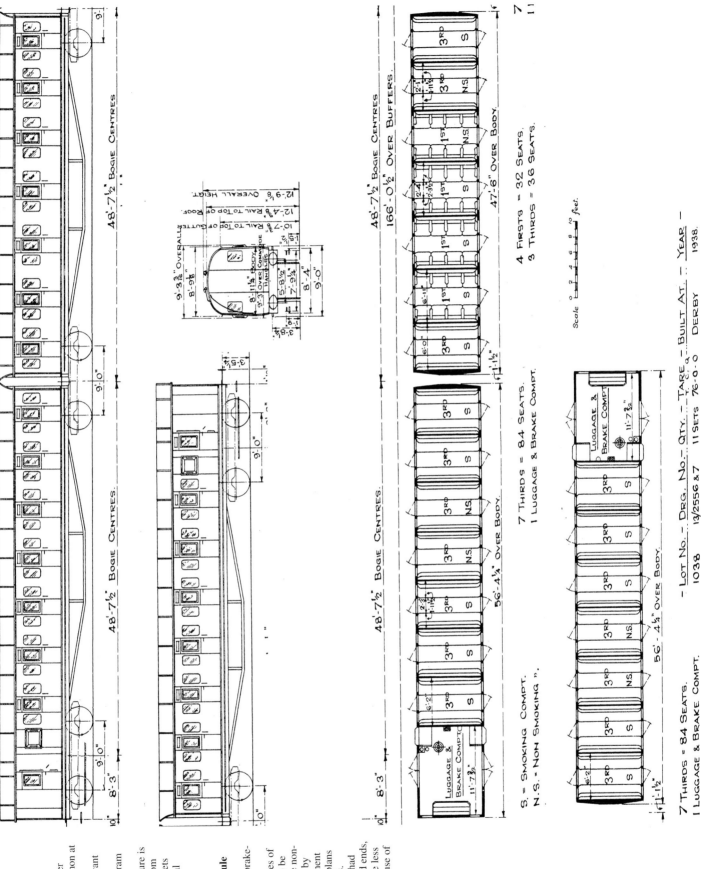

Figure 53 Non-corridor Articulated Set D1995

This diagram (drawn to a rather better standard than was common at the time — see Authors' Introduction) offers most relevant details of this unique design. Because of its length, the diagram has had to be 'split' into two sections. The only known picture is that reproduced on page 83 from which it can be seen that the sets displayed entirely conventional Period III design features.

Figure 54 Articulated Vestibule Stock D1965/1966/1967

This drawing, essentially the brake-ended version to D1965, was prepared to allow all three types of articulated vestibule 'twins' to be appreciated. Elevations for the non-brake versions can be derived by 'reversing' the right-hand element of the version drawn and the plans indicate the internal variations. Although not shown, the sets had standard Period III gangwayed ends, the overall height being a little less than normal bogie stock because of the new form of chassis construction.

Drawing: D. Jenkinson

87

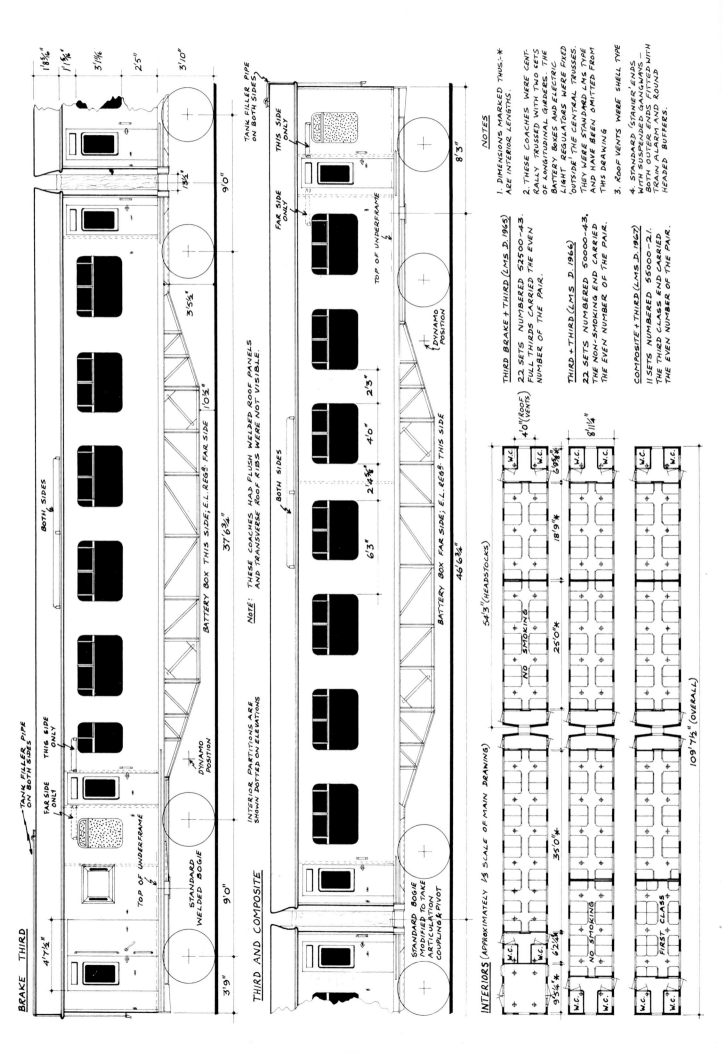

BRAKE THIRD

TANK FILLER PIPE ON BOTH SIDES

FAR SIDE ONLY   THIS SIDE ONLY

DYNAMO POSITION

TOP OF UNDERFRAME

STANDARD WELDED BOGIE

3'9"   9'0"

1 8⅝" 1 5¼" 3 1¹¹⁄₁₆" 2 5" 3'10"

9'0"   3 5½"   1 0½"

BATTERY BOX THIS SIDE; E.L. REGS. FAR SIDE

37'6¾"

4'7½"

BOTH SIDES

NOTE: THESE COACHES HAD FLUSH WELDED ROOF PANELS AND TRANSVERSE ROOF RIBS WERE NOT VISIBLE.

INTERIOR PARTITIONS ARE SHOWN DOTTED ON ELEVATIONS

THIRD AND COMPOSITE

TANK FILLER PIPE ON BOTH SIDES

THIS SIDE ONLY

FAR SIDE ONLY

FAR SIDE ONLY   THIS SIDE ONLY

BOTH SIDES

TOP OF UNDERFRAME

DYNAMO POSITION

STANDARD BOGIE MODIFIED TO TAKE ARTICULATION COUPLING & PIVOT

8'3"

2'3" 4'0" 2'4⅝" 6'3"

BATTERY BOX FAR SIDE; E.L. REGS. THIS SIDE

46'6¾"

9'0"

NOTES

1. DIMENSIONS MARKED THUS :-* ARE INTERIOR LENGTHS.

2. THESE COACHES WERE CENTRALLY TRUSSED WITH TWO SETS OF LONGITUDINAL GIRDERS. THE BATTERY BOXES AND ELECTRIC LIGHT REGULATORS WERE FIXED 'OUTSIDE' THE CENTRAL TRUSSES. THEY WERE STANDARD LMS TYPE AND HAVE BEEN OMITTED FROM THIS DRAWING.

3. ROOF VENTS WERE SHELL TYPE

4. STANDARD (STANIER) ENDS WITH SUSPENDED GANGWAYS – BOTH OUTER ENDS FITTED WITH TRAIN ALARM AND ROUND HEADED BUFFERS.

THIRD BRAKE + THIRD (LMS D.1965)

22 SETS NUMBERED 52500-43. FULL THIRDS CARRIED THE EVEN NUMBER OF THE PAIR.

THIRD + THIRD (LMS D.1966)

22 SETS NUMBERED 50000-43. THE NON-SMOKING END CARRIED THE EVEN NUMBER OF THE PAIR.

COMPOSITE + THIRD (LMS D.1967)

11 SETS NUMBERED 55000-21. THE THIRD CLASS END CARRIED THE EVEN NUMBER OF THE PAIR.

INTERIORS (APPROXIMATELY ⅓ SCALE OF MAIN DRAWING)

4 0" (ROOF VENTS)

6 9⅞"

18'9¾"

8 11¼"

W.C.   W.C.

NO SMOKING

25'0"*

54'3" (HEADSTOCKS)

35'0"*

W.C.   W.C.

6 2¼"

9 3¼"*

W.C.   W.C.
NO SMOKING

W.C.   W.C.

FIRST CLASS

W.C.   W.C.

109'7½" (OVERALL)

88

Chapter 4. The 'Coronation Scot' Sets

*Introduction; The 1937 Sets; The 1939-40 Sets; The Postwar Story;
The 1939-40 Stock Described; Conclusions.*

The inter-company rivalry in the matter of speed in the 1930s is too well known to need any amplification here and, of course, it led principally to the ultra-high-speed services and trains on the East Coast route which, with its matching Class A4 4-6-2 locomotives, tended to steal much of the limelight.

It was not to be expected that the LMS would remain entirely unmoved in the face of all this activity from King's Cross and after the announcement by the LMS of its forthcoming 1937 high-speed service, the train and its engine were awaited with more than the usual interest. It duly appeared in the famous blue and silver livery and achieved immediate fame by the hair-raising speed trial down Madeley bank when the LMS temporarily wrested the steam locomotive speed record from the LNER at the cost of a new set of crockery for the dining cars and more than a few red faces in high places! The only commendable thing about this escapade seems to have been the leading bogie on the locomotive which literally saved the day for the LMS. When the 'Coronation Scot' service as such was seen to be on a 6½-hour Euston-Glasgow timing it appeared to some as though the LMS had conceded defeat to its rivals. Add to this the fact that the coaches themselves were mostly reconditioned existing vehicles, albeit of the latest style, and it is not surprising that the story gained currency that the LMS had provided an answer to the LNER very much on the cheap.

This may, in some respects, have been true. Not everyone on the LMS was anxious to promote this gimmicky approach to travel and any form of ultra-special service such as the 'Coronation Scot' must inevitably demand a greater proportion of the company's time and energy than a more normal service would do. Although the authors have not been able to trace the 'Coronation Scot' train right back to its source, the evidence which has been scrutinised does suggest that permission to build trains may have been granted only if this could be achieved at low cost. Even the streamlining of the locomotives seems to have been a rather half-hearted last-minute affair and although much has been made of the 'true aerodynamic form' of the streamline casing and the wind tunnel testing of the shape, this may well have been no more than an accidental by-product of cloaking Stanier's masterpiece to satisfy the publicity department. Apart from the sloping smoke-box top, there was precious little difference between the de-streamlined and non-streamlined 'Coronation' class 4-6-2s as was readily apparent from 1945 onwards.

Something better than the 1937 trains would have emerged in 1940 had not the world been at war. Thus the 'Coronation Scot' ceased to run and, like its LNER contemporaries, was never to be seen as such again. However, this book is about LMS coaches and although the train itself may have had an unhappy history, the coaches built for it were some of the finest vehicles ever made for the LMS and thus deserve special consideration.

THE 1937 SETS

The 1937-39 'Coronation Scot' service was operated by nine-coach sets of the latest Stanier-pattern coaches which had been specially converted for the task. Three complete sets were provided (two working and one spare) and the train ran to the following formation:

BFK / FK / RFO / RK / RTO / RTO / RK / RTO / BTK

Although all the third class open coaches were 42-seaters, thus qualifying for the RTO classification, they were used for all-the-way travelling. They were, moreover, the only 42-seater open third class coaches of Period III styling.

Most of the coaches selected for the sets were taken from the latest batches of new stock and were completely refitted inside and, except for the kitchen cars, were equipped with a pressure heating and ventilation system. There were no spare corridor firsts or first brakes available so these coaches were built new for the service. The total cost of providing the coaches was quoted as £27,000 which must be considered very low in relation to the average cost of £2,000-£2,500 per coach had new vehicles been built. If one allows roughly half of this figure of £27,000 for the six new vehicles, the conversion of the remaining 21 averaged out at some £700 per coach.

This aspect of the 1937 coaches has tended to foster the impression that, apart from the blue and silver livery, the coaches were little different from ordinary LMS vehicles. As far as appearance and body styling was concerned this was so but by no stretch of the imagination could the interiors be so glibly dismissed. The perpetuation in the kitchen cars of gas cooking and gas lighting was also logical since the LMS had had unhappy experience of electric cooking in its experimental 1933 kitchen cars and doubtless the involvement with those vehicles caused the company to prefer its traditional and well-proved system. As the largest provider of dining car facilities in the country it presumably had sufficient experience to draw upon.

Within the train, the first class compartments seated but two-a-side and were most tastefully and comfortably finished, while the open saloons were equally spacious. The coaches were trimmed with matched wood veneers and facing of selected Empire timber, this being true to LMS tradition, while upholstery was in soft and restful shades of blue, brown and green. Lighting in the vestibule cars was by tubular strip supplemented by table lamps and in the compartments, bell pushes were provided for calling the attendant. In some respects, although less modern and radical than their LNER counterparts, they probably did not date so quickly as did the East Coast coaches.

The fact is that in the middle 1930s, the average LMS long-distance stock was so far ahead of that of most of the country that there probably seemed no real need to build special vehicles for the 'Coronation Scot' service. After all, the LMS had long abandoned outside compartment doors on its corridor coaches, which idea was still being perpetuated elsewhere, and moreover had been giving armrests to the third class passenger for years.

Admirers of the LNER trains will, doubtless, feel that the above remarks are tainted with prejudice but it does seem to the authors that contemporary writers, in giving rightful praise to Gresley's magnificent coaches, gave less than their due share of credit to the 1937 'Coronation Scot' trains. The LNER sets were superb trains and certainly unsurpassed for comfort but it cannot be denied that the normal wood-panelled LNER stock was not really suitable for conversion to the streamline image whereas LMS flush-sided stock could more readily be thus treated. Furthermore, it is a matter of personal taste whether the stainless steel and chromium trimmings of the LNER trains were preferable to the wood veneers of the LMS coaches. Even so, the fact that all the first class passengers in the LNER trains had individual single seats probably gave them the edge in passenger appeal. Moreover, they were a complete breakaway from anything the LNER had hitherto built whereas the LMS sets were merely luxury developments of an already well-established trend and therefore probably seemed less progressive.

The coaches themselves are listed in Volume 2 where we deal with the individual coach types but the formation of the sets themselves is tabulated at the end of this chapter. The coaches were laid up for the duration of the war, two sets at Horwich and one at Lostock Hall. They re-entered general service in 1947 but not as set trains.

THE 1939-40 SETS

Some sources have claimed that dissatisfaction with the 1937 coaches was the main reason behind the building of the ill-fated 1939-40 'Coronation Scot' stock but perusal of contemporary records does not bear this out. The authors have found no recorded evidence that they were built because the 1937 stock was considered inferior or inadequate, although this may have been a contributory factor.

In October 1937, the LMS decided to exhibit a complete 'Coronation Scot' train and locomotive in 1939 at the proposed New York World Fair. In early November 1937, the Chief Operating Manager stated that in this case a new corridor first and brake first would be needed if a new set of coaches was contemplated 'as there are no suitable vehicles of these types which can be withdrawn from our existing stock without detriment to our ordinary business'. The implication behind this statement can only be that the original intention was to exhibit a 1937-type train.

At the end of November, the LMS Executive Committee resolved to build a complete new 'Coronation Scot'-type train with a sleeping car to replace one of the kitchens. The cost of the train was to be charged to the 'Coronation Scot' suspense account and brought into the renewal programme for the year it was due to enter service in Great Britain, namely 1940. Stanier was invited to proceed with the design on the lines agreed and no mention was ever made of the necessity to build a better train to compete with those of the LNER.

By the beginning of December, the first proposed designs for the new train had been sketched out. It was to be a 10-coach set made up of three articulated triplets and a single coach arranged as follows:

BFK+FO+FO/ /RFO (with cocktail lounge and bar)+RK+RTO (with buffet)/ /TO+TO+TO/ /BTK

The articulated triplets would have two 65ft sections and a 51ft 6in centre portion, while the loose brake was to be the normal 57ft length. Several objections were raised to some of the design features and these can be summarised as follows:

a.   The first FO should be an FK, first class passengers not liking to travel in open coaches!
b.   The second FO should be a semi-RFO thus balancing the number of first class compartments and dining seats.
c.   The buffet should be in the leading TO, not the RTO, and this would give more third class dining seats.

The second proposal followed shortly afterwards and the layout was as follows:

BFK+FK+Semi-FK and cocktail lounge/ /RFO+RK+RTO/ /Semi-RTO+TK+TK/ / BTK

This all-corridor formation (except for the dining areas) was to remain a feature of all future schemes considered and differed basically from the 1937 trains in having separate third class dining seats. Thus, more seat units would have to be provided for the same number of passengers and hence the desire to save weight by articulation. The main objection to the planned interior layout seemed to be that the walk to the toilets — which were to be segregated 'Ladies' and 'Gentlemen' — could be excessive under certain circumstances! At the same time as this proposal was submitted, Stanier also proposed an identical train made up of 10 separate coaches and this idea seemed to be his own preferred choice:

'If the train is made up as an articulated train . . . the total weight of the train would be 309 tons, but we have no experience of articulated trains in this high-speed work. Further, the articulation must be the LMS type otherwise you will not get the seating arrangement, and this is an entirely new type which has not been tried out yet, and is only being used on the three-car light unit, which will be out early in January, and until this arrangement is thoroughly tested, I would not recommend our using it on a special train of this kind'.

This is the first mention in the files of the 'LMS type' of articulation and, indeed, the earlier general service articulated stock had been built on the Gresley principle. Stanier obviously preferred the idea of separate coaches and therefore asked the commercial side which of the 10 cars they were prepared to omit to keep the weight around the 300-ton mark. However, the operating staff were not keen on losing space so Stanier tried again. This time he produced the first twin articulated scheme which would have been formed as follows:

BFK+FK/ /Semi-FK and cocktail lounge+RFO/ /RK+RTO/ /Semi-RTO+TK/ /TK+BTK

This had the same layout as the preceding suggestion and provision was also made for an optional twin pair (presumably TK+TK) which could be added to make a 12-coach set at peak loading periods. The designed length was 59ft 5¼in per coach.

This was still not quite what was wanted although Stanier had agreed to improve the distribution of the toilets and dispense with separate Ladies' and Gentlemen's toilets. He was, therefore, asked to prepare a set 11-coach train (five pairs plus a loose third) with a further loose third for strengthening and this was done. At the same time it was resolved that for the American tour the Semi-RTO+TK would be omitted and a sleeping car would be marshalled between the corridor first and the cocktail lounge.

When this 11-coach set plus extra corridor third was sketched out, the main objection seemed to be that the loose thirds were to be 57ft long and the operating side felt that this might not be as roomy as the 59ft 5¼in dimension of the articulated halves. Stanier therefore produced a 59ft 5¼in loose third design. At the same time, the extra twelfth coach was, after all, deemed unnecessary and the 11-coach formation was finally settled.

Incredible though it may seem, all these design studies took place during December 1937, and 1938 was ushered in with the train formation more or less decided. Stanier had suggested a complete open third instead of the semi-open third but the Board preferred the original scheme.

It was not until February 1938 that the obvious anomaly that would exist in 1940 (when the new set was to be introduced to run with the 1937 sets) seemed to receive any attention. The Chief Commercial Manager and the Chief Operating Manager therefore wrote a joint letter to Vice-President Lemon from which the following extract is relevant:

' . . . it would be undesirable for the following reasons to utilise the new train in conjunction with two of the existing design and layout:

1.) It would be inconsistent to have trains of different type in a service of this kind. Were two trains of different type in use at one time we should have the new train leaving Euston Monday, Wednesday and Friday and the old type train on Tuesday and Thursday in one week, and the reverse in the following week . . .

2.) Whereas in one train every third class seat is reserved, in the other the dining seats are fluid.

3.) To enable reservation to be effected for the different types of train on different days, there would require to be assurance some weeks ahead which train would be in service on any particular day . . . any attempt at reservation in such circumstances would be fraught with danger from errors by the reservation clerks.

'In the circumstances will you kindly say that you agree to the building of two further trains as now proposed in the 1939 Carriage Renewal Programme for the "Coronation Scot" Service, in which case the existing "Coronation Scot" vehicles could be painted the standard colour and remarshalled and used in the "Royal Scot" services.'

The American train photographed from the first class end with twin BFK+FK leading. Note the distinctive shape of the guard's lookout and the absence of droplights in the double door of the brake portion. All the cars in the train were branded on the outside 'Lounge Car', 'Dining Car', etc with the sole exception of the leading BFK+FK. The Club car seems to have been omitted at the far end!

It will be noted that no mention was made of the superior nature of the 1939/40 coaches nor were comparisons drawn with the LNER sets. One must, therefore, conclude that the design of the trains was occasioned solely by the New York Fair and the decision to build three sets was mainly for operating convenience. Doubtless, however, the LMS publicity men were happy enough at the prospect of a new train for them to advertise when it did enter revenue service.

During early 1938 the design of seating was discussed, the Company not liking the idea of proposed loose chairs in the diners, while Stanier asked whether, for appearance sake, the double doors to the brake ends might be built without drop-lights. This was agreed subject to there being windows at the coach ends.

By May 1938, preparations for the American tour were well under way and a diagram of the proposed train was submitted. This showed that only seven of the new-style coaches together with a sleeping car were intended for the USA, viz: BFK+FK/ /Semi-FK (with cocktail lounge)+RFO/ /RK+RTO/ /SLF/ /BTK. The reason for the reduction in number of vehicles from the American formation originally envisaged (see above) has not been ascertained — possibly it may have had something to do with the time available for building the coaches. However, the proposed loose brake third was a new development and, as this had played no part in any of the original design studies, it was queried. No reason can be discovered why it was proposed unless it was because the articulated TK+BTK could not be built in time. The train had to have a brake end and possibly a loose brake third of the new type seemed the quickest solution.

Stanier was accordingly asked if, on return from America, the loose brake end was to be articulated with its corridor third partner but he replied that it was not and would go into general service on return. The remaining coaches of the American train (Semi-RTO+TK/ /TK/ /TK+BTK) would be built during 1939 and added to the other six vehicles when they came back from the USA.

The idea of a non-standard 'one-off' brake third was not particularly welcome and by July 1938 the proposal had been changed to that of a 'Club Car' brake coach which was the form in which it was finally built. Presumably this would give the opportunity for further displaying LMS coach-building techniques and after the American tour it could be used in the Manchester-Blackpool Club Car trains.

There was a certain amount of trouble in getting the first class sleeping car away from the traffic people during the summer of 1938 because it was needed in service. However, after the summer services were concluded, Car 377 was sent to Derby Works for the necessary modifications to provide staff sleeping accommodation.

Thus, by the autumn of 1938, the American train was all but ready for its transatlantic venture. Nowhere has been found mention of the reasons for the decision to change the livery from the blue/silver of the 1937 sets to the red and gold scheme of the USA tour train but this was done and in this guise, after display at Euston, the train was safely shipped to America in January 1939.

With the American train safely away, the CME then turned to the question of the remaining coaches to be built for the 1940 sets and to complete the American train. He suggested that for the two new 1940 sets, the articulated kitchen car and vestibule third diner should be made as separate vehicles and he also suggested that the Commercial Department might examine closely the general desirability of perpetuating the cocktail lounge in the British trains. The Commercial Manager's letter to acting Vice-President Davies on this issue makes amusing reading:

'. . . the question arises as to whether the Cocktail Bar should be perpetuated in the three new Coronation Scot trains which will eventually be put into service between Euston and Glasgow Central.

'The vehicle with the Cocktail Bar is marshalled in the first class portion of the train and we do not consider it would be sound to allow third class passengers to make use of the Cocktail Bar as to do so they would have to pass through the Vestibule First diner.

'We understand that the L.N.E. Company have experimented with a Cocktail Bar on their Scotch services but the bar had to be taken away and the vehicles concerned altered, owing to the third class passengers making use of it for beer drinking and disturbing the convenience of first class and other passengers . . .'

In February 1939, Vice-President Hartley agreed to the conversion of the cocktail lounge of the American train to a semi-open first on its return to Britain and also instructed that the matching vehicles for the new 1940 sets should be built from the outset as semi-open firsts. Thus the final formations of the envisaged 1940 Coronation Scot trains were as follows:

a. American Train   BFK+FK/ /Semi-RFO+RFO/ /RK+RTO/ /Semi-RTO+TK/ /TK/ /TK+BTK
b. Two new sets   BFK+FK/ /Semi-RFO+RFO/ /RK/ /RTO/ /Semi-RTO+TK/ /TK/ /TK+BTK

By this time, international affairs were overruling all other matters and the building of the 1940 coaches, then under construction, was suspended. In April 1941, the authority for the building of the 'Coronation Scot' stock was cancelled.

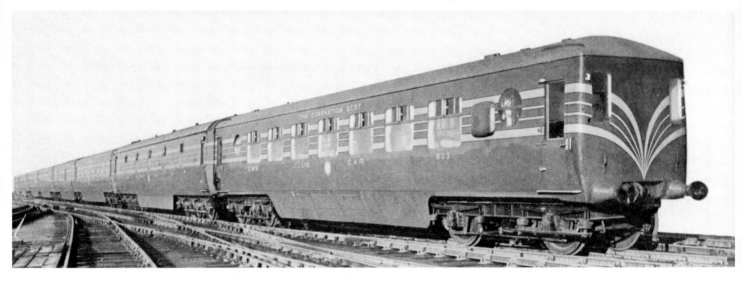

The American train photographed from the Club Car end. This picture clearly shows the difference in profile between the 1939/40 stock and the traditional LMS stock as exemplified by the sleeping car which is the second vehicle in the train. On return from America the panels between the bogies were removed below footboard level.

The luxury two-a-side compartments of the 1939 articulated 'Coronation Scot' set. The coach is not identified but is probably No 56000/1.

Interior view of the vestibule first class dining coach of the American train.

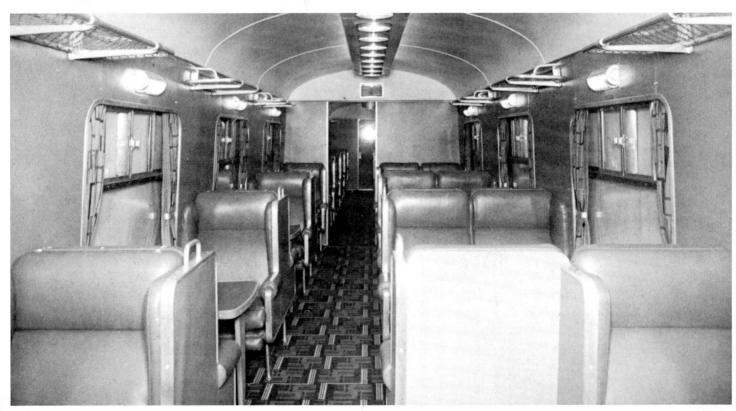

THE POSTWAR STORY

For three years the LMS was concerned with larger issues than prestige trains but by April 1944 the situation was such that the CME, now Mr. C. E. Fairburn, could write to the Chief Operating Manager as follows:

'. . . I have now got some details available for the "Coronation Scot" coaches which were held up when war broke out. The situation is as follows:

'The number of coaches is 25 and we have got all the underframes complete with bogies for these and a certain amount of bodywork had been done on 11 of the vehicles. Fourteen are corridor but only two are loose vehicles, the other 12 being matched with other vehicles as articulated twins.

    Underframes with bodies erected   - 8
    Underframes with floor only   - 2

'So far as the material side is concerned, we have material as follows . . .'

There then follows a long list of supplies which were in hand for the coaches. The CME's letter concludes:

'You will see that there is a number of these cars that we could finish reasonably quickly; the limiting item seems to be key sheeting, of which we have got a supply for five only. We have not been able to get this for other vehicles but just recently we have reason to believe that the position may have eased somewhat on that . . .

'I should be glad to have your views on the matter as to whether you think we should open up this lot number again or not. Under existing circumstances where material is tight it seems unfortunate to leave this material lying and it would be better converted into vehicles as far as possible.'

It should be noted that the 25 vehicles referred to did not include either of the kitchen cars for the 1940 trains but referred to all the other coaches designated for the new trains. The initial response to Mr Fairburn's proposal was not particularly hopeful:

'. . .Under the circumstances, I consider it would not be sound to proceed with the construction of these "Coronation Scot" trains during the war, because if they were to be turned out it would be necessary for them to be put on one side and stabled under cover until the "Coronation Scot" trains, with all they entail in regard to limiting travel to the seats provided, are re-introduced after the war . . .

'It is my view that immediately after the war, and not till then, consideration should be given to the completion of the 25 vehicles to which you refer . . .'

The CME seems to have anticipated something like this sort of reply for in his next submission he introduced further facts in support of his desire to recommence building the coaches:

'. . .the real difficulty I see in adopting the policy proposed by you is that no account has been taken of the time that these Coronation Coaches will probably be required to be constructed . . . if they are required in any period, say, from one to four years after the war and perhaps even longer, they will just be required at the time when our shops are really doing all they can to provide standard coaches.

'All these coaches are special in every way . . .and to introduce them into the Works at a time when we are trying as near as possible to mass produce, would I am afraid have a very serious effect on our rate of production of standard coaches.

'If we could commence almost immediately and proceed as far as labour and materials permit, we would expect to get the bulk of the work done before we started on standard coaches . . .'

The operating manager was still not over keen on the idea but appreciated Fairburn's point and he replied that he had no objection to the work proceeding provided that suitable covered storage space could be found for the completed coaches until they were needed in service. The resumption of work was, of course, subject to approval from the LMS Board since authority for building had been cancelled. Thus, in a memorandum to the Board on 21 April 1944, the President of the Executive (W. V. Wood) wrote as follows:

'During the interval between the expiry of certain aircraft contracts and the date at which materials will be available to begin the construction of the 800 coaching vehicles for which authority is asked at this Board, it would be convenient if the CME could proceed as far as possible with the completion of the "Coronation Scot" coaches. This would enable him to employ any carriage building staff previously engaged on aircraft work and it would be a useful way of re-training them on actual carriage building of which they have done practically none for five years . . . the work on the "Coronation Scot" coaches would cease immediately material for the 800 vehicles began to be available.

'The approval of the Board is asked for the resumption of work on the "Coronation Scot" coaches on the above conditions.'

Authority for resumption on these terms was granted on 27 April 1944 and in the autumn of the same year, the partially completed coaches were returned from store at Abergavenny and Spondon to Derby Works. Construction recommenced almost at once but progress was slow. The aim was to have them finished before the anticipated large-scale postwar building started but in the event, several more years were to pass before the coaches finally took to the rails. Postwar replacement of general service coaches was obviously given top priority and from the leisurely rate of progress on the 'Coronation Scot' coaches one must conclude that work was suspended on them many times during the 1945-49 period.

By mid-1945, the first of the vehicles were approaching partial completion and were scheduled to be placed again in store — destined once more for Abergavenny. By 1946, only 11 coaches had been part completed — they were without seats, some fittings and external paint and the first nine consisted of the following vehicles:

Type	Running Numbers
Artic BTK+TK	56500-56501
Artic Semi-TO+TK	56300-56301
Artic BFK+FK	56002-56003
Loose TK	2148
Loose RTO	9517-9518

These coaches completed the American train and provided certain vehicles of the later sets. They were shortly joined by the last of the BFK+FK twins (56004-56005). On 29 May 1946, a recommendation was made which helped to seal the fate of the new vehicles. The Chief Operating Manager wrote to Vice-President G. L. Darbyshire in some detail explaining his views on the matter of high-speed trains and the paragraphs relating to the 'Coronation Scot' sets ran as follows:

Postwar 'Coronation Scot'-type corridor third to D2019, No 2148.

'. . .My considered view is that is will be some considerable time before we shall be in a position on the LMS to contemplate the introduction of such high speeds as existed prewar because of the effect of the war-time years on the maintenance of our rolling stock and track.

'. . .to introduce ultra high speed working with permanent way slacks of a more severe nature than existed prewar would mean bad time-keeping and result in an outcry from the public on the score of unpunctuality . . .

'In view of the facts brought out in this memorandum I recommend that the three "Coronation Scot" sets painted blue with silver lining which have been stored since September 1939, should be repainted in the standard colours and the vehicles forming these trains should be utilised in our best passenger trains in the same way as any other stock . . .

'If this is agreed, consideration can then be given to what is to be done with the red and gold "Coronation Scot" vehicles which are now being returned to us from America and the other vehicles . . .which were authorised to be built for forming three new "Coronation Scot" trains.'

This suggestion was agreed and the 1937 sets were brought into use for general service. The new CME, Mr H. G. Ivatt, was asked about the possibility of converting the first class coaches of the 1937 sets to three-a-side seating but stated that this could not be done in the stipulated time available as it would need new seats to be made. However, he also stated that some of the American coaches could likewise be made quickly available for general service if required. With regard to the incomplete coaches, Ivatt stated:

'. . .The whole of these coaches . . .can be taken in hand this autumn, when it is anticipated that the work in connection with Ambulance Train Vehicles (conversion and restoration) will be dropping off. But this means the whole of the 25 vehicles could be completed in time for the summer timetable — 1947 — without interference with the planned production of other new coaches.'

Ivatt also stated that the incomplete first class coaches could be altered to seat three-a-side without much additional expense.

The partly completed coaches were, therefore, sent back yet again from Abergavenny during the winter of 1946-7 and consideration was now given as to how best to employ them on completion. By this time, one gets a strong impression from the documentary evidence that the LMS regarded the coaches as something of a millstone round its neck. The non-gangwayed brake ends were not really suitable for general service but the Chief Operating Manager decided, one feels somewhat resignedly, that he was prepared to accept the position '. . . rather than recommend that further expenditure be incurred in altering them to standard ends with gangway connection.'

Excluding the Club brake and the articulated kitchen pair, there were 29 vehicles to find services for and in February 1947 all 29 were offered to the Central Division, the Chief Operating Manager commenting:

'. . .it is desirable to find some suitable service in which as many as possible of them can be kept in sets which are not normally subject to change in formation, etc.

'In particular, the two brake vehicles for each of the three intended "Coronation Scot" sets form part of a twin articulated with the outside end bowed and not fitted with a gangway and if it can be avoided it is desirable that these be not used in main line services, where the necessity frequently arises for attaching other vehicles outside the brake.

'. . .I shall be obliged if you will give early consideration to the possibility of making use of any of these coaches in any appropriate residential service between Manchester (Victoria) and Blackpool or Southport . . . I am particularly anxious that you should find use for the units which embody the vehicles with bowed ends if at all practicable.'

No doubt to the relief of the operating staff, the Central Division stated that it could use 23 of the coaches in set trains on the Manchester-Southport services and could absorb all the non-gangwayed brake ends. Thus, as the coaches were finished they were sent to Lostock Hall for stabling until sufficient were available for forming into sets.

The remaining six coaches not allocated to the Central Division (Semi-RFO+RFO; Semi-RTO+TK; loose TO and loose TK) were offered to the Western Division which said it could use the first class pair on one of the Liverpool-Euston turns and could place the third class coaches in the Wolverhampton-Euston services. In the event, the four third class coaches were not utilised because of their low seating capacity. One was stored at Abergavenny Junction (the open third) and the other three went to Craven Arms.

Postwar semi-RTO+TK to D2017 Nos 56302/3. This was one of the articulated types not built for the 1939 tour train.

The first recorded working of the 1939-40 stock in this country was in October 1947 when the following set was formed to work a Blackpool-Liverpool residential turn: BFK+FK/ /Semi-TO+TK/ /TK+BTK. The firsts were the American pair and the thirds were the coaches built to complete the American train. From this point onwards, the balance of the stock was completed during the autumn and winter of 1947-8 except for the two outstanding TK+BTK pairs which did not emerge until 1949 and 1951. Table 4c, appended after this chapter, lists the known workings to which the coaches were allocated on first entering service although they later became somewhat scattered.

The articulated RK+RTO and the Club Brake saloon were nobody's friends at first but the Club Car eventually found its way onto the North Wales Land Cruise train along with a number of other rather unusual vehicles. The Kitchen twin was placed in store at Craven Arms on return from the USA and while at Craven Arms it lost a bogie to the Chairman's saloon No 45005 in 1947. It would appear that unequal axle loading was causing distortion to the underframe and it ultimately went into Derby Works for attention. No recorded working for the kitchen pair has been located and it may never have left Derby again as it was scrapped in early 1952.

THE 1939-40 STOCK DESCRIBED

All the 1939-40 stock, whether articulated or loose, was built to a common 59ft 5¼in length which was occasioned by the maximum permissible distance between point locking bars on the articulated pairs; the loose coaches were built to matching dimensions. Externally the coaches were quite distinctive — even apart from the original livery of the American set. Body framing was of steel with solebar and cantrail combined in one unit, and the angle between roof and sides at the cantrail was rather sharper than the orthodox Period III coach. Views of the American train show a clear distinction between the profile of the sleeping car and the 1939-40 stock proper.

The underframes were centrally trussed on all the coaches and the whole sub-structure was of welded construction, Windows were double-glazed and on the American train the bodyside panelling was carried down between the bogies to obscure the underframes. India rubber fairings covered the gaps between the coaches of the American set and were painted to match the train.

Another characteristic styling point was the circular pattern of toilet windows. These were, in effect, the precursors of the porthole style although not exactly similar. They had a central horizontal bar and the upper half hinged inwards. Similar matching windows, but without hinged top sections, were placed on the sides opposite the toilets to balance the appearance. The guard's lookout on the brake ends was also of a new shape — impossible to describe in words but clear enough from pictures. All main windows were of Period III style with shorter sliding portions rather like the postwar pattern. Brake ends were slightly bow-ended and without gangway connections.

The American train carried the crimson and gold 'Coronation Scot' livery and the gold stripes converged to a 'V' at the outer ends of the train as they also did on the front of the locomotive. Postwar coaches were built without the lower bodyside fairings and had the standard LMS livery, some of the later coaches also being outshopped without LMS markings where they post-dated Nationalisation. The American coaches were altered to match this style when they went into service in this country.

Inside, the vehicles followed traditional LMS practice: first class compartments seated four and thirds seated six, while all open saloons were designed as diners and thus seated two-and-one each side of the gangway with a one-and-one arrangement adjacent to the entrances. The familiar LMS wood veneers were extensively employed but in the dining saloons the LMS did make some concessions to the fashions of the day — whether this was a good thing or not is hard to say. Walls were faced in leather (grey in the first and green

in the thirds) while seats were also leather upholstered (dull pink in the firsts and brown in the thirds). The cocktail lounge of the American train was a patriotic example of the decor of the later 1930s with blue leather wall facings, blue carpets, red and white curtains and ivory ceiling. The club saloon had brown oak facings and coral pink(!) leather armchairs. However, colour schemes apart which are, after all, a matter of personal preference, the vehicles themselves were superlatively comfortable and well-thought-out designs. The corridor thirds were particularly luxurious having but six compartments, 6ft 6in between partitions.

Telephones were fitted in the compartments of the American train but were later removed and never put into the postwar coaches. Although Ivatt had considered the conversion of the two-a-side seating to three-a-side, this was not carried out and the postwar firsts were built with two-a-side compartments as well. Finally, the kitchen car of the American train was not of the usual LMS gas cooking type but was fitted with a solid fuel cooking range designed to burn smokeless fuel. It is not known if the two loose kitchen cars would have been similar had they ever been built. Perhaps the LMS intended to use the 60ft all-electric kitchen cars of 1933 — we shall never know.

Left: Third class compartment interior of Nos 56302/3.

Below: Interior view of the first class dining area of the semi-open firsts built after the war. It is believed to be the interior of Nos 56102/3. Note the postwar reversion to traditional LMS finishes compared with the adjacent picture.

CONCLUSIONS

Thus was concluded the complicated and rather sad story of the 'Coronation Scot'. It was a train conceived at the zenith of British steam railway operating and but for the war might well have attracted fresh laurels with the new coaches. However, this was not to be and, after the war, changing conditions and attitudes saw to it that not even a partial revival of the streamline age could be attempted. Nevertheless, the 1939-40 coaches were rather too good to waste — as indeed were the LNER streamline sets — and one wonders why none of these vehicles was ever re-formed for the Anglo-Scottish services. Although a high-speed timing might not have been possible, one feels that limited accommodation luxury trains would have attracted custom and been of inestimable publicity value to the railway service during those early postwar austerity years and might have helped to offset the high construction costs of such specialised vehicles. This lack of enterprise is even more surprising when one recalls the very early postwar reintroduction of the much heavier, and even more wasteful of space, Pullman trains.

TABLE 4a: THE 1937 'CORONATION SCOT' SETS

The 1937 sets were made of coaches to the following coach diagrams, details of which are given in Volume 2:

Corridor Brake First	D1961	three built Wolverton 1937 (Lot 1063)
Corridor First	D1960	three built Wolverton 1937 (Lot 1062)
Vestibule First Diner	D1902	three converted Wolverton 1937 (Lot 734)
Kitchen Only Car	D1912	six converted Wolverton 1937 (Lot 956)
Vestibule Third Diner	D1981	nine converted Wolverton 1937 ex-D1904 (Lots 804/5)
Corridor Brake Third	D1905	three converted Wolverton 1937 (Lot 898)

Set Formations (Note: One source claims that the 'reserve' set ran on LNWR bogies. This is not confirmed nor is it known which set was the official 'reserve'.)

BFK	FK	RFO	RK	RTO	RTO	RK	RTO	BTK
5052	1069	7507	30084	8996	8993	30086	8961	5812
5053	1070	7508	30089	9003	9006	30085	9004	5792
5054	1071	7509	30087	8950	9029	30088	8931	5814

TABLE 4b: THE 1939-40 'CORONATION SCOT' COACHES

Note: All coaches were built at Derby and had the following over-body dimensions: 59ft 5¼in x 9ft 2⅜in x 12ft 2⁷⁄₁₆in. Bogie centres were 51ft 9in for the articulated pairs and 41ft 11½in for the loose coaches. Articulated pairs were 120ft long over body. The loose coaches were plated 60ft long and brake ends were 9ft 3⅛in over projections.

Type	Diag	Lot	Qty	Date	Weight	Running Numbers	Withdrawals First	Last	Remarks
Twin BFK+FK	2014	1148*	1 set	1939	57T	56000-56001	-	1/65	Plated 58T.
		1176A	2 sets	1947	57T	56002-56005	4/65	11/65	
Twin-Semi-FK+RFO	2015	1149*	1 set	1939	58T	56100-56101	-	2/64	Initially with a cocktail lounge.
Twin-Semi-RFO+RFO	2138	1177A	2 sets	1848	55T	56102-56105	4/64	11/65	The postwar version of D2015.
Twin RK+RTO	2016	1150*	1 set	1939	66T	56200-56201	-	4/52	First coaches scrapped.
Twin-Semi-RTO+TK	2017	1151A	1 set	1947	58T	56300-56301	-	3/66	
		1179A	2 sets	1948	57T	56302-56305	4/65	11/65	
Twin BTK+TK	2018	1153A	1 set	1947	58T	56500-56501	-	12/66	56502/3 in service in 1949.
		1181A	2 sets	1951	58T	56502-56505	13/63	6/64	
TK	2019	1152A	1	1947	33T	2148	-	10/67	Oval buffers. Lot 1180A plated 31T.
		1180A	2	1949	33T	2149-2150	13/66	11/67	
Club Car	2020	1164*	1	1939	31T	823	-	4/63	
RTO	2153	1178A	2	1947	30T	9517-9518	9/67	13/67	Oval buffers.

*Coaches to USA in 1939.

TABLE 4c: FIRST RECORDED WORKINGS OF 1939-40 'CORONATION SCOT' STOCK IN BRITAIN

Coach Numbers	Date to traffic	Time	Details of Working From	To
56000-56001	6 October 1947	09.00	Blackpool	Liverpool
		16.40(SX)	Liverpool	Blackpool
		13.10(SO)		
56002-56003	9 February 1948	07.50(SX)	Southport	Manchester
		08.05(SO)	Southport	Manchester
		16.10(SX)	Manchester	Southport
		11.25(SO)	Manchester	Southport
56004-56005	1 December 1947	08.55	Southport	Manchester
		17.22(SX)	Manchester	Southport
		13.50(SO)	Manchester	Southport
56100-56101	not known	not known but believed allocated to same set as 56002/3.		
56102-56103	9 February 1948	10.00(SX)	Southport	Manchester
		08.30(SO)		
		18.10(SX)	Manchester	Southport
		12.45(SO)		
56104-56105	about mid-1948	between Euston and Wolverhampton†		
9517	26 July 1948	as for 56102/3		
9518	to store Dec 1947			
56300-56301	6 October 1947	as for 56000/1		
56302-56303	26 July 1948	07.43(SX)	Blackpool	Manchester
		17.03(SX)	Manchester	Blackpool
56304-56305	to store May 1948			
2148	1 December 1947	as for 56004/5		
2149	not Known	allocated to Central Division		
2150	to store, date unknown			
56500-56501	6 October 1947	as for 56000/1		
56502-56503*	May 1949	as for 56102/3		
56504-56505*	not known	allocated to Central Division		

* These coaches are shown in the LM diagram book as having entered service in 1951 and are quoted as such in Table 4b above. The 1951 date applies only to the last pair of coaches (56504/5).

† Not, apparently, between Euston and Liverpool as planned — see p95.

An evocative reminder of the only 'Coronation Scot' trains which went into revenue service — the silver and blue 1937 sets. The main picture, a classic Eric Treacy shot, shows the southbound train descending Shap behind No 6220 *Coronation* itself, while the detail picture shows converted Kitchen Car No 30084 in its special livery — note the retained gas lighting, a standard feature of LMS 50ft kitchen cars.

Postwar Twin BFK+FK No 56004/5. Compare with the view of the similar prewar pair on page 91.

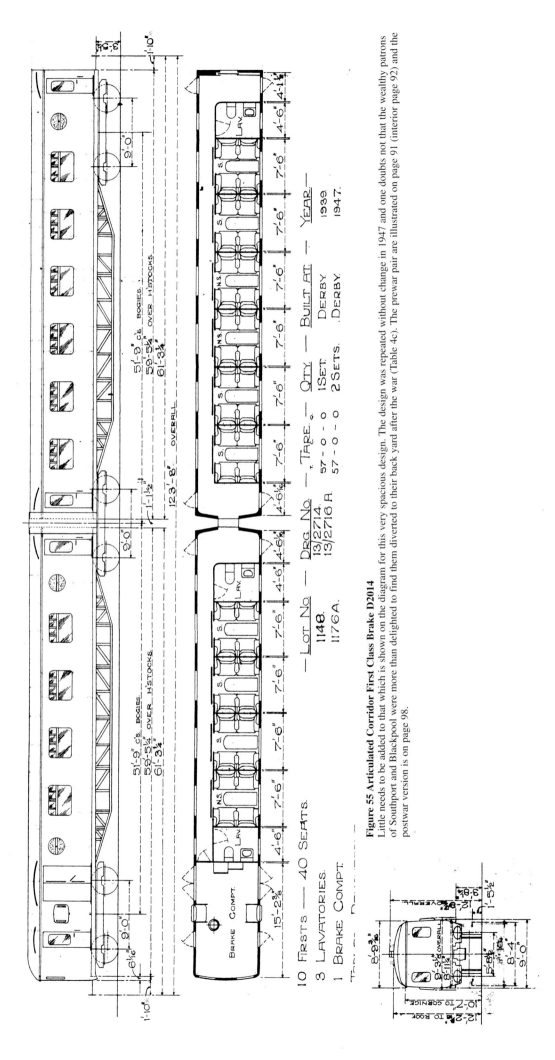

10 FIRSTS — 40 SEATS.
3 LAVATORIES.
1 BRAKE COMPT.

— LOT NO —	DRG. NO. —	TARE. —	QTY. —	BUILT AT. —	YEAR —
1148.	13/2714.	57 - 0 - 0	1 SET.	DERBY	1939
1176A.	13/2716 A	57 - 0 - 0	2 SETS.	DERBY	1947.

Figure 55 Articulated Corridor First Class Brake D2014

Little needs to be added to that which is shown on the diagram for this very spacious design. The design was repeated without change in 1947 and one doubts not that the wealthy patrons of Southport and Blackpool were more than delighted to find them diverted to their back yard after the war (Table 4c). The prewar pair are illustrated on page 91 (interior page 92) and the postwar version is on page 98.

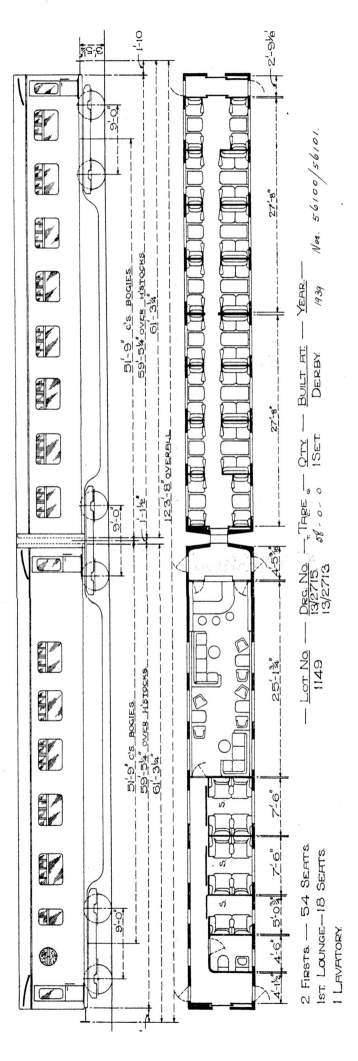

2 FIRSTS — 54 SEATS.
1ST. LOUNGE — 18 SEATS.
1 LAVATORY.

— LOT NO — DRG. NO — TARE — QTY — BUILT AT — YEAR —
   1149   13/2715   58-0-0 1 SET. DERBY   1939
             13/2713   Nos. 56100/56101.

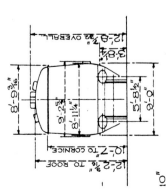

Figure 56 Articulated Corridor First Lounge & First Diner D2015
This diagram shows the 'one-off' articulated full first which went to the USA with the open portion originally arranged as a lounge bar. It is a moot point whether the postwar derivation (see next page) would, had it gone into the sort of service for which originally intended, have proved quite as agreeable as this elegant arrangement. But — see also page 93 — the cocktail bar was suppressed in the postwar version and the prewar example was altered to match. An interior view can be found on page 92.

100

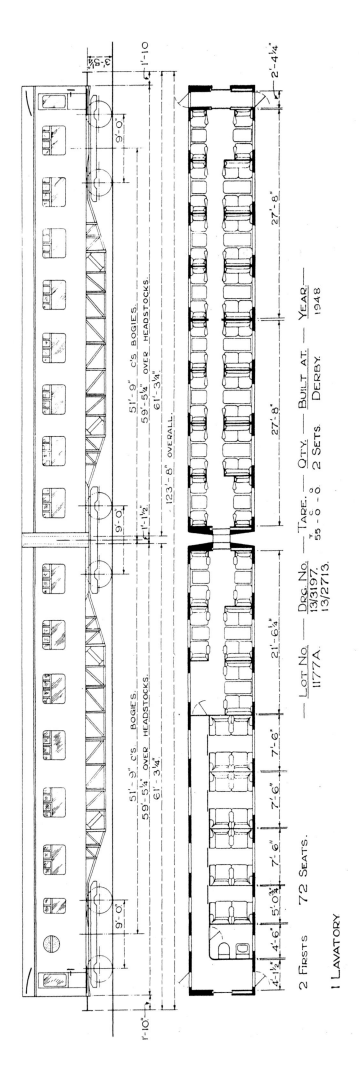

2 FIRSTS   72 SEATS.

1 LAVATORY

— LOT NO. —	— DRG. NO. —	— TARE. —	— QTY. —	— BUILT AT. —	— YEAR —
1177A.	13/3197. 13/2713.	T C Q 55 - 0 - 0	2 SETS.	DERBY.	1948

Figure 57 Articulated Corridor First Class Vestibule D2138
This was the postwar development of D2015 (last page), its out-of-sequence diagram number clearly indicating later thinking. The suppression of the cocktail bar allowed an extra first class compartment to be offered but, surprisingly, like its prewar equivalent, the sets built to this design still contained only one lavatory compartment for a notional 72-seat capacity. Presumably this was felt adequate considering the more than sufficient provisioning in the non-dining parts of the planned formations. The slightly restyled interior of this type is illustrated on page 96.

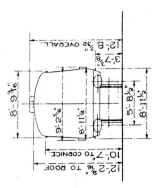

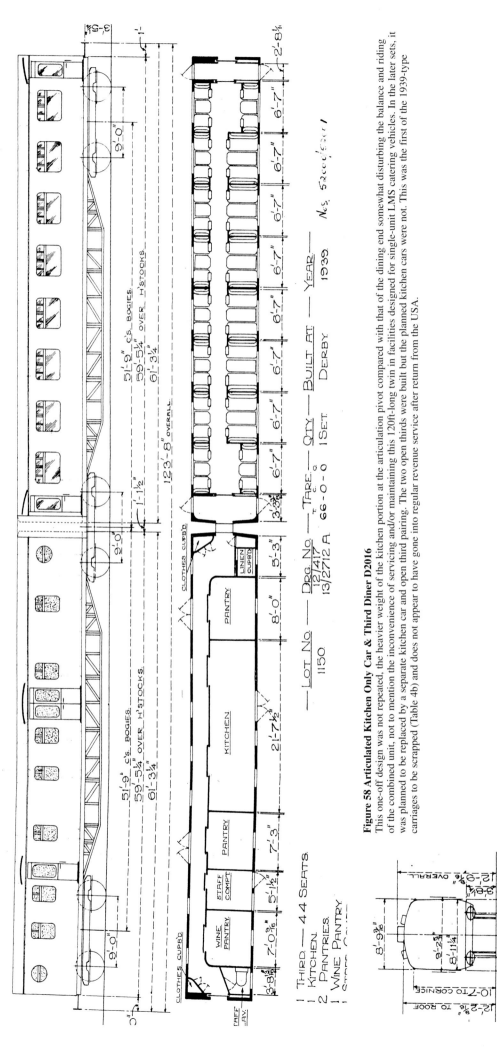

Figure 58 Articulated Kitchen Only Car & Third Diner D2016

This one-off design was not repeated, the heavier weight of the kitchen portion at the articulation pivot compared with that of the dining end somewhat disturbing the balance and riding of the combined unit, not to mention the inconvenience of servicing and/or maintaining this 120ft-long twin in facilities designed for single-unit LMS catering vehicles. In the later sets, it was planned to be replaced by a separate kitchen car and open third pairing. The two open thirds were built but the planned kitchen cars were not. This was the first of the 1939-type carriages to be scrapped (Table 4b) and does not appear to have gone into regular revenue service after return from the USA.

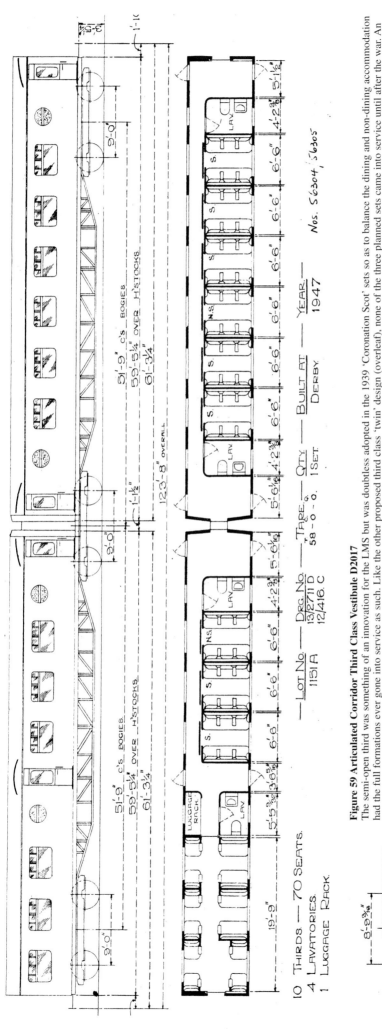

10 THIRDS — 70 SEATS.
4 LAVATORIES.
1 LUGGAGE RACK.

LOT No.	DRG. No.	TARE.	QTY	BUILT AT	YEAR
1151 A	13/2711 D 12/416 C	58 – 0 – 0	1 SET	DERBY	1947

Nos. 56304, 56305

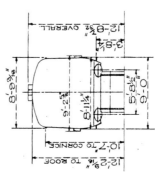

Figure 59 Articulated Corridor Third Class Vestibule D2017

The semi-open third was something of an innovation for the LMS but was doubtless adopted in the 1939 'Coronation Scot' sets so as to balance the dining and non-dining accommodation had the full formations ever gone into service as such. Like the other proposed third class 'twin' design (overleaf), none of the three planned sets came into service until after the war. An exterior view is offered on page 95.

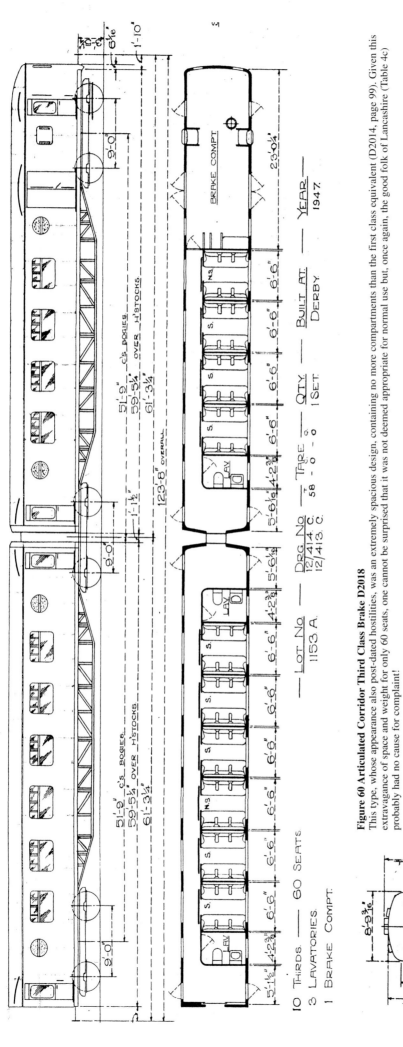

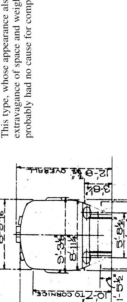

— LOT Nº — DRG. Nº — TARE — QTY. — BUILT AT — YEAR —
1153 A.   12/414. C.   58 - 0 - 0   1 SET.   DERBY   1947.
          12/413. C.

10 THIRDS. — 60 SEATS.
3 LAVATORIES.
1 BRAKE COMPT.

Figure 60 Articulated Corridor Third Class Brake D2018
This type, whose appearance also post-dated hostilities, was an extremely spacious design, containing no more compartments than the first class equivalent (D2014, page 99). Given this extravagance of space and weight for only 60 seats, one cannot be surprised that it was not deemed appropriate for normal use but, once again, the good folk of Lancashire (Table 4c) probably had no cause for complaint!

104

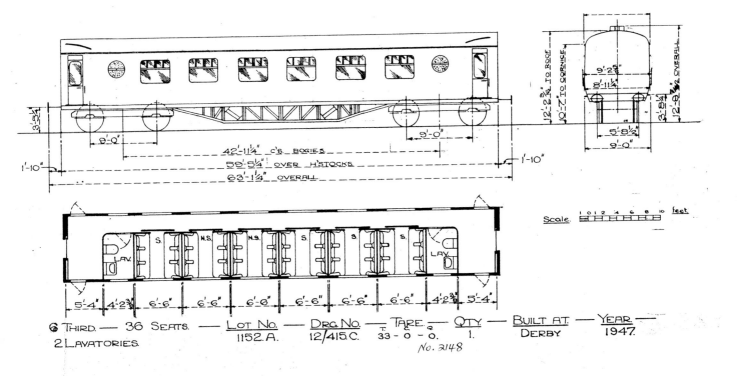

Figure 61 Third Class Corridor D2019
This design represented the so-called 'strengthener' which would have made the full 11-unit formation had the train gone into service as planned. Its layout was exactly the same as the non-brake half of D2018 (opposite) and the full corridor element of D2017, between which two twins it would have been marshalled. All were built after the war and the authors recall encountering one of them at Carstairs in the mid-1960s, shortly before withdrawal, on a local service in Scotland — most surprising but very agreeable! One of them is illustrated on page 94.

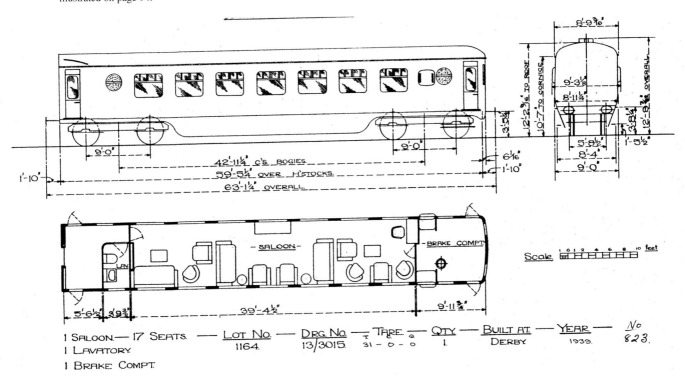

Figure 62 Club Saloon D2020
This was the surprising outcome of the decision not to build a 'loose' brake third for the American train — see page 91. Although its diagram number is in sequence with those of all the other prewar designs, it is not known how the LMS intended to use this one-off carriage had the three full 1939-40 sets gone into postwar Anglo-Scottish service as originally planned. As it was, after its return from the USA it saw occasional use on club and cruise trains during the early BR period. It is shown in its original livery on page 92.

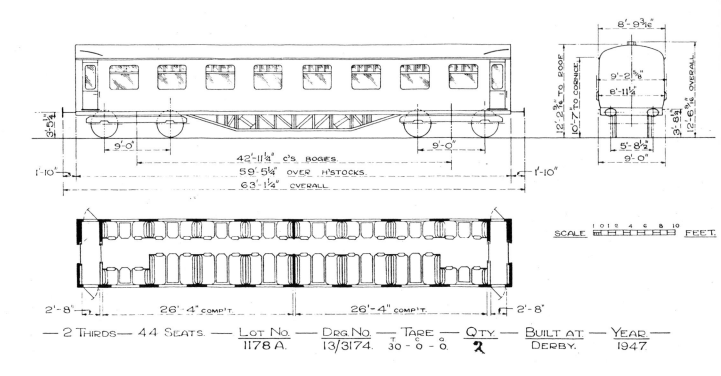

2 THIRDS — 44 SEATS. — LOT NO. — DRG. NO. — TARE — QTY. — BUILT AT — YEAR. —
1178 A.   13/3174.   30 - 0 - 0.   2   DERBY.   1947

Figure 63 Vestibule Third Class Diner D2133
As with D2138 (page 101) the out-of-sequence diagram number for this type denotes that it was something of an afterthought. Its layout was identical to that of the passenger half of D2016 (page 102) and in the second and third sets, this type plus a loose kitchen car would have been offered instead of the articulated twin of the original 1939 set. The appended illustration shows No 9518 when new in standard postwar LMS livery. As with many of these carriages, it first went into service between Manchester and Southport.

Chapter 5 - Passenger Brake Vans

Introduction; World War 1 Conversions; Period I Designs; Period III Designs;
World War 2 Conversions.

The terms Periods I, II and III, while suitable for most vehicles described in this work, are not quite comprehensive enough when considering the passenger full brakes built to LMS diagrams. Considerable numbers of full brakes were built as conversions from older stock which had seen a variety of previous uses. The section headings in this chapter, therefore, reflect this fact.

WORLD WAR 1 CONVERSIONS

The first vehicles to be considered are not really LMS standards at all, although they were all given LMS diagrams. They consisted of a number of ex-pre-Grouping coaches which had been in government service during World War 1 as ambulance trains. Following their release, some were converted at Newton Heath and others at Wolverton, a policy which was to be repeated in large measure at the end of World War 2 some 22 years later.

There were 63 vehicles concerned spread over eight LMS diagrams. The coaches appear largely to have eluded photographers and only one official photograph has come to light. From the diagrams issued it is possible to give a generalised statement about the more obvious differences between the various types and for ease of reference, these details have been incorporated into Table 5a which covers these conversions.

The only general comment which can be made is that most of the diagrams were fully beaded (except D1713/4) and all would have been given the full livery when converted.

PERIOD I DESIGNS

The construction of LMS standard full brakes began with D1778 in 1925. This was a typical Period I design and was built to a 50ft length. This length remained standard with but few exceptions for LMS bogie brakes and appears to have been a case of the LMS adopting an LNWR standard length as it did for so many of its standard types. The vans themselves had a central guard's lookout with a single door to the right of it. Flanking this central feature were two pairs of double doors. This arrangement of doors and lookout was to remain unchanged in all subsequent designs of LMS standard bogie full brakes.

Two coaches from D1778 were converted to Bullion Vans 44597/9 in 1953. These were Nos 30414/58 and were finally withdrawn in 1966. The conversion was to D2183.

The need for passenger full brakes must have been somewhat urgent during the middle 1920s, and 1926 saw the introduction of the first of an eventual 360 all-steel brakes built by outside contractors. These coaches were to D1715 and lacked conventional underframes. They were in all respects contemporary with and structurally similar to the open stock referred to in Volume 2. They were of the same length and layout as the orthodox Period I full brakes and all but one were finished in fully lined livery when new.

The exception was old No 7898 (later 30562), one of the batch built by the Birmingham Railway Carriage & Wagon Company to Lot 291. This coach was given a vitreous enamelled steel body. The idea was to reduce the time spent in shops — especially paint shops — and after the many difficulties were overcome, the vehicle entered traffic. The usual standard finish, including numbers and letters, was achieved but the process seems to have been incapable of producing the lining out. Thus it entered service in plain crimson hue. No paint was used above the chassis except around the door margins and gangways. All side and roof panels were enamelled. The experiment does not seem to have been a success and no evidence has been located that any other coaches were similarly treated. The all-steel brakes exhibited small but noticeable differences between batches. This took the form of presence or absence of outside rivets, horizontal reinforcement strips and so on. The differences generally related to the works where built and some are listed in Table 5b.

An accident to the 'Royal Highlander' at Dinwoodie in 1928 revealed the fact that the all-steel brake marshalled at the front of the train had absorbed a great deal of the impact and thus had minimised the damage to the passenger-carrying coaches. The LMS therefore

Period I 'all-steel' BG to D1715 No 7898, later 30562. This was the experimental vehicle given an unlined enamel finish but its style (eg steel roof and lack of conventional under-frame) was typical of all the 1925/6 full brakes.

Period III six-wheeled full brake No 32977 (D2000). Note the beading strips at the waist and above the window. These vehicles later became more familiarly known as 'Stove R'.

made an attempt to marshal as many trains as possible with these steel brakes at the outer ends. As may be expected, the complications of carriage rostering rendered the scheme somewhat abortive in many cases. However, this story may have had some bearing on the eventual adoption in this country of integral steel construction for passenger stock in later years. The final batch of all-steel brakes entered service in 1930 and no further full brakes were built until after Stanier had taken office.

PERIOD III DESIGNS

The first Period III full brakes appeared almost as soon as Stanier had arrived on the LMS. These were to D1796 and appeared in 1932 and 1933 and were six-wheel vehicles. In their later years they became known as 'Stove R'.

An interesting feature of these vans is that the diagram clearly shows short rainstrips on the roof over the doors which suggest that the design had been thought out before Stanier took office. The vehicles in fact were built with the characteristic Stanier ribbed roof and it seems possible that, just as in other matters, so in coaches, the CME started innovating almost as soon as he arrived.

Another externally distinguishing aspect of these coaches was the two strips of steel beading above and below the windows. These were, presumably, to cover the steel panel joints and were to become a typical feature of the prewar Stanier full brake in all its guises. It seems odd that the passenger-carrying coaches of contemporary design did not exhibit these beading strips and no reason can be offered why the brakes had this feature. Eventually, the full brakes also omitted the beading strip, the first diagram to do so being D2007.

When first built, D1796 carried lamps over the guard's lookout but these were later removed to conform with standard Stanier practice as there was no longer any need for fully braked trains of passenger-type stock to carry side lamps. During World War 2 and following complaints from the guards, these vehicles were fitted with stoves.

At the same time as Wolverton was building D1796, Derby began to produce the 50ft Period III full bogie brake to D1854. These were identical in size and layout to the Period I designs but exhibited the Period III full brake styling as first seen on the six-wheel brakes — including the horizontal beading strips and side lamps.

Further six-wheelers followed to D2000 in 1938. These were 9ft 0in wide as opposed to the 8ft 9in of D1796 but the only real difference was a change in position of the guard's brake wheel to the centre of the coach. The diagram does not show any horizontal beading strip on D2000.

As with the preceding examples, the next 50ft design overlapped the construction of six-wheel brakes. This was D2007 which became numerically the largest LMS full brake diagram. It hardly differed from D1854 and it is difficult to deduce why a new diagram was issued. Some later lots of D2007 were rated as having 12T carrying capacity but not all were thus distinguished. There were also slight external detail changes such as the omission of the beading in later lots (believed Lot 1357 upwards). The building of these 50ft brakes went on well into the war years and they were some of the very few LMS coaches to be built between 1940 and 1945.

Another wartime variant was D2100. These were 57ft brakes built on second-hand underframes. The general layout was identical to the 50ft vans. The building of 57ft vans seems a little odd — especially during the war — and the most likely solution seems to be that vans were needed and old underframes were available, hence the new design. These 57ft coaches were rated as 12T carrying capacity except for the two vehicles Nos 31900-1 which were 8T. This latter pair were given the underframes of the ex-LNWR Royal Train coaches Nos 5154-5 which had been given new underframes in 1937! The chassis for the remainder of this 57ft series came from war-damaged coaches. The 57ft brakes did not have horizontal beading strips.

A pointer to the reason for the sudden building of 57ft vans is given by the consecutive Lot 1357/8 on the 50ft diagram D2007. These total 114 coaches which is an unusual figure. However, with the 57ft vans to Lot 1359, the total rises to 150 which is much more typical of the LMS. It is felt reasonable to postulate that the 57ft vans may have been ordered as 50ft vehicles on D2007 but wartime economy made it cheaper to utilise spare 57ft underframes and thus save quite a quantity of new rolled steel section.

After the war, the final 50ft diagram was issued. This was D2171 and appeared in 1948. These coaches were contemporary with the porthole stock and were rated as 12T carrying capacity. They had no raised outside beading strip and were given postwar torpedo ventilators. They were otherwise all but identical to the prewar 50ft Period III types.

Period III standard full brake No 30965 (D2007). Note the beading strips at the waist and above the windows. This distinctive feature of many Period III full brakes was absent from later lots to this diagram.

The wartime Period III full brake to D2100 built to 57ft length as opposed to the standard 50ft. The coach depicted is No M31972M as running in 1965. The general arrangement was identical to the 50ft types. *R. J. Essery*

World War 2 LMS ambulance train No 8 — converted from Period I corridor stock. The first four vehicles, in order, started life as the following types: BTK (D1696); TO (D1692); CK (D1694); CK (D1694). Vehicles of this ambulance coach type were selected for conversion to full brakes.

Thus, in summary, although several diagrams were issued for Period III full brakes, there were really only two types, the 50ft standard and the six-wheelers. The 57ft batch was, it is felt, no more than a wartime expedient and not, therefore, of any crucial significance in design terms.

WORLD WAR 2 CONVERSIONS

As has been mentioned in Volume 2 (Chapters 3/4) a considerable number of early LMS standard Period I gangwayed stock was requisitioned by the government at the beginning of World War 2 for conversion into ambulance trains. When released from this role they were further converted into full brakes to two separate diagrams (D2129 and D2130). Since there were more than two types of Period I coach involved, the exterior arrangement of these converted brakes displayed a bewildering variety of styles. As far as can be seen, both the brake van diagrams involved coaches from all the Period I types concerned.

It is possible to give only the most general description of these conversions in the space available, although full details do exist and the history of most of the coaches involved can be traced.

Both diagrams had the guard located at one end of the vehicle, both diagrams were 57ft over headstocks and 9ft 0in wide over body, but D2130 is shown as 2¼in higher overall. D2130 had lookouts and two opposite inward-opening doors at one end, two outward-opening double doors close to the lookouts and two offset outward-opening double doors about three-quarters of a coach length from the guard's end. D2129 had the guard's seat on the opposite side to D2130 and the first pair of double-opening doors were offset and about one third of a coach length from the guard. The double doors furthest from the guard in this diagram were opposite each other. Finally, D2129 is shown as having the single doors near the outlook as opening outward. Many of these converted full brakes still showed signs of their original Period I types and reasonably characteristic examples of them are shown in the accompanying pictures.

As with the World War 1 conversions, these latter-day conversions are listed separately and will be found in Table 5c.

Post-World War 2 ex-ambulance full brake No M31731M as running in 1964. This was the D2129 version and prior to becoming an ambulance the coach was Period I TO No 8561 (D1692). Perceptive readers will note that in this, and the next picture, the inward/outward opening door arrangement was not quite as per diagram and the authors guess that other examples were similar.

The D2130 ex-ambulance full brake as running in 1965. This coach, No M31775M, was originally Period I CK No 3672 (D1694). As can be seen, quite a substantial amount of its original panelling survived both the ambulance and the brake conversion.

TABLE 5a: LMS PASSENGER BRAKE VANS I — WORLD WAR 1 CONVERSIONS

Diag	Lot	Qty	Date	Built	Dimensions (L x W x H)	Weight	Running Numbers	Withdrawals First	Last	Remarks
1713	64	16	1924	N. Heath ⎫	56ft x 9ft 0in x 12ft 5in	26T	31971-31986	2/54	12/60	Ex-LYR Ward-Personnel cars
	360	1	1929	N. Heath ⎭		25T	32017	-	12/59	
1714	69	30	1924	N. Heath	56ft x 9ft 0in x 12ft 5in	26T	31987-32016	10/53	2/63	Ex-LYR Ambulance Staff cars
1773	Part 70	2	1924	Wolverton	45ft x 9ft 3in x 12ft 7½in	21T	31953-31954	1/37 (31954)	12/47 (31953)	Ex-LNWR Ward cars (with clerestory)
1774	Part 70	1	1924	Wolverton	57ft x 8ft 11in x 12ft 5½in	26T	32018	-	12/51	Ex-LNWR Brake/Infections car
1776	Part 70	2	1924	Wolverton	50ft x 8ft 11in x 12ft 5½in	24T	31956-31957	1/56 (31956)	12/56 (31957)	Ex-LNWR Pharmacy car
1777	Part 70	9	1924	Wolverton	54ft x 8ft 11in x 12ft 5½in	25T	31958-31966	5/55	2/59	Ex-LNWR Ward cars
1780	88	1	1924	Wolverton	49ft x 8ft 11in x 12ft 3in	24T	31955	-	6/47	Ex-LNWR Pharmacy car
1711	90	1	1924	Wolverton	57ft x 8ft 11in x 12ft 5½in	26T	32019	-	12/57	Ex-LNWR Brake/Infections car

TABLE 5b: LMS PASSENGER BRAKE VANS II — STANDARD DESIGNS

Diag	Lot	Qty	Date	Built	Dimensions (L x W x H)	Period	Running Numbers	Withdrawals First	Last	Remarks
1778	218	75	1925/6	Wolverton ⎫	50ft x 9ft 3in x 12ft 4¾in	I	30400-30474	5/61	4/67	Lot 405 Plated 9ft 0in wide, Nos 30414 and 30458 to Bullion Vans 1953. Lot 405 may, originally, have contained 50 coaches.
	219	25	1926	N. Heath ⎬			30475-30499	10/59	9/67	
	405	49	1928	Wolverton ⎭			30500-30548	4/63	12/67	
1715	291	50	1926/7	B'ham C&W ⎫	50ft x 9ft 3in x 12ft 4¾in	I (All steel)	30549-30598	3/60	10/67	• plus 31948. Layout identical to D1778 but no conventional underframe — merely a battery support bracket at one side. Lot 292 was heavily riveted, remainder had less rivets but a prominent waist strip. The Birmingham C&W vehicles also had a top strip above the windows. All varieties had short rainstrips over the doors rather than a single end-to-end rainstrip.
	292	50	1927	Met C&W			30599-30648	11/58	12/66	
	344	50	1928	Camm/Laird			30649-30698	3/57	one (30654) extant 1968	
	345	50	1927/8	B'ham C&W			30699-30747*	12/58	9/67	
	460	50	1929	B'ham C&W			30748-30797	8/58	4/68	
	461	50	1929	Camm/Laird			30798-30847	2/60	a few extant in 1968	
	536	30	1930	Metro Cammell			30848-30877	3/65		
	537	30	1930	B'ham C&W			30878-30907	7/63	1/68	
1796	664	25	1932	Wolverton	31ft x 8ft 9in x 12ft 4¾in (six-wheel)	III	32900-32924	3/65	majority extant 1968.	Very early Stanier vehicles. Outshopped in full livery with torpedo vents. Beading strips at waist and above windows.
	669	50	1933	Wolverton			32925-32974	9/63		
1854	665	25	1932/3	Derby	50ft x 9ft 0in x 12ft 4⅝in	III	30908-30932	8/64}	a few still extant	First Stanier version of the standard 50ft van. Lots 665/686 had full livery and torpedo vents. Lot 780 had torpedo vents but probably simple livery. Beading strips as with D1796.
	686	25	1933	Derby			30933-30957	4/66}	extant	
	780	6	1934	Wolverton			30958-30963	2/66	6/67	
2000	1091	25	1938	Wolverton	31ft x 9ft 0in x 12ft 4⅝in (six-wheel)	III	32975-32999	13/66	majority extant 1968.	Officially 3in wider than D1796 but both types had standard 8ft 6in-wide body. Handbrake repositioned compared with D1796. Most had standard Period III shell vents but some had torpedo type.
	1262	20	1940	Wolverton			33000-33019	8/64		
2007	1096	25	1938	Wolverton	50ft x 9ft 0in x 12ft 4⅝in	III	30964-30988	3/65		No apparent difference to D1854. From Lot 1260 upwards many were rated at 12T carrying capacity (standard value 8T). Lots 1260/1 all plated 1939. Beading strips on bodyside seem to have finished with Lot 1305. Lot 1358 had second-hand underframes.
	1097	25	1938/9	Wolverton			30989-31013	3/65		
	1198	25	1939	Wolverton			31014-31038	11/67	virtually all extant 1968.	
	1260	20	1940	Derby			31039-31058	5/66		
	1261	50	1939/40	Wolverton			31059-31108	8/66		
	1304	50	1940/41	Derby			31109-31158	5/66		
	1305	50	1941	Wolverton			31159-31208	6/67		
	1357	110	1941	Wolverton			31210-31319	10/65		
	1358	4	1944	Wolverton			31320-31323}	All extant 1968.		
	1444	25	1947	Wolverton			31324-31348}			
2100	Part 1359	2	1944	Wolverton	57ft x 9ft 0in x 12ft 4⅝in	III	31900-31901	9/66 (31901) 31900 extant 1968		The 57ft wartime version on second-hand underframes. All rated 12T capacity except 31900/1 which were 8T. This pair were given the underframes of ex-LNWR Royal coaches Nos 5154/5. No beading on body side of this design.
	Part 1359	34	1944	Wolverton			31902-31935	All extant 1968.		
2171	1508	25	1949/50	Wolverton	50ft x 9ft 0in x 12ft 4⅝in	III	31349-31373}	All extant (except for accident withdrawals) in 1968		The postwar 50ft design. All rated 12T capacity but no fundamental differences from D1854/D2007. Exteriors had no raised beading strip. The vans had BR-type torpedo vents all outshopped without LMS markings (many probably in BR livery from new).
	1563	25	1949	Derby			31374-31398}			
	1579	15	1950	Derby			31399-31413	5/68} Most extant		
	1588	15	1950	Wolverton			31414-31428	3/65} 1968		

Addendum

Not surprisingly, the passenger full brakes were generally the longest lived by far of LMS-pattern gangwayed coaches, many receiving either a full BR blue or BR blue/grey repaint. Many were still in service into the 1980s, but a large number were converted to non-gangway form.

TABLE 5c: LMS PASSENGER BRAKE VANS III — WORLD WAR 2 CONVERSIONS

Two diagrams were involved (D2129/D2130), both being 57ft x 9ft 3in but D2129 was 12ft 7¼in high and D2130 was 12ft 9½in high (both measured over roof vents). There were no standard details to the designs as such, except that all had originated from Period I wood-panelled gangwayed stock. The coaches were numbered in the 31700-31871 series with the following gaps: 31794-6; 31828; 31839; 31845; 31859; 31863 and 31867. This gave 163 actual vehicles, 81 of which were converted to D2129, the remainder to D2130. The numbers did not run consecutively through the diagrams so the following table is listed in number order not diagram order. The conversions took place at Derby and Wolverton between 1946 and 1949. All were scrapped by the end of 1967.

Running Number	Original Coach	Type of ambulance vehicle from which converted	Brake Van Diagram
31700	TO No 7827	Ward Car	D2129
31701	TO No 8150	Ward Car	D2130
31702	TO No 7875	Not known	D2129
31703	TO No 8139	Ward Car	D2130
31704	TO No 8154	Ward Car	"
31705	TO No 8090	Ward Car	"
31706	TO No 8076	Ward Car	"
31707	TO No 7838	Ward Car	D2129
31708	TO No 7852	Not known	"
31709	TO No 7848	Ward Car	"
31710	TO No 7856	Not known	"
31711	TO No 8089	Ward Car	D2130
31712	TO No 8131	Ward Car	"
31713	TO No 8101	Ward Car	"
31714	BTK No 5261	Ward and Brake Car	D2129
31715	BTK No 5254	Ward and Brake Car	"
31716	CK No 3623	Spare Car	"
31717	TO No 8525	Spare Car	"
31718	BTK No 5294	Spare Car	"
31719	BTK No 5328	Spare Car	D2130
31720	TO No 8557	Ward Car	D2129
31721	TO No 8574	Ward Car	"
31722	TO No 8489	Ward Car	"
31723	TO No 8486	Ward Car	"
31724	TO No 8457	Ward Car	"
31725	TO No 8492	Ward Car	"
31726	TO No 8471	Ward Car	"
31727	TO No 8549	Ward Car	"
31728	TO No 8483	Ward Car	"
31729	TO No 8576	Ward Car	"
31730	TO No 8513	Ward Car	"
31731	TO No 8561	Ward Car	"
31732	TO No 8522	Ward Car	"
31733	TO No 8551	Ward Car	"
31734	TO No 8460	Ward Car	"
31735	TO No 8510	Ward Car	"
31736	TO No 8474	Ward Car	"
31737	TO No 8535	Ward Car	"
31738	TO No 8534	Ward Car	"
31739	TO No 8533	Ward Car	"
31740	TO No 8506	Ward Car	"
31741	TO No 8502	Ward Car	"
31742	TO No 8536	Ward Car	"
31743	TO No 8580	Not known	"
31744	TO No 8381	Ward Car	D2130
31745	TO No 8411	Ward Car	"
31746	TO No 8364	Ward Car	"
31747	TO No 8470	Ward Car	D2129
31748	TO No 8503	Ward Car	"
31749	TO No 8365	Ward Car	D2130
31750	TO No 8573	Ward Car	D2129
31751	TO No 8369	Ward Car	D2130
31752	TO No 8370	Ward Car	"
31753	TO No 8575	Ward Car	D2129
31754	TO No 8367	Ward Car	D2130
31755	TO No 8421	Ward Car	"
31756	BTO No 9879	Ward and Brake Car	"
31757	BTO No 9882	Ward and Brake Car	"
31758	BTO No 9870	Ward and Brake Car	"
31759	BTO No 9872	Ward and Brake Car	"
31760	BTO No 9878	Ward and Brake Car	"
31761	BTO No 9871	Ward and Brake Car	"
31762	BTO No 9880	Ward and Brake Car	"
31763	BTO No 9886	Ward and Brake Car	"
31764	BTO No 9863	Ward and Brake Car	"
31765	BTO No 9865	Ward and Brake Car	"
31766	BTO No 9888	Ward and Brake Car	"
31767	BTO No 9835	Ward and Brake Car	D2129
31768	CK No 3640	Personnel Car	"
31769	CK No 3647	Personnel Car	"
31770	CK No 3699	Personnel Car	"
31771	CK No 3696	Personnel Car	"
31772	CK No 3666	Personnel Car	"
31773	CK No 3687	Personnel Car	"
31774	CK No 3686	Personnel Car	"
31775	CK No 3672	Personnel Car	"
31776	CK No 3662	Personnel Car	"
31777	CK No 3591	Personnel Car	"
31778	CK No 3676	Personnel Car	D2130
31779	CK No 3682	Personnel Car	D2129
31780	CK No 3681	Ambulance Kitchen Car	"
31781	CK No 3700	Ambulance Kitchen Car	"
31782	CK No 3661	Ambulance Kitchen Car	"
31783	CK No 3665	Ambulance Kitchen Car	"
31784	CK No 3680	Ambulance Kitchen Car	"
31785	CK No 3698	Ambulance Kitchen Car	"
31786	CK No 3669	Ambulance Kitchen Car	"
31787	CK No 3692	Ambulance Kitchen Car	"
31788	CK No 3695	Ambulance Kitchen Car	D2130
31789	CK No 3689	Ambulance Kitchen Car	D2129
31790	CK No 3683	Ambulance Kitchen Car	"
31791	CK No 3668	Probably Ambulance Kitchen Car	"
31792	TO No 8390	Spare Car	D2130
31793	TO No 8454	Spare Car	"
31794-6	Number series vacant		

Note: From this point onwards it is not possible to state the type of ambulance vehicle from which each full brake was converted. However, the two diagrams for the full brakes indicate that the following additional types of ambulance coach were also involved: kitchen and mess cars; brake infection and boiler cars; pharmacy cars; brake and stores cars; brake, stores and boiler cars; dressing and baggage cars.

Running Number	Original Coach	Type of ambulance vehicle from which converted	Brake Van Diagram
31797	TO No 8458		D2129
31798	TO No 8484		"
31799	TO (No 8498?)		"
31800	TO No 8413		D2130
31801	TO No 8436		"
31802	TO No 8455		"
31803	TO No 8339		"
31804	TO No 8269		"
31805	TO No 8389		"
31806	TO No 8493		D2129
31807	TO No 8518		"
31808	TO (No 8393?)		D2130
31809	TO No 8336		"
31810	TO No 8374		"
31811	TO No 8468		D2129
31812	TO No 8358		D2130
31813	TO No 8529		D2129
31814	TO No 8577		"
31815	TO No 8563		"
31816	TO No 8542		"
31817	TO No 8447		D2130
31818	TO No 8299		"
31819	TO No 8482		D2129
31820	TO No 8378		D2130
31821	TO No 8379		"
31822	TO No 8579		D2129
31823	TO No 8388		D2130
31824	TO No 8516		D2129
31825	TO (No 8435?)		D2130
31826	TO No 8463		D2129
31827	BTO No 9869		"
31828	Number vacant		"
31829	BTO (No 9860?)		"
31830	BTO No 9883		D2130
31831	BTK No 5316		"
31832	BTK No 5242		"
31833	BTK No 5237		"
31834	BTK No 5231		"
31835	BTK No 5257		"
31836	BTK No 5337		"
31837	BTK (No 5230?)		"
31838	BTK No 5250		"
31839	Number vacant but allocated to BTK No 5235 lost overseas		"
31840	BTK No 5311		"
31841	BTK No 5262		"
31842	BTK No 5282		"
31843	BTK No 5259		"
31844	BTK No 5275		"
31845	Number vacant but allocated to BTK No 5310 lost overseas		"
31846	BTK No 5241		"
31847	BTK No 5304		"
31848	BTK No 5255		"
31849	BTK No 5260		"
31850	BTK No 5301		"
31851	BTK No 5273		"
31852	BTK No 5253		"
31853	BTK No 5265		"
31854	BTK No 5281		"
31855	BTK No 5228		"
31856	BTK No 5271		"
31857	BTK No 5333		"
31858	BTK No 5315		"
31859	Number vacant		"
31860	BTK No 5324		D2129
31861	BTK No 5341		D2130
31862	BTK No 5302		"
31863	Number vacant		"
31864	BTK No 5297		"
31865	BTK No 5278		"
31866	BTK No 5267		"
31867	Number vacant		"
31868	CK No 3648		"
31869	CK (No 3678?)		D2129
31870	CK No 3634		D2130
31871	CK No 3705		D2129

TABLE 5d: THE 1933 RENUMBERING OF LMS PASSENGER BRAKE VANS

The following number lists are given in the same carriage diagram order as Table 5b for standard designs and are, of course, applicable only to pre-1934 examples. The pre-1934 numbers of the ex-World War 1 conversions, their post-1933 numbers being somewhat randomly disposed (see Table 5a), are offered in the single list form which the LMS also adopted. In 1933 they were given a continuous sequence from 31953-32019 and it is assumed that the precise order of their 1933 numbers reflected the actual dates of conversion to full brake form, regardless of specific diagram.

New Number	Old Number	New Number	Old Number	New Number	Old Number	New Number	Old Number	New Number	Old Number
Ex-Ambulance Vehicles		32013	5565	30451	6518	30514	439	30574	7059
		32014	5566	30452	6520	30515	442	30575	7061
		32015	5567	30453	6522	30516	2543	30576	7062
31953	512	32016	5568	30454	6523	30517	2376	30577	7063
31954	532	32017	5899	30455	6528	30518	2837	30578	7064
31955	2955	32018	261	30456	6530	30519	2881	30579	7065
31956	280	32019	3083	30457	6532	30520	2894	30580	7066
31957	296			30458	6534	30521	2896	30581	7067
31958	19	**LMS Standard**		30459	6537	30522	2949	30582	7068
31959	52	**Vehicles**		30460	6538	30523	3081	30583	7069
31960	60	**D1778**		30461	6542	30524	5408	30584	7070
31961	83			30462	6544	30525	5486	30585	7071
31962	103	30400	9	30463	6558	30526	5487	30586	7072
31963	173	30401	18	30464	6583	30527	5500	30587	7073
31964	237	30402	66	30465	6594	30528	5509	30588	7088
31965	242	30403	74	30466	6606	30529	6314	30589	7090
31966	255	30404	96	30467	6614	30530	6315	30590	7123
31967	2012	30405	114	30468	6629	30531	6321	30591	7137
31968	2013	30406	145	30469	6639	30532	6326	30592	7155
31969	2014	30407	183	30470	6646	30533	6422	30593	7157
31970	2015	30408	197	30471	6669	30534	6446	30594	7158
31971	5407	30409	231	30472	6881	30535	6453	30595	7371
31972	5438	30410	235	30473	6882	30536	6457	30596	7390
31973	5458	20411	259	30474	6883	30537	6459	30597	7399
31974	5502	30412	273	30475	6301	30538	6462	30598	7443
31975	5506	30413	275	30476	6313	30539	6467	30599	486
31976	5523	30414	288	30477	6328	30540	6470	30600	798
31977	5524	30415	291	30478	6337	30541	6473	30601	809
31978	5526	30416	292	30479	6340	30542	6487	30602	6323
31979	5527	30417	297	30480	6347	30543	6489	30603	6336
31980	5528	30418	299	30481	6359	30544	6997	30604	6343
31981	5529	30419	305	30482	6360	30545	7384	30605	6439
31982	5530	30420	311	30483	6368	30546	7442	30606	6444
31983	5532	30421	314	30484	6395	30547	7460	30607	6455
31984	5535	30422	325	30485	6443	30548	7468	30608	6501
31985	5537	30423	372	30486	6454			30609	6509
31986	5538	30424	381	30487	6463	**D1715**		30610	6557
31987	5539	30425	6302	30488	6468			30611	6720
31988	5540	30426	6329	30489	6471	30549	6205	30612	6761
31989	5541	30427	6345	30490	6496	30550	6218	30613	6774
31990	5542	30428	6348	30491	6499	30551	6219	30614	6809
31991	5543	30429	6349	30492	6500	30552	6220	30615	6813
31992	5544	30430	6350	30493	6519	30553	6221	30616	6814
31993	5545	30431	6351	30494	6539	30554	6222	30617	6854
31994	5546	30432	6356	30495	6541	30555	6223	30618	6864
31995	5547	30433	6362	30496	6551	30556	6224	30619	6866
31996	5548	30434	6375	30497	6552	30557	6225	30620	6874
31997	5549	30435	6388	30498	6559	30558	6226	30621	6878
31998	5550	30436	6434	30499	6569	30559	6227	30622	6879
31999	5551	30437	6436	30500	34	30560	7896	30623	7969
32000	5552	30438	6445	30501	77	30561	7897	30624	7970
32001	5553	30439	6447	30502	172	30562	7898	30625	7971
32002	5554	30440	6466	30503	178	30563	6995	30626	7972
32003	5555	30441	6493	30504	187	30564	6996	30627	7973
32004	5556	30442	6494	30505	199	30565	6997	30628	7974
32005	5557	30443	6497	30506	202	30566	6998	30629	7975
32006	5558	30444	6502	30507	208	30567	7052	30630	7976
32007	5559	30445	6510	30508	213	30568	7053	30631	7977
32008	5560	30446	6511	30509	224	30569	7054	30632	7978
32009	5561	30447	6512	30510	283	30570	7055	30633	7979
32010	5562	30448	6513	30511	316	30571	7056	30634	7980
32011	5563	30449	6514	30512	326	30572	7057	30635	7981
32012	5564	30450	6515	30513	327	30573	7058	30636	7982

New Number	Old Number	New Number	Old Number	New Number	Old Number	New Number	Old Number	New Number	Old Number
30637	7983	30708	7232	30779	5517	30850	194	32910	2866
30638	7984	30709	7234	30780	5518	30851	436	32911	2867
30639	7985	30710	7248	30781	6215	30852	565	32912	2869
30640	7986	30711	7251	30782	6490	30853	571	32913	2876
30641	7987	30712	7271	30783	6503	30854	2208	32914	2878
30642	7988	30713	7272	30784	6657	30855	2788	32915	2880
30643	7989	30714	7274	30785	6661	30856	2839	32916	2882
30644	7991	30715	7353	30786	7389	30857	2919	32917	2883
30645	7992	30716	7354	30787	7432	30858	2931	32918	2884
30646	7994	30717	7453	30788	7454	30859	2950	32919	2886
30647	7995	30718	7516	30789	7456	30860	2965	32920	2888
30648	7996	30719	7557	30790	7458	30861	2976	32921	2892
30649	745	30720	7560	30791	7469	30862	3021	32922	2893
30650	1519	30721	7580	30792	7904	30863	3096	32923	2895
30651	1810	30722	7583	30793	8124	30864	3100	32924	2897
30652	3373	30723	7589	30794	8136	30865	3113		
30653	3577	30724	7850	30795	8137	30866	3119	**D1854**	
30654	3655	30725	7967	30796	8146	30867	3122		
30655	3667	30726	7997	30797	8147	30868	3130	30908	7
30656	3696	30727	8001	30798	4282	30869	3143	30909	13
30657	3776	30728	8003	30799	8149	30870	4753	30910	20
30658	3778	30729	8006	30800	8150	30871	4754	30911	29
30659	4628	30730	8008	30801	8158	30872	4755	30912	51
30660	4694	30731	8009	30802	8166	30873	4756	30913	53
30661	4706	30732	8010	30803	8175	30874	5463	30914	58
30662	4843	30733	8012	30804	8177	30875	6488	30915	59
30663	5196	30734	8122	30805	8179	30876	7006	30916	70
30664	5256	30735	8125	30806	8645	30877	7435	30917	71
30665	5263	30736	8131	30807	8646	30878	6	30918	73
30666	5265	30737	8134	30808	8647	30879	320	30919	88
30667	5280	30738	8148	30809	8648	30880	573	30920	97
30668	5290	30739	8161	30810	8649	30881	1615	30921	107
30669	5307	30740	8178	30811	8650	30882	1631	30922	110
30670	5424	30741	8181	30812	8651	30883	1632	30923	112
30671	5664	30742	8182	30813	8652	30884	1645	30924	125
30672	5676	30743	539	30814	8653	30885	1666	30925	341
30673	5987	30744	2852	30815	8654	30886	1678	30926	378
30674	6160	30745	2854	30816	8655	30887	1687	30927	382
30675	6263	30746	2913	30817	8656	30888	1691	30928	397
30676	6266	30747	3001	30818	8657	30889	1694	30929	400
30677	6316	30748	166	30819	8658	30890	1703	30930	455
30678	6341	30749	167	30820	8659	30891	1752	30931	577
30679	6354	30750	193	30821	8660	30892	2832	30932	588
30680	6358	30751	360	30822	8661	30893	3000	30933	471
30681	6405	30752	518	30823	8662	30894	3027	30934	557
30682	6448	30753	2844	30824	8663	30895	3112	30935	558
30683	6458	30754	2870	30825	8664	30896	4757	30936	578
30684	6486	30755	2890	30826	8665	30897	4758	30937	605
30685	6531	30756	2918	30827	8666	30898	4759	30938	612
30686	6545	30757	2943	30828	8667	30899	5993	30939	622
30687	6550	30758	3018	30829	8668	30900	5998	30940	623
30688	6563	30759	3026	30830	8669	30901	6012	30941	697
30689	6564	30760	3029	30831	8670	30902	6015	30942	708
30690	6574	30761	3043	30832	8671	30903	6069	30943	726
30691	6592	30762	3086	30833	8672	30904	6079	30944	959
30692	6611	30763	3090	30834	8673	30905	6080	30945	1025
30693	6612	30764	3097	30835	8674	30906	7281	30946	1027
30694	6556	30765	3114	30836	8675	30907	7306	30947	1031
30695	285	30766	3142	30837	8676			30948	1032
30696	295	30767	3144	30838	8677	**D1796**		30949	1040
30697	546	30768	3146	30839	8678			30950	1043
30698	566	30769	3147	30840	8679	32900	2842	30951	1044
30699	6625	30770	5403	30841	8680	32901	2848	30952	1061
30700	6769	30771	5416	30842	8681	32902	2849	30953	1073
30701	6783	30772	5447	30843	8682	32903	2851	30954	1081
30702	6848	30773	5454	30844	8683	32904	2853	30955	1087
30703	6851	30774	5455	30845	8684	32905	2858	30956	1089
30704	6877	30775	5457	30846	8685	32906	2859	30957	1123
30705	7136	30776	5476	30847	8586	32907	2860		
30706	7201	30777	5481	30848	175	32908	2861		
30707	7219	30778	5482	30849	176	32909	2862		

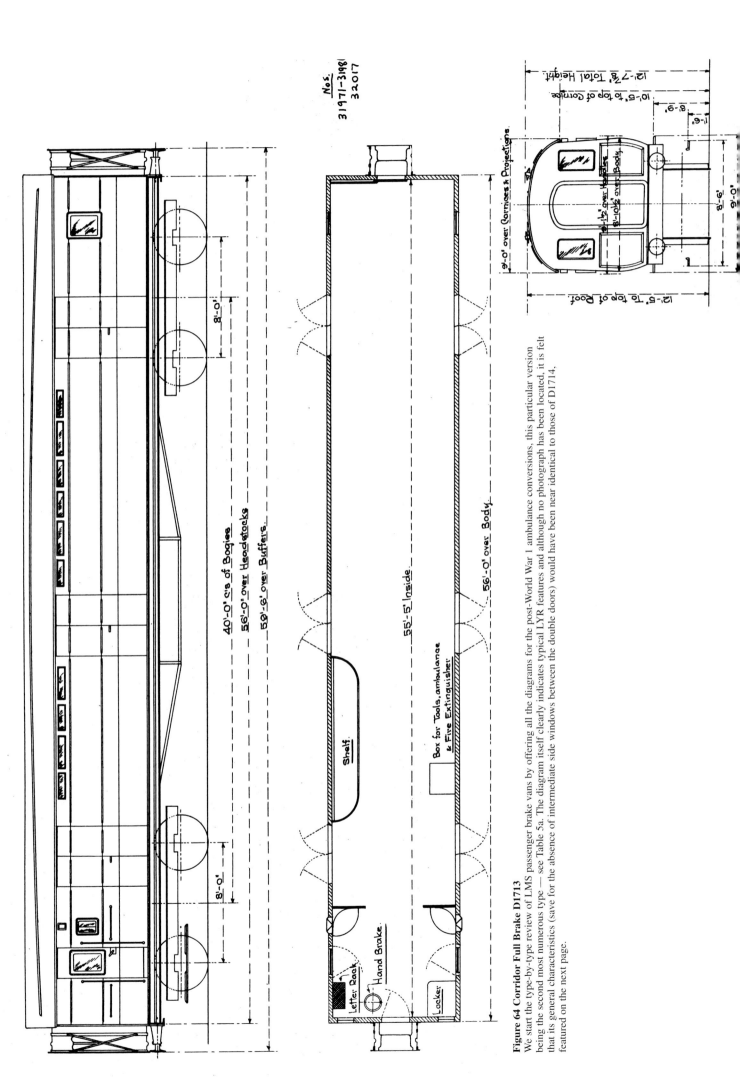

Figure 64 Corridor Full Brake D1713

We start the type-by-type review of LMS passenger brake vans by offering all the diagrams for the post-World War 1 ambulance conversions, this particular version being the second most numerous type — see Table 5a. The diagram itself clearly indicates typical LYR features and although no photograph has been located, it is felt that its general characteristics (save for the absence of intermediate side windows between the double doors) would have been near identical to those of D1714, featured on the next page.

Nos. 31971-31981 32017

40'-0' c's of Bogies

56'-0" over Headstocks

59'-6' over Buffers

8'-0'

8'-0'

55'-5' Inside

56'-0' over Body.

Shelf.

Box for Tools, ambulance & Fire Extinguisher.

Hand Brake.

Letter Rack

Locker.

12'-7⅜' Total Height

10'-6" to top of Cornice

8'-9'

1'-6'

9'-0' over Cornices & Projections

13'-1½' over handles

8'-10½' over Body.

8'-6'

9'-0'

12'-5' To top of Roof.

115

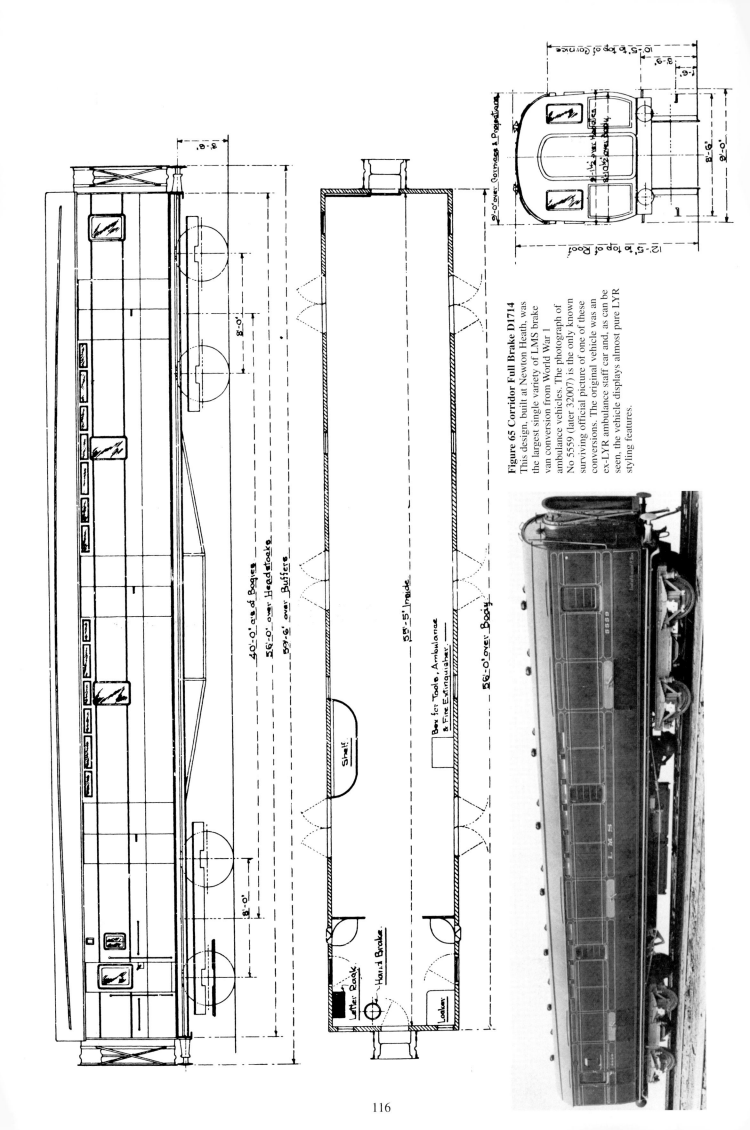

Figure 65 Corridor Full Brake D1714
This design, built at Newton Heath, was the largest single variety of LMS brake van conversion from World War 1 ambulance vehicles. The photograph of No 5559 (later 32007) is the only known surviving official picture of one of these conversions. The original vehicle was an ex-LYR ambulance staff car and, as can be seen, the vehicle displays almost pure LYR styling features.

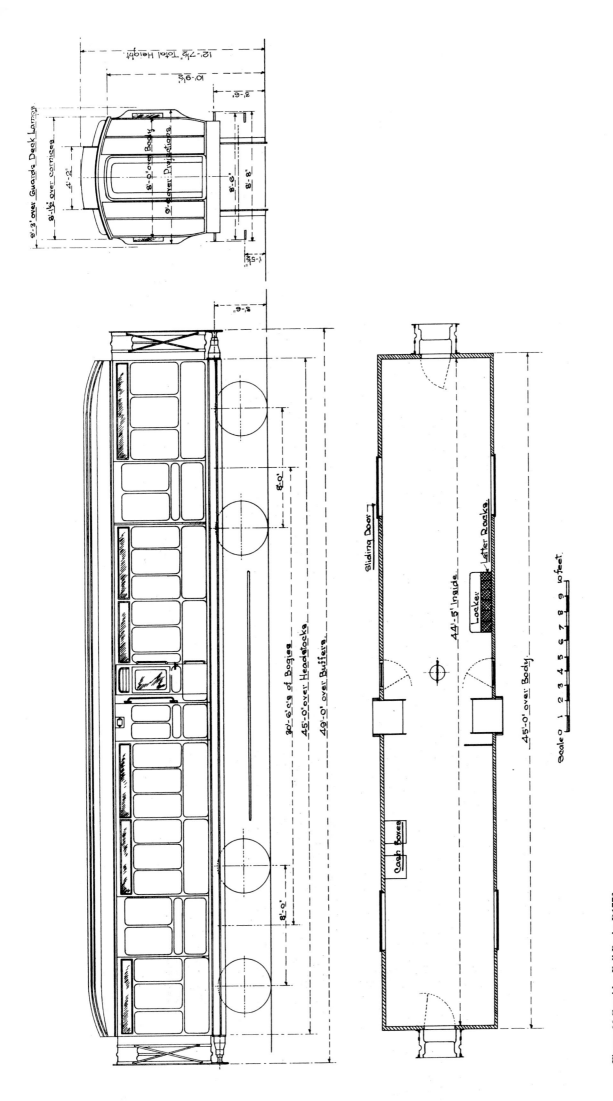

Figure 66 Corridor Full Brake D1773

This rather attractive clerestory design with sliding doors and central lookout originated on the LNWR in 1902, being designated as a cycle van to LNWR D381B. Converted to ward cars during World War 1, they were mostly reinstated as full brakes after 1918, the majority regaining their original LNWR diagram identity in this revised form. This pair, however, were presumably reinstated after the Grouping and thus given LMS series diagram numbers on conversion to full brake.

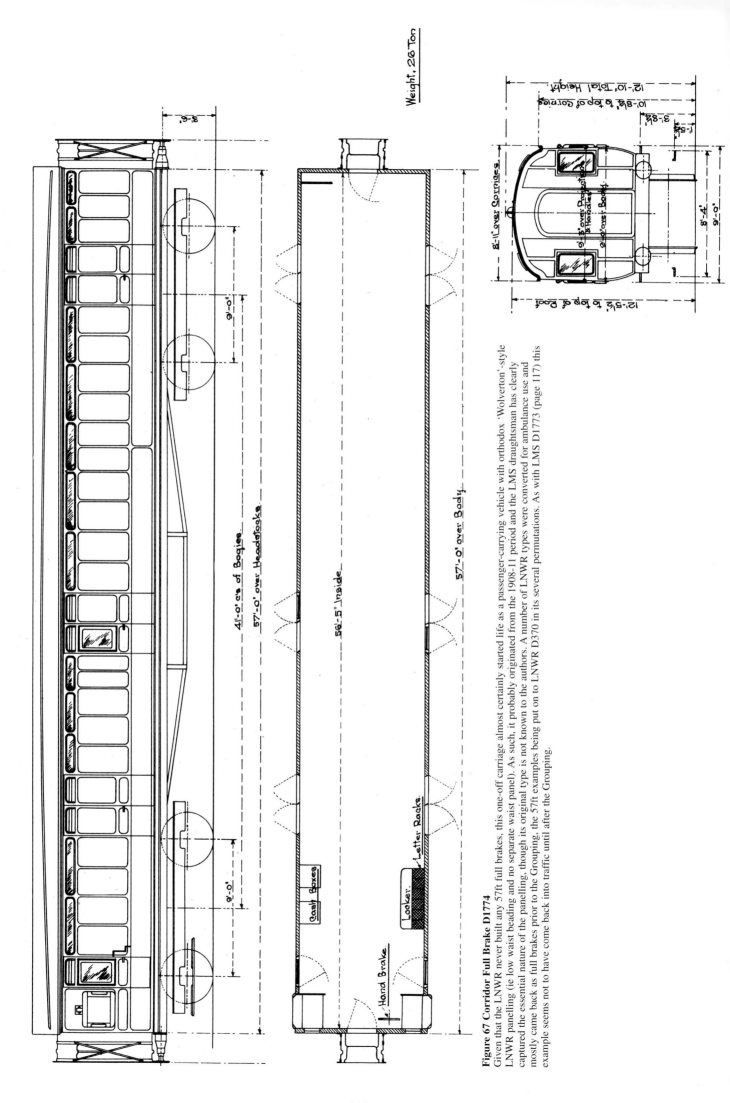

Weight, 26 Ton

3'-6"

9'-0"

41'-0' c'rs of Bogies.

57'-0' over Headstocks.

9'-0'

56'-5" inside

57'-0' over Body

Cash Boxes

Locker.

Letter Rack.

Hand Brake

8'-11' over Carriages.

12'-10' Total Height

10'-8¾' to top of Cornice

3'-8¾'

1'-0"

8'-4'

9'-0'

10'-3' over Projections & Handles.

9'-10' over Body.

12'-5½' to top of Roof.

Figure 67 Corridor Full Brake D1774

Given that the LNWR never built any 57ft full brakes, this one-off carriage almost certainly started life as a passenger-carrying vehicle with orthodox 'Wolverton'-style LNWR panelling (ie low waist beading and no separate waist panel). As such, it probably originated from the 1908-11 period and the LMS draughtsman has clearly captured the essential nature of the panelling, though its original type is not known to the authors. A number of LNWR types were converted for ambulance use and mostly came back as full brakes prior to the Grouping, the 57ft examples being put on to LNWR D370 in its several permutations. As with LMS D1773 (page 117) this example seems not to have come back into traffic until after the Grouping.

118

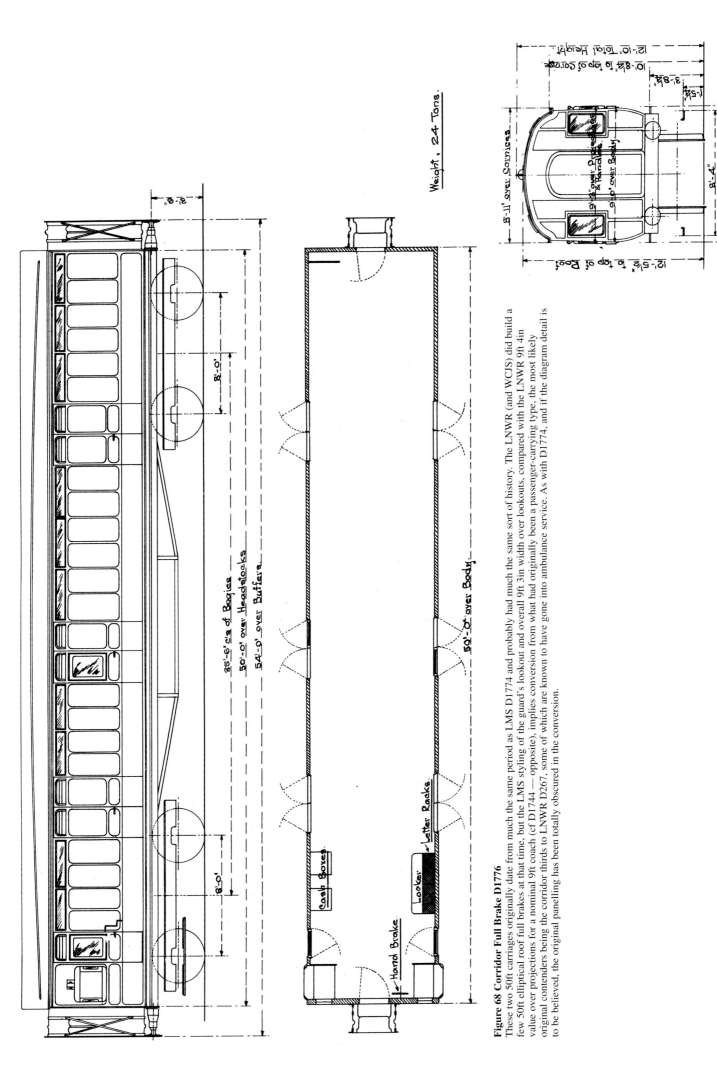

Weight, 24 Tons.

8'-0" over Cornices

10'-8½" to top of Cornice

12'-10' Total Height

3'-8½"

1'-5½"

9'-3 over Droplights & Handles

9'-10' over Body

8'-4"

9'-0"

12'-5½" to top of Roof

8'-2"

8'-0"

8'-0"

35'-6' c'rs of Bogies

50'-0" over Headstocks

54'-0' over Buffers

50'-0" over Body

Letter Racks

Locker

Cash Boxes

Hand Brake

Figure 68 Corridor Full Brake D1776

These two 50ft carriages originally date from much the same period as LMS D1774 and probably had much the same sort of history. The LNWR (and WCJS) did build a few 50ft elliptical roof full brakes at that time, but the LMS styling of the guard's lookout and overall 9ft 3in width over lookouts, compared with the LNWR 9ft 4in value over projections for a nominal 9ft coach (cf D1744 — opposite), implies conversion from what had originally been a passenger-carrying type, the most likely original contenders being the corridor thirds to LNWR D267, some of which are known to have gone into ambulance service. As with D1774, and if the diagram detail is to be believed, the original panelling has been totally obscured in the conversion.

119

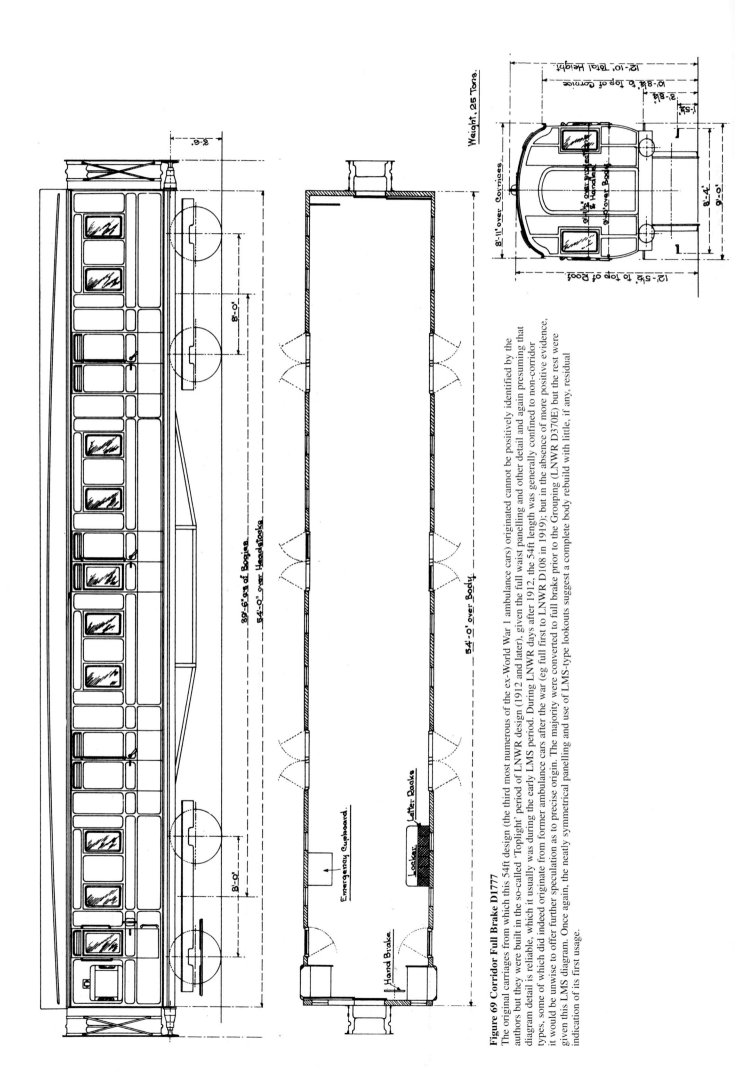

Weight, 25 Tons.

Figure 69 Corridor Full Brake D1777

The original carriages from which this 54ft design (the third most numerous of the ex-World War 1 ambulance cars) originated cannot be positively identified by the authors but they were built in the so-called 'Toplight' period of LNWR design (1912 and later), given the full waist panelling and other detail and again presuming that diagram detail is reliable, which it usually was during the early LMS period. During LNWR days after 1912, the 54ft length was generally confined to non-corridor types, some of which did indeed originate from former ambulance cars after the war (eg full first to LNWR D108 in 1919); but in the absence of more positive evidence, it would be unwise to offer further speculation as to precise origin. The majority were converted to full brake prior to the Grouping (LNWR D370E) but the rest were given this LMS diagram. Once again, the neatly symmetrical panelling and use of LMS-type lookouts suggest a complete body rebuild with little, if any, residual indication of its first usage.

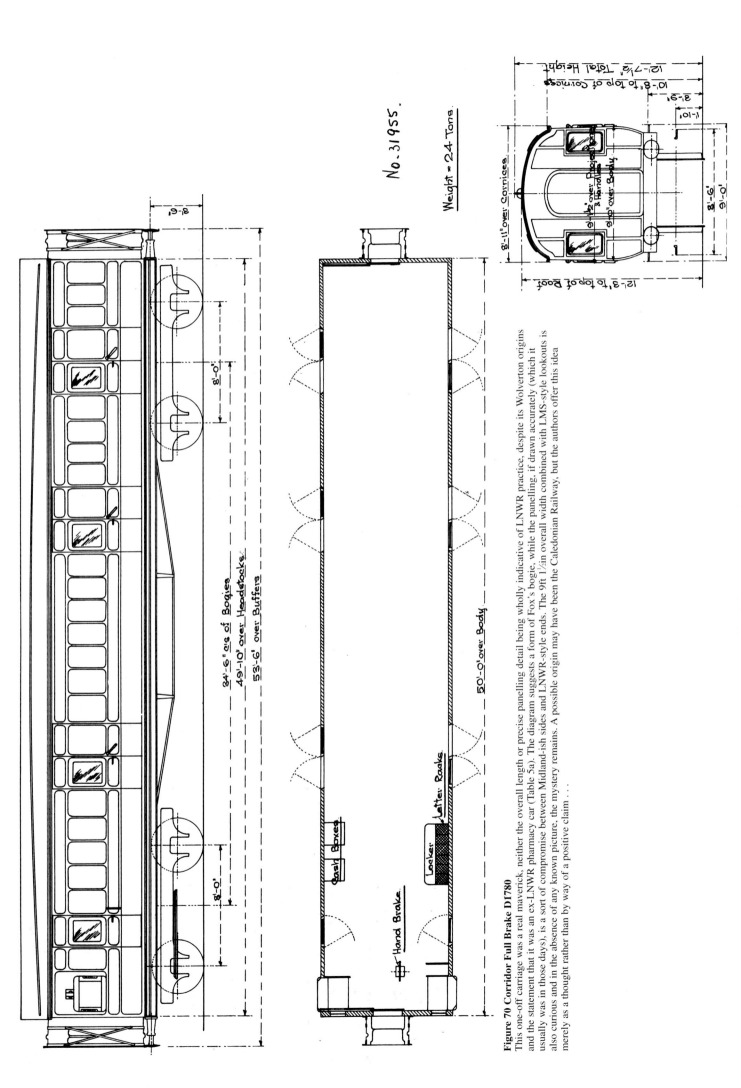

No. 31955.

Weight = 24 Tons.

Figure 70 Corridor Full Brake D1780

This one-off carriage was a real maverick, neither the overall length or precise panelling detail being wholly indicative of LNWR practice, despite its Wolverton origins and the statement that it was an ex-LNWR pharmacy car (Table 5a). The diagram suggests a form of Fox's bogie, while the panelling, if drawn accurately (which it usually was in those days), is a sort of compromise between Midland-ish sides and LNWR-style ends. The 9ft 1½in overall width combined with LMS-style lookouts is also curious and in the absence of any known picture, the mystery remains. A possible origin may have been the Caledonian Railway, but the authors offer this idea merely as a thought rather than by way of a positive claim . . . .

121

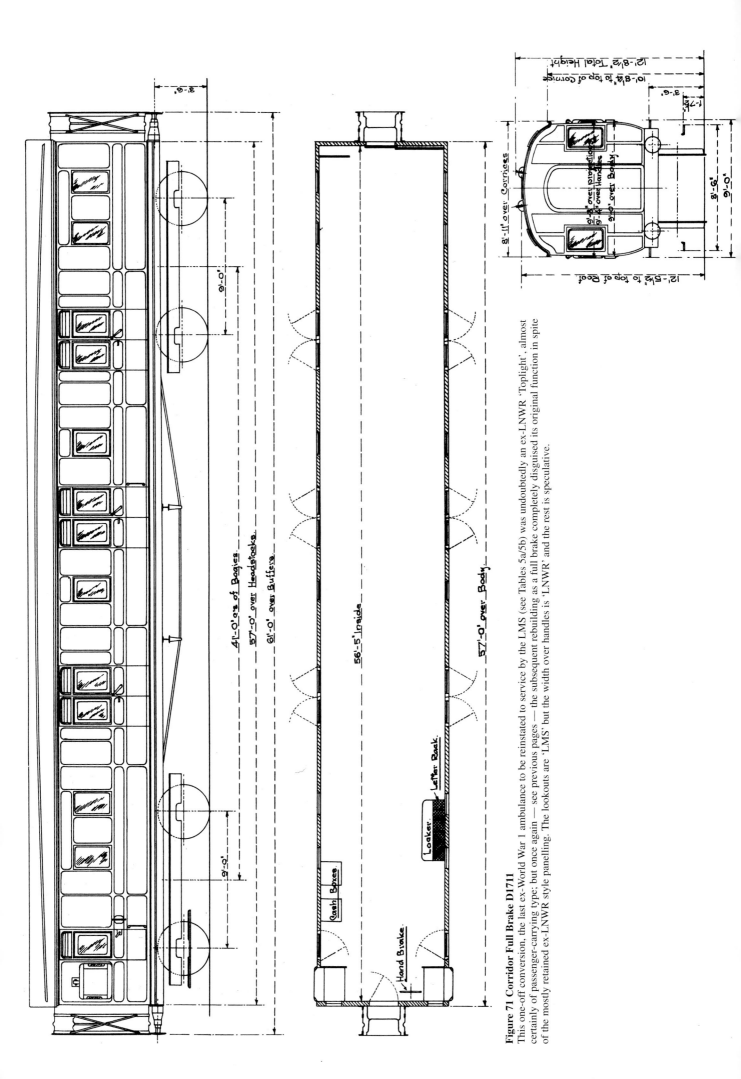

Figure 71 Corridor Full Brake D1711

This one-off conversion, the last ex-World War 1 ambulance to be reinstated to service by the LMS (see Tables 5a/5b) was undoubtedly an ex-LNWR 'Toplight', almost certainly of passenger-carrying type; but once again — see previous pages — the subsequent rebuilding as a full brake completely disguised its original function in spite of the mostly retained ex-LNWR style panelling. The lookouts are 'LMS' but the width over handles is 'LNWR' and the rest is speculative.

Figure 72 Corridor Full Brake D1778

The LMS Period I 50ft full brake to D1778, although not the most numerous of the several 50ft diagrams, undoubtedly established the style for all subsequent full brakes to LMS design. As can be seen from the picture of No 5509 (later 30528), these coaches were all given the fully lined livery, probably lined in gold rather than yellow in order to match the gangwayed stock with which they most often ran. Note the non-standard torpedo ventilators of this Wolverton-built example.

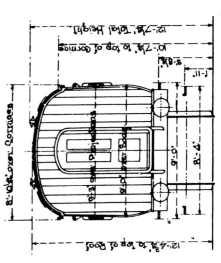

123

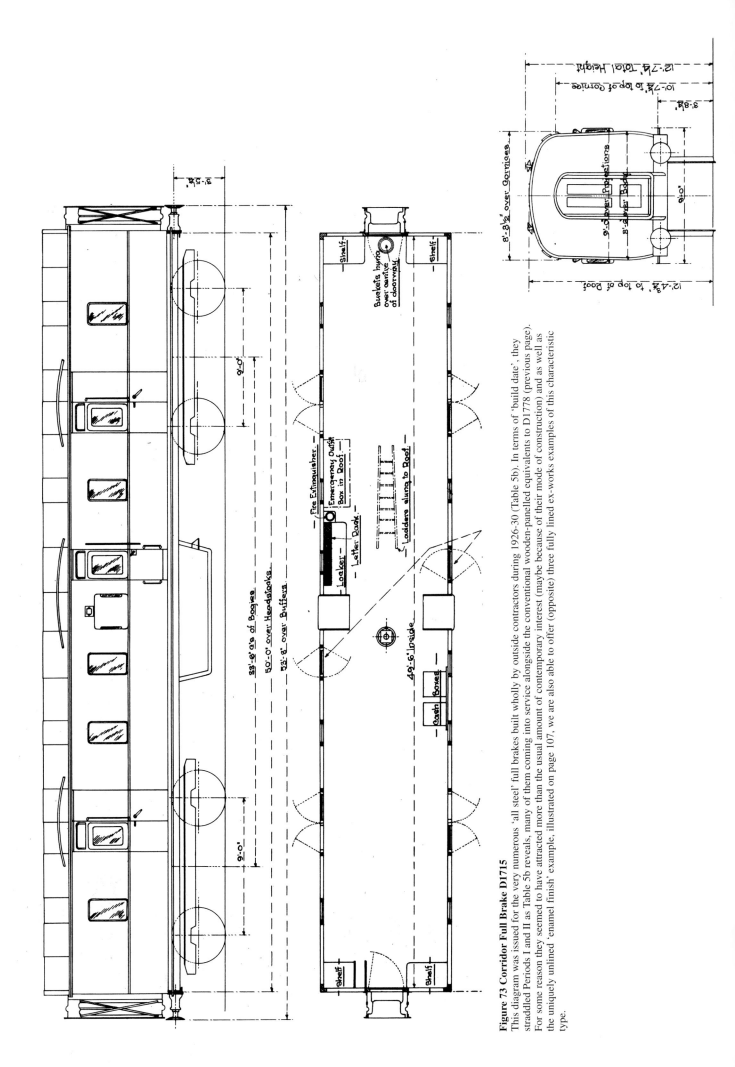

Figure 73 Corridor Full Brake D1715

This diagram was issued for the very numerous 'all steel' full brakes built wholly by outside contractors during 1926-30 (Table 5b). In terms of 'build date', they straddled Periods I and II as Table 5b reveals, many of them coming into service alongside the conventional wooden-panelled equivalents to D1778 (previous page). For some reason they seemed to have attracted more than the usual amount of contemporary interest (maybe because of their mode of construction) and as well as the uniquely unlined 'enamel finish' example, illustrated on page 107, we are also able to offer (opposite) three fully lined ex-works examples of this characteristic type.

This first view shows LMS No 6996, later 30564, from the original 1926-7 batch of all-steel brakes from Birmingham C&W. The fully lined livery is pure 'Period I' save for the absence of the customary two-tone roof treatment (black and grey — see Volume 1) which seems, instead, to have been replaced by a plain grey treatment. The white wheel tyres were arguably a bit up-market for a full brake, but were not unique — see final view, below.

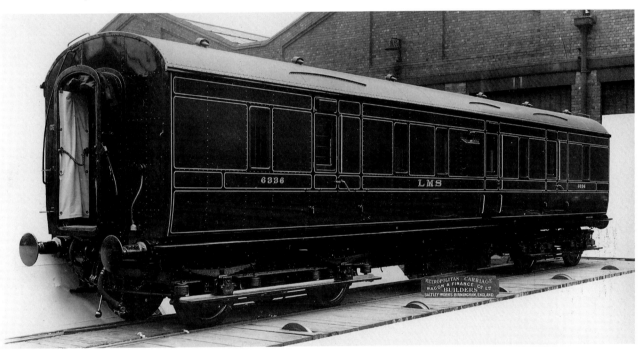

This official Metropolitan Carriage Wagon & Finance Co Ltd view of LMS No 6336, later 30603, shows one of the earlier 1927 examples of D1715 from this firm in what was still the standard 'Period I' livery, near-identical to that of No 6996 (above). Note, however, the additional visible surface riveting compared with the Birmingham batch and the fact that the roof of this example seems to have been given a sort of silver-grey paint finish — but no white tyres . . .

This third view shows No 4755, later 30872, from Metro-Cammell in 1930 when low-waisted Period II designs were normal for passenger-carrying gangwayed stock. It is likely that the high-waisted nature of a full brake probably prompted the traditional 'Period I' livery but the insignia positioning (and numeral style) is in the Period II arrangement and there are subtle changes (eg roof rainstrips and length of battery boxes) compared with the previous examples. The underframe treatment (including bogies, wheels and tyres) seems to have retained a works grey finish while the roof colour is indeterminate, though not two-tone (probably plain grey).

Figure 74 Corridor Full Brake D1796

Although six-wheel full brakes were very common amongst the LMS constituent companies, the LMS itself did not build any until 1932. D1796 was one of the very first Stanier carriage diagrams and, as with all the early Stanier stock, was given the full livery. This particular design also had torpedo ventilators and side lights above the lookouts. It was also one of the few Stanier designs to emerge before the major renumbering scheme and early examples had old series numbers such as 2860, illustrated, which later became 32907. These vehicles lasted a long time and were later fitted with stoves.

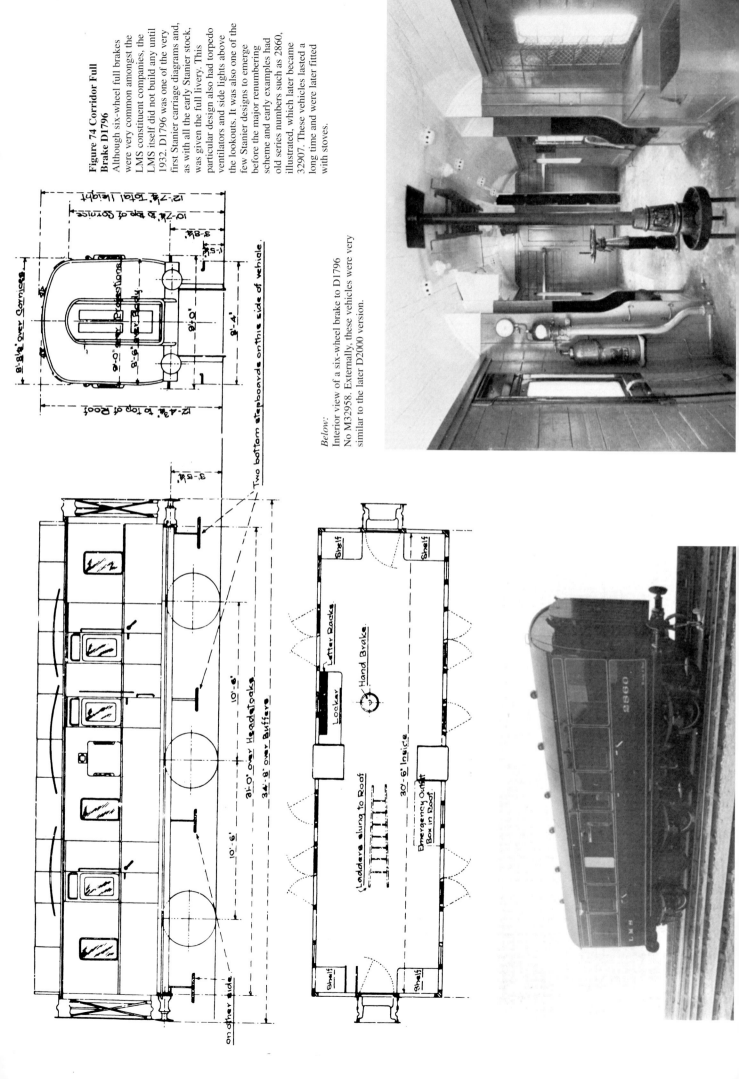

Below:
Interior view of a six-wheel brake to D1796 No M32958. Externally, these vehicles were very similar to the later D2000 version.

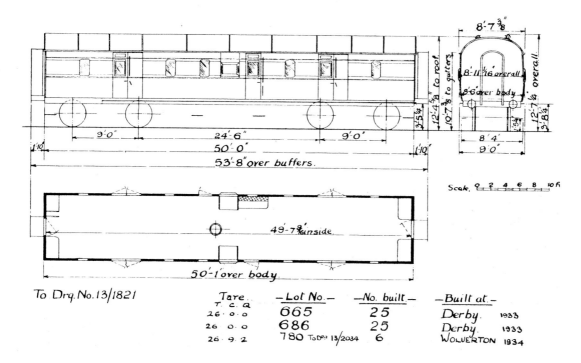

To Drg. No. 13/1821

Tare T. C. Q	— Lot No. —	— No. built —	— Built at —
26 · 0 · 0	665	25	Derby. 1933
26 · 0 · 0	686	25	Derby 1933
26 · 9 · 2	780 ToD⁰ 13/2034	6	WOLVERTON 1934

Figure 75 Corridor Full Brake D1854

This somewhat basic diagram (typical of the mid-1930s changes) shows the general features of the first Period III full brakes, built only in modest numbers — see Table 5b. Unfortunately, no picture can be offered but, as with D1796, these were some of the very few Period III types to have pre-1933 numbers.

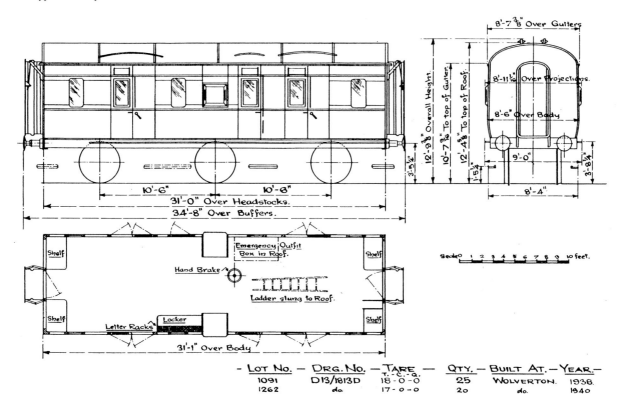

— Lot No. —	Drg. No.	Tare T.·C.·Q.	Qty.	— Built At. —	Year. —
1091	D13/1813D	18 - 0 - 0	25	Wolverton.	1938.
1262	do	17 - 0 - 0	20	do.	1940

Figure 76 Corridor Full Brake D2000

This six-wheel diagram was all but identical to D1796 and it is hard to see why a new diagram was issued for no more than a minor shift of hand-brake position. As with the D1796 examples, they were later fitted with stoves, thus becoming the familiar 'Stove R' of more recent times — 'R' being the LMS code for a full brake. The type is pictured on page 108.

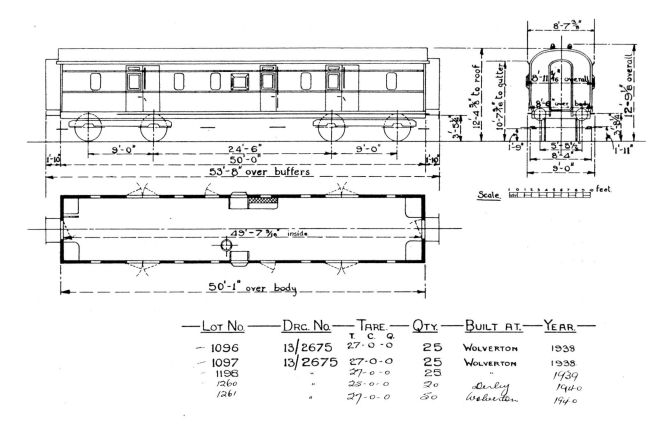

Lot No.	Drg. No.	Tare. T. C. Q.	Qty.	Built At.	Year.
1096	13/2675	27-0-0	25	Wolverton	1938
1097	13/2675	27-0-0	25	Wolverton	1938
1198	"	27-0-0	25	"	1939
1260	"	25-0-0	20	Derby	1940
1261	"	27-0-0	50	Wolverton	1940

Figure 77 Corridor Full Brake D2007

This design was, marginally, the most numerous of the LMS standard 50ft full brakes and is illustrated on page 109. There was no significant difference between these and the D1854 versions (see previous page) apart from the upgraded carrying capacity of some of the D2007 examples (see Table 5b) and these were the types which, ultimately, became the last LMS-design carriages in BR revenue service, albeit usually stripped of gangways in their final years.

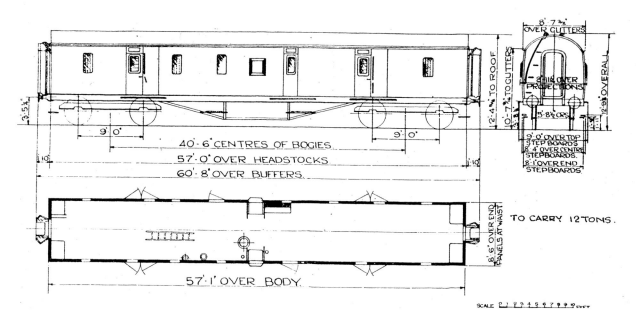

Figure 78 Corridor Full Brake D2100

Illustrated on page 109, these were the only standard 57ft full brakes built by the LMS. Using second-hand underframes and maybe allowed to be built (1944) for that reason alone given the urgent need for such vehicles, only their length distinguished them from their normal Period III equivalents — and they lasted just as long.

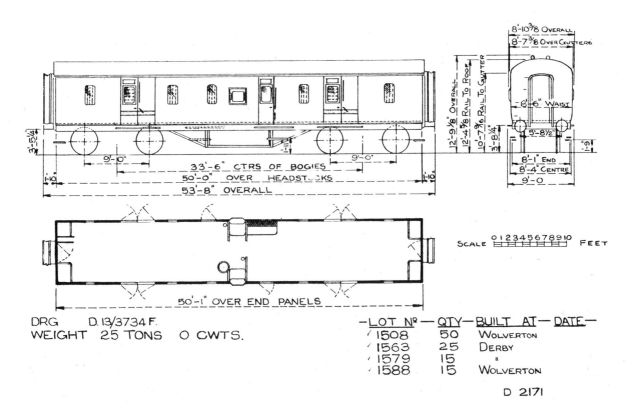

DRG   D.13/3734 F.
WEIGHT 25 TONS   O CWTS.

LOT №	QTY	BUILT AT	DATE
1508	50	WOLVERTON	
1563	25	DERBY	
1579	15	"	
1588	15	WOLVERTON	

D 2171

Figure 79 Corridor Full Brake D2171
This, the final LMS standard 50ft full brake diagram, was issued for the post-BR build of the type, though apart from carrying capacity, it was in no way significantly changed from the earlier D1845/2007 versions covered previously. The diagram itself implies that 50 examples were intended for Lot 1508 but, as Table 5b indicates, only 25 were actually built to that lot number. The illustration shows No M31374 (the first example from Lot 1563 — Derby 1949) in its typical original early BR livery — note the BR-type roof ventilators.

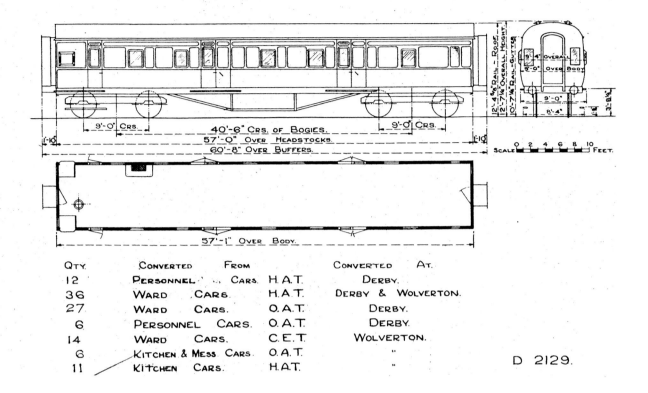

QTY.	CONVERTED FROM		CONVERTED AT.
12	PERSONNEL CARS.	H.A.T.	DERBY.
36	WARD CARS.	H.A.T.	DERBY & WOLVERTON.
27	WARD CARS.	O.A.T.	DERBY.
6	PERSONNEL CARS.	O.A.T.	DERBY.
14	WARD CARS.	C.E.T.	WOLVERTON.
6	KITCHEN & MESS CARS.	O.A.T.	"
11	KITCHEN CARS.	H.A.T.	"

D 2129.

Figures 80/81 Corridor Full Brake D2129/2130

We conclude this full brake survey as we began with ambulance conversions, but this time from a generation later: World War 2. Typical examples are illustrated on page 110, full running number details are offered in Table 5c (page 112) and on this page are the somewhat basic diagrams themselves. They do not give too many clues as to precise type origin, nor do we believe that such detail as is shown is much more than generally representative of the vehicles. It was clearly a 'cheap and cheerful' operation at the time, as may well have been the similar exercise after World War 1, but it no doubt made economic sense. Given the stylistic variations of the original vehicles, we reckon that the main reason for two diagrams was probably a function of the different double-door positions, D2129 (upper) having the first pair somewhat further away from the guard's end than D2130 (lower).

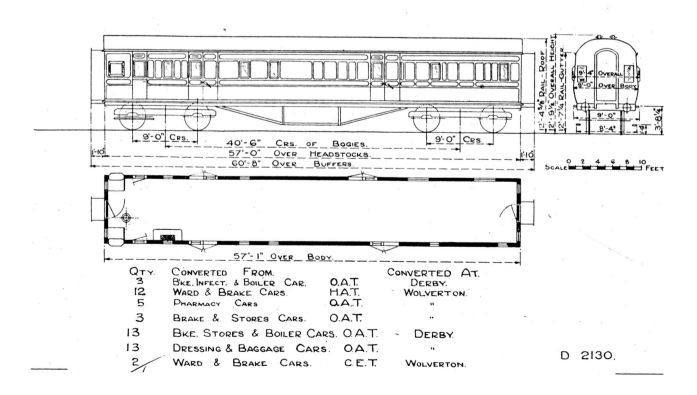

QTY.	CONVERTED FROM.		CONVERTED AT.
3	BKE. INFECT. & BOILER CAR.	O.A.T.	DERBY.
12	WARD & BRAKE CARS.	H.A.T.	WOLVERTON.
5	PHARMACY CARS	O.A.T.	"
3	BRAKE & STORES CARS.	O.A.T.	"
13	BKE. STORES & BOILER CARS.	O.A.T.	DERBY.
13	DRESSING & BAGGAGE CARS.	O.A.T.	"
2	WARD & BRAKE CARS.	C.E.T.	WOLVERTON.

D 2130.

Chapter 6 - Post Office Vehicles

In the LMS/LMR carriage diagram book there are listed 68 GPO vehicles built to no less than 20 separate diagrams. Of these 20 diagrams, two account for some 36 of the 68 coaches involved so it will be readily appreciated that unlike most other LMS-design coaches, it is not really possible to make any form of valid generalisation about Post Office coaches, other than to say that they were of two basic types: stowage and sorting vans.

As far as the authors can deduce, the reasons for this variety probably stem from the operation of the vehicles themselves. Firstly, Post Office vehicles generally seem to have been built as planned replacements on a one-for-one basis for vehicles scheduled to be withdrawn. Thus, the replacement coach often had to satisfy the requirements of the service being operated by the coach/coaches scheduled for withdrawal. This probably meant, in turn, that many vehicles were tailor-made for specific services. This would undoubtedly give one possible reason for the number of one-off diagrams and the often quite trivial but bewildering differences in such matters as interior fittings and so forth which these vehicles displayed.

Unfortunately, however, it has not been possible to find any evidence of the utilisation of Post Office coaches which sheds much light on the situation and the only information which has survived is that pertaining to the coaches themselves which is summarised, as far as it is known, in Table 6.

Turning now to the vehicles themselves, it is possible to make a few comments which are generally applicable to most LMS Post Office coaches. The division into Periods I, II and III was only immediately noticeable in the method of roof construction adopted — there being no fully beaded LMS Post Office coaches. Full livery was adopted for the pre-1934 built examples when new but this was only a transitory difference.

As far as there was a typical design it is represented by D1792 (Fig 83). These were 60ft coaches and the diagram was current from 1930 to 1939 so it contains both Period II and Period III coaches. Internally, the layout was typical of all LMS *sorting* coaches. The corridor connection was offset and the sorting racks were on the non-corridor side. From the outside the racks could be distinguished by 'bulges' in the exterior panelling. The corridor side of the coach carried the pick-up net which was located at the right-hand end of the coach. Most LMS sorting coaches had a lavatory on the shelf side at the same end as the pick-up nets. However, a few individual coaches did not have this lavatory — even though it was shown on the diagram.

Deviations from this style in such diagrams as D1908 and D1970 were mainly in the nature of variations in length from the normal 60ft or slight alterations to the interior. One presumes that the length deviations which justified fresh diagrams were probably made to enable the coaches to run on lines with a more limited loading gauge than would clear the standard 60ft coach.

Some sorting carriages were not fitted with pick-up apparatus although carrying the recessed body side panelling where it would be fitted. Some of these coaches may have originally had the nets but this is not known with certainty. Detail differences where known are given in the summary table but there are gaps in the available information.

There were rather fewer stowage vans built to LMS design than sorting vans; in general they were shorter in length although there were some 60ft examples. In so far as there was an interior design for these vehicles, it took the form of the occasional provision of such features as wardrobes (for the GPO staff?), lavatories, folding tables, ovens and so forth. In general, however, these vehicles usually possessed a completely unfurnished interior and such fittings as were provided, if any at all, occupied but a small proportion of the floor space. Most vehicles in the stowage category were of standard LMS lengths (eg D1793), but there were two noteworthy exceptions.

D1883 was built in 1933 and was a 42ft vehicle. In some respects it was similar to the 42ft luggage/parcels van of the same vintage (see Volume 1) except that D1883 had gangway connections and tumblehome sides rather than end loading doors and flat sides. D1876 of the same year was also a little odd. This was a six-wheel full brake but it had no interior fittings at all and no gangway connection.

Post Office sorting van No 3242, later 30232, was the first LMS TPO vehicle to be built (D1794) and was a 'one-off' coach. Apart from the LMS standard underframe, it was very much in the LNWR/WCJS tradition as regards body styling. Even the LMS gave its pseudo-panelling an LNWR look by the semi-circular ends to the waist lining panels.

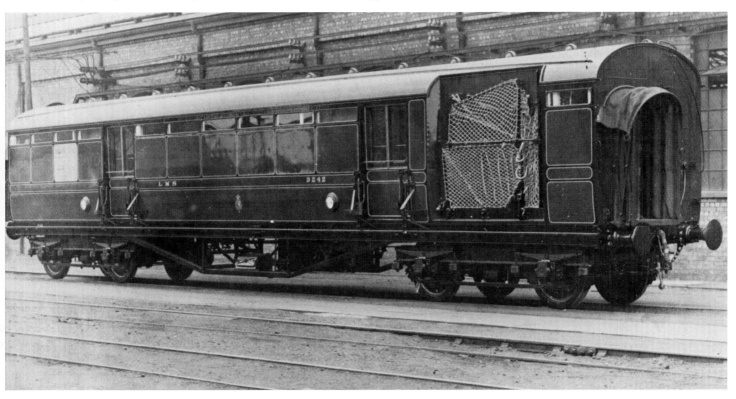

Both these unusual coaches were 'one-offs' and no reason for their very marked deviation from standard practice can be adduced. The LMS did not even distinguish them with the title of Stowage Van — they were simply 'Vans'.

Although the 1932/3 renumbering placed GPO vehicles in the 30200-30399 series, a quick perusal of the tables will indicate that there was no logic in the numbering of individual coaches. Some carried the numbers of the vehicles they replaced which would have been logical if universally applied but this was not so. For example 30307-8 eventually replaced 30261-2!

The only other point to make in this general discussion on GPO coaches is the very late date at which LMS-design vehicles in this category were emerging. D2193 has, it is believed, the highest LMS series lot number to be issued for a passenger-rated vehicle.

Many LMS-design GPO vehicles outlived their passenger-carrying contemporaries and it is conceivable that, pro rata, more GPO type coaches survived to receive the BR blue/grey livery than any other group of LMS-design coaches. For this reason, withdrawal dates are not usually known.

TABLE 6: SUMMARY TABLE OF LMS STANDARD GPO VEHICLES

Note: In the case of those examples built before the 1933 renumbering, essentially D1792 (page 134) and D1793 (page 144), the earlier running numbers are given with these two types.

Type	Diag	Lot	Qty	Date	Built	Dimensions (L x W x H) (See Footnote)	Weight	Period	Running Numbers	Withdrawals First	Withdrawals Last	Remarks
POS	1794	472	1	1929	Wolverton	57ft x 8ft 8in x 12ft 5½ in	31T	II	30232			The 'standard' LMS-pattern GPO sorting coach. Change to simple livery came with Period III Lot 772. Lots 502/611/877 did not have a toilet. These coaches were often plated as 9ft 10in wide (presumably measured over the pick-up equipment). Nos 30250/51 had the pick-up equipment removed at least by 1957 and several more followed suit.
POS	1792	502	3	1930	Wolverton	60ft x 8ft 8in x 12ft 4¼ in	32T	II (Flush)	30233-30235			
		564	3	1931	Wolverton		33T	II (Flush)	30266-30268			
		Part 611	3	1931	Wolverton		32T	II (Flush)	30213-30215	8/48		
		Part 611	3	1931	Wolverton		32T	II (Flush)	30246-30248			
		612	1	1931	Wolverton		33T	II (Flush)	30314			
		772	3	1934	Wolverton		32T	III	30216-30218			
		773	1	1934	Wolverton		32T	III	30219			
		877	3	1935	Wolverton		32T	III	30220-30222	5/48		
		987	1	1936	Wolverton		34T	III	30230			
		1059	3	1937	Wolverton		33T	III	30249-30251			
		1197	3	1939	Wolverton		33T	III	30289-30291			
POS	1908	774	1	1934	Wolverton	57ft x 8ft 8in x 12ft 4⅜ in	30T	III	30204			Basically a 57ft version of D1792 but no lavatory.
POS	1970	1052	2	1937	Wolverton	60ft x 8ft 8in x 12ft 4⅜ in	33T	III	30223-30224			A genuine Period III version of D1792 but with slightly altered interior.
POS	2043	1238	1	1939	Wolverton	60ft x 8ft 8in x 12ft 4⅜ in	32T	III	30225			As for D1970 but without lavatory.
POS	2175	1443	2	1947	Wolverton	60ft x 8ft 8in x 12ft 4⅜ in	31T	III	30292-30293			Lot 1443 originally listed on D2043. Not fitted with pick-up apparatus.
		1606	1	1950	Wolverton		31T	III	30281			
POS	2140	1488	3	1948	Wolverton	60ft x 8ft 8in x 12ft 4⅜ in	31T	III	30294-30296			Virtually as for D2043 but slightly altered interior fittings. No 30277 replaced 30294.
		1604	2	1950	Wolverton		32T	III	30277-30278			
POS	2167	1507	2	1949	Wolverton	60ft x 8ft 8in x 12ft 4⅜ in	32T	III	30269-30270			As for D2140 but fitted with lavatory.
		1559	3	1950	Wolverton		33T	III	30271-30273			
		1560	1	1950	Wolverton		33T	III	30274			
		1619	3	1950	Wolverton		32T	III	30297-30299			
POS	2185	1620	3	1954	Wolverton	57ft x 8ft 8in x 12ft 4⅜ in	30T	III	30300-30302			No pick-up gear but fitted wardrobe and lavatory.
POS	2188	1673	1	1954	Wolverton	60ft x 8ft 8in x 12ft 4⅜ in	30T	III	30303			Fitted extra tables plus heating stove and oven. No pick-up gear but fitted with lavatory.
POS	2191	1674	2	1954	Wolverton	60ft x 8ft 8in x 12ft 4⅜ in	Not known	III	30307-30308			Coaches had recesses for pick-up nets but the latter were not fitted.
POS	2193	1689	2	1957*	Wolverton	57ft x 8ft 8in x 12ft 4⅜ in	33T	III	30309-30310			Basically a 57ft design with both pick-up apparatus and lavatory. BR-type toplights.
POT	1793	479	3	1930	Wolverton	50ft x 8ft 6in x 12ft 4⅜ in	28T	II (Flush)	30210-30212	8/48		Recessed side but no net. Mail delivery apparatus fitted. Fitted shelves and two sliding doors each side. No 30211 had nets by 1958.
POT	1937	883	1	1935	Wolverton	50ft x 8ft 6in x 12ft 4⅜ in	27T	III	30341			Completely empty interior but lavatory at right-hand end looking at corridor side of vehicle.
POT	2052	1297	1	1940	Wolverton	50ft x 8ft 6in x 12ft 4⅜ in	25T	III	30280			As for D1937 but wardrobe in place of lavatory. No 30280 built for M&NEJPS.
		1433	1	1946	Wolverton		25T	III	30282			
POT	2172	1561	1	1950	Wolverton	60ft x 9ft 2¼ in x 12ft 4⅜ in	29T	III	30275			Fitted with lavatory and guard's compartment. Width quoted over handles as this was a normal profile diagram rather than the standard Post Office type.
		1603	1	1950	Wolverton		29T	III	30276			
		1672	1	1954	Wolverton			III	30306			
POT	2176	1605	1	1950	Wolverton	60ft x 8ft 6in x 12ft 4⅜ in	30T	III	30279			Fitted with net, wardrobe, sink, oven and folding tables.
POT	2187	1671	1	1954	Wolverton	57ft x 9ft 3in x 12ft 4⅜ in	Not known	III	30305			Empty interior except for water boiler and wardrobe. Normal profile vehicle and width is quoted over handles.
VAN	1853	662	1	1933	Wolverton	42ft x 8ft 6in x 12ft 4⅜ in	25T	III	30304			Probably full livery when new. No interior fittings at all.
VAN	1867	703	1	1933	Wolverton	31ft x 8ft 9in x 12ft 4⅜ in (six-wheel)	16T	III	30391		12/65	No gangway — probably full livery when new. To parcels van (12/52).

Note: In this table, width is quoted over **body** (excluding projections) unless otherwise stated in 'Remarks' column. Most LMS Post Office coaches were 8ft 6in at waist plus a 2in projection on the sorting side, giving an overall 8ft 8in dimension.

* Official date. The coaches actually appeared in 1958 and were given the last LMS series numbers to be allocated.

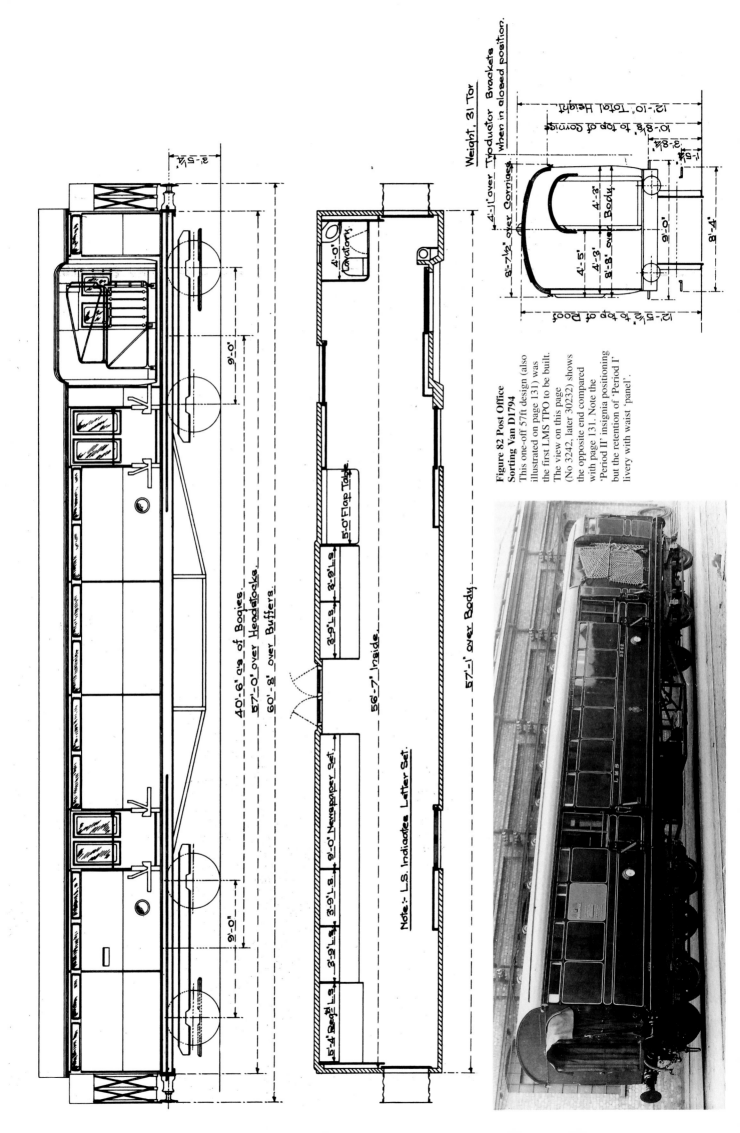

Figure 82 Post Office Sorting Van D1794

This one-off 57ft design (also illustrated on page 131) was the first LMS TPO to be built. The view on this page (No 3242, later 30232) shows the opposite end compared with page 131. Note the 'Period II' insignia positioning but the retention of 'Period I' livery with waist 'panel'.

Weight, 31 Ton

40'-6" c's of Bogies.
57'-0" over Headstocks.
60'-8" over Buffers.

9'-0"
9'-0"

8'-5½"

4'-0" Lavatory.

5'-0" Flap Table.
3'-9" L.S. 3'-9" L.S. 9'-0" Newspaper Set.
5'-4" Reg'd L.S. 3'-9" L.S.

56'-7" Inside.

57'-1" over Body.

Note:- L.S. Indicates Letter Set.

4'-1" over Tipductor Brackets when in closed position.

12'-10" Total Height.
10'-8⅝" to top of Carriage.

8'-7½" over Carriage.

4'-1" over Carriage.

4'-5'
4'-3'
8'-8' over Body.

4'-2'

9'-0'

3'-8¾'

8'-4"

12'-5½" to top of Roof.

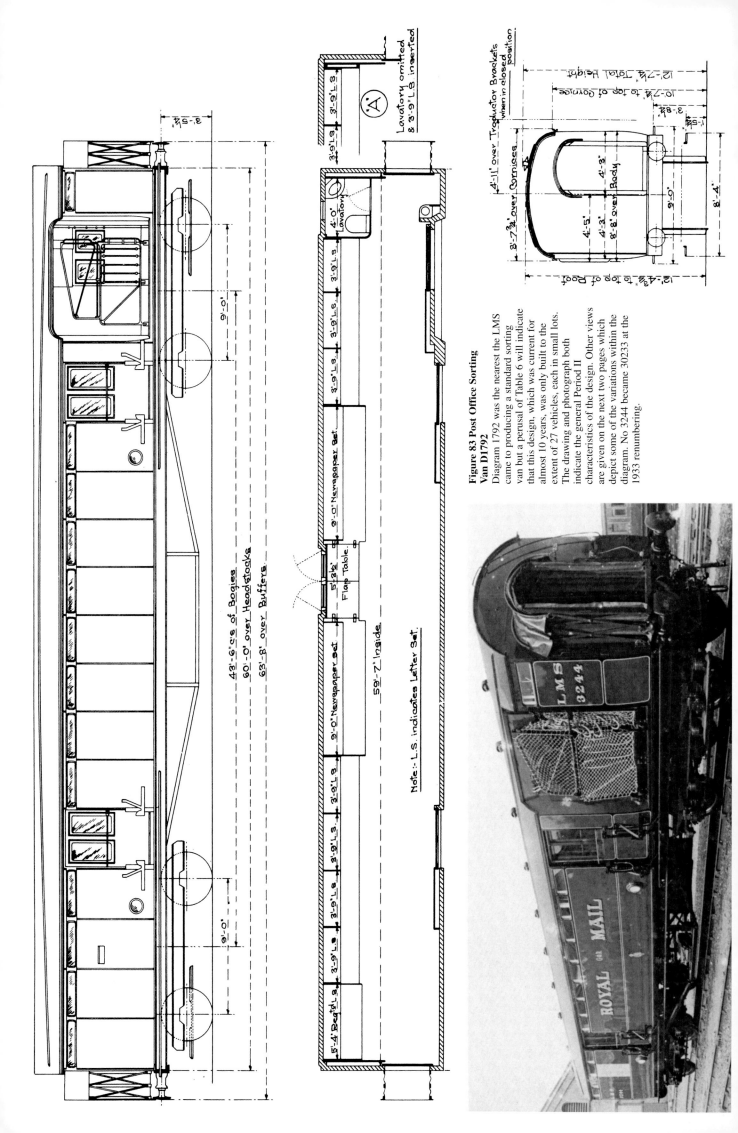

Figure 83 dimensions and labels:

3'-5¾"

9'-0"

43'-6" c/c's of Bogies
60'-0" over Headstocks
63'-8' over Buffers

9'-0"

3'-9' L.S   3'-9' L.S
4'-0' Lavatory
9'-0' Newspaper set   3'-9' L.S   3'-9' L.S   3'-9' L.S   3'-9' L.S   3'-9' L.S
5'-2½'
Flap Table.
9'-0' Newspaper set
59'-7" Inside.
5'-4' Regd. S   3'-9' L.S   3'-9' L.S   3'-9' L.S

'A'

Lavatory omitted
& 3'-9" L.S inserted

Note:- L.S. indicates Letter Set.

4'-11' over Traductor Brackets when in closed position.
8'-7¾' over Cornices
12'-7¾ Total Height.
10'-7¾' to top of Cornice.
3'-8¾'
1'-5"
12'-4¾" to top of Roof.
9'-0' to top of Roof
4'-5'
4'-3'
4'-3'
8'-8' over Body
9'-0"
8'-4"

Figure 83 Post Office Sorting Van D1792

Diagram 1792 was the nearest the LMS came to producing a standard sorting van but a perusal of Table 6 will indicate that this design, which was current for almost 10 years, was only built to the extent of 27 vehicles, each in small lots. The drawing and photograph both indicate the general Period II characteristics of the design. Other views are given on the next two pages which depict some of the variations within the diagram. No 3244 became 30233 at the 1933 renumbering.

Opposite side view of No 3244 (Figure 83) showing the letter sorting 'bulges'.

POS No 3241, later 30314, to D1792 shows an example built without pick-up nets or traductor brackets but still with the recessed side where the net would be fitted. It is not known if nets were fitted later.

This view of POS No 3251 (later 30266) shows the sorting side view of a D1792 post office when fitted with toilet compartment. No 3241 (above) was of this type. Pictures indicate that toilets were often fitted to those coaches without pick-up nets but whether this was a standard distinction is not known.

Interior view of LMS No 30217 when new — one of the first
three Period III examples to D1792, built to Lot 772 in 1934.

PRE-1933 RUNNING NUMBERS FOR D1792
(see also Table 6)

Lot Number	1933 Number	Original Number
502	30233	3244
	30234	3247
	30235	3250
564	30266	3251
	30267	3252
	30268	3258
611	30213	1895
	30214	1896
	30215	1897
	30246	1902
	30247	1903
	30248	1904
612	30314	3241

Opposite page top to bottom:
LMS No 30314 (formerly 3241) of D1792 from the letter rack
(or 'off' side) showing the retention of fully lined livery after
renumbering. This carriage dated from 1931 and was fitted with a
lavatory compartment at the far end. *Authors' Collection*

No M30250M was one of three Period III TPOs built to D1792
in 1937. It is shown here from the letter rack side in typical BR
livery of the late 1950s/early 1960s, by which time the pick-up
gear on the far side had been removed to give a similar
appearance to the carriage shown in the next view.
Authors' Collection

LMS No 30289 was the first of the last three TPOs to be built to
D1792 (Lot 1197, Table 6), appearing in 1939 without pick-up
nets as shown here. Whether nets were subsequently fitted is not
known, but since many former LMS TPOs ran for several years
in later life without pick-up gear (see previous view), this
example is likely to have been one of them.

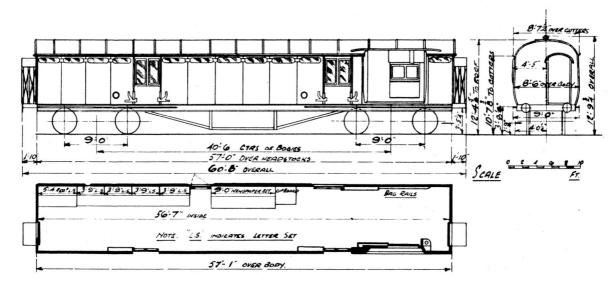

Figure 84 Post Office Sorting Van D1908

This was the first TPO diagram to be issued under the 'utility' regime — see Introduction — and was for a solitary 57ft example, otherwise similar to D1792. It was probably needed for some service where a 60ft version would not be acceptable and appears to have been allocated No 3217 in the old number series (or may have replaced an older vehicle with that number) but is unlikely ever to have carried it. The appended view, taken when new, clearly has the new series No 30204 painted on both roof and far bulkhead.

Opposite side view of No 3244 (Figure 83) showing the letter sorting 'bulges'.

POS No 3241, later 30314, to D1792 shows an example built without pick-up nets or traductor brackets but still with the recessed side where the net would be fitted. It is not known if nets were fitted later.

This view of POS No 3251 (later 30266) shows the sorting side view of a D1792 post office when fitted with toilet compartment. No 3241 (above) was of this type. Pictures indicate that toilets were often fitted to those coaches without pick-up nets but whether this was a standard distinction is not known.

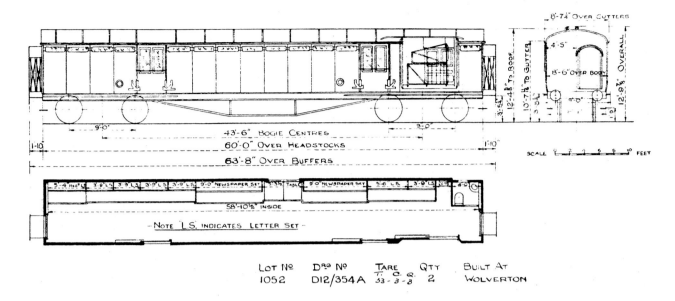

Lot No.	Drg No.	Tare T. C. Q.	Qty	Built At
1052	D12/354A	33 - 3 - 3	2	Wolverton

Figure 85 Post Office Sorting Van D1970

This is the genuine Period III version of D1792 (page 134) though its slightly changed interior compared with that diagram probably explains why Period III carriages continued to be built to D1792 at the same time. An interior view will be found on page 145.

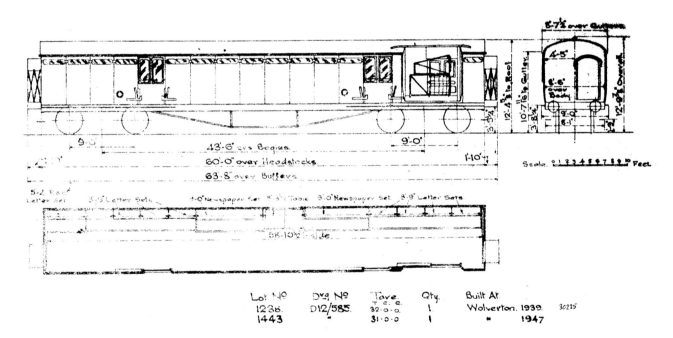

Lot No.	Drg No.	Tare T. C. Q.	Qty	Built At
1238	D12/585	32 - 0 - 0	1	Wolverton. 1939.
1443	"	31 - 0 - 0	1	" 1947

Figure 86 Post Office Sorting Van D2043

This diagram was issued as the non-lavatory version of D1970, unlike the earlier D1792 which covered both types. Lot 1443 was originally intended to be this type but was actually built to D2175 (next page).

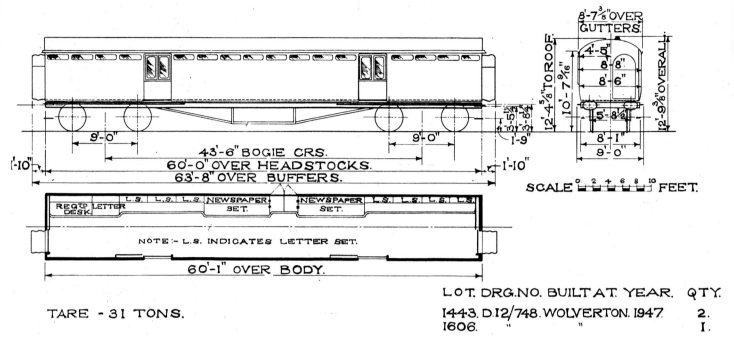

SCALE 0 2 4 6 8 10 FEET.

TARE - 31 TONS.

NOTE:- L.S. INDICATES LETTER SET.

60'-1" OVER BODY.

LOT.	DRG.NO.	BUILT AT.	YEAR.	QTY.
1443.	D.12/748.	WOLVERTON.	1947	2.
1606.	"	"		I.

Figure 87 Post Office Sorting Van D2175
This diagram covered the last sorting vans to be built for the LMS itself, though Lot 1006 was not built until 1950. This design was never fitted with pick-up apparatus.

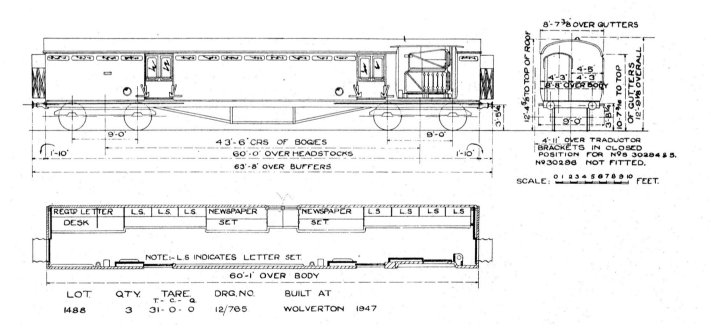

SCALE: 0 1 2 3 4 5 6 7 8 9 10 FEET.

NOTE:- L.S INDICATES LETTER SET.

60'-1" OVER BODY

LOT.	QTY.	TARE. T - C. - Q.	DRG.NO.	BUILT AT
1488	3	31- 0- 0	12/785	WOLVERTON 1947

Figure 88 Post Office Sorting Van D2140
This diagram, essentially equivalent to D2175 but fitted with pick-up nets, was intended to be built during LMS days but the planned three examples did not appear until 1948, two more being built in 1950.

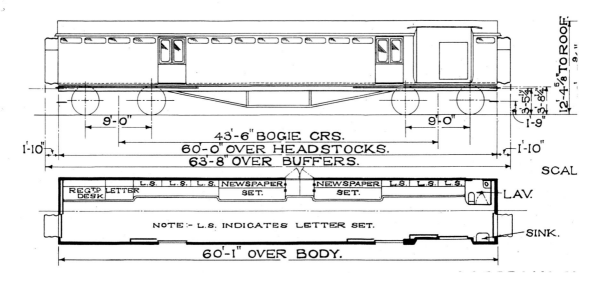

9'-0"   43'-6" BOGIE CRS.   9'-0"

60'-0" OVER HEADSTOCKS.

63'-8" OVER BUFFERS.

1'-10"   1'-10"

12'-4⅝" TO ROOF

3'-5¼"
3'-8¼"
1'-9"

SCAL

| REGD DESK | LETTER | L.S. | L.S. | L.S. | NEWSPAPER SET. | NEWSPAPER SET. | L.S. | L.S. | L.S. | LAV. |

NOTE:- L.S. INDICATES LETTER SET.

SINK.

60'-1" OVER BODY.

TARE - 32 TONS   0 CWT.   0 QRS.

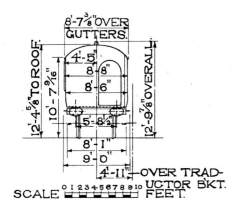

8'-7⅜" OVER GUTTERS.

4'-5"
8'-8"
8'-6"
5'-8½"
8'-1"
9'-0"

12'-4⅝" TO ROOF
10'-7⁹⁄₁₆"
12'-9⅞" OVERALL

4'-11" OVER TRAD-UCTOR BKT.

SCALE 0 1 2 3 4 5 6 7 8 9 10 FEET.

Figure 89 Post Office Sorting Van D2167
Some of the LMS series diagrams improved in quality during BR days and this one was issued to cover the lavatory version of D2140 (opposite, bottom). After D1792, it eventually became the second most numerous of the LMS-design sorting vans and the appended photograph shows No M30273M (built 1950) from the 'off' side during the early 1960s. *Authors' Collection*

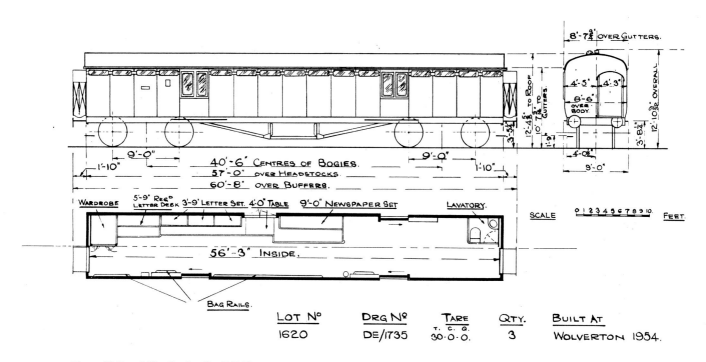

Figure 90 Post Office Sorting Van D2185
This 57ft type, again presumably built for some specific service, had no pick-up apparatus but, unusually, was fitted with a wardrobe compartment as well as lavatory.

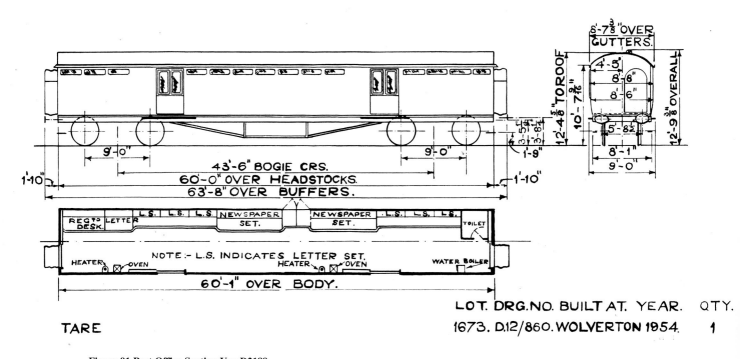

Figure 91 Post Office Sorting Van D2188
This one-off type again had no pick-up gear but the presence of additional heating and cooking facilities again suggests some sort of dedicated service.

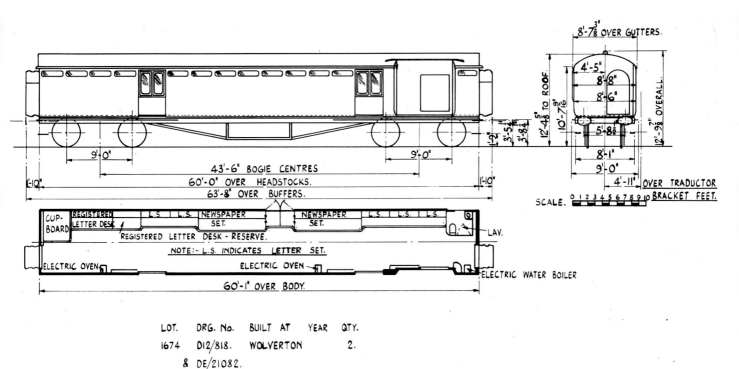

Figure 92 Post Office Sorting Van D2191
This was the final LMS-pattern 60ft sorting van to be built. Like some of the earlier Period III TPOs, this design was fitted with recesses for pick-up apparatus but as far as we are aware, the latter was never fitted.

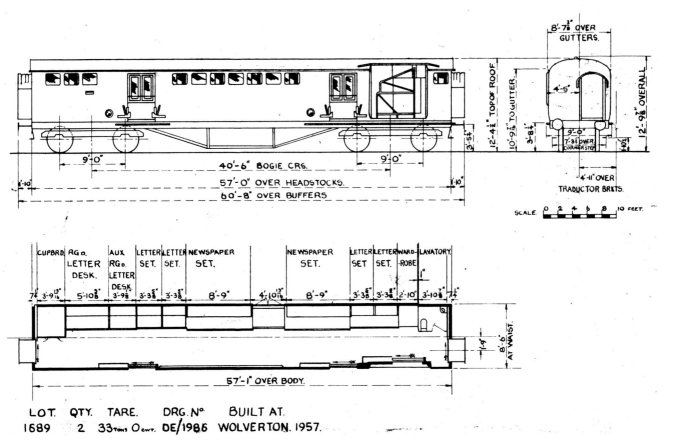

LOT.   QTY.   TARE.   DRG.Nº   BUILT AT.
1689   2   33 tons 0 cwt. DE/1986   WOLVERTON. 1957.

Figure 93 Post Office Sorting Van D2193
The very last LMS-style TPO reverted to a 57ft length and displayed BR-type upper windows. As far as is known, they were the last carriages to be allocated LMS series running numbers (30309-10) when they entered service in 1958.

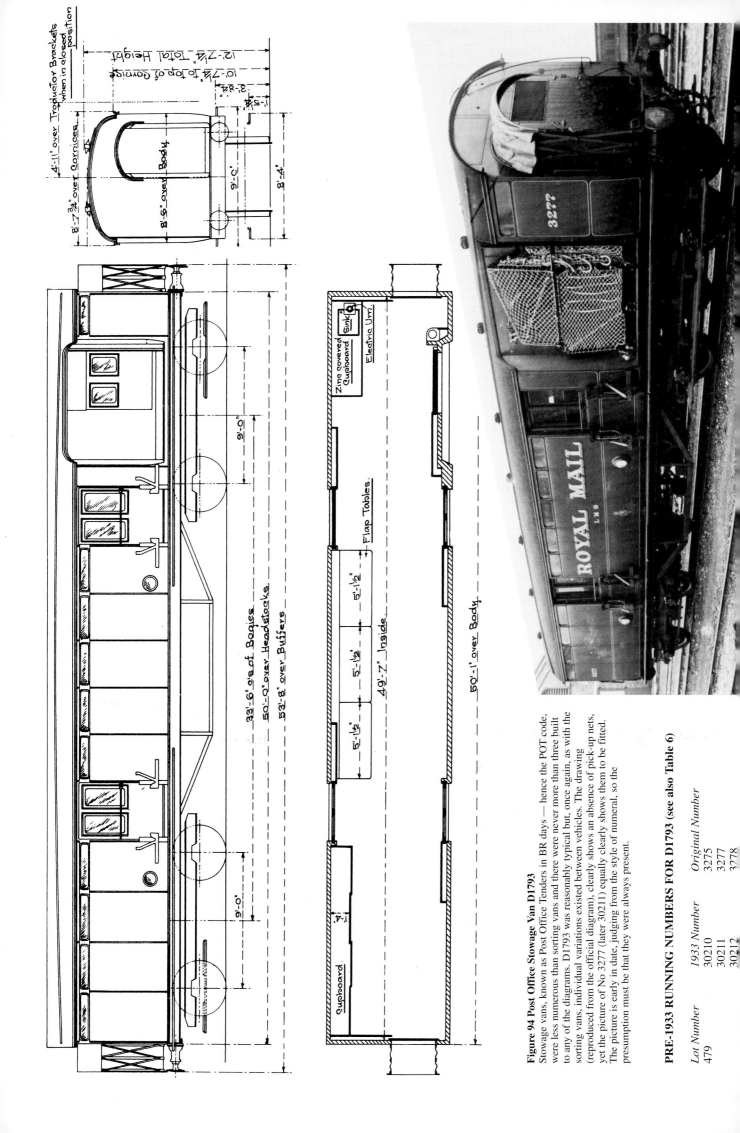

Figure 94 Post Office Stowage Van D1793

Stowage vans, known as Post Office Tenders in BR days — hence the POT code, were less numerous than sorting vans and there were never more than three built to any of the diagrams. D1793 was reasonably typical but, once again, as with the sorting vans, individual variations existed between vehicles. The drawing (reproduced from the official diagram), clearly shows an absence of pick-up nets, yet the picture of No 3277 (later 30211) equally clearly shows them to be fitted. The picture is early in date, judging from the style of numeral, so the presumption must be that they were always present.

PRE-1933 RUNNING NUMBERS FOR D1793 (see also Table 6)

Lot Number	1933 Number	Original Number
479	30210	3275
	30211	3277
	30212	3278

Interior of sorting coach No 30224, photographed from the end fitted with pick-up apparatus. The coach itself (D1970) was a Stanier version of the standard sorting coach.

This view of POT No 3275 (later 30210) shows the opposite side of D1793 to the view at Figure 94. This coach, the first example to the diagram, is thought not to have had pick-up nets.

Stowage van No M30275, built in 1949 to D2172. This shows the general styling of Period III GPO vehicles.

LMS No 3275 (later 30210) was the first example of D1793 to be built. It too had recesses for pick-up nets but this ex-works view shows it with traductor arms in place for lineside delivery — ie exactly as indicated on the diagram. It is not known whether it eventually assumed the form of No 3277 (page 144) or remained as shown here. The services on which these three vans were used are not known to the writers. *Authors' Collection*

The third example to D1793 was LMS No 3278, later 30212. This view shows the 'off' side of the carriage, there being no reason to suppose that it was any different on the other side to the first two examples, but whether or not it had pick-up nets is not known. Logically, a vehicle classified as a stowage van and devoid of letter sorting racks would be less likely to have pick-up nets, though capable of dispatching completed bundles of mail via the traductor arms.

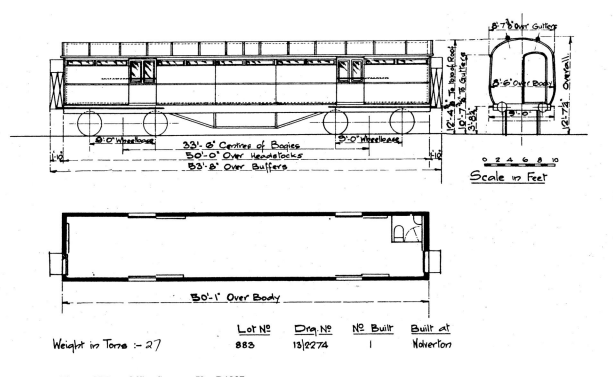

Weight in Tons :- 27

	Lot Nº	Drg. Nº	Nº Built	Built at
	883	13\2274	1	Wolverton

Figure 95 Post Office Stowage Van D1937
An unremarkable one-off Period III 50ft van with no interior furniture whatsoever, nor any facility for picking up or setting down mail.

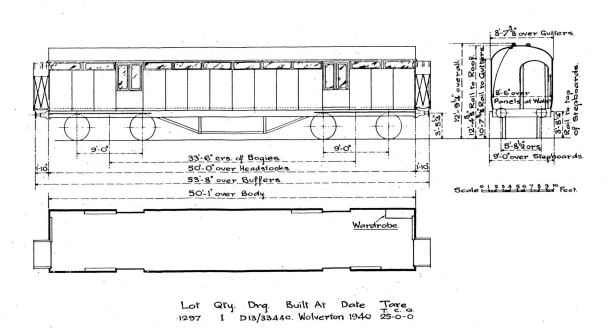

Lot	Qty.	Drg.	Built At	Date	Tare T. C. Q.
1297	1	D13/3344c.	Wolverton	1940	25-0-0

Figure 96 Post Office Stowage Van D2052
This design was much as D1937 save for the substitution of a wardrobe for the lavatory. Both examples seem to have been built as replacements for former Midland postal vehicles, No 30280 going into the M&NE postal fleet replacing old No 1987 (which carriage may also have been the first No 30280 before scrapping). No 30282 replaced old No 1905 from the Midland fleet but other details are not known.

147

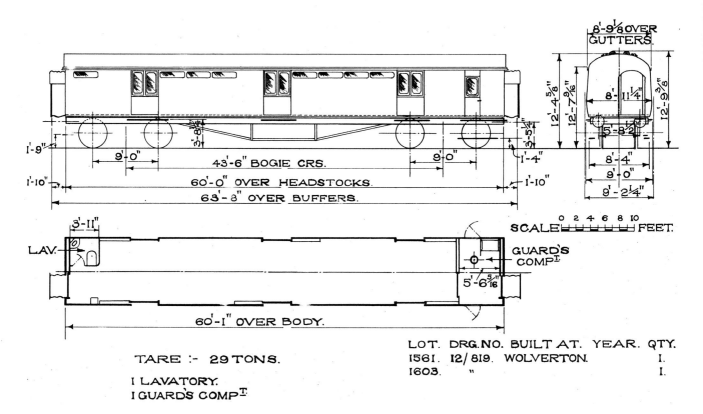

Figure 97 Post Office Stowage Van D2172
This 60ft design, which emerged in BR days, was unusual in having a guard's compartment, but was otherwise a straightforward stowage van. An exterior view is on page 145.

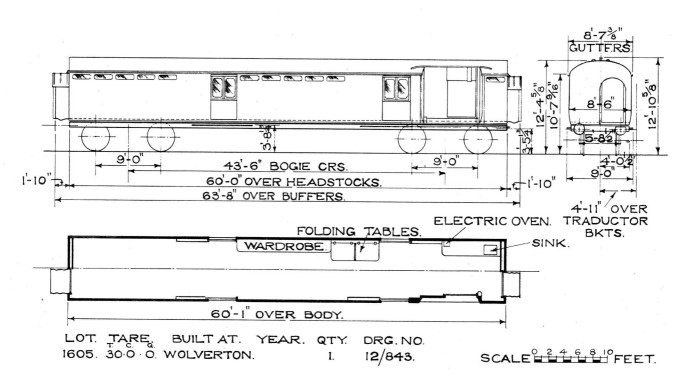

Figure 98 Post Office Stowage Van D2176
This one-off 60ft design emerged in 1950, presumably for some specific service. It was rather lavishly equipped for a stowage van and appears to have received a full set of trackside pick-up and delivery apparatus.

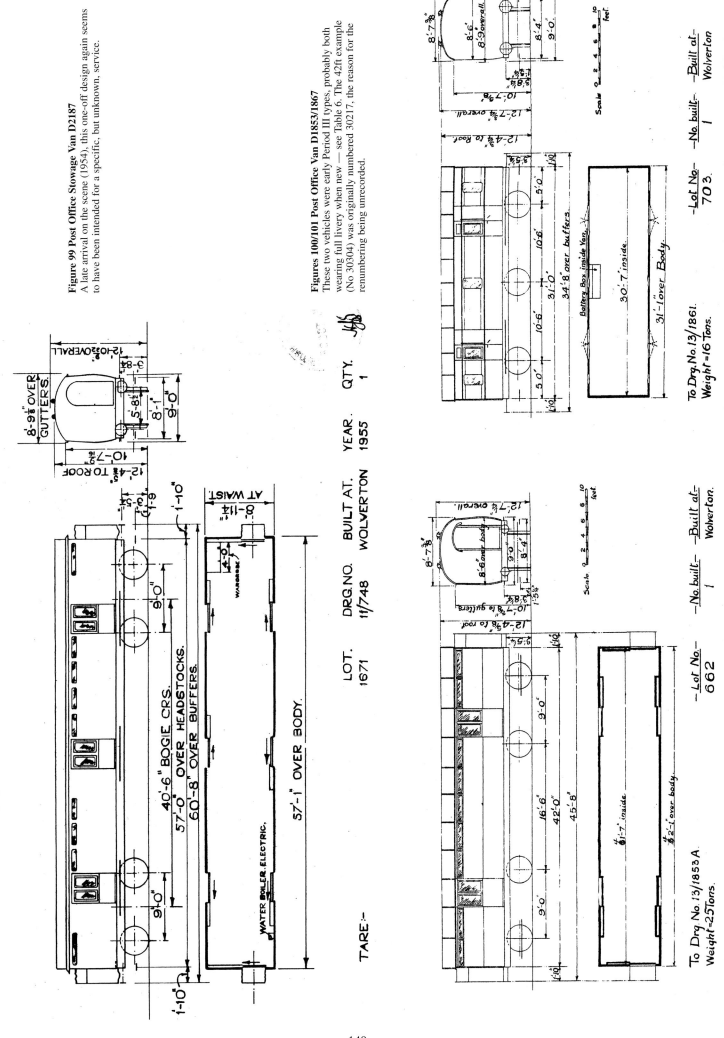

Figure 99 Post Office Stowage Van D2187
A late arrival on the scene (1954), this one-off design again seems to have been intended for a specific, but unknown, service.

Figures 100/101 Post Office Van D1853/1867
These two vehicles were early Period III types, probably both wearing full livery when new — see Table 6. The 42ft example (No 30304) was originally numbered 30217, the reason for the renumbering being unrecorded.

QTY.	YEAR.	BUILT AT.	DRG.NO.	LOT.
1	1955	WOLVERTON	11/748	1671

149

Chapter 7 - Special Saloons

Introduction; Club Saloons; District Engineers' Saloons; Royal Saloons; Chairman's Saloons; Summary Table

It seems to have been almost a sacred doctrine of the British railway system that included amongst the oldest passenger vehicles owned by a railway company should be the bulk of its special saloons. This may have reflected a fondness for the traditional on the part of top management or possibly it was a realistic appraisal by the company officials that a special saloon ran a very low mileage and therefore took a long time to wear out! Be that as it may, the LMS followed the tradition and managed to make do with pre-Grouping vehicles for a very long time after Grouping. In fact, only two saloons — both travelling clubs — were built before the war. What was perhaps most surprising was the fact that the bulk of the special saloons which the LMS *did* build, entered service during the wartime period when most normal carriage construction had ceased in the national interest. Just how the LMS managed to get away with the building of these highly specialised vehicles at that time is not known and speculation is outside the scope of this book.

The saloons built by the LMS were few in number and are best considered by types in chronological order of building.

CLUB SALOONS (OR CLUB CARS)

The travelling 'club' was a notable feature of railway working on parts of the LMS, particularly the North West, and both the LNWR and LYR had set aside special vehicles for this purpose. The LMS continued the practice and its activities took two forms: the conversion of older stock and the building of more coaches. Most conversion was of pre-Grouping stock — for example, some of the first class 65ft 6in coaches of the LNWR 'American Boat Train' sets — and only one example of the conversion of a standard coach has been traced. This was Period I vestibule first No 3572 (original pre-1933 number) which was converted into a club saloon. It became 818 at the 1932/3 renumbering. As far as is known, it was little if any altered from its original state except that, being a club saloon, it would now be for the sole use of an exclusive clientele.

Only two club saloons were actually built as such by the LMS. These were Nos 822 and 823, the latter being, of course, the 1939 'Coronation Scot' club car brake whose history is given in Chapter 4. Although this car seems to have been something of an afterthought, the same cannot be said of No 822 which was a genuine type-designed vehicle for the prewar Manchester-Blackpool service. It was built in 1935 to D1922 and was a 60ft Period III coach. Inside the car were three separate saloons, each equipped with individual armchairs and tables, and attendant's compartment. Patrons had their own 'reserved' seats in the car.

Club services never regained much popularity after the war and several LMS club cars and saloons found their way on to such services as the 'North Wales Land Cruise' where many of them served out their time. Nos 818, 822 and 823 were among the coaches thus used.

DISTRICT ENGINEERS' SALOONS

Some neat 50ft District Engineers' saloons were built during and after the war, all but the first to D2046. They had inspection saloons at each end which were connected by a side corridor which ran alongside the centre portion of the coach which was occupied by a lavatory, guard's compartment and a small kitchen/pantry. These coaches were preceded into service by the odd one out to D2045. This was probably a prototype for the D2046 version and the only significant difference was that this car was fitted with two lavatories.

No reason can be offered why so many, relatively speaking, of these saloons were built, nor why they were allowed to be constructed during the war years.

LMS Club Car No 822 built in 1935 for the Manchester-Blackpool service. Note the supplementary wording adjacent to the doors and the distinctive roof board.

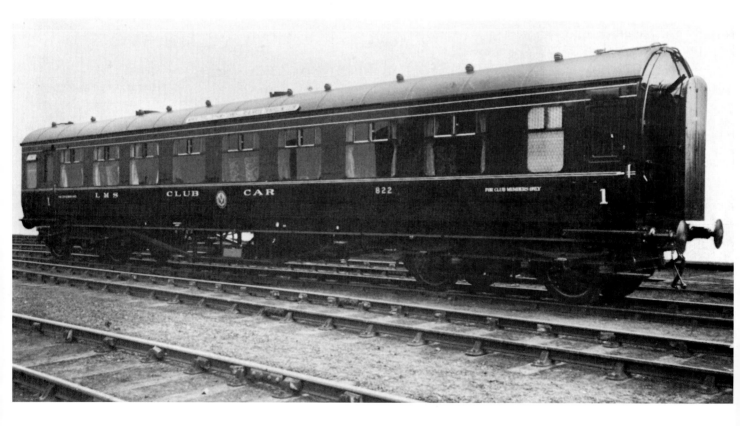

LMS District Engineer's saloon No 45026. Note the ascending steps below the guard's door.

ROYAL SALOONS

The fact that King George V and his son preferred the LNWR colours to those of the LMS and were thus instrumental in keeping the royal train in its traditional livery until the 1939-45 war is well known. Equally well known is the fact that the train was finally repainted in LMS livery to make it less conspicuous during World War 2. However, conspicuous or not, the magnificent LNWR saloons built originally for King Edward VII and Queen Alexandra were wood panelled and, therefore, highly vulnerable to air attack. Since safety of the monarch appears to have been the major consideration in the repainting of the train, it seems reasonable to assume that similar motives may have been the reason why the LMS was allowed to build new Royal saloons in 1941 with full armour plating. It is, of course, quite conceivable that the LMS would have wished to build new saloons anyway — although in all conscience it is hard to envisage much improvement on the LNWR pair — but no evidence has been located of any prewar activity in this direction. The principal saloons built in 1941 are, of course, still in existence under NRM custodianship.

Three vehicles were built on 12-wheel chassis. Two were the royal saloons themselves (Nos 798/799) and the third was a convertible sleeping, brake and power car. The chassis of the coaches are 67ft 6in over headstocks but the coaches are 69ft over the end panels since they have bowed ends. They were the only LMS-built coaches to be constructed with drophead buffers, buckeye couplers and Pullman-type gangways. All three have slightly recessed end vestibule entrance doors. When new, the two royal saloons were fitted with armour-plated shutters over the windows but these features were later removed. The coaches were originally finished in standard LMS lake with a modified form of the simple lining. There was a waist line as on standard stock but this was taken round the entrance doors at the inner and upper edges. The LMS emblem appeared twice on each side of the coach. Windows on the coaches are mostly of standard Stanier 4ft 0in pattern but only a few are fitted with sliding ventilators. Side/end panel junctions are rounded off and the solebar is completely concealed by the lower bodyside panelling. All exterior grab handles, etc, are of plated finish.

HM The King's Royal Saloon No 798 from the outside, showing protective wartime armour plating.

HM The Queen's Saloon No 799 in LMS days without the armour-plated shutters. The layout of the lining in this picture was faithfully copied when the saloon assumed the current Royal claret colour during the 1950s.

The two royal saloons are almost identical except that the interior arrangements are opposite handed. Basically, each coach contains a suite of rooms (bedroom, bathroom and lounge) together with attendant's accommodation. The entrance vestibules are extremely wide and spacious as befits the nature of the coaches. It is believed that the coaches were designed to be marshalled with the two day saloons adjacent to each other. Needless to say, the interiors of these vehicles are sumptuous in the extreme. Just about every possible refinement was incorporated into the design and mere words cannot do justice to them. They were fit in every way to replace the original LNWR coaches, although it could be argued that the fashion style of the 1940s compares unfavourably with the pre-Grouping designs which they replaced.

In 1954-5, the LMS royal saloons, together with the brake and power car, were finished in the royal train livery, described as claret, but which is, in fact, a dark purple lake shade very close to the old LNWR colour. The lining style was the same as in LMS days but rendered in vermilion and black rather than yellow and black. The royal saloons remained in use until 1977 when replaced by new BR Mk III vehicles. When finally withdrawn, they had been in service for almost as long as the LNWR pair they replaced. The two Chairman's saloons, Nos 45005/6, were also still in use in 1977 as sleeping cars in the Royal Train.

Interior view of HM The King's Lounge of Royal Saloon No 798.

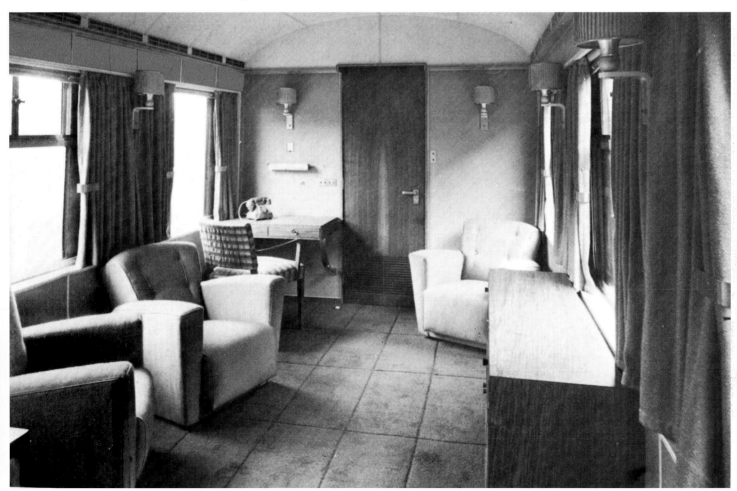

CHAIRMAN'S SALOONS

In 1942, two identical Chairman's saloons were built to D2066. Two views of these 60ft coaches are given overleaf and the coaches were orthodox Period III-styled vehicles. It is not known why they were allowed to be built during the war unless it was to act as mobile headquarters in connection with some aspect or other of wartime railway administration. At the same time it must be stated that there were surely enough pre-Grouping saloons for this purpose if it was the reason. Thus, their origin is something of a mystery.

The saloons did not survive for long in their original state, being altered in 1948 into combined sleeping-cum-day saloons (see pages 162-3). Presumably in 1948, the continued existence of a 'Chairman's' saloon was something of an anachronism! The cars still survive in their rebuilt form, however, and prior to their withdrawal were frequently employed in the royal train whose livery they carried. They replaced some of the elderly ex-LNWR coaches which continued to be part of the royal train long after the newer royal saloons had been replaced by the 1941 LMS vehicles and were originally converted for the use of HRH The Princess Elizabeth and The Duke of Edinburgh. (NB. See also caption overleaf.)

Interior view of the No 1 Saloon end of an unidentified District Engineer's Saloon to D2046. The BR-style upholstery cloth suggests a recent retrim and, compared with the diagram itself, a second large window seems to have replaced the outer door on the left-hand wall.

TABLE 7: SUMMARY OF LMS-BUILT SPECIAL SALOONS

Type	*Diag*	*Lot*	*Qty*	*Date*	*Built*	*Dimensions* (L x W x H)	*Weight*	*Running Numbers*	*Withdrawals First*	*Withdrawals Last*	*Remarks*
Club	1922	851	1	1935	Derby	60ft x 9ft 3in x 12ft 4⅝in	32T	822	—	4/63	'Coronation Scot' Car
Club	2020	1164	1	1939	Derby	59ft 5¼in x 9ft 2⅝in x 12ft 2 9/16in	31T	823	—	4/63	
District Engineer	2045	part 1221	1	1940	Wolverton	50ft x 9ft 3in x 12ft 4⅝in	31T	45043	—	8/66	
District Engineer	2046	part 1221	2	1940	Wolverton		31T	45044-5			
		1264	3	1941	Wolverton		31T	45046-8		Some extant in preservation.	
		1327	3	1942	Wolverton	50ft x 9ft 3in x 12ft 4⅝in	30T	45028-30			
		1356*	3	1944	Wolverton		31T	45020/1/6	1968		
		1432*	2	1947	Wolverton		31T	45035-6	8/66		
King's Saloon	2054	1167	1	1941	Wolverton	69ft x 9ft 0in x 12ft 10⅞in	56T	798}			
Queen's Saloon	2055†	1168	1	1941	Wolverton	69ft x 9ft 0in x 12ft 10⅞in	57T	799}			Quoted height for Royal Saloons is the overall value.
Brake & Power	2056	1229	1	1941	Wolverton	69ft x 9ft 0in x 12ft 8½in	52T	31209}	(later 2910, see page 157)		
Chair-man's (as built.)	2066	1323	1	1942	Wolverton	60ft x 9ft 3in x 12ft 4¼in	38T	45005}	All extant (1977), later disposal not always known		
		1331	1	1942	Wolverton		38T	45006}			
Chair-man's (altered)	2136	1323	1	1948	Wolverton	60ft x 9ft 3in x 12ft 4¼in	39T	45005}			
Chair-man's (altered)	2137	1331	1	1948	Wolverton	60ft x 9ft 3in x 12ft 4¼in	41T	45006}			45005/6 built on second-hand underframes from war-damaged coaches.

*Recessed door handles on these lots and only 9ft 2in wide.
†When the steel shutters were removed the saloon diagrams were renumbered 2054A and 2055A respectively.

Exterior and interior views of the Chairman's saloons taken at the time of conversion in 1948. They became regular constituents of the London Midland Region Royal Train until well into the late 1970s when, like Nos 798/799, their general incompatibility with more modern air-braked stock caused them to be withdrawn. However, they have been privately preserved — current whereabouts not known.

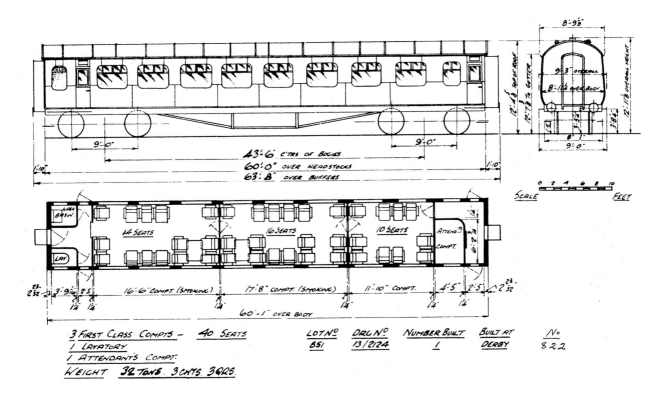

Figure 102 First Class Club Saloon D1922
This diagram should be read in conjunction with the exterior view on page 150. It was built on a standard 60ft underframe and it is an interesting sign of changing times that 75% of the accommodation was for smokers . . .

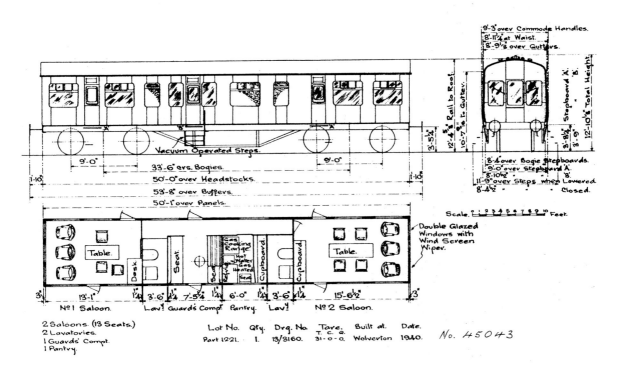

Figure 103 District Engineer's Saloon D2045
This was the prototype 50ft Period III inspection saloon which was built to the same lot number as the first two examples of D2046 (overleaf) but no further 'two lavatory' versions were built to this design.

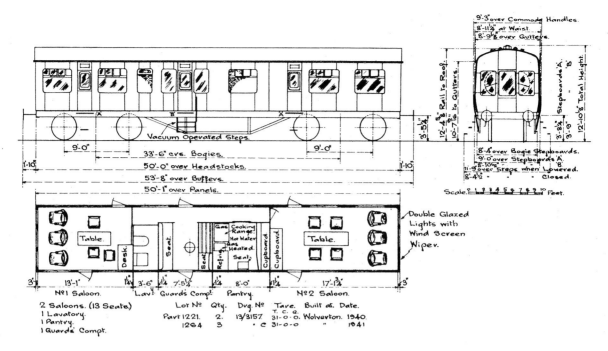

Figure 104 District Engineer's Saloon D2046
This 50ft type rapidly superseded the prototype version, the removal of one lavatory allowing an enlargement of the No 2 Saloon and kitchen areas, the latter having been very cramped in D2045. The appended view shows the No 2 Saloon end of a non-identified example, undoubtedly the same carriage as illustrated on page 153, from which it can be seen that the extra length allowed more seats to be fitted if need be. The precise internal arrangement of these carriages varied and there may have been some later structural changes. Some are privately preserved.

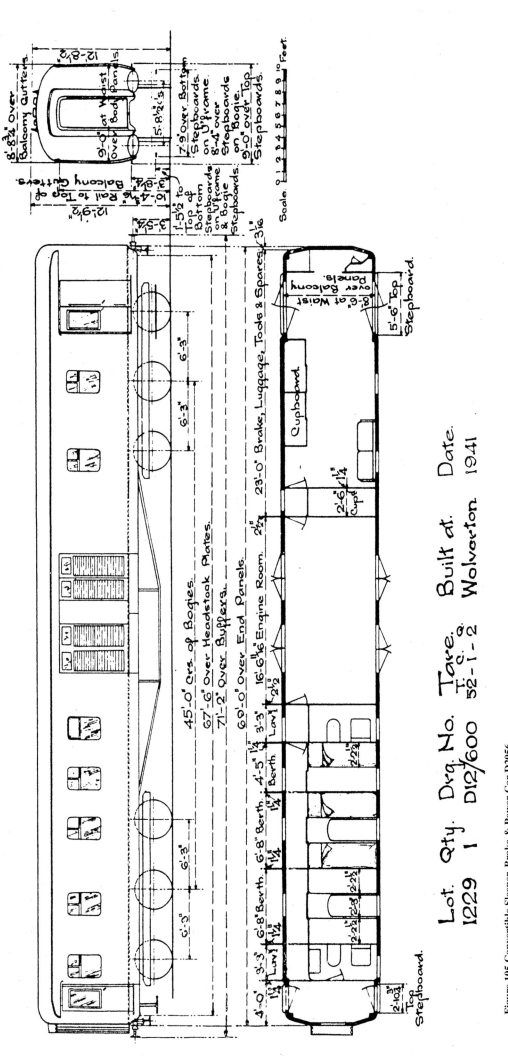

Scale 0 1 2 3 4 5 6 7 8 9 10 Feet.

Lot. Qty. Drg. No. Tare. Built at. Date.
1229 1 D12/600 52-1-2 Wolverton 1941
T. C. Q.

Figure 105 Convertible Sleeper, Brake & Power Car D2056
This unique vehicle, styled to match the two new principal saloons (next pages), reflected the growing self-contained nature of the LMS Royal Train during the war, the central portion being devoted to an engine compartment for an on-train electrical power generator. The rest of the carriage was to accommodate the travelling technicians and other railway staff who always accompanied the train, it being possible to sleep 10 *in extremis*, each compartment having double-tier bunks. The car was technically superseded in 1977 but was held in reserve for a few years afterwards, being renumbered 2910 in the BR Royal Train number series in 1983. It was eventually purchased privately for preservation in 1989 but was scrapped in 1991. In spite of the somewhat sub-standard nature of the drawing, we offer it at 3mm=1ft scale to allow the detail to be seen. An official view of this carriage was taken but we have been unable to discover a copy.

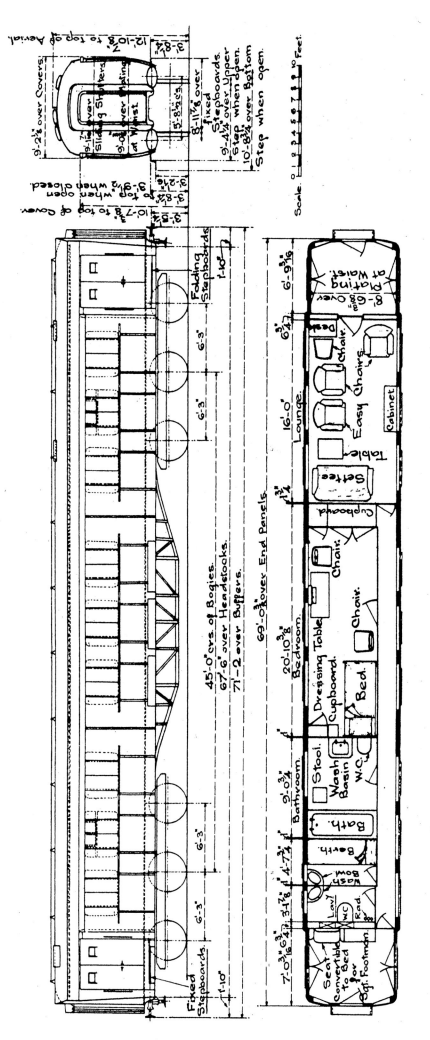

Lot. Qty. Drg. No. Tare. Built at. Date.
1167. 1. W1/1402. T.C.a. Wolverton. 1941. No. 798
56 - 8 - 2.

Figure 106 HM The King's Saloon No 798 D2054/2054A

Two diagrams were raised both for this vehicle and its partner, the original being the armour-plated version which added about four tons to the weight. They are believed to have been the heaviest locomotive-hauled carriages ever built to run in Britain at that time (and probably since) and the diagrams are self-explanatory. We have again been able to offer this vehicle at 3mm scale. Exterior and interior views are on pages 151/2.

After King George VI died in 1952, this saloon was used by HRH The Duke of Edinburgh until 1977 and it is believed to have been at his request that the 'Royal Claret' colour scheme was adopted, c1954-5. At some time during the 1954-7 period, the small end berth and lavatory were combined to form a single larger 'suite' for the Duke's valet and it is in this form that the carriage was preserved by the NRM in 1978.

One of the authors was privileged to be responsible for the restoration to museum condition of these carriages (basically an external repaint only) and, to add interest, it was decided to repaint one of them into original LMS colours. No 798 was selected so that it could resume its *primus inter pares* status, since when it has reverted to being called the King's Saloon ('His' and 'Hers' were the unofficial railway terms!). The same author was also probably the last person to ride in this carriage when it came on its own wheels to York from Wolverton, where it had been repainted in 1979. After some years on show in York, it was transferred to the Glasgow Museum of Transport just in time for its grand reopening in 1987 and can still (2000) be seen there.

158

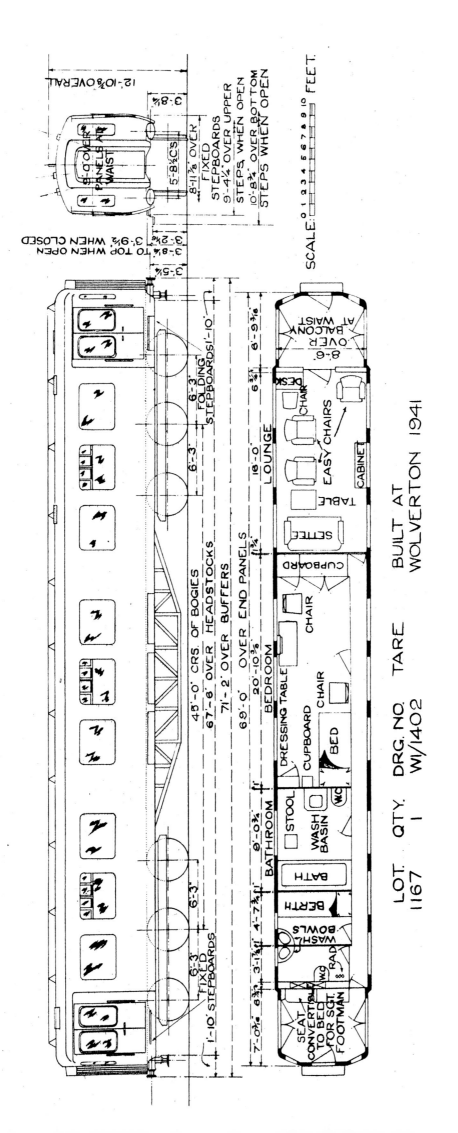

12'-10⅞" OVERALL

3'-8¾"

8'-0" OVER PANELS AT WAIST

5'-8½" C'S

8'-11⅞" OVER FIXED STEPBOARDS
9'-4¼" OVER UPPER STEPS WHEN OPEN
10'-8¾" OVER BOTTOM STEPS WHEN OPEN

3'-8¾" TO TOP WHEN OPEN
3'-2⅜" 3'-9½" WHEN CLOSED

3'-5¼"

6'-3" FOLDING STEPBOARDS 1'-10"

6'-3"

8'-9⅟₁₆"

OVER BALCONY AT WAIST

6'-3"

45'-0" CRS. OF BOGIES
67'-6" OVER HEADSTOCKS
71'-2" OVER BUFFERS
69'-0" OVER END PANELS

18'-0"
LOUNGE

6¾"

8'-6"

DESK
CHAIR
EASY CHAIRS
CABINET
TABLE
SETTEE
CUPBOARD

20'-10⅞"
BEDROOM

CUPBOARD
DRESSING TABLE
CHAIR
CHAIR
BED
WC

9'-0¾"
BATHROOM

STOOL
WASH BASIN
BATH

4'-7¾"
BERTH

3'-¾"
WASH BOWLS

7'-0⅞" 6¾" 3'-1¾"

6'-3"

6'-3" FIXED STEPBOARDS

SEAT CONVERTIBLE TO BED FOR SGT. FOOTMAN
WC
RAD'R

SCALE: 0 1 2 3 4 5 6 7 8 9 10 FEET.

LOT. 1167   QTY. 1   DRG. NO. W1/1402   TARE   BUILT AT WOLVERTON 1941

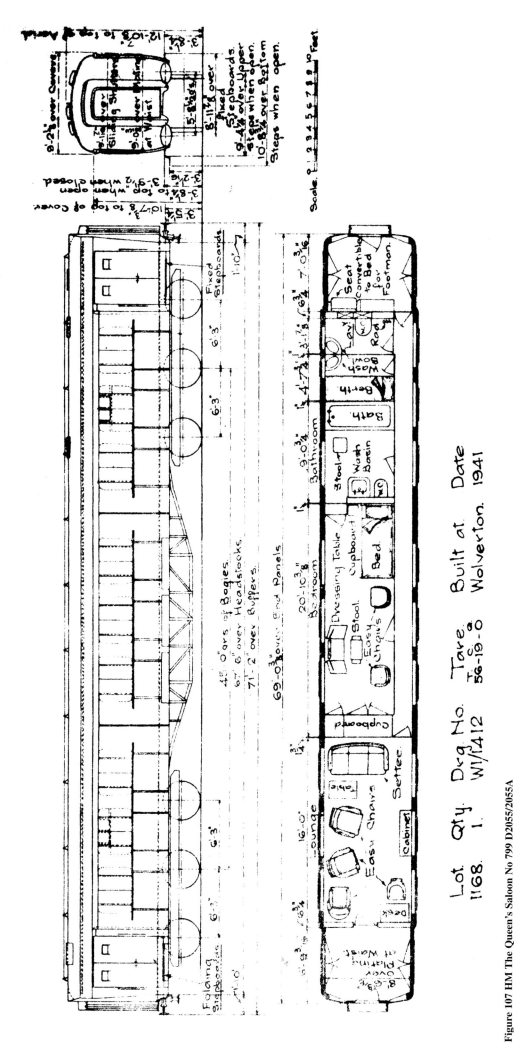

Figure 107 HM The Queen's Saloon No 799 D2055/2055A

The history of this carriage is much the same as for No 798. Built for HM Queen Elizabeth (later the Queen Mother) in 1941, it became the principal saloon on the accession of her daughter to the throne in 1952. Like No 798, the two small compartments were later combined into a larger area for the Queen's dresser and the carriage has been preserved in the exact style (including external livery) in which it ran during its final 20 or more years in service. The appended drawing offers another external view of the carriage in LMS days (see also page 152) and the saloon is currently displayed at York. As with No 798, the drawings are to 3mm scale.

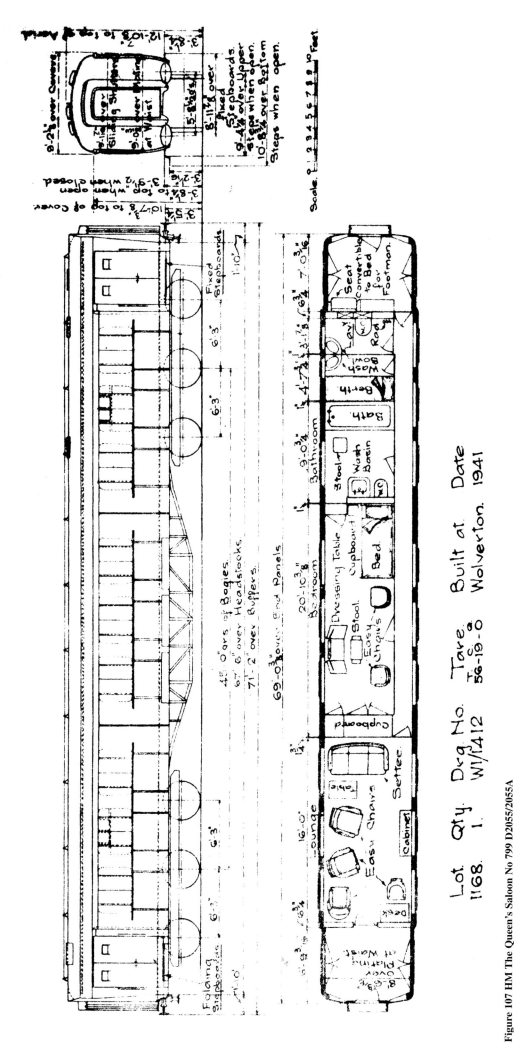

160

55A

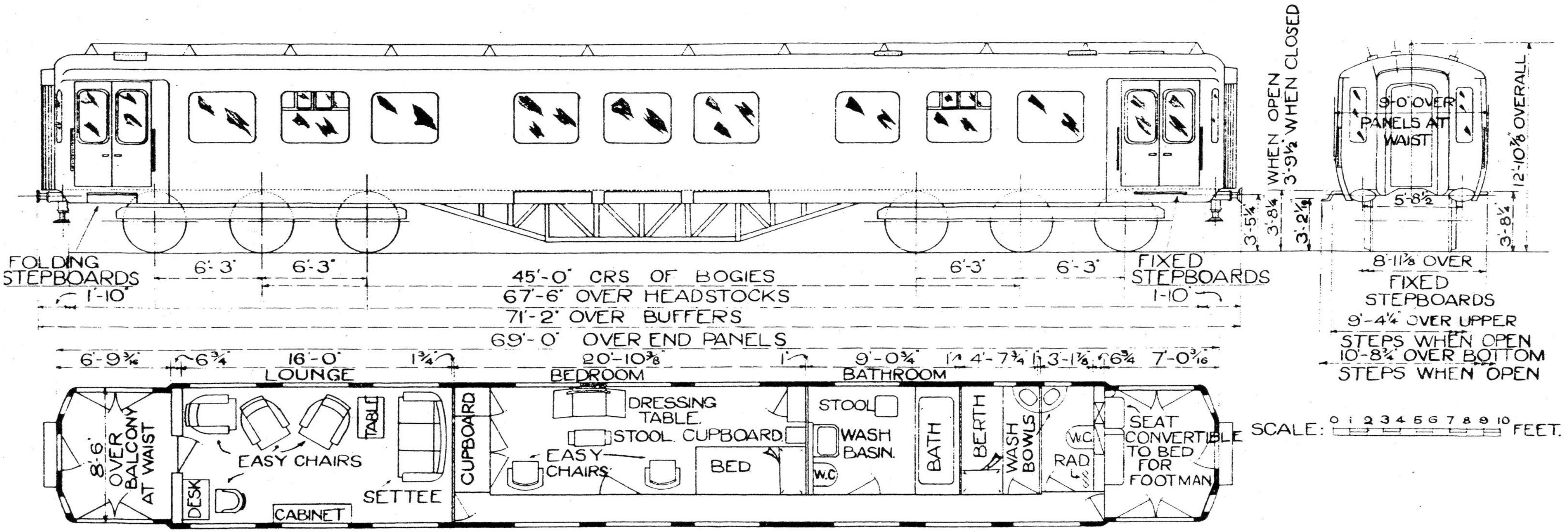

WHEN OPEN
3'-9½" WHEN CLOSED
9'-0" OVER PANELS AT WAIST
12'-10⅞" OVERALL
5'-8½"
3'-5¼"
3'-8¼"
3'-2⅛"
3'-8¼"
FOLDING STEPBOARDS
1'-10"
6'-3"
6'-3"
45'-0" CRS OF BOGIES
67'-6" OVER HEADSTOCKS
71'-2" OVER BUFFERS
69'-0" OVER END PANELS
6'-3"
6'-3"
FIXED STEPBOARDS
1'-10"
8'-11⅛" OVER FIXED STEPBOARDS
9'-4¼" OVER UPPER STEPS WHEN OPEN
10'-8¾" OVER BOTTOM STEPS WHEN OPEN
6'-9³⁄₁₆"
6¾"
16'-0"
LOUNGE
1¾"
20'-10⅜"
BEDROOM
1"
9'-0¾"
BATHROOM
1¼
4'-7¾
1
3'-1⅛
6¾
7'-0³⁄₁₆"
8'-6" OVER BALCONY AT WAIST
DESK
EASY CHAIRS
TABLE
CABINET
SETTEE
CUPBOARD
DRESSING TABLE
STOOL
CUPBOARD
EASY CHAIRS
BED
STOOL
WASH BASIN
W.C
BATH
BERTH
WASH BOWLS
W.C
RAD
SEAT CONVERTIBLE TO BED FOR FOOTMAN
SCALE: 0 1 2 3 4 5 6 7 8 9 10 FEET.

Overleaf:
Figure 108 Chairman's Saloon D2066/2136/2137
These two carriages, illustrated on page 154, started out identically styled to D2066 but, on conversion, assumed slightly different internal arrangements for which two new diagrams were issued. All three versions are offered here at 3mm scale in view of the relative clarity of the drawings. Originally used by HRH The Princess Elizabeth and HRH The Duke of Edinburgh between 1948 and 1952, they then went into general Royal Train use for the Royal Household and other senior staff. When the Royal Train was extensively re-equipped from 1977 onwards (generally by BR Mk III types), they became largely redundant and, not being principal saloons (which were not allowed to be disposed of other than to the NRM), were allowed to be privately purchased for preservation. Their location was not known to the writers at the time of compilation (1999), nor whether they can be viewed.

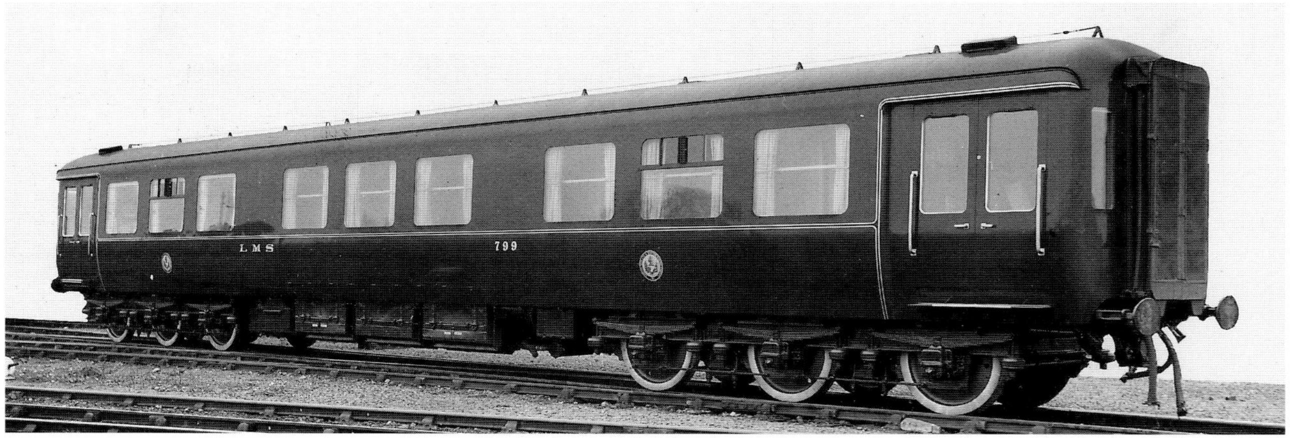

L M S
799

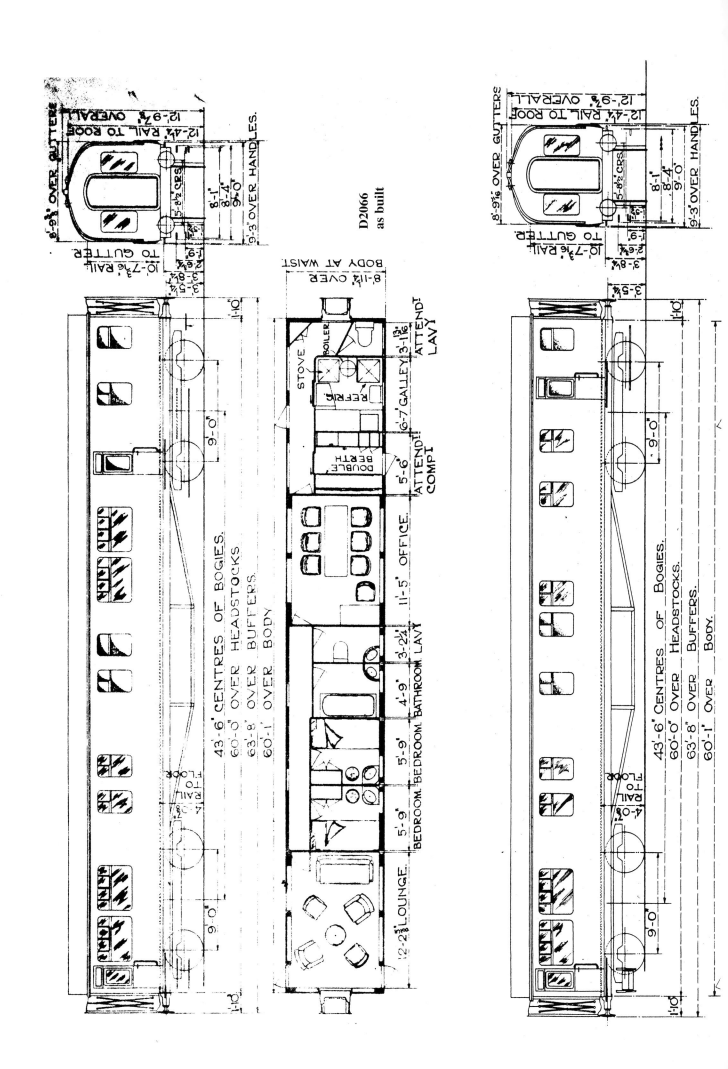

D2066
as built

162

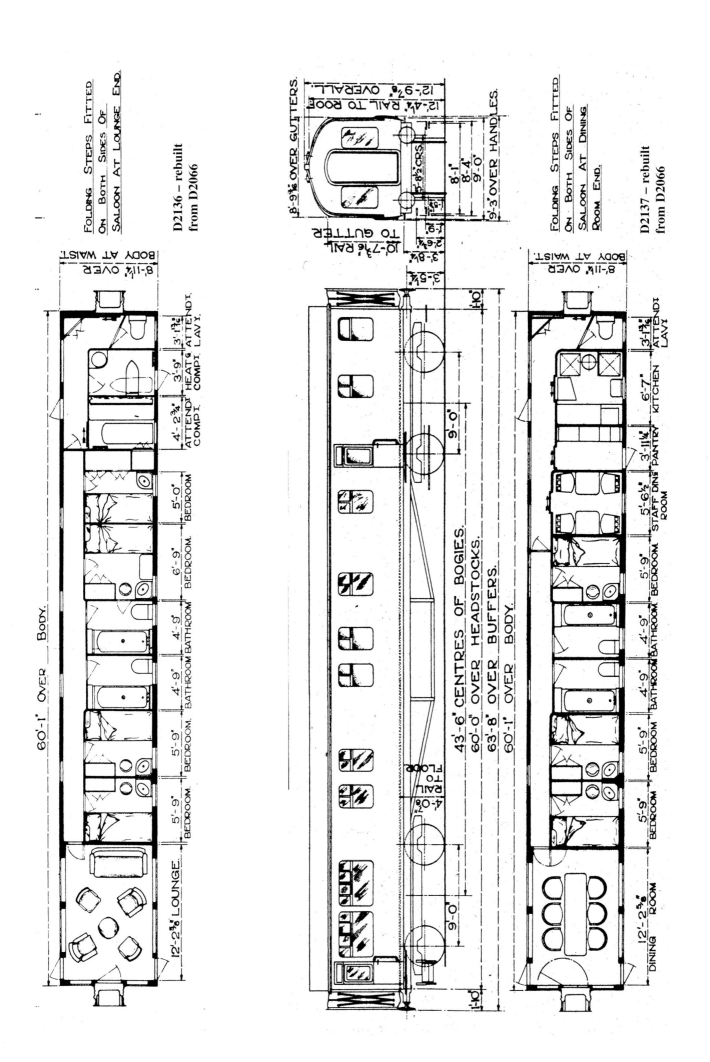

FOLDING STEPS FITTED
ON BOTH SIDES OF
SALOON AT LOUNGE END.

**D2136 – rebuilt
from D2066**

BODY AT WAIST.
8'-11⅛" OVER

60'-1" OVER BODY.

3'-1¹³⁄₁₆" HEAT'G ATTEND'T COMP'T LAV'Y.
4'-2¾" ATTEND'T COMP'T
5'-0" BEDROOM.
6'-9" BEDROOM.
4'-9" BATHROOM.
5'-9" BEDROOM.
5'-9" BEDROOM.
12'-2⅝" LOUNGE.

8'-9¾" OVER GUTTERS.

12'-9⅞" OVERALL.
12'-4⅜" RAIL TO ROOF

5'-8½" CRS.

8'-1"
8'-4"
9'-0"
9'-3" OVER HANDLES.

10'-7⅞₆" RAIL TO GUTTER.

3'-8¾"
2'-6½"
1'-9¼"
3'-5¾"

9'-0"

43'-6" CENTRES OF BOGIES.
60'-0" OVER HEADSTOCKS.
63'-8" OVER BUFFERS.
60'-1" OVER BODY.

4'-0⅞" RAIL TO FLOOR.

9'-0"

1'-10"

FOLDING STEPS FITTED
ON BOTH SIDES OF
SALOON AT DINING
ROOM END.

**D2137 – rebuilt
from D2066**

BODY AT WAIST.
8'-11⅛" OVER

3'-1¹³⁄₁₆" ATTEND'T LAV'Y.
6'-7" KITCHEN
3'-11¼" PANTRY
5'-6½" STAFF DIN'G ROOM
5'-9" BEDROOM.
4'-9" BATHROOM.
5'-9" BEDROOM.
12'-2⅝" DINING ROOM.

163

Chapter 8 - Electric Multiple-Unit Stock

Introduction; London Suburban Electric Stock; Liverpool-Southport Electric Stock;
MSJA Electric Stock; Mersey-Wirral Electric Stock

The self-propelled vehicles listed in the LMS diagram book fall into convenient self-contained categories which will be taken as the basis for this discussion. In summary, the types to be considered are as follows:

Electric multiple-unit stock

London suburban stock	- all compartment type
Liverpool-Southport stock	- a mixture of compartment and open types
MSJA stock	- all compartment type
Mersey-Wirral stock	- all open type

Other self-propelled stock

Steam Railcars }
Internal Combustion vehicles } See Chapter 9

The electric multiple-unit coaches accounted for the bulk of the vehicles built.

LONDON SUBURBAN ELECTRIC STOCK

The London electrified lines of the LMS consisted of the former LNWR routes between Broad Street and Richmond and between Euston and Watford with their associated links and branches. The electrification was initiated in 1911 and was in large measure completed some two months before the Grouping with the electrification of the Croxley Green branch. It was built and remained for many years a 630V dc four-rail system and its history is very well recorded already in *London's North Western Electric* by Atkinson and Adams, published in 1962 by the Electric Railway Society. Interested readers are referred to this very excellent account.

By the time the LMS came into existence, the North Western Electric already possessed a considerable number of vehicles composed of Siemens and Oerlikon centre-corridor open types but the expansion of services necessitated further provision of stock at a fairly early stage after 1923. Not surprisingly, this was of standard LMS non-corridor style and the first batches entered service in 1927.

Three varieties of coach were provided: 17 third class driving motor coaches, 12 composite trailers and 12 third class driving trailers. They ran as three-car sets with five spare motor cars, but the stock was never kept in regular formations. All coaches were steel panelled but carried full Period I LMS livery (ie with painted waist panel). The motor coaches were 59ft over headstocks, a unique dimension for LMS standard stock, with an equally unique bogie centre dimension of 39ft 6in (Figure 109). The electrical equipment, by GEC, was based on that of the LNWR Oerlikon sets with which the LMS coaches were designed to run in multiple, when necessary. The motor cars had four 280hp traction motors each. The trailers were of standard 57ft length and in every way similar to the contemporary locomotive-hauled stock.

Close-up of the composite trailer, No 5717, later 29608, from the three-car set at Figure 109.

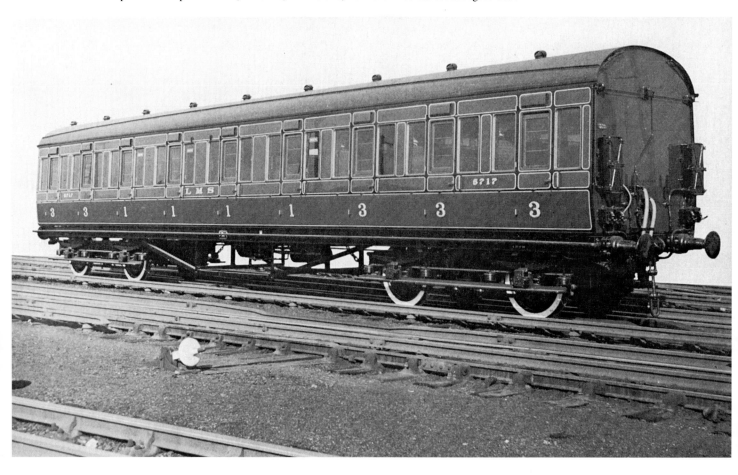

In 1929, this initial batch of LMS-design coaches was supplemented by a fourth type — this time a third class non-driving trailer of which 10 were supplied. These were used to make up some seven-car trains by being placed either 'inside' a three-car set or between two three-car sets. The coaches were again orthodox 57ft LMS types with fully lined livery.

The last batch of LMS stock for the North Western Electric system was a repeat order in 1932 for the first three types of coach; the electric traction motors were now, however, 320hp rather than 280hp. This new stock, again in full livery but this time without waist 'panel', made it possible to dispense with some of the seven-car trains by running a more frequent service with six-car formations. The number of coaches provided was slightly variable, 13 driving trailers being built but only eight motor cars. Since there were five spare motors from the 1927 batch, 13 sets could be formed. However, instead of ordering 13 composite trailers to go with the driving ends, only 10 were provided, three of the 1929 third class trailers (now no longer needed for seven-car sets) being converted to make up the 13 new three-car sets. The conversion was confined to reupholstery of the firsts and all nine compartments remained the same size. One more third class trailer of the 1929 batch was transferred to the MSJA system in 1939 which left six of the original 10 still running as thirds on the London lines. These too became surplus when seven-car trains ceased to run in 1941 (coincident with the abolition of first class on the system) but were not actually withdrawn until the advent of BR stock in 1957. Although LNWR saloon stock was gradually withdrawn after this date, the LMS compartment stock survived more or less intact until it too was withdrawn en bloc when timetable rationalisation rendered it redundant in 1963. It is interesting to recall that plans issued in 1933 foreshadowed the use of sliding door stock on the London area lines. In the event this was not pursued but the idea was adopted later for the Southport and Wirral lines.

TABLE 8a: SUMMARY OF LONDON SUBURBAN ELECTRIC STOCK

Type	Diag	Lot	Qty	Date	Built	Dimensions (LxWxH)	Running Numbers	Withdrawals First	Last
Motor Brake Third	1727	Part 235	17	1927	Met C&W	59ft x 9ft 2¼in x 12ft 5⅜in	28001-28017	6/62	11/63
	1847	636	8	1933	Wolverton	59ft x 9ft 2¼in x 12ft 4¾in	28018-28025	11/63	11/63
Composite Trailer*	1691	Part 237	12	1927	Clayton Wagons Ltd	57ft x 9ft 2¼in x12ft 5⅜in	29600-29611	2/57	11/63
	1846	622	10	1933	Wolverton	57ft x 9ft 2¼in x 12ft 5⅜in	29612-29621	11/63	11/63
Driving Trailer Third	1728	Part 236	12	1927	Midland Ry C & W Ltd	57ft x 9ft 2¼in x 12ft 5⅜in	28800-28811	11/63	11/63
		623	13	1933	Wolverton		28812-28824	11/63	11/63
Third Trailer†	1684	464	10	1929	Wolverton	57ft x 9ft 2¼in x 12ft 5⅜in	29400-29409	2/57	11/63

* Downgraded to third in 1941.

† Subsequent history as follows:

> 29400/7/8 altered to composite becoming 29622-4 in order (2/33).
> 29401 transferred to MSJA becoming MSJA 153 in 1939.

Note: In all probability, the three coaches of D1684 which were altered to composite never carried their 1933 series **third** class numbers since the conversion approximately coincided with the 1932/3 renumbering.

Right:
Close-up of the end of a third class trailer from the 1929 batch.

Below:
Motor bogie from one of the London area sets.

Five-coach train of Liverpool-Southport compartment stock as running in BR days in unlined green livery.

LIVERPOOL-SOUTHPORT ELECTRIC STOCK

The Liverpool-Southport line was originally electrified on the 550V dc system, later being altered to the more common 630V dc supply; apart from this, the first LMS coaches built for use on the line were compartment vehicles identical to those provided in 1927 for the London suburban area. In fact, the coaches were built at the same time, to the same diagram and lot numbers. Eleven three-coach sets (motor brake third/composite trailer/driving trailer third) were provided, plus an extra composite trailer. Five of the non-driving trailers were later transferred to the MSJA system as all thirds in 1939 — presumably they could be spared as a result of the large-scale building of open stock for the Southport line. In 1953, one each of the motor thirds and driving trailer thirds were converted at Derby as baggage cars for use on the system, part of the electrical equipment and traction motors being transferred from the motor coach to the driving trailer to form a second motor coach.

In 1939, the first of a considerable order for open stock was placed in service on the Southport line with English Electric equipment. These were very long coaches (66ft 6in) and moreover were 9ft 3in wide over body and 9ft 7in overall since the Liverpool-Southport line's loading gauge was more generous than elsewhere; indeed the original LYR stock for the line was 10ft wide. Four varieties were produced: motor brake thirds, trailer thirds, trailer composites and driving trailer composites, of which the driving coaches were bow-ended at the driving end. The motor coaches were fitted with four 180hp traction motors. The 1939 Liverpool-Southport stock was of lightweight all-steel welded construction in which the car body from underframe to roof formed a single girder structure; motor coaches for example weighed only 41 tons and trailer cars 24 tons compared with 56 tons and 28 tons respectively for 1927/33 stock.

The driving trailer composites were an insertion of a type not allowed for the 1932/3 LMS block number scheme and, in consequence, their numbers were allocated towards the end of the non-driving composite series. When new, the coaches were finished in a modified form of the simple LMS coach livery. They were painted all crimson with a yellow/black/yellow line along the waist but *no* lining above the windows. Insignia was of standard LMS pattern. The driving coaches also carried the coach number on the front as indeed did most Liverpool area electric stock.

Electric baggage car No 28497. This coach was originally Liverpool-Southport driving trailer third No 29106.

Three-car set in LMS livery as built. This was the first set to enter service; later ones were given the 1940-style scroll pattern running numbers. The leading vehicle is a driving trailer composite (No 29866) and the centre car a trailer third (No 29545).

Motor brake third No M28315 in BR livery — unlined green.

Interior view of the first class seating area of driving trailer composite No 29885.

The quantities of each type built — see Table 8b — allowed for the formation of 34 three-car sets (motor third/trailer third/driving trailer composite) and 25 two-car sets consisting of a motor third plus trailer (16 thirds and nine composites). It will be appreciated, therefore, that not all sets had the same number of first and third class seats.

It may have been this imbalance between the seating accommodation which caused the somewhat confusing postwar rebuilding of the nine trailer composites (Nos 29812-20). Six were built as trailer thirds (Nos 29812-7) and, at a later stage, the other three were rebuilt as driving trailer composite (Nos 29818-20) along with one of the six which already had become 'all third'. Curiously, no diagrams were ever issued for these conversions. At the completion of this conversion operation, the final tally of coaches was as follows:

Motor thirds	- 59 (all as built)
Trailer thirds	- 55 (50 as built plus five downgraded trailer composites)
Driving trailer composites	- 38 (34 as built plus four ex-trailer composites)

By 1968, five motor and two non-driving trailers had been withdrawn from this total and the remaining stock was formed into 38 three-car sets, 15 two-car sets and a spare motor. The sets remained permanently formed almost in their original 1939 formations.

The open coaches seated two each side of the gangway in the first class sections and had a three-and-two arrangement in the thirds (later seconds). They also had a proportion of longitudinal seats adjacent to the entrance which were of sliding-door-type opening on to a reasonably sized passenger standing area. Except in respect of the surviving two-class accommodation, the interior arrangement was reminiscent of the London Transport Metropolitan and District line sets. The exterior styling was, of course, rather different and was shared only with the Mersey-Wirral sets — see page 171.

TABLE 8b: SUMMARY OF LIVERPOOL-SOUTHPORT ELECTRIC STOCK

Type	Diag	Lot	Qty	Date	Built	Dimensions* (L x W x H)	Running Numbers	Withdrawals First	Last	Remarks
Compartment stock										
Motor Brake Third	1727	Part 235	11	1927	Met. C&W	59ft x 9ft 2¼in x 12ft 5⅜in	28300-28310	3/53	7/63	
Composite Trailer†	1691	Part 237	12	1927	Clayton Wagons Ltd	57ft x 9ft 2¼in x 12ft 5⅜in	29800-29811	1939	7/63	
Driving Trailer Third	1728	Part 236	11	1927	Midland Ry C & W Ltd	57ft x 9ft 2¼in x12ft 5⅜in	29100-29110	4/53	7/63	see footnotes
Baggage car	2178	Part 236	1	1953	Derby	57ft x 9ft 2³/₈in x 12ft 5⅜in	28497Å	-	2/66	
	2179	Part 235	1	1953	Derby	59ft x 9ft 2³/₈in x 12ft 5⅜in	28496¤	-	2/66	
Open stock										
Motor Brake Third	2012	1073	59	1939	Derby	66ft 5¼in x 9ft 3in x 11ft 5in	28311-28369			The open stock was actually delivered to service during the 1939-43 period.
Composite Trailer#	2009	1076	9	1939	Derby	66ft 5¼in x 9ft 3in x 11ft 5in	29812-29820	See footnotes		
Third Trailer	2011	1074	50	1939	Derby	66ft 5¼in x 9ft 3in x 11ft 5in	29545-29594			
Driving Trailer Composite	2013	1075	34	1939	Derby	66ft 5¼in x 9ft 3in x 11ft 5in	29866-29899			

* Width of open stock is quoted over body. Over handles it was almost 9ft 7in.
† The following coaches transferred to MSJA in 1939, No 29800/2/3/8/11 becoming MSJA 154-8.
Å Originally No 29106 (D1728)
¤ Originally No 28300 (D1727)
Subsequent rebuilding as follows:
        No 29812-7 rebuilt to all third and renumbered No 29595-9; No 29544 in same order.
        No 29818-20 rebuilt to driving trailer composite becoming No 29863-5 in same order.
        No 29597 (originally No 29814) rebuilt to driving trailer composite and numbered No 29862.
        Note: The withdrawn coaches by 1968, all as a result of damage, were as follows:
        Motor brake thirds (later seconds): No 28320/1/5/9/46.
        Third trailers (later seconds): No 29576; 29544 (ex-29817).

Third class seating in third class trailer No 29545.

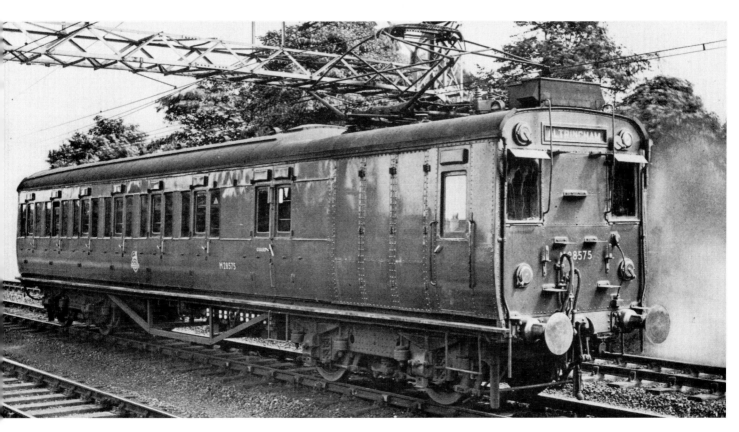

Motor brake third No M28575 as running in BR livery without louvres on the side doors (MSJA No 5).

MSJA ELECTRIC STOCK

The Manchester South Junction & Altrincham Railway was nominally an independent concern until 1947. It was owned jointly by the LMS and LNER and when it was electrified in 1931, it became the first line to be converted to the 1500V dc overhead system.

The stock for running the electrified services was of LMS standard style but, uniquely, all three varieties of coach were built on 58ft underframes — the only LMS diagrams of this length. The stock was built by Metropolitan-Cammell with Metrovick equipment and presented an orthodox Period II non-corridor appearance except for the lowered roof where the pantographs were fixed; 22 three-car sets were built (motor brake third/composite trailer/driving trailer third) plus two spare motors. All the motor cars were equipped with four 330hp traction motors. All the stock was given MSJA numbers and livery. The latter employed a mid-green body colour which was lined in LMS Period II style (ie full lining but no waist panel). The coaches also carried the MSJAR monogram and coat of arms. In 1948, the coaches were numbered into LMS (now LMR) 1932/3 block series and both these and the MSJA numbers are given in the summary table.

In 1939, a decision was made to strengthen some of the peak trains to seven cars and, for this purpose, eight trailer thirds were acquired. Two were built for the task at Wolverton, one came from the London suburban area and five from the Liverpool-Southport line. In style, all matched the original MSJA stock — except that they were 57ft long — and they were repainted and renumbered in the MSJA series. The experiment was not successful and the eight coaches had a mixed history afterwards. One was converted to a driving trailer (No 74) to replace an accident victim (No 57). No diagram was issued although the coach was 57ft not 58ft long. Six of the remaining seven were stored out of use for a long time, while the seventh acted as a spare coach. In 1954, six were converted to locomotive-hauled coaches, renumbered and transferred away from the MSJA area. One of the latter even turned up in a Euston-Bletchley-Northampton local set for a time.

A driving motor (No 28575) and a composite trailer (No 29664) were withdrawn in 1963 following a collision but apart from these, the stock remained virtually unchanged until late 1966 when the number of three-car sets was reduced to 16. These remained in service throughout the 1960s and gave to the railway enthusiast his last opportunity of regularly riding in pure prewar LMS-type compartment stock. Two survive in private ownership, converted for locomotive haulage.

Third class trailer No 151 (MSJA series) showing the MSJA livery. This was one of two cars built at Wolverton in 1939 to supplement those transferred from the London and Liverpool areas. In spite of the late date of building it was given full lining and Period II styling. The body colour was light green and the coaches carried the MSJAR monogram and crest.

First class compartment interior of MSJA trailer composite No 104.

TABLE 8c: SUMMARY OF MSJAR ELECTRIC STOCK

Type	Diag	Lot	Qty	Date	Built	Wt	Dimensions (L x W x H)	MSJA Nos	LMS Series Numbers	Withdrawals First	Last
Motor Brake Third	1724	504	24	1931	Met-Camm	57T	58ft x 9ft 3in x 12ft 4¾in	1-24	28571-28594	12/63	not known
Composite Trailer	1726	505	22	1931	Met-Camm	30T	58ft x 9ft 3in x 12ft 4¾in	101-122	29650-29671	12/63	not known
Driving Trailer Third*	1725	506	22	1931	Met-Camm	31T	58ft x 9ft 3in x 12ft 4¾in	51-56	29231-29236	13/48	not known
								57	Accident		
								58	29237		
								59-72	29239-29252		
Trailer Third†	1684	1158	2	1939	Wolverton	28T	57ft x 9ft 2¼in x 12ft 5⅝in	151-152	29390-29391	See Note 1	

* One more driving trailer (MSJA 74) rebuilt from trailer third No 153 (below) and renumbered 29238 in 1948.
† Six more trailer thirds as follows: 153 was ex-London Suburban No 29401 and later became driving trailer 74. 154-8 were ex-Liverpool-Southport composite trailers 29800/2/3/8/11 (D1691). In 1948, these five became 29392-29396.

Notes:
1. In 1954, trailer thirds Nos 29390-5 (ex-MSJA 151/2/4-7) were altered to locomotive-hauled stock and renumbered 12278-83 in the LMS series non-corridor third class number block. 29396 withdrawn period 7/66.
2. All the renumbering of the MSJA stock into the LMS block series took place after Nationalisation so the coaches were given the appropriate 'M' prefixes and suffixes with effect from the renumbering date.

LMS-built three-car Mersey-Wirral set when new. Note the non-standard LMS insignia and absence of lining above the window. The waist lining was carried on a raised beading strip. The picture shows a driving trailer third leading.

BR-built three-car set with motor brake third leading. Note by comparison with Plate 211 the absence of waist beading and the outward-facing solebar channel.

MERSEY-WIRRAL ELECTRIC STOCK

The system of suburban electrification, on the 650V dc third rail system, originated as two separate concerns which made an end-on junction at Birkenhead Park. East of this location and below the river to Liverpool, the lines belonged to the Mersey Railway while the remainder was LMS (ex-Wirral Railway) property. The Mersey Railway was electrified in 1903 but the Wirral lines to West Kirby and New Brighton were not converted until 1938. Both halves of the system lost independent identity in 1948.

The new stock for the 1938 electrification built by the LMS to supplement existing Mersey Railway stock took the form of 19 three-car sets (motor brake third/composite trailer/driving trailer third). The motor thirds had four 135hp traction motors. The coaches were all of open pattern with styling almost identical to that exhibited by the 1939 Liverpool-Southport stock (above). In fact, it is possible that the Mersey-Wirral stock set the pattern for the coaches built for the Southport line. There were, however, a few differences worthy of note. The Mersey-Wirral coaches were much shorter than the Southport vehicles being 58ft over headstocks (driving coaches) or 56ft over headstocks (non-driving trailers). There were two seats each side of the gangway (third class) or two-and-one (first class). The overall width over foot boards, however, was no less than 9ft 11in. Like the Southport sets, the Wirral stock was of lightweight construction, motor coaches taring 36 tons and trailers only 20 tons. The coaches had sliding doors and longitudinal seating adjacent to the entrance area. The combination of shorter body and narrower width made a considerable difference to the seating capacity compared with the Southport coaches.

The stock was finished in the same modified version of the simplified LMS livery as described for the Liverpool-Southport stock, but was given non-standard sans serif insignia edged in black. The coaches were assembled in sets in correct number order but two driving trailers and two non-driving trailers were destroyed at Birkenhead during the war.

In 1956-7, the ex-Mersey Railway stock was scrapped and replaced by 24 further sets of the LMS type. The main differences between these and the 1938 coaches were in external detail. The 1956 stock had slight detail changes in the windows, no raised beading strip along the waist and was built with an *outward*-facing solebar channel. The passenger-open push-buttons for the sliding doors were on the doors themselves on 1938 stock but on the bodysides on the 1956 stock. Along with the 24 new sets, opportunity was also taken to replace the war losses mentioned above. Unlike the LMS sets, the formation of the BR-built sets, although normally remaining unchanged, was not in any particular order of running numbers. The actual running numbers of the 1956 sets did not run consecutively with the LMS-built coaches but were in the correct number blocks.

The building of the Mersey-Wirral open stock was a joint venture between the Birmingham Railway Carriage & Wagon Company and Metropolitan-Cammell. The former firm built the driving trailers, Metro-Cammell the motors and the two works shared the non-driving trailers.

First class interior of one of the LMS-built composite trailers.   Third, now second, class interior of BR-built motor brake third No 28371.

TABLE 8d: SUMMARY OF LMS-DESIGN MERSEY-WIRRAL ELECTRIC STOCK

	Type	Diag	Lot	Qty	Date	Built	Wt	Dimensions (L x W* x H)	Running Numbers
Motor Brake Third	2004	1009	19	1938	Met-Camm	36T		58ft x 9ft 1in x 11ft 5in	28672-28690
		1685	24	1956	Met-Camm	37T ⎱			28371-28394
Composite Trailer	2005	1012	11	1938	Birmingham	20T ⎰		56ft x 9ft 1in x 11ft 5in	29702-29712
		1010	8	1938	Met-Camm		20T ⎱		29713-29720
		1682	10	1956	Birmingham		20T ⎟		29821-29830
		1684	2	1956	Birmingham		20T ⎟		29831-29832†
		1686	14	1956	Met-Camm		20T ⎰		29833-29846
Driving Trailer Third	2006	1011	19	1938	Birmingham	21T ⎱			29721-29289
		1681	24	1956	Birmingham	22T ⎰		58ft x 9ft 1in x 11ft 5in	29131-29514
		1683	2	1956	Birmingham	22T}			29155-29156†

* Width is quoted over handles. Over footboards the stock measured 9ft 1in and over body it was 8ft 8in.

† These lots built as replacements for wartime losses as follows:
Composite trailers: Nos 29708: 29717 (which ran with motors 28678: 28687).
Driving trailers: Nos 29277: 29286 (which ran with motors 28678: 28687).

TABLE 8e: THE 1933 RENUMBERING OF LMS STANDARD ELECTRIC STOCK

Note: The 1933 renumbering allocated rather widely separated number blocks for the London and Liverpool area carriages, albeit that the same diagrams were involved in most cases. This was mainly so that within each generic type, the pre-1923 electric stock from the LNWR and LYR respectively could be numbered immediately after the LMS types alongside which they ran. Pre-1933 numbers for LMS-built stock were mostly somewhat random in the London area, whereas in the Liverpool area pre-1933 numbers generally formed a consecutive series. The following lists separate them out according to area — see also Tables 8a/8b — but note also that the MSJA stock (Table 8c) did not receive LMS series numbers until after Nationalisation and these are therefore included in Table 8c itself.

New Numbers	Old Numbers
Motor Brake Third D1727	
London Area Stock	
28001-6	4605-10
28007	5801
28008	8800
28009-17	8880-88
Liverpool Area Stock	
28300-10	8889-99
Motor Brake Third D1847	
London Area Stock*	
28018	2019
28019-20	2025-6
28021	2031
28022	2039
28023	2121
28024	2234
28025	2253

*Allocated but may not have been carried — see caption to Fig. 110.

New Numbers	Old Numbers
Composite Trailer D1691	
London Area Stock	
29600-3	4615-8
29604-9	5713-8
29610-1	10679-80
Liverpool Area Stock	
29800-11	10682-93

New Numbers	Old Numbers
Composite Trailer D1846	
London Area Stock*	
29612	1886
29613	1892
29614	1895
29615	1898
29616	1901
29617	1905
29618	1912
29619	1917
29620-1	1922-3

*Allocated but may not have been carried — see ex-works view of 28819 at Figure 113

New Numbers	Old Numbers
Driving Trailer Third D1728	
London Area Stock	
28800-3	4611-4
28804-11	5236-43
28812	1931
28813	1934
28814	1939
28815	1952
28816	1956
28817	1959
28818-9	1964-5
28820	1968
28821	1971
28822	1976
28823	1984
28824	1993
Liverpool Area Stock	
29100-6	5244-50
29107-9	5358-60
29110	10020

New Numbers	Old Numbers
Third Trailer D1684	
London Area Stock	
29400-9	14403-12#

#Believed correct; LMS list is only part complete.

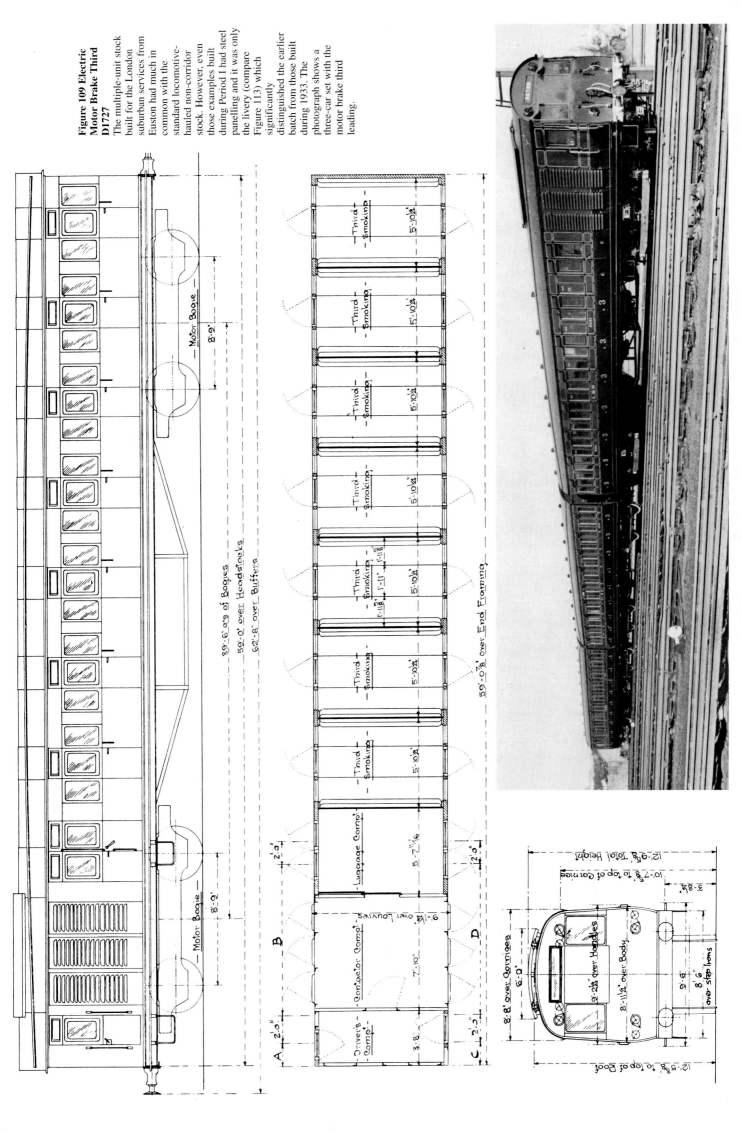

Figure 109 Electric Motor Brake Third D1727

The multiple-unit stock built for the London suburban services from Euston had much in common with the standard locomotive-hauled non-corridor stock. However, even those examples built during Period I had steel panelling and it was only the livery (compare Figure 113) which significantly distinguished the earlier batch from those built during 1933. The photograph shows a three-car set with the motor brake third leading.

Motor Bogie

8'-9"

Motor Bogie

8'-9"

39'-6" c'rs of Bogies

59'-0" over Headstocks

62'-8" over Buffers

Third Smoking 5'-10¼"

Third Smoking 5'-10¼"

Third Smoking 5'-10¼"

Third Smoking 5'-10¼"

Third Smoking 5'-10¼"

Third Smoking 5'-10¼"

Third Smoking 5'-10¼"

1'-11½" 5' 1'-11"

Luggage Comp'. 5'-7"¹⁶

59'-0⅞" over End Framing

A 2'-0"

B

Conductor Comp'. 9'-1¼" over Louvres

C 2'-3"

D 2'-0"

Driver's Comp'. 3'-8"

7'-10"

12'-9⅝" Total Height

10'-7⅜" to top of Cornice

3'-8½"

8'-8" over Carriages

6'-0"

9'-2¼" over Handles

8'-11¼" over Body

2'-6"

8'-6" over Step Irons

12'-5⅜" to top of Roof

This official Metropolitan C&W picture shows D1727 No 8898 (later 28309) of the Liverpool-Southport series. As far as can be judged, save for original livery, the succeeding D1847 (London area only — below), was largely identical in style.

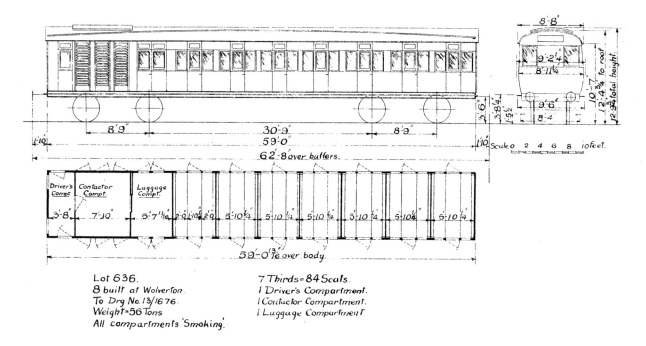

Lot 636.
8 built at Wolverton.
To Drg No.13/1676.
Weight=56 Tons
All compartments 'Smoking'.

7 Thirds=84 Seats.
1 Driver's Compartment.
1 Contactor Compartment.
1 Luggage Compartment.

Figure 110 Electric Motor Brake Third D1847

This sub-standard diagram was issued for the final batch of carriages to Lot 636 (Table 8a). It was essentially Period II in character, but given that the earlier D1727 also had steel panelling, there was no significant difference (all essential dimensions are identical) and it is hard to understand why a new diagram was raised, given that their contemporary driving trailers were inserted on the original diagram applicable to that type (Figure 113). Their original livery saw a suppression of the painted waist panel compared with D1727 and they were originally finished as per the contemporary driving trailer shown at Figure 113. Also, they probably carried their 1933 series running numbers from new.

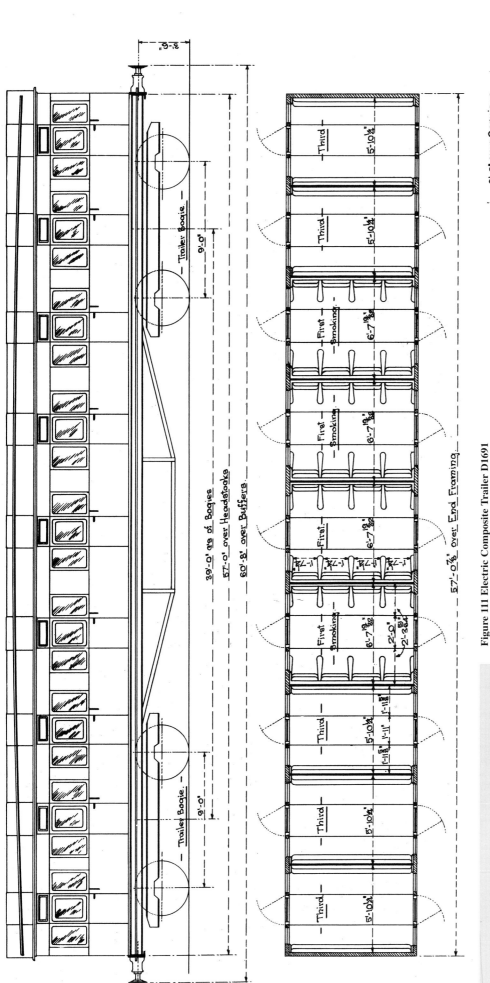

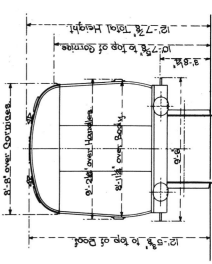

Figure 111 Electric Composite Trailer D1691

Although mounted on the standard 57ft underframe, the 4F + 5T layout of these carriages made them subtly different from the standard 3F + 6T layout of the contemporary locomotive-hauled stock. It is also perhaps worth noting that the first class armrests could be folded away to give five per side at busy times — shades of the Cathcart Circle stock, see Chapter 2. The accompanying view (an enlarged portion of an alternative view of the full set shown at Figure 109) shows No 5717 (later 29608) when first put into service. In 1939, some of them were transferred to MSJAR stock and downgraded to all third — see notes to Tables 8b/8c.

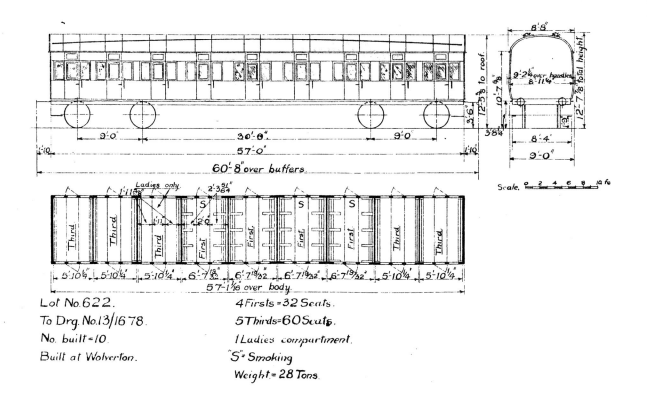

Lot No. 622.
To Drg. No. 13/1678.
No. built = 10.
Built at Wolverton.

4 Firsts = 32 Seats.
5 Thirds = 60 Seats.
1 Ladies compartment.
"S" = Smoking
Weight = 28 Tons.

Figure 112 Electric Composite Trailer D1846

As with D1847 — page 174 — this sub-standard diagram was raised for what, save for original livery, was an exact repeat of the previous type down to the very last fraction of an inch in compartment dimensions and, once again, the precise reason for the new diagram is obscure. No picture can be offered but the general styling of these 10 carriages was exactly as shown for the matching driving trailers, illustrated at Figure 113 (opposite).

This interesting, albeit less than perfectly exposed, official picture prompts a number of observations. Superficially, it looks like the opposite side of a standard three-coach set from the London area as illustrated at Figure 109. Motor Third No 28006 (formerly 4610) leads followed by the usual Trailer Composite/Driving Trailer Third pairing. However, on closer scrutiny, the Trailer Composite's running number (29623) reveals it to have been one of the former trailer thirds (29407, formerly 14410 — Tables 8a/8c) while the driving trailer third (almost certainly No 28814) is from the later series with 'Period II' livery — see Fig.113. This was therefore one of the 'hybrid' sets formed up in 1932 — see text, page 165 — and probably accounts for the picture being taken, although it cannot be dated: the set is clearly not ex-works. The retention of the fully lined livery until full repainting after the 1933 renumbering was not unusual on LMS standard stock, but it is perhaps worth commenting that the 'London Electrics' (including ex-LNWR types) usually retained their fully lined livery until the war years.

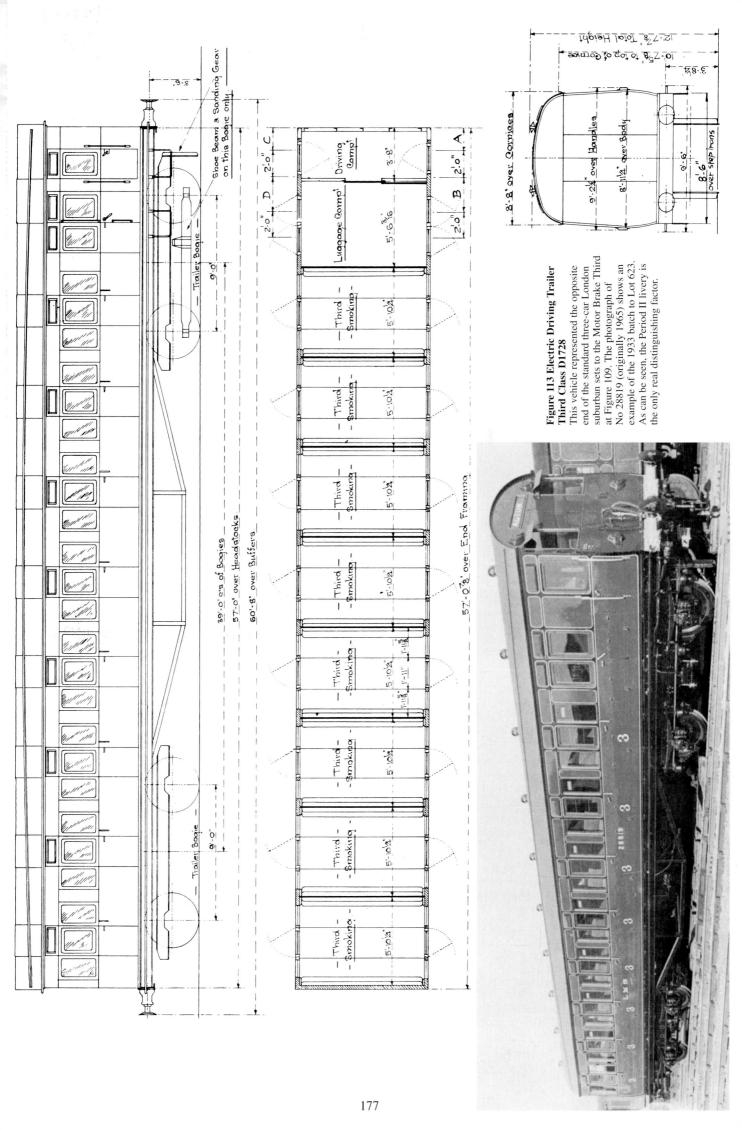

Figure 113 Electric Driving Trailer Third Class D1728

This vehicle represented the opposite end of the standard three-car London suburban sets to the Motor Brake Third at Figure 109. The photograph of No 28819 (originally 1965) shows an example of the 1933 batch to Lot 623. As can be seen, the Period II livery is the only real distinguishing factor.

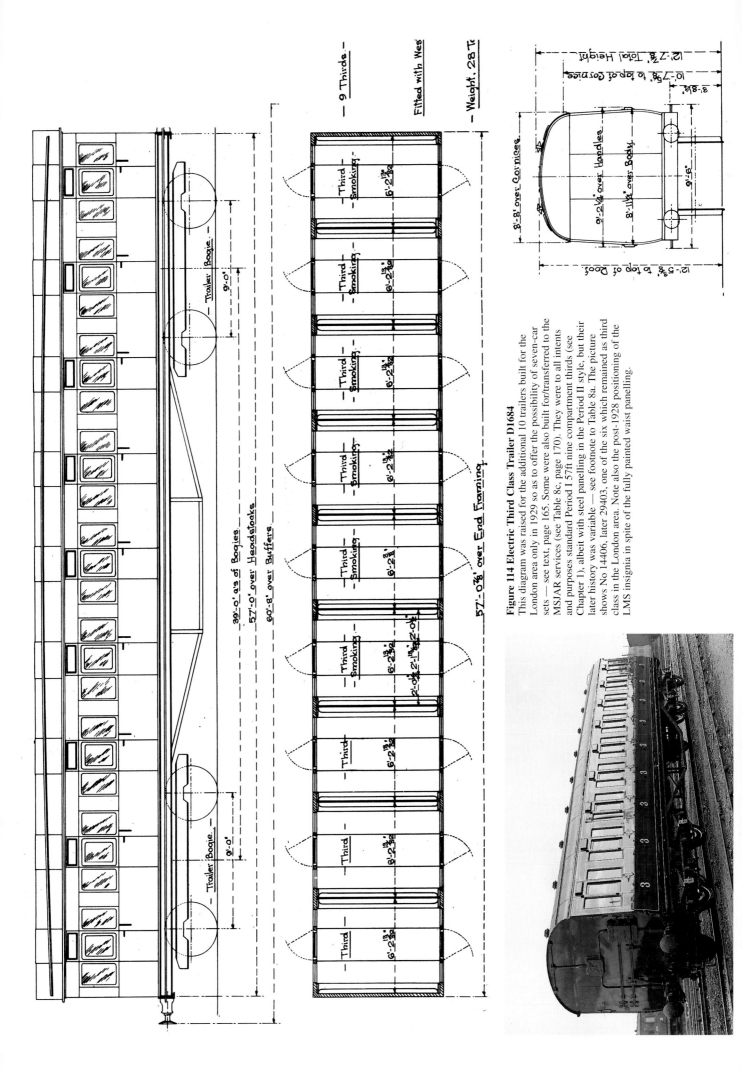

Figure 114 Electric Third Class Trailer D1684

This diagram was raised for the additional 10 trailers built for the London area only in 1929 so as to offer the possibility of seven-car sets — see text, page 165. Some were also built for/transferred to the MSJAR services (see Table 8c, page 170). They were to all intents and purposes standard Period I 57ft nine compartment thirds (see Chapter 1), albeit with steel panelling in the Period II style, but their later history was variable — see footnote to Table 8a. The picture shows No 14406, later 29403, one of the six which remained as third class in the London area. Note also the post-1928 positioning of the LMS insignia in spite of the fully painted waist panelling.

9 Thirds.

Fitted with Wes

Weight, 28 T

9'-0' Trailer Bogie.

9'-0' Trailer Bogie.

39'-0' c's of Bogies.

57'-0' over Headstocks.

60'-8' over Buffers.

57'-0⅞' over End Framing.

Third Smoking. 6'-2¹³⁄₃₂'

Third Smoking. 6'-2¹³⁄₃₂'

Third Smoking. 6'-2¹³⁄₃₂'

Third Smoking. 6'-2¹³⁄₃₂'

Third Smoking. 6'-2³⁄₈'

Third Smoking. 6'-2¹³⁄₃₂'

2'-0' 2'-1¹³⁄₁₆' 2'-0'

Third. 6'-2¹³⁄₃₂'

Third. 8'-2¹³⁄₃₂' 2'-0'

Third. 6'-2¹³⁄₃₂'

8'-8' over Cornices.

10'-7⅝' to top of Cornices.

12'-7⅞' Total Height.

3'-8¼'

9'-6'

9'-2¼' over Handles.

8'-11¼' over Body.

12'-5⅜' to top of Roof.

Given the date of their introduction to service at the outbreak of World War 2, ex-works official pictures of the trend-setting Liverpool-Southport sliding-door electric stock are, unsurprisingly, rather rare. However, the expansion of this survey compared with the original single-volume work allows us to offer such other views as have been located, additional to those on pages 167/8 of the main narrative.

The two external views show typical three-car sets photographed from the Motor Brake Third end, the first of them (car No 28311 leading) being a posed opposite end view of the set also illustrated at the top of page 167. The second view, taken from the rear of a train in service moving away from the photographer (note the tail lamp), is of a similar set with the later scroll-type insignia. This was only the fifth set to be put into service and may well have been the first to display this slight change of style.

The interior view cannot be identified positively, but is undoubtedly the central portion of a third class trailer to D2011 (page 182), the 3 + 2 seating combined with four bays between doors being unique to this type. It is likely, however, that it is the first of the series, No 29545, another interior view of which is given on page 168.

It is also worth mentioning that because of their importance in the context of multiple-unit electric stock development (eg sliding doors, etc) plus their integral form of construction, the NRM elected to preserve a pair of these carriages in fully working order — see also Figures 115/118. This was done in 1980 at the time of the 150th anniversary of the Liverpool & Manchester Railway and they were subsequently restored to LMS external condition at Steamport, Southport.

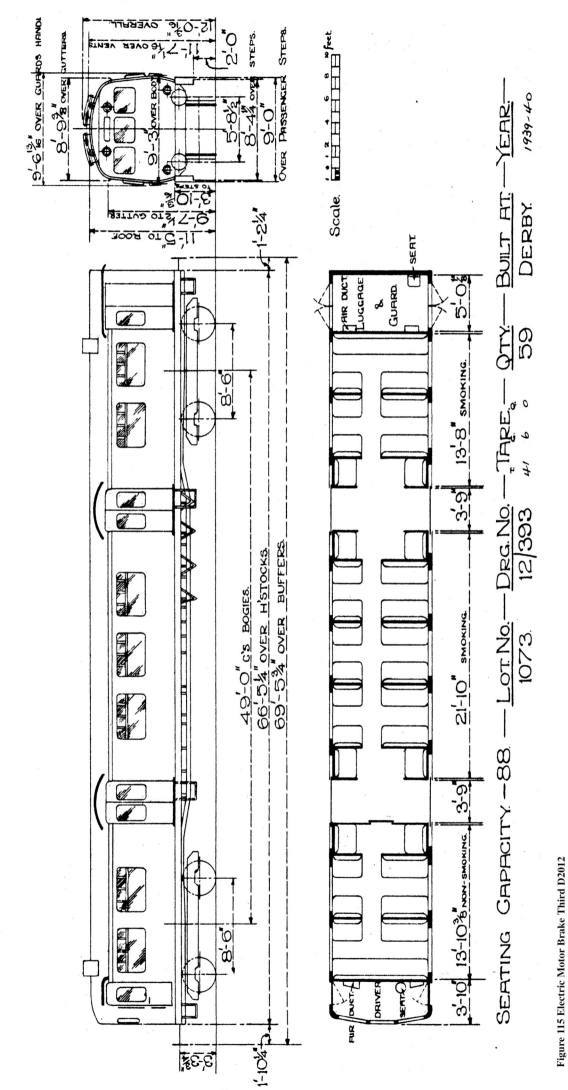

Figure 115 Electric Motor Brake Third D2012
The relatively clean nature of the diagrams issued for the sliding-door electric stock for the Liverpool-Southport area allows a somewhat larger scale of reproduction than for most of the later LMS types so we offer the next few pages at 3mm=1ft scale. On this page is featured the numerically largest type, which figured in both the three-car and two-car sets — see text, page 168. The diagram is self-explanatory and external views are offered on the previous page. No 28361 is preserved in the National Collection (see also D2013 overleaf).

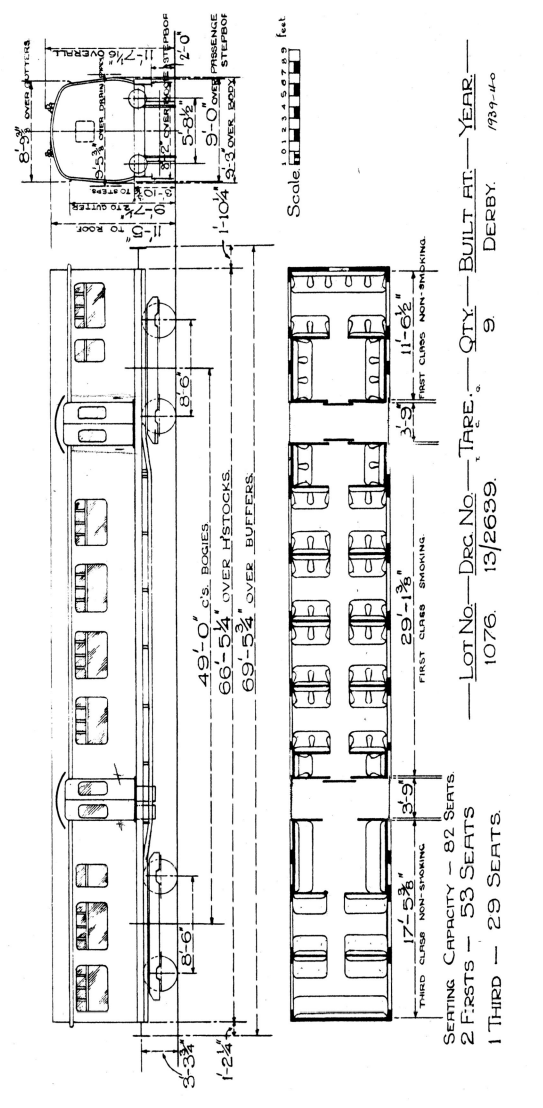

Figure 116 Electric Composite Trailer D2009

This was the least common of the sliding-door Liverpool-Southport types and they did not last long in the form in which built where they accounted for the trailer element of about one third of the original two-car sets. Structurally and dimensionally they were not too dissimilar from the trailer thirds and driving trailer composites (overleaf) which allowed their subsequent postwar conversion to both these forms, described in more detail on page 168, including Table 8b.

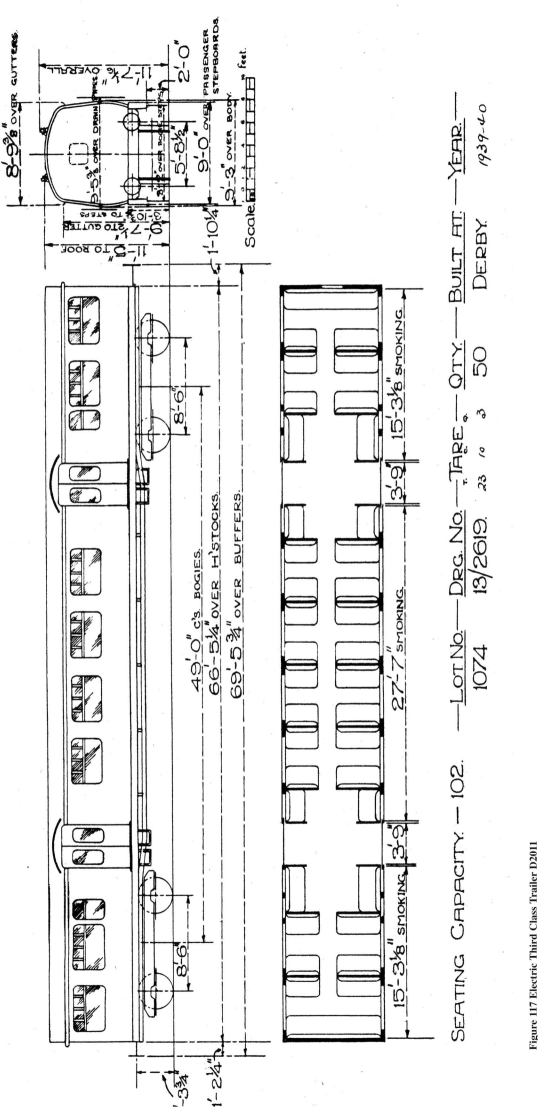

Figure 117 Electric Third Class Trailer D2011

This type formed the 'middle' element of the original three-car units plus some two thirds of the trailer element of the original two-car sets, examples being present in the centre of the formations shown on pages 167 and 179. They remained unchanged for the whole of their working life and the diagram is self-explanatory as to detail. Five of the former trailer composites (previous page) were later converted to this type — see page 168.

SEATING CAPACITY.	— 102.	— LOT No.	— DRG. No.	— TARE.	— QTY.	— BUILT AT	— YEAR.
		1074	13/2619.	23 ᵗᵒ 3	50	DERBY.	1939-40

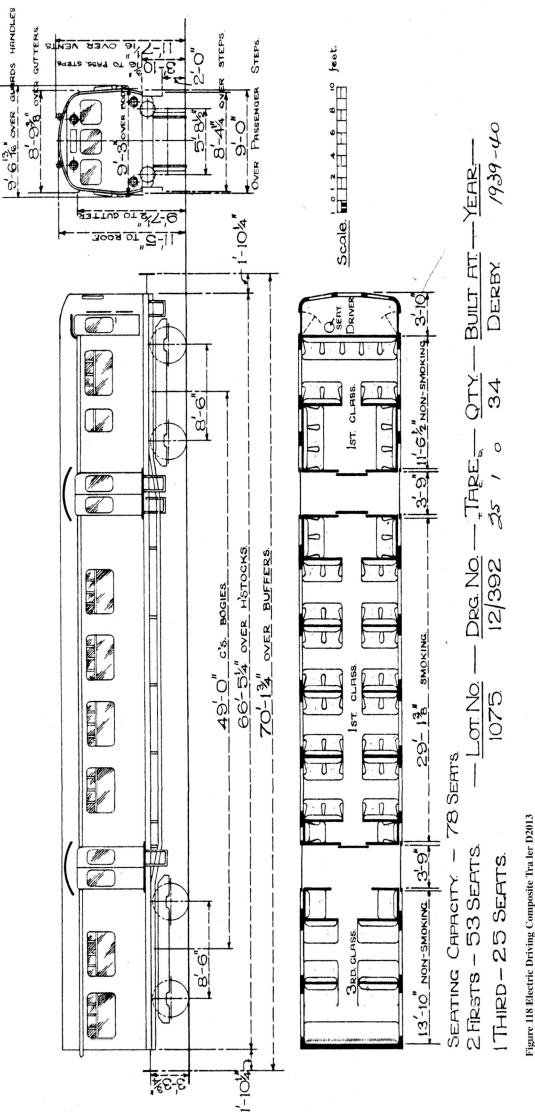

SEATING CAPACITY — 78 SEATS.

2 FIRSTS — 53 SEATS.   — LOT No. — DRG. No. — TARE. — QTY. — BUILT AT. — YEAR. —

1 THIRD — 25 SEATS.   1075   12/392   25 1 0   34   DERBY.   1939-40

Figure 118 Electric Driving Composite Trailer D2013
This was a new generic type to which four of D2009 (page 181) were later converted — see page 168. The relatively high number of first class seats in these sets was undoubtedly a result of the prosperous hinterland which they served along the Lancashire coast north of Liverpool. One of them (29–96), along with Motor Third No 28361 has been preserved by the NRM as a typical pairing of these important carriages.

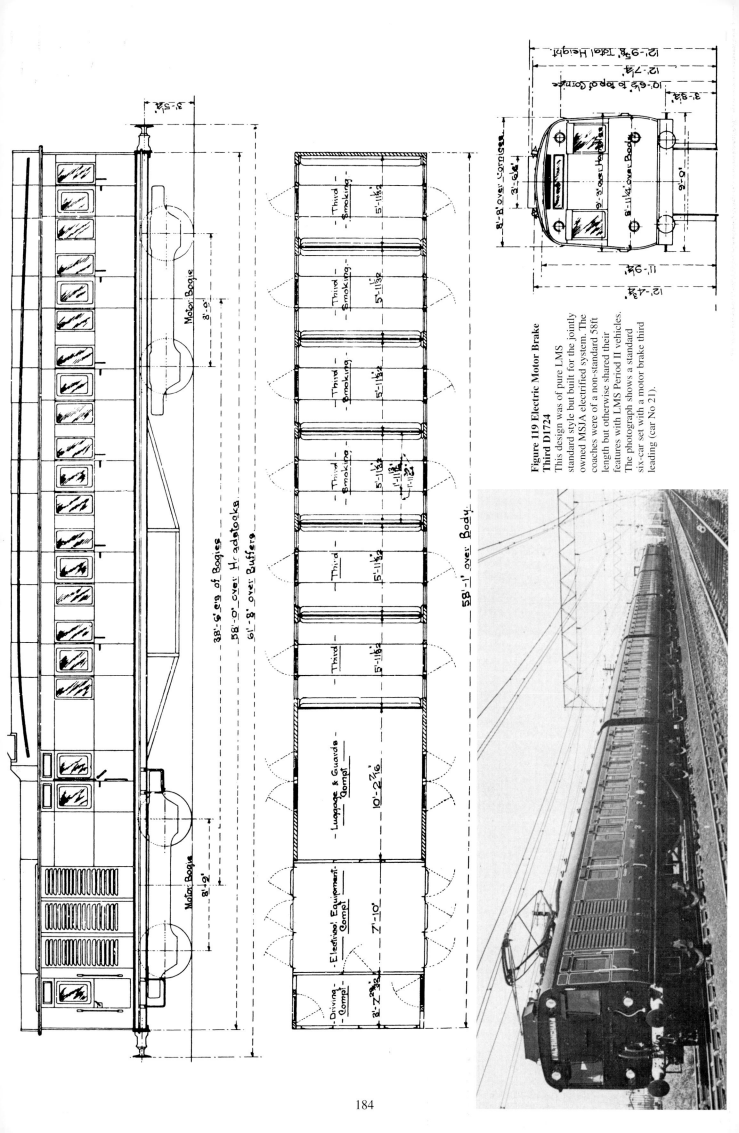

Motor Bogie

8'-0"

38'-6" c/s of Bogies

58'-0" over Headstocks

61'-8" over Buffers

Motor Bogie

8'-2"

3'-5½"

Third Smoking 5'-11½²
Third Smoking 5'-11½²
Third Smoking 5'-11½²
Third Smoking 5'-11½²
Third 5'-11½²
Third 5'-11½²

1'-11½
1'-11½

Luggage & Guards Compt 10'-2⅛⁶

Electrical Equipment Compt 7'-10'

Driving Compt 8'-2'2³²⁄₃₂

58'-1" over Body.

12'-9⅝" Total Height
12'-7¾'
10'-6½" to top of Cornice
8'-8' over Cornices
3'-6¼'
9'-3" over Handles
8'-11¼" over Body
2'-0'
11'-9½'
12'-4⅜'

Figure 119 Electric Motor Brake Third D1724

This design was of pure LMS standard style but built for the jointly owned MSJA electrified system. The coaches were of a non-standard 58ft length but otherwise shared their features with LMS Period II vehicles. The photograph shows a standard six-car set with a motor brake third leading (car No 21).

184

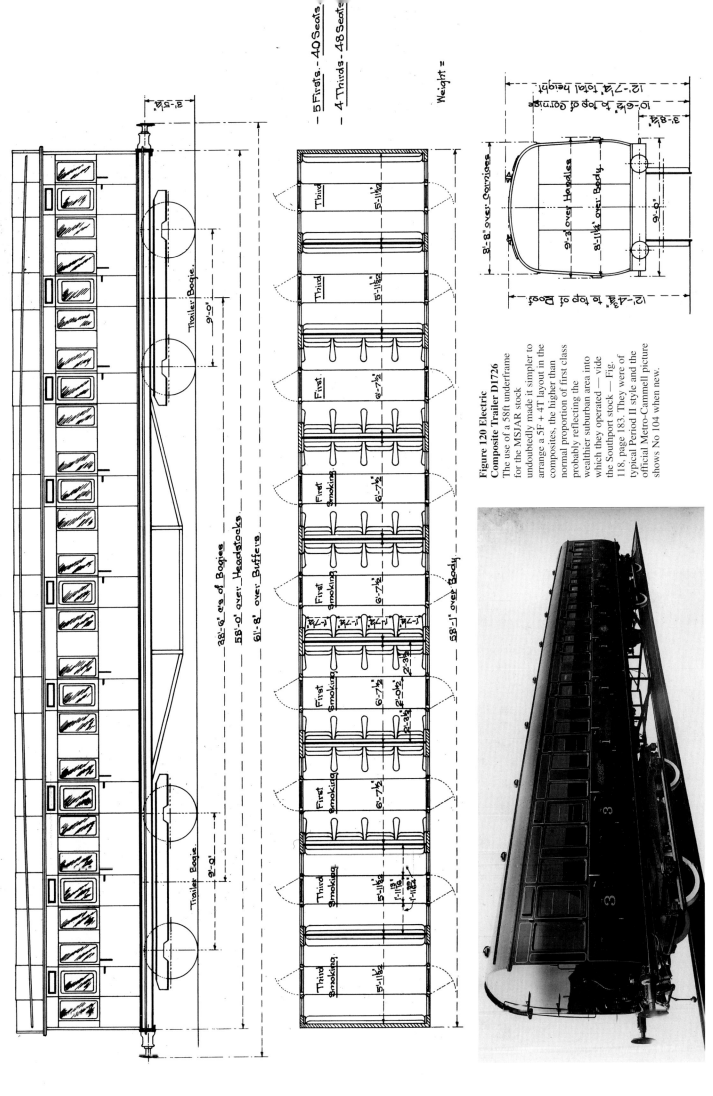

Figure 120 Electric Composite Trailer D1726
The use of a 58ft underframe for the MSJAR stock undoubtedly made it simpler to arrange a 5F + 4T layout in the composites, the higher than normal proportion of first class probably reflecting the wealthier suburban area into which they operated — vide the Southport stock — Fig. 118, page 183. They were of typical Period II style and the official Metro-Cammell picture shows No 104 when new.

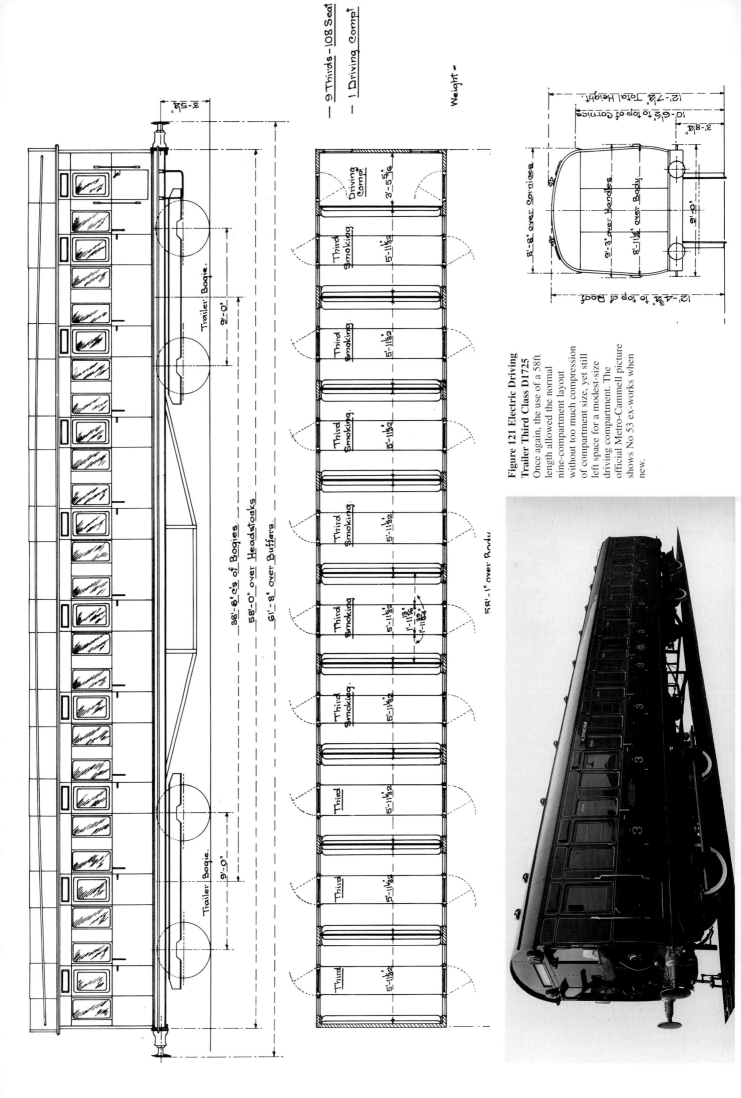

9 Thirds – 108 Seat
1 Driving Compt

Weight =

Trailer Bogie.

9'-0"

38'-6" c's of Bogies.

58'-0" over Headstocks.

61'-8" over Buffers.

Trailer Bogie.

9'-0"

3'-5⅜"

Driving Compt

3'-5⅜"

Third Smoking   5'-11½₂"

Third Smoking   5'-11½₂"

Third Smoking   5'-11½₂"

Third Smoking   5'-11½₂"

Third Smoking   5'-11½₂"

Third Smoking   5'-11½₂"

1'-11⅜"
1'-1⅜"

Third Smoking   5'-11½₂"

Third   5'-11½₂"

Third   5'-11½₂"

Third   5'-11½₂"

58'-1" over Body.

12'-4¾" to top of Roof.

12'-7⅜" Total Height.

10'-6½" to top of Cornice

8'-8" over Cornices

9'-3" over Handles

3'-8¾"

8'-11¼" over Body

9'-0"

Figure 121 Electric Driving Trailer Third Class D1725
Once again, the use of a 58ft length allowed the normal nine-compartment layout without too much compression of compartment size, yet still left space for a modest-size driving compartment. The official Metro-Cammell picture shows No 53 ex-works when new.

186

As with the Liverpool-Southport stock, the extra space available in this revised survey enables us to offer further views of the MSJAR stock than could previously be accommodated. The first picture shows a close-up view of Motor Brake Third No 3 to D1724, ex-works at Metro-Cammell, while the second picture features a standard three-car set with Driving Third Class Trailer No 64 to D1725 leading — probably taken when it was about to go into service ex-works.

The final view shows a typical six-car formation from the Motor Brake Third end, though the carriage numbers cannot be identified. Note (see also page 184) that when running in six-car formation, the sets were arranged so that the motorised cars were at the extreme outer ends.

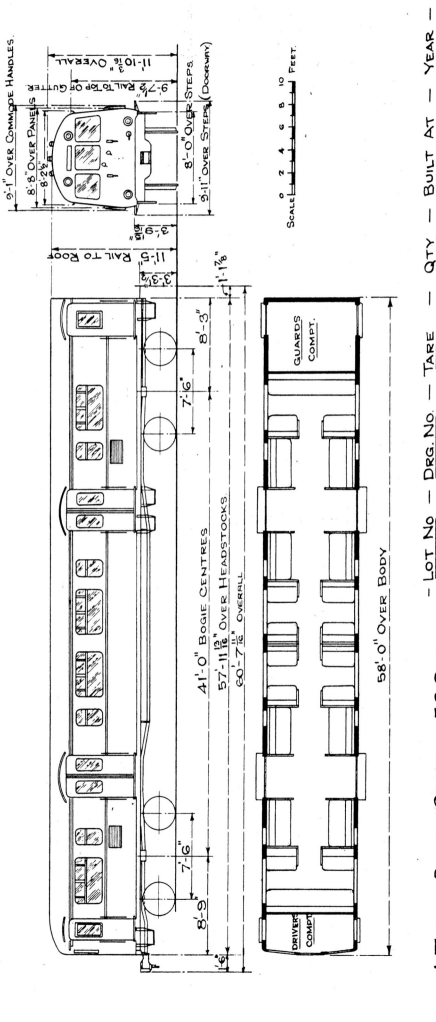

1 THIRD CLASS COMPT. = 58 SEATS.
1 DRIVERS COMPT.
1 GUARDS COMPT.

— LOT No —	DRG. No. —	— TARE —	QTY —	BUILT AT —	YEAR —
		T. C. Q.			
1009	12/486	36 – 0 – 0	19	METRO CAMMELL	1938.

Figure 122 Electric Motor Brake Third D2004
As with the sliding-door Liverpool-Southport stock, the relatively clear nature of the diagrams for the Mersey-Wirral types allows their reproduction at 3mm=1ft scale. The diagram itself is self-explanatory and the official Metro-Cammell picture shows the first of the series, No 28672, ex-works when new.

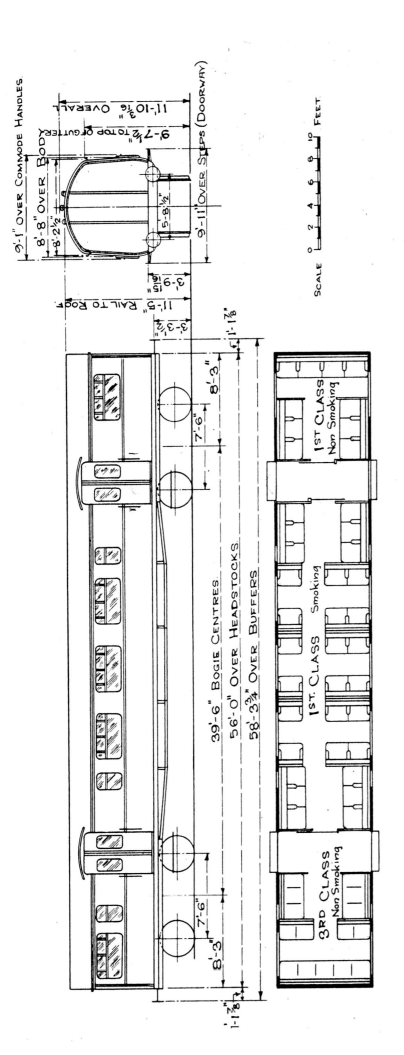

9'-1" OVER COMMODE HANDLES.

11'-10 3/16" OVERALL.

9'-7 1/2" TO TOP OF GUTTER

8'-8" OVER BODY

8'-2 1/2"

3'-9 15/16"

11'-3" RAIL TO ROOF

9'-11" OVER STEPS (DOORWAY)

5'-8 1/2"

3'-3 1/2"

1'-1 7/8"

8'-3"

7'-6"

39'-6" BOGIE CENTRES.

56'-0" OVER HEADSTOCKS.

58'-3 3/4" OVER BUFFERS.

7'-6"

8'-3"

1'-1 7/8"

SCALE

FEET

0 2 4 6 8 10

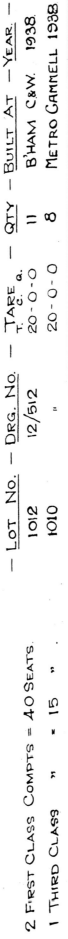

1ST CLASS Non Smoking

1ST CLASS Smoking

3RD CLASS Non Smoking

	— LOT NO.	— DRG. NO.	— TARE			— QTY	— BUILT AT	— YEAR.
			T. C. Q.					
	1012	12/512	20- 0- 0			11	B'HAM C&W.	1938.
	1010	"	20- 0- 0			8	METRO CAMMELL	1938

2 FIRST CLASS COMPTS = 40 SEATS.

1 THIRD CLASS   "   "   = 15   "   .

Figure 123 Electric Composite Trailer D200 5
Once again this diagram is self-explanatory, though it is again worth noting the high proportion of first class, the Wirral area being another part of Merseyside where a fair amount of prosperous trade could safely be anticipated. The official Metro-Cammell view shows the first of the series, No 29713, to be built by that company.

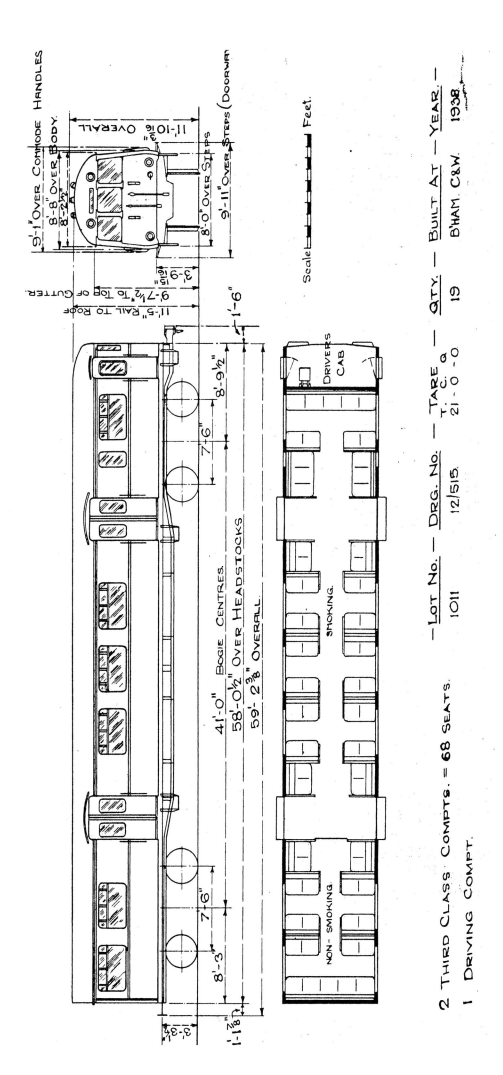

Scale |——————| Feet.

9'-1" OVER COMMODE HANDLES
8'-8" OVER BODY.
8'-2½"
11'-10³⁄₁₆" OVERALL.
8'-0" OVER STEPS.
9'-11" OVER STEPS (DOORWAY)
3'-9¼"
9'-7½" TO TOP OF GUTTER.
11'-5" RAIL TO ROOF.
1'-6"

DRIVERS CAB

SMOKING.

NON-SMOKING.

8'-9½"
7'-6"
41'-0" BOGIE CENTRES.
58'-0½" OVER HEADSTOCKS.
59'-2⅜" OVERALL.
7'-6"
8'-3"
3'-3⅜"
1'-1½"

— LOT No. —	DRG. No. —	— TARE — T. C. q	QTY. —	BUILT AT —	YEAR. —
1011	12/515	21-0-0	19	B'HAM. C&W.	1938

2 THIRD CLASS COMPTS. = 68 SEATS.
1 DRIVING COMPT.

Figure 124 Electric Driving Trailer Third Class D2006
The third of the Mersey-Wirral types was somewhat similar in appearance to the motorised cars of D2004, save that the central portion had three single windows, while the lack of a guard's compartment allowed an extra 10 seats to be present. A photograph of this type can be seen at the head of a three-car set on page 170.

190

Chapter 9 - Steam Railcars and Internal Combustion Vehicles

This imposing LMS publicity picture was taken to mark the introduction of the experimental articulated three-car diesel unit in 1938. As with the contemporary articulated 'Coronation Scot' sets (see Chapter 4) with which the diesel unit had much in common as far as carriage development was concerned, World War 2 was to prevent further progress on what was undoubtedly the most significant contribution made by the LMS in terms of self-propelled internal combustion passenger-carrying stock. Its strikingly modern appearance would not look out of place on the later 20th century railway and one can only speculate what might have happened had circumstances been different. It is quite properly credited to the Stanier regime and is posed alongside one of the best of the pre-Stanier LMS steam designs: 'Patriot' class 4-6-0 No 5507 *Royal Tank Corps*.

STEAM RAILCARS

The LMS experimented with steam railcars for about 10 years but does not seem to have found them as useful as did the LNER. One could argue that a steam railcar is a locomotive but the LMS inserted its examples in the passenger stock diagram book and numbered them in the coach series — thus their inclusion in this book.

There were 14 steam railcars built for LMS of which 13 were to one design (D1779), the last one to be acquired being to D1842. All were of the Sentinel type and double-ended. D1779 was chain driven and had the motive power end articulated to the passenger saloon (see Figure 125), but D1842 was a rigid vehicle with shaft drive. Both versions were the same length and the main difference in layout was that the luggage compartment of D1842 was at the powered end of the car. The interior saloon of both types of railcar seated 44 passengers in seats arranged two each side of the gangway. The cars were third class only.

Unlike the LNER, the LMS bestowed neither special livery nor distinctive names to the Sentinel railcars and all were turned out in standard full lined livery and insignia. They were allotted 29xxx series numbers in 1932/3 but it is not possible to say if all carried these numbers since most were withdrawn around 1935.

Rigid steam railcar No 4349, later 29913 (D1842). This picture shows the style of livery adopted with all the steam railcars.

Little contemporary evidence has survived about the use to which the LMS put its Sentinels other than pictures which show them to have operated as far afield as Strathpeffer and Highbridge. It seems reasonably clear that they were an attempt to stem the tide of the motor omnibus in the more remote areas of the system.

Prototype Details

D1779   — Articulated steam railcar
           13 built in 1926/7 to Lot 312 by the Sentinel Wagon Works and Metro-Cammell. Allocated numbers 29900-12 in 1932/3. Weight: 21T.
           All withdrawn in 1935 except 29910 (1937). 29900 was a prototype and ran on hire for several years.

D1842   — Rigid steam railcar.
           One built in 1930 to Lot 576 by Sentinel Wagon Works and Metro-Cammell. Weight 25T. Given number 29913 in 1932/3 and withdrawn 13/39.

INTERNAL COMBUSTION VEHICLES

The remaining self-propelled vehicles built by the LMS were, like the steam railcars, somewhat experimental designs of the 1930s. The first to be considered were three Leyland four-wheel railcars built to D2132 in 1933 and in some ways akin to the BR railbuses of 25 years later. One suspects from the diagram number that it was allocated some time after the cars were in service, possibly after some modification. Their appearance is best appreciated by the perusal of pictures — a sort of cross-breed between the contemporary Leyland Titan double-deck bus and a single-deck Blackpool tram. Their lot number was 760, they weighed just over 10 tons and were numbered 29950-2.

They seated 40 third class passengers — all in pairs of seats either side of the gangway — in two saloons either side of the centre entrance. The seats faced outwards from the centre of the car and the driver sat in a small compartment at the left-hand side facing forward. The livery is not known with certainty but the light bands of colour at waist and skirt level were probably cream, with LMS red as the base colour.

The Leyland railcars are recorded as having entered service in mid-1934 and initially worked in the Accrington, Blackburn, Lower Darwen, Preston and Hamilton districts in turn. Their subsequent history is not known but they were withdrawn in 1951.

Leyland railcar No 29950 to D2132. Note the general resemblance to the maker's contemporary omnibus designs.

Diesel articulated unit, coach 80000 leading. Later, the sheeting between the bogies was removed and the driving cab windows slightly altered by fitting with external wire 'screens'. The LMS crest was placed on each unit in the plain panel to the side of the entrance doors about halfway between waist and cantrail.

The final unit to be considered in this chapter is the experimental three-car articulated diesel train of 1938 to D1996. This design was the prototype for the 'LMS' system of articulation by means of a double pivot alluded to in Chapter 4 and was also yet another attempt to combat growing road competition over shorter distances. Little is known of the train since it entered revenue service only six months before the 1939-45 war and was stored during the latter event. In its few months of service it was allocated to Bedford.

The design was very distinctive and very much in the 'streamline' image of the 1930s. Its markedly rounded nose was very reminiscent of more recent Continental stock and its livery was somewhat striking — bright red and cream with a dividing band of black and probably a silver roof. The overall length over body was 182ft, the end components of the set being 64ft long and the centre portion 52ft long. Bogie centres were 52ft 6in-53ft-52ft 6in. Bogies were of a new design and the set was powered by six 125hp engines mounted under the floor (two per car), each driving a single axle via a torque converter. Bodyside panels were carried down between the bogies in the manner of the 1939 'Coronation Scot' train which toured America although, in the case of the railcar, these panel extensions seem to have been cut back at an early stage.

The outer cars each seated 54 third class passengers in two saloons. The endmost saloon seated 26 and contained a small lavatory while the inner saloon seated 28. Most seats were transverse with reversible seat backs. Between the passenger saloons and the driver was a small luggage and brake compartment. Entry was gained by air-operated sliding doors at the centre of the car only. The middle vehicle of the set was a composite. At one end was a 30-seat third class saloon with lavatory and luggage racks and at the other end was a 24-seat first class saloon. The two were separated by the entrance vestibule. The third class seats in the centre vehicle all had reversible seat backs but the LMS diagram shows the firsts to have been arranged in varied fashion, some facing each other and others as for the thirds. In all parts of the train, the seats were arranged in pairs on each side of the gangway. The driving cab was very capacious and the driver was centrally placed.

It is not possible to say whether the LMS intended to multiply the design.* It anticipated in many respects the present-day DMU style of vehicle but no evidence has been located by the authors which would indicate whether or not enough data was obtained about the experiment to lead to any valid conclusions. It remained out of use until 1949 when it was converted to a two-car maintenance train for the MSJA electric line. The two outer ends were articulated on one bogie, the roof was flattened and the driving cabs were also given flat ends. All passenger seats were removed and semi-standard buffers were fitted. All but two engines were removed but the method of propulsion was unchanged. The set moved to Longsight in 1959 and was still there, derelict, in late 1967.

When new, the articulated set weighed 73 tons and was numbered 80000/1/2. After conversion, the two outer ends (80000/2) tared 54 tons and were renumbered M19885/6 in the departmental stock series.

*Another set *was* marked on the diagram but was never built.

193

'In service' views of LMS self-propelled stock are somewhat rare, but the extra space in this revised survey allows us to offer a couple of pictures which space precluded in the original single-volume edition. The first view shows the original articulated Sentinel railcar to D1779 in somewhat scruffy condition at Perth in 1932, running as No 2232 (pre-1933 series) — whether or not it carried lining or LMS ownership markings is anyone's guess. The view is from the opposite side to that at Figure 125 (opposite) but unfortunately, the authors have no record of the whole pre-1933 number series for these cars. *T. J. Edgington Collection*

The second view shows the three-car diesel unit to D1996 as it is believed to have gone into traffic on the old Midland main line, the 'stone guards' over the cab windows and the more substantial buffers being the main changes from the original form. There are, however, no signs of conventional couplings, the lack of which would, presumably, have been rectified had any further units been built, the idea being to run them in multiple if need be.

FOOTNOTE

The LMS was also involved with several other experiments in the internal combustion field during the 1930s, principal amongst which were the Karrier 'Ro-Railer' (a fairly typical contemporary road bus adapted to run on rails as well as road), two separate experiments with pneumatic-tyred vehicles and a modest involvement with Armstrong Whitworth's diesel-electric railcar developments. None of these seem to have been entered into the LMS carriage diagram book but since our first single-volume survey was published, a historical overview of early British Railcars has appeared in print (in which these vehicles are included for those who would know more) and which, as far as we know, is still available: *British Railcars 1900-1950* — Jenkinson/Lane, Atlantic Transport Publishers, 1996.

It would therefore be inappropriate to rework this material here, but for the sake of completeness, we do include a few captioned illustrations on page 198, immediately following the diagram details for this chapter.

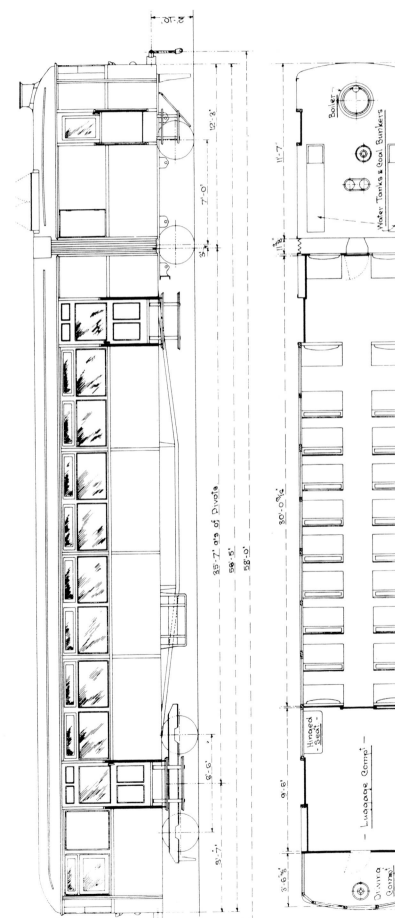

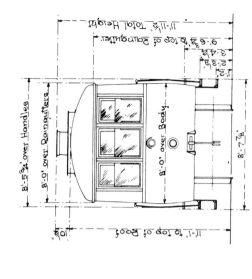

Figure 125 Sentinel-Cammell Steam Railmotor D1779

Thirteen of these 'articulated' steam railmotors were built for the LMS and the picture appended on this page is believed to be of the first one delivered (No 29900) before receiving LMS livery or insignia. When fully painted, the cars were broadly similar to the rigid railcar illustrated.

Figure 126 Sentinel-Cammell Steam Railmotor D1842
By the time a diagram was issued for the solitary rigid-framed Sentinel railcar, the 'utility' drawing office phase had set in — see Introduction — so the best we can do here is to offer a 2mm scale version. However, we are able to add another works picture of this 'one-off' unit which gives additional detail and which should be studied alongside the broadside view on page 192. As stated in the text, we can offer no good reason why this car, along with its articulated equivalents (previous page), did not enjoy as much success (or last as long) as those very similar units which the LNER found so useful at much the same time.

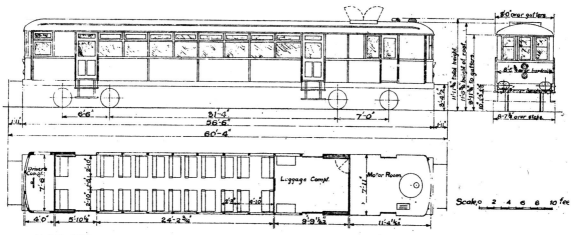

Lot No.576.
1 built at Nottingham by Cammel Laird &Co.Ltd.   4349 | 22913.
To seat 44 passengers.
Weight – 25 Tons.

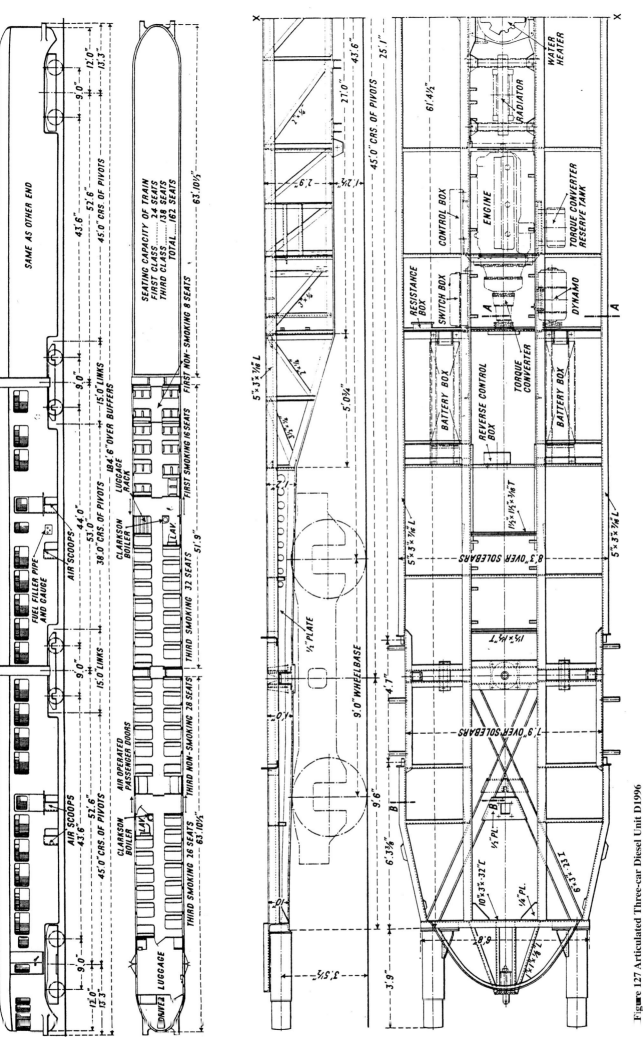

SEATING CAPACITY OF TRAIN
FIRST CLASS ..... 24 SEATS
THIRD CLASS ..... 138 SEATS
TOTAL ..... 162 SEATS

Figure 127 Articulated Three-car Diesel Unit D1996

The official LMS diagram for this unit is not particularly clear so, instead, we have chosen to use some of the drawings issued in the contemporary technical press. The detailed drawing of underframe detail is at 7mm=1ft scale while the conventional side elevation/plan, fully dimensioned, shows most of the normal diagram information at something under ⅛ in=1ft (exact value indeterminate). Studying the internal layout of this unit, one cannot but remark on its general similarity in concept with that which BR later adopted in its original non-suburban DMUs of the mid-1950s, not to mention the much later Class 158 cross-country units of the last decade or so of the 20th century. Perhaps the most surprising feature, given its implied medium-distance role, is that the LMS seemed not to have anticipated any form of catering provisioning. We are accustomed to this sort of thing in the modern era but it was not the LMS way of doing things — the feeble travelling refreshment trolley propelled down the aisle was way in the future! But at least the LMS did offer two-class travel ...

197

During 1931-2, Armstrong-Whitworth built three experimental diesel-electric railcars – at that time a relatively new venture as far as Britain's railways were concerned. They were initially tested on the LNER and, in due course, purchased by that company to run alongside its better-known Sentinel steam railcar fleet. However, while under A-W ownership, the second example was additionally tested on the LMS in 1933 with an experimental 12-seat luxury interior (including kitchen facilities) as the 'Armstrong-Shell Express' between London and the British Industries Fair at Castle Bromwich. This operation only ran for two weeks but was the first diesel powered express service in Britain. It is seen here at Wolverton in February 1933 in its distinctive blue and cream maker's livery. It went back to the LNER, reverted to its original high seat density and was renamed *Northumbrian* later that year.

Following an earlier experiment with a French-built railcar fitted with rubber-tyred wheels in 1932 and known as *La Micheline*, the LMS (sponsored by Armstrong-Siddeley Motors Ltd who provided the engine unit), introduced a 56-seat, 16-wheel pneumatic tyred railcar onto its Oxford to Cambridge service in 1935. As with the earlier experiment, the Michelin tyre company was again heavily involved. Inscribed 'Coventry Railcar' and probably painted red and cream, it ran for several years on the LMS but was never owned by the company. Its light weight (little more than eight tons) and performance (c.70mph in near total silence) were both very impressive but unlike France, where this type of vehicle became quite well known, the idea never took hold in Britain and the ultimate fate of this car is not known to the authors. It is seen here at Cambridge c.1936.

Appendix - Summary of Drawing References for LMS Standard Carriage Stock (including the types featured in Volumes I and II)

This appendix gives, as far as we are able to do so, the reference numbers of all the official works drawings of LMS carriage and non-passenger coaching stock. It is compiled in ascending order of diagram numbers (see also first sub-heading on page 7), this being by far the simplest way of facilitating cross-reference to the main text in both this and the previous two volumes. As well as drawing reference number(s), we have included the formal LMS lot book description together with the lot numbers themselves and the page number in the LMS diagram book. The latter should not be confused with the actual diagram number itself, but it is helpful information for those who wish to study matters further, since it indicates the exact order in which the various types were arranged in the diagram book: ie usually grouped into specific categories. We also offer some additional comments by way of further explanation.

In 1923, the newly formed LMS adopted, to all intents and purposes, the former Midland Railway system of diagram books and diagram number sequence. Following the Grouping, the carriage and wagon drawings produced at Derby were a continuation of the Midland's own numerical sequence. This began in 1873 with drawing No 1 and continued up to drawing No 6701, dated 21 January 1927. Thereafter, the LMS appears to have originated a new number sequence, viz: 11/xxxx; 12/xxxx; 13/xxxx, etc. The LMS did, however, start a new 'Lot' list in 1923 (Lot No 1 of D1353) and this list continued to be added to (without a fresh start in 1927) well into BR days.

Although a copy of the original Midland Railway drawing register survives at the National Railway Museum, York, we have been unable to discover the whereabouts of the later LMS or BR carriage and wagon drawing registers. This means that we are uncertain of the exact number of drawings produced or the logic behind the numbering system adopted in 1927. But at some date after 1923 (by inference, 1927 onwards?) a number of former Midland drawings were renumbered by the LMS, now receiving 'two part' numbers of the newly introduced type (above). We speculate, but cannot prove, that these renumberings generally related to newer vehicles which would be expected to continue to feature prominently in LMS affairs for some time. However, some very early component drawings from the 1880s were also included in the renumbering scheme.

During the LMS era a number of drawings were also produced at Wolverton and these had their own numbering sequence, presumably continuing from that of the old LNWR. Additionally, a handful of Newton Heath drawings, produced after 1923, also feature in the LMS lot list. From their reference numbers, these too would seem to have been in direct continuation from the pre-Grouping (LYR) series.

The use of diagram books, containing simplified drawings, usually showing side, end and plan views, dates from c1900 and applied to passenger, non-passenger, goods and specially constructed vehicles, both revenue and non-revenue. Diagrams were often the first step towards the production of new types and copies of diagrams exist which illustrate vehicles which were never in fact built — more than a few authors and model makers have been led astray by this fact alone . . . Usually, all diagrams received a separate identification number on both the Midland and the LMS, although the earliest example of a Midland Railway goods stock diagram book uses page number references only, the latter system being common on the LNWR and LYR to mention but two. Generally, once given, the diagram numbers remained constant and, as such, are more commonly understood than page reference numbers by students of MR and LMS rolling stock practice. However, there are a few examples of vehicles whose diagram numbers also changed — eg some late Midland designs, later adopted as LMS standard types, did have their original diagram number altered after 1923.

With the increasing availability of copies of the original drawings, we felt we should take this opportunity to publish the most comprehensive list which we were able to compile, based on the surviving lot book evidence. In it, the quoted lot book vehicle description is often different from that shown on the diagram itself or used by us in these volumes. We should also point out that since some of the final entries from Lot 1400 onwards are sketchy and not entirely legible, we are uncertain if everything was recorded accurately. This transcription difficulty apart, we are as near certain as can be that the following list is accurate; but we accept full responsibility for any odd errors which readers may find (we hope there are none) and ask that they be advised to us via the publisher.

For the benefit of the readers who may be unfamiliar with works drawings, vehicles were constructed in accordance with a specification which included a number of component drawings. For example, the main or 'general arrangement' drawing could simply specify the component drawing numbers concerned, or these component drawings may only appear on the schedule of drawings for a particular lot. Such was the standardisation of LMS carriage building that it was regularly presumed that the carriage works supervisors would know exactly what was intended to fill in the detail, so to speak; in consequence there was no point in redrawing every single component (eg a standard door or window type) for every new type introduced.

Sometimes the lot book gives both body and underframe drawing numbers but in the case of the underframes, separate component drawings were provided for bogies, wheels, buffing and drawgear, etc. Also, it was not unheard of for a new drawing to be issued for later lot numbers within a single diagram — usually to cover the sort of change which, though it may have affected some precise aspect of the construction of the vehicle, did not affect its overall dimensions or operational role. This alone may well account for some of the detailed differences which we have noted in the 'Remarks' columns of our summary tables within the individual book chapters.

Finally, at the time of compiling this list (September 1999), it is clear that very many carriage and wagon drawings have survived, and current endeavours being undertaken by the National Railway Museum to catalogue these drawings should ensure that such material as remains is recorded so that in due course it may be made available in some form to interested persons.

LMS Diagram No	Lot Book Description	LMS Diagram Book Page No	Lot	Drawing Nos
1353	57ft Third Vestibule	106	Lots 1/16/21/94	DRG 5554
1654	Corridor First Brake	147	Lot 326	DRG 13/1038
1684	57ft Electric Trailer Third	378	Lots 464/1158	DRG 13/1240
1685	57ft Third Brake	304	Lots 127/290/398/448	DRG 6026
1686	57ft Composite	251	Lots 126/389/446	DRG 6001
1691	57ft Electric Trailer Composite	365	Part Lot 237	DRG (Not recorded in the lot book)
1692	57ft Third Vestibule	107	Lots 154/302/343/355/375/431	DRG 6070
1693	57ft Vestibule Third Brake	120	Lots 303/328	DRG 6070 & 6072
1694	57ft Corridor Composite	161	Lots 30/72/120/157/207	DRG W1/814*
1695	57ft Corridor Third	199	Lots 9/71/95/147/158/388	DRG 5681
1696	57ft Corridor Third Brake	216	Lots 125/148/412	DRG 6073
1697	50ft Kitchen Car	130	Lots 65/100/153/234/382/627	DRG 5970
1698	54ft Corridor First	135	Lot 29	DRG (Not recorded in the lot book)
1699	57ft Third Vestibule Diner	83	Lot 156	DRG 6102
1700	57ft Non-Corridor Third	278	Lots 102/103/124/231/305/361	DRG 6021
			Lots 390/410/447/492/510	DRG 13/506
1701	57ft Composite Non-Corridor	247	Lots 33/81/122/247/322	DRG 6640
1702	57ft Third Brake (Non-Corridor)	302	Lots 82/141/230/289/335/356	DRG 6029
1704	56ft Passenger Brake Van	322	Lots 64/360	DRG Newton Heath 10362
1705	68ft First Sleeper	2	Lot 146	DRG 1/878*
1706	57ft Vestibule Diner	75	Lot 411	DRG 11/191
1709	60ft Third Sleeper	20	Lots 418/428/469	DRG 12/169
			Lot 579	DRG 12/107
1710	52½ft Corridor Third	198	Lot 87	DRG W4/1409*
1711	57ft Passenger Brake Van	330	Lot 90	DRG W4/1433*
1712	57ft Corridor Third Brake	215	Lot 91	DRG W4/1434*
1713	56ft Passenger Brake Van	322	Lots 64/360	DRG Newton Heath 10362
1714	56ft Passenger Brake Van	323	Lot 69	DRG Newton Heath 10368
1715	50ft Passenger Brake Van	332	Lots 291/292/344/345/460/461/563/537	DRG 13/1041
1716	60ft Corridor Composite	164	Lot 450	DRG 12/115
1717	57ft Corridor First Brake	148	Lots 477/625	DRG 13/1281
1718	68ft First Diner	30	Lot 478	DRG 11/210

* Wolverton drawings shown thus throughout the list

1719	57ft First Corridor Vestibule Carriage	87	Lot 379	DRG 13/1105
1720	60ft Corridor Composite Brake	183	Lots 490/550	DRG 12/136
1721	60ft Third Vestibule Diner	84	Lots 491/519	DRG 12/137
1723	57ft Non-Corridor Second Brake	293	Lot 513	DRG (Not recorded in the lot book)
1724	Electric Motor Car Third (58ft)	342	Lot 504	DRG 13/1255
1725	Electric Driving Trailer Car Third (58ft)	391	Lot 506	DRG 13/1256
1726	Electric Trailer Car Composite (58ft)	366	Lot 505	DRG 13/1257
1727	59ft Electric Motor Car Third	341	Lot 235	DRG (Not recorded in the lot book)
1728	57ft Electric Driving Trailer Third	390	Lots 236/623	DRG 13/1677
1730	Corridor Third Brake (57ft)	217	Lots 507/508/542	DRG 13/1277
			Lot 578	DRG 13/1520
1731	57ft Non-Corridor Composite	253	Lot 512	DRG (Not recorded in the lot book)

LMS Diagram No	Lot Book Description	LMS Diagram Book Page No	Lot	Drawing Nos
1732	57ft Non-Corridor Composite	252	Lot 511	DRG (Not recorded in the lot book)
1733	57ft Non-Corridor Third Brake	305	Lot 509	DRG (Not recorded in the lot book)
1734	57ft Non-Corridor Composite	254	Lots 526/581	DRG 13/944
1735	57ft Non-Corridor Third Brake	306	Part Lot 527 Lot 562	DRG 13/1356
			Lot 621	DRG 11/198
			Lots 647/649	DRG 13/1772
			Lots 681/687	DRG 13/1836
1736	57ft Non-Corridor Composite	255	Lot 529	DRG 13/648
1737	57ft Non-Corridor Third Brake	307	Lot 530	DRG 13/484
1738	60ft Third Vestibule	109	Part Lot 522	DRG 12/140
1739	68ft First Sleeper	1	Lot 62	DRG W4/1350*
1741	57ft First Lounge Brake	49	Lot 378	DRG 13/1106
1742	57ft First Vestibule	91	Lots 80/138/155/293	DRG 5819
1743	68ft Vestibule Diner	39	Lot 28	DRG (Not recorded in the lot book)
1744	57ft Vestibule Composite	98	Lots 2/93	DRG 5555
1745	57ft Third Vestibule	108	Lots 183/184/185	DRG 12/116
1746	57ft Vestibule Third Brake	119	Lots 181/182	DRG (Not recorded in the lot book)
1747	57ft Corridor First	136	Lot 246	DRG (Not recorded in the lot book)
1748	57ft Corridor First	137	Lot 325	DRG (Shown as 1748 which is the diagram number)
1751	57ft Corridor Composite	162	Lot 101	DRG W4/1450*
1752	57ft Corridor Composite	163	Lot 139	DRG (Not recorded in the lot book)
1754	57ft Corridor Composite Brake	180	Lot 31	DRG W1/813*
1755	57ft Corridor Composite Brake	181	Lot 208	DRG (Not recorded in the lot book)
1756	57ft Corridor Third	196	Lots 7/8	DRG 5400
1758	57ft Corridor Third Brake	214	Lot 11	DRG 5824
1759	Bogie First Non-Corridor	228	Lot 12 Part Lot 96	DRG 5476
1760	Bogie First Non-Corridor	230	Lots 212/213	DRG 6074
1761	57ft First Class	231	Lot 249	DRG (Not recorded in the lot book)
1762	54ft Non-Corridor First	232	Lots 129/331/394/432	DRG 6074
1763	54ft Non-Corridor Composite	245	Lots 13/97	DRG 5338
1764	54ft Non-Corridor Composite	246	Part Lot 96	DRG 5476
1765	54ft Non-Corridor Composite	248	Lots 130/332/395/433	DRG 5991
1766	57ft Non-Corridor Composite	303	Lots 216/217	DRG 6082
1767	57ft Non-Corridor Composite	250	Lot 229	DRG 6122
1768	54ft Second	276	Lot 14	DRG 5336} This is how it appeared
	54ft Third Non-Corridor Third	276	Lots 60/78/98	DRG 5336} in the lot book
1769	54ft Non-Corridor Third	277	Lot 131	DRG 5336
			Lots 333/396/434	DRG 6386
1770	54ft Third Brake	300	Lot 15	DRG 5478
			Lot 61	DRG Newton Heath 10408
			Lot 99	DRG 5478
1771	54ft Third Brake	301	Lots 79/128	DRG 5932
1772	54ft Third Brake	303	Lots 132/214/215/334	DRG 6082
			Lots 397/435	DRG 13/1052
1773	45ft Passenger Brake Van	324	Part Lot 70	DRG (Not recorded in the lot book)
1774	57ft Passenger Brake Van	325	Part Lot 70	DRG (Not recorded in the lot book)

LMS Diagram No	Lot Book Description	LMS Diagram Book Page No	Lot	Drawing Nos
1776	50ft Passenger Brake Van	327	Part Lot 70	DRG(Not recorded in th book)
1777	54ft Passenger Brake Van	328	Part Lot 70	
1778	50ft Passenger Brake Van	331	Lots 218/219/405	DRG 6093
1779	Steam Rail Motor Car	403	Lot 312	DRG (Not recorded in the lot book)
1781	68ft Composite Sleeper	11	Lot 543	DRG 11/212A†

† Later to D1844. In our previous work we have shown Lot 571 as being allocated to this diagram. The lot book shows 571 as being a 59ft Trailer Third Brake but it does not appear in the diagram book index.

LMS Diagram No	Lot Book Description	LMS Diagram Book Page No	Lot	Drawing Nos
1782	60ft Corridor Third	200	Lot 551	DRG 11/232
1783	57ft Non-Corridor Third Brake	308	Lot 553	DRG 13/1408
			Lot 641	DRG 13/1408A
1784	57ft Non-Corridor Third Brake	279	Lots 523/528/554	DRG 13/1353
			Lots 580/642	DRG 13/1353B
1785	57ft Non-Corridor Composite	256	Lot 555	DRG 13/1409
			Lot 643	DRG 13/1409B
1786	57ft Non-Corridor Composite	257	Lot 556	DRG 13/1409
			Lot 644	DRG 13/1409B
1788	54ft Non-Corridor Composite	258	Lot 559	DRG 13/1411
			Lot 820	DRG 13/2085
1789	54ft Non-Corridor Third	280	Lot 560	DRG 13/1412
			Lot 821	DRG 13/2083
1790	57ft Non-Corridor Third Brake	309	Part Lot 527	DRG 13/1356
1791	60ft Corridor Composite	165	Lot 531	DRG 12/143
1792	Post Office Sorting Van (60ft)	411	Lot 502	DRG 12/133
			Lot 564	DRG 16/489
			Lot 611	DRG 12/133
			Lot 612	DRG 12/157
			Lot 772/773/872	DRG 12/253
			Lot 987	DRG 12/253
			Lot 1059	DRGs 12/254D & 12/253B
			Lot 1197	DRGs 12/253 & 12/556
1793	50ft Post Office Stowage	425	Lot 479	DRG 13/1270
1794	57ft Post Office Sorting Van	410	Lot 472	DRG 1/1047
1795	60ft Third Vestibule	110	Part Lot 522	DRG 12/140
			Lot 628	DRG 12/192
1796	31ft Passenger Brake Van	333	Lots 664/669	DRGs 12/1813 & 13/1814
1797	57ft Non-Corridor Second Brake	294	Lot 557	DRG 13/1356
			Lot 645	DRG 13/1356C
1810	68ft Restaurant Kitchen Car First	31	Lots 525/616	DRG 11/210
1811	68ft Composite Restaurant Kitchen	40	Lot 617	DRG 11/238
1841	54ft Non-Corridor Third Brake	310	Lot 501	DRG 13/1413
1844	See Diagram 1781			
1845	57ft Corridor First Brake	149	Part Lot 582	DRG 13/1519
1846	57ft Composite Trailer	367	Lot 622	DRG 13/1678
1847	59ft Third Motor Car	343	Lot 636	DRG 13/1676
1848	57ft Buffet Car	45	Lot 646	DRG 12/213

LMS Diagram No	Lot Book Description	LMS Diagram Book Page No	Lot	Drawing Nos
1849	57ft Composite Non-Corridor	259	Lots 650/684	DRG 13/1779
			Lot 704	DRG 13/1840B
1850	60ft Corridor Composite Brake	184	Part Lot 658	DRG 12/221
1851	57ft Corridor Third Brake	218	Lot 659 Part Lot 692	DRG 13/1802
1852	57ft Corridor Third Brake	219	Part Lot 692	DRG 13/1802
1853	42ft Post Office Van	430	Lot 662	DRG 13/1853A
1854	50ft Passenger Brake Van	334	Lots 665/686/780	DRG 13/1821
1855	60ft Kitchen Car	131	Lot 670	DRG 12/235
1856	57ft Third Driving Trailer	311	Lot 688 Part Lots 850/1037	DRG 13/1836C
1857	68ft First Kitchen Diner	32	Lot 689	DRG 11/260
1858	57ft Non-Corridor First	234	Lots 693/778	DRG 13/1903
			Lot 778	DRG 13/2029
1859	60ft Corridor Composite	166	Lot 694	DRG 12/229
1860	57ft Corridor Third	201	Lot 695	DRG 13/1846
1861	68ft Third Kitchen Diner	44	Lot 685	DRG 11/258
1862	57ft Vestibule Corridor	99	Lot 697	DRG 12/242
1863	65ft Third Sleeper	21	Lot 699	DRG 12/233
1867	31ft Post Office Mail Van	439	Lot 703	DRG 13/1861
1868	33ft Motor Car Van	14§	Lot 85	DRG 13/815
1869	Bogie Parcels Van	25§	Lot 250	DRG 13/536
1870	Luggage & Parcels Van	23§	Lots 690/750/751	DRG 14/2172A
			Lots 848/863/864/1050	DRG 14/2471
1871	Covered Combination Truck	10§	Lots 111/123	DRG W/495*
1872	Covered Combination Truck	11§	Lot 363	DRG 13/1096
			Lots 406/532/594/661	DRG 1096A
			Lots 746/747	DRG 13/1096B
1873	Fruit & Milk Van	20§	Lots 112/233/364/663	DRG 13/974
1874	Covered Milk Van	21§	Lots 304/442	DRG 13/1020
1875	Theatrical Scenery Van	28§	Lots 134/160	DRG 13/448
1876	Prize Cattle Van	6§	Lots 227/318/377	DRG 13/459
1877	Prize Cattle Van	7§	Lots 463/598/855	DRG 11/208
			Lot 1638	DRG 11/208 Body
				13/1231 Under Frame
1878	Horse Box	1§	Lot 232	DRG 11/118
1879	Horse Box	2§	Lots 463/493/584/657	DRG 11/172
1880	Aeroplane Van	18§	Lots 229/407	DRG 12/22
1881	Theatrical Scenery Van	30§	Lot 400	DRG 12/102
1882	Theatrical Scenery Van	29§	Lot 308	DRG 13/706
1883	Ventilated Refrigeration Van (Meat)	34§	Lot 133	DRG 6429

§ Non-passenger coaching stock diagram book page number shown thus throughout the list

1884	Fish Van	36§	Part Lot 105	DRG 5937
1885	Fish Van	36A§	Lots 66/Part Lot 105/Lots 336/339	DRG 6220
1886	Fish Van	36B§	Lots 589/592	DRG 12/164
1887	Fish Van	36C§	Lot 660	DRG 12/212A
			Lot 691	DRG 12/212B

LMS Diagram No	Lot Book Description	LMS Diagram Book Page No	Lot	Drawing Nos
1898	60ft Corridor Composite	161	Lots 728/729	DRG 12/251
1899	57ft Corridor Third	202	Lots 730/731/795/796/797/798/ 799/800/801/802/803/846	DRG 13/1972
			Lots 896/897	DRG 13/2299
			Lot 998	DRG 13/2299A
			Lots 1089/1090	DRG 13/2299B
			Lot 1190	Shown as DRG 13/2299; probably an error and should be 13/2299B
1900	68ft Kitchen Diner	33	Lots 737/865	DRG 11/266
			Lots 914/1046	DRG 11/266E
1901	68ft Third Kitchen Diner	46	Lot 733	DRG 11/267
1902	65ft First Vestibule Diner	67	Lots 734/1187	DRG 11/252
1903	57ft Vestibule Composite	100	Lots 735/853	DRG 11/269
			Lot 1049	DRG 11/269B
			Lot 1101	DRG 11/269E
1904	57ft Vestibule Third	112	Lot 736	DRG 13/1989
1905	57ft Corridor Third Brake	220	Lots 737/738/739/740/794/858/859	DRG 13/1995
			Lots 898/899	DRG 13/2316
			Lots 910/911	DRGs 13/1995D & 13/2316
1906	57ft Non-Corridor Third	282	Lots 682/683	DRG 13/1481
			Lots 743/847/1194/1195	DRG 13/2023
1906A	57ft Non-Corridor Third	282A	Lots 906/907	DRG 13/2023B
			Lots 1036/1043/1044	DRGs 13/2023D & 13/2011F
			Lot 1094	DRG 13/2023E
1907	57ft Non-Corridor Third Brake	313	Lots 744/745	DRG 13/2011
1908	57ft Post Office Sorting Van	412	Lot 774	DRG 11/262
1909	57ft Corridor First (Luxury)	138	Lot 793	DRG 13/2021
1910	57ft Corridor First Brake	150	Lot 776	DRG 13/2067
			Lot 1093	DRGs 13/2067 & 13/2650A
1911	60ft Corridor Composite Brake	185	Lot 777	DRG 12/262
1912	50ft Kitchen Car	132	Lots 779/956	DRG 12/272
			Lots 1039/1081	DRG 12/308C
			Lot 1128	DRG 12/308D
1913	57ft Third Vestibule Brake	121	Lot 806	DRG 13/2014
1914	54ft Non-Corridor Composite Brake	314	Lot 822	DRG 13/2084
1915	57ft Third Vestibule	113	Lots 843/857	DRG 13/2088
			Lots 894/953/954	DRG 13/2253
1915A	57ft Third Vestibule	113A	Lot 996	DRG 13/2253B
1916	57ft Third Vestibule Brake	122	Lot 844	DRG 13/2105
1917	60ft First Vestibule	92	Lot 845	DRG 12/280
			Lot 909	DRG 12/280B
			Lot 995	DRG 12/280C
1920	57ft First Corridor	138A	Lot 775	DRG 13/2021
1921	57ft Non-Corridor Composite	261	Lots 741/742/849	DRG 13/2003
1921A	57ft Non-Corridor Composite	261A	Lots 901/1047	DRG 2003B
			Lot 1102	DRG 13/2003E

LMS Diagram No	Lot Book Description	LMS Diagram Book Page No	Lot	Drawing Nos
			Lots 1449/1450/1576	DRG 13/3808
1922	60ft First Club Saloon	70	Lot 851	DRG 13/2124
1923	68ft Third Kitchen Diner	47	Lot 852	DRG 11/270
			Lot 903	DRG 11/270A
			Lot 1034	DRG 11/270E
1925	60ft Corridor Composite	168	Lots 856/862	DRG 12/300
			Lots 912/913	DRGs 12/322 & 12/1300C
1926	69ft First Sleeper	3	Lot 876	DRG 12/289
			Lot 935	DRG 12/289C (Fabricated 1947)
1928	Milk Tank Under Frame	24D§	Lots 931/932	DRG 12/294
1929	8-ton Covered Combination Truck	12§	Lot 860	DRG 13/2102
			Lot 999	DRG 13/2102A
1930	57ft Corridor First (Luxury)	139	Lot 904	DRG 13/2252A
			Lots 1041/1092	DRG 13/2252C
1932	62ft Corridor Composite Brake	186	Lot 861	DRG 12/296
			Lot 908	DRGs 12/296B & 12/311B
1936	Insulated Milk Van	22§	Lot 887	DRG 13/2080C
1937	Post Office Storage Van	426	Lot 883	DRG 13/2274
1938	68ft Restaurant Car	47	Lot 905	DRG 11/275A
			Lot 1405	DRG 11/275F
1939	60ft Corridor Composite Brake	184A	Part Lot 658	DRG 12/221
1946	57ft Third Vestibule Brake	123	Lots 895/955/997	DRG 13/2288
			Lot 997	DRG 13/2288D
1947	69ft Composite Sleeper (Fabricated)	12	Lot 934	DRGs 12/310 & 12/313
1948	Buffet Car (57ft)	45A	Lot 902	DRG 13/2345
1952	Horse Box	3§	Part Lot 854	DRG 11/172
1955	31ft Sausage Van	37§	Lot 986	DRG 13/2422
1956	Horse Box	12§	Lots 317/696/748/749 Part Lot 854	DRG 11/172
1957	50ft Sausage Van	38§	Lot 984	DRG 13/2362A
1960	57ft Corridor First (Luxury)	140	Lot 1062	DRG W1/1326*
1961	57ft Corridor First Brake	151	Lot 1063	DRG W1/1325*
1962	57ft Corridor First Brake (Luxury)	149A	Part Lot 582	DRG 13/1519
1963	57ft Corridor Third Brake	221	Lot 956	DRG 13/2406
1964	57ft Non-Corridor Third Brake	315	Lot 900	DRG 13/2011E
1964A	57ft Non-Corridor Third Brake	315A	Part Lot 1057	DRGs 15/2486B & 13/2557
			Lots 1080/1087	DRG 13/2627A
			Lot 1441	DRG 13/3686
			Lot 1485	DRG 13/3686A
			Lot 1634	DRGs 13/3686 &13/3029
1965	Articulated Vestibule Third & Vestibule Third Brake	124	Lot 1000	DRGs 13/2450 & 13/2451
1966	Two Third Vestibule Articulated	114	Lot 1001	DRG 13/2451
1967	Articulated Vestibule Third & Vestibule Composite	101	Lot 1002	DRGs 13/2451 & 13/2452
1968	57ft Corridor Third Brake	223	Lots 1035/1082/1083/1175/1192	DRG 13/2492 The same DRG was probably used for Lots 1408/1409/1410 but the writing on the lot list is illegible.

LMS Diagram No	Lot Book Description	LMS Diagram Book Page No	Lot	Drawing Nos
1969	60ft Corridor Composite	169	Part Lot 531	DRG 12/358
			Lots 1099/1100	DRG 12/358B
			Lots 1189/1190	DRG 12/358
1970	60ft Post Office Sorting Van	413	Lot 1052	DRG 12/354
1971	57ft Corridor Third Brake	222	Lot 976	DRG 13/2387
1972	Horse Box	5§	Lot 1040	DRGs 6525 & 6291
			Lot 1088	DRGs 6525 & 6291A
1977	Under Frame for Road Rail Milk Tank	24E§	Lot 1008	DRGs 14/2796 U/Frame & 12/339 Body
1981	57ft Third Vestibule	112A	Part Lots 804/805	DRG W1/1346*
1982	Fish Van	36D	Lot 456	DRG 5669
1984	57ft Vestibule Composite	99A	Lot 725	DRG 13/2149
1989	2000-Gallon Road Rail Milk Tank Wagon Underframe	48§	Lot 878	DRG 14/2539
1990	Frame for Road Rail Milk Tank Six-Wheel Underframe for Road Rail Milk Tanks C.W.S	49§	Lot 1240 Lot 1491	DRGs 14/2796 & 12/339 DRG 14/4399
1991	3000-Gallon Milk Tank	44§	Lot 613	DRG 14/1799
1992	2000-Gallon Milk Tank Underframe	43§	Part Lot 1077	DRG 14/2861A
1993	3000-Gallon Milk Tank Underframe	45§	Part Lot 1077	DRG 14/2862A
1994	3000-Gallon Milk Tank	46	Lots 596/599/615/631/632/633/ 640/651/656/668	DRG 14/1745
			Lots 705/727/781/782/791	DRG 14/2164
			Lots 812/874/875/881/882/893/936/ 1067/1068/1129	DRG 14/2164A
			Lots 1172/1232	DRG 14/3494
			Lot 1306	DRG 3669
			Lots 1328/1378	DRG 14/3818
			Lot 1434	DRG 14/3818A
1997	57ft Non-Corridor First	235	Lot 1048	DRG 13/2029A
			Lot 1632	DRG DE/1602
1999	57ft Vestibule Third	115	Lot 1084	DRG 13/2624A
			Lot 1127	DRG 13/2624B
			Lots 1188/1400/1401/1402/1438	DRG 13/2624
2000	31ft Corridor Brake Van (Six wheels)	335	Lots 1091/1262	DRGs 13/1813D & 13/1814
2001	50ft Refrigerator or Sausage Van	38A§	Lots 1125/1157	DRG 11/299
2002	59ft Refrigerator or Cream Van	41§	Lot 1156	DRG 11/299
2004	58ft Third Electric Motor Car (Wirral)	344	Lot 1009	DRG 12/486
			Lot 1685	No details recorded in the lot book
2005	56ft Composite Trailer Motor Car (Wirral)	368	Lots 1010/1012	DRGs 12/512 & 25377
			Lots 1682/1684/1686	No details recorded in the lot book
2006	58ft Third Driving Trailer Motor Car (Wirral)	392	Lot 1011	DRGs 12/515 & 25376
			Lots 1681/1683	No details recorded in the lot book
2007	50ft Passenger Brake Van (Corridor)	336	Lots 1096/1097/1198/1260/1261	DRG 13/2675
			Lots 1304/1305	DRGs 11/410 & 13/2675

LMS Diagram No	Lot Book Description	LMS Diagram Book Page No	Lot	Drawing Nos
	50ft Passenger Brake Van (Corridor) *continued*		Lots 1357/1358	DRG 13/3575
			Lot 1444	DRG 13/3734
2008	57ft Vestibule Third Brake	125	Lots 1085/1174	DRG 13/2633
2009	66½ft Trailer Composite (L&S)*	369	Lot 1076	DRGs 12/394 & 14/3086
2010	62ft Corridor Composite Brake	187	Lot 1098	DRGs 12/311E & 12/408
2011	66½ft Third Trailer Car (L&S)*	329	Lot 1074	DRGs 12/382 & 14/3086
2012	66½ft Third Electric Motor Car (L&S)*	345	Lot 1073	DRGs 12/388 & 13/2640
2013	66½ft Composite Driving Trailer (L&S)*	393	Lot 1075	DRGs 12/376 & 14/3086

[designer — set at bottom of page: *Liverpool & Southport Railway]

LMS Diagram No	Lot Book Description	LMS Diagram Book Page No	Lot	Drawing Nos
2014	Articulated Corridor First Brake & Corridor First	141	Lot 1148	DRGs 13/2714 & 13/2716
2015	Articulated Corridor First Lounge & First Diner	48	Lot 1149	DRGs 13/2713 & 13/2715
2016	Articulated Kitchen Car & Third Diner	46A	Lot 1150	DRGs 12/417 & 13/2712A
2017	Articulated Corridor Third Diner & Corridor Third	213	Lot 1151A	DRGs 12/416 & 13/2711A
2018	Articulated Corridor Third & Corridor Third Brake	212	Lot 1153A	DRGs 12/413 & 12/414
2019	Corridor Third (59½ft)	203	Lot 1152A	DRG 12/415C
2020	59½ft Club Saloon	71	Lot 1164	DRG 13/3015
2021	60ft Vestibule Third	116	Lot 1126	DRG 12/403
2023	Luggage & Parcels Van	23A§	Lot 1051	DRG 14/3032
2026	Motor Car Van	15§	Lots 1154/1636	DRGs 13/2665 & 13/2623
2027	10-Ton Open Carriage Truck	53§	Lots 1185/1263	DRG 11/385
2032	6-Ton Motor Car Van	16§	Part Lot 35	DRG W2 1406*
2043	60ft Post Office Sorting Van	414	Lot 1238	DRGs 12/584 & 12/585
2045	Inspection Saloon 2 Lavatories	51	Part Lot 1221	DRG13/3160
2046	Inspection Saloon 1 Lavatory	52	Part Lot 1221 Lots 1264/1327	DRG 13/3157
			Lot 1356	DRG 13/3157B
			Lot 1432	DRG 13/3157
2052	50ft Post Office Storage Van	427	Lot 1297	DRG 13/3344
			Lot 1433	DRG 13/3344E
2054	HM The King's Saloon	54	Lot 1167	DRG W1/1402*
2055	HM The Queen's Saloon	55	Lot 1168	DRG W1/1412*
2059	Fish Van	36E§	Lot 1299	DRG 12/611
2107	Four-Wheeled Fish Van Fitted	36F§	Lot 1390	DRGs 13/3618 U/Frame 12/699 Body
2115	Fish Van	36G§	Lots 1428/1445/1509	DRGs 13/37154 U/Frame 13/3706 Body
2119	Corridor Third	170	Lots 1405/1406/1407	DRG 13/3673
			Lot 1436	DRG 13/3673G
			Lot 1447	DRG 13/3673E
			Lots 1483/1484	DRG 13/3673G
2122	Non-Corridor Third Class (Push & Pull)	316	Lots 1442/1577	DRG 13/3884
2123	Corridor Third Brake	224	Lot 1448	DRG 13/3782